REA

DO NOT REMOVE
CARDS FROM POCKET

ALLEN COUNTY PUBLIC LIBRARY
FORT WAYNE, INDIANA 46802

You may return this book to any agency, branch,
or bookmobile of the Allen County Public Library.

DEMCO

Historian of the Strange

Pu Songling and the
Chinese Classical Tale

Historian of the Strange

Pu Songling and the
Chinese Classical Tale

Judith T. Zeitlin

Stanford University Press   Stanford, California   1993

Stanford University Press
Stanford, California
© 1993 by the Board of Trustees
of the Leland Stanford Junior University
Printed in the United States of America

CIP data are at the end of the book

Frontispiece: Anonymous Song painting of an immortal.
Reproduced by permission of the Palace Museum, Beijing.

To my parents,
George and Froma Zeitlin

In 811, the sixth year of the Yuanhe reign period, Zhang journeyed to Huaiyang, where he stopped for the night at the government inn. The official in charge of the inn threw a banquet for the guests at which the following drinking game was decided upon: those present would take turns recounting a strange experience that had befallen them, being obliged to drink a forfeit if the experience were judged insufficiently strange.

—Li Fuyan, *Sequel to Records of the Strange and the Mysterious*

Acknowledgments

I have accumulated many debts in the preparation of this book, and I express my gratitude to the teachers, colleagues, friends, and institutions who have so generously helped me: to Patrick Hanan, who directed this study in its first incarnation as a doctoral dissertation; to Stephen Owen, for his inspiration and critical involvement throughout; to Yuan Shishuo and Ma Ruifang of the Chinese department of Shandong University for sharing their expertise and resources on Pu Songling, and to Lu Fan for helping to make my stay at Shandong University fruitful; to Jonathan Spence and the Society for the Humanities at Yale for their help and support during the postdoctoral year I spent revising the manuscript. I especially thank Allan Barr for his advice in the initial stages of this project and for his meticulous reading of the final manuscript and Ellen Widmer for her help in navigating rare book collections and for sharing rare materials and unpublished works of her own with me. A number of other readers took time from their own work to make valuable suggestions on the manuscript at various stages of the project: Valerie Hansen, Sue Naquin, Joanna Handlin Smith, Sarah Queen, Cynthia Zarin, Nancy Berliner, Marston Anderson, Ariel Zeitlin, and Froma Zeitlin.

I gratefully acknowledge the financial support of the American Council of Learned Societies, the Mrs. Giles S. Whiting Foundation, and the National Resource Council. I also thank Eugene Wu and the staff of the Harvard-Yenching Library, especially Sidney Tai; Mi-chu Wiens and the staff of the Chinese collection at the Library of Congress; and the staff of the Rare Book Rooms of the Shandong Provincial Library, the Beijing Library, and the Academy of Sciences Library in Beijing. Jinhua Emma Teng provided crucial assistance with the last stages of the manuscript and the index. Finally, I thank Helen Tartar and John R. Ziemer, my editors at Stanford University Press, for their invaluable editorial assistance and support.

My biggest debt of all is to Wu Hung, who shared my obsession with Pu Songling for so long and who contributed so much intellectually and emotionally to this study. Without him this book would never have been written.

J.T.Z.

Contents

Note on Citations and Abbreviations

The chapter (*juan*) and page numbers provided in the text are keyed to Zhang Youhe's *Liaozhai zhiyi huijiao huizhu huiping ben*. Pu Songling's own preface is paginated separately from the tales, as are the various prefaces, colophons, and poems to the book that follow Pu Songling's preface. Citations with *juan* numbers refer to the tales; citations without *juan* numbers refer to the prefatory materials.

I use a colon to separate a volume number and a page number and a period to separate a *juan* number and a page number.

Unless otherwise indicated, all translations are my own.

The following abbreviations are used throughout the text (see the Selected Bibliography, pp. 283–300, for complete bibliographic data):

DMB	Goodrich and Fang, *Dictionary of Ming Biography, 1368–1644*
ECCP	Hummel, *Eminent Chinese of the Ch'ing Period (1644–1912)*
HJAS	*Harvard Journal of Asiatic Studies*
IC	Nienhauser, *The Indiana Companion to Traditional Chinese Literature*
Liaozhai	Pu Songling, *Liaozhai zhiyi huijiao huizhu huiping ben*
MQSB	Ming Qing xiaoshuo shanben congkan
PSLJ	Pu Songling, *Pu Songling ji*
PSLK	*Pu Songling yanjiu jikan*
TPGJ	*Taiping guangji*
ZL	Zhu Yixuan, *Liaozhai ziliao huibian*

Historian of the Strange

Pu Songling and the
Chinese Classical Tale

Introduction

Like many of his contemporaries, Pu Songling (1640–1715) gave himself a number of names, of which two are intimately related to his writing. In accord with prevailing practice, he used a scholarly sobriquet, Liaozhai—the Studio of Leisure or Studio of Conversation—to designate the title of his masterpiece, *Liaozhai's Records of the Strange* (*Liaozhai zhiyi*), or simply *Liaozhai,* a collection of nearly five hundred tales that constituted his life's work. In a somewhat more arresting step, Pu Songling derived a second and more evocative literary name, *Yishi shi*—the Historian of the Strange—from an ancient tradition. Many scholars have pointed out that he modeled this epithet after the title Grand Historian of Sima Qian of the second century B.C. and have found a connection between the two titles not only in their similar wording but also in their parallel usage: Sima Qian employed "Grand Historian" when commenting on his historical narratives; Pu Songling called himself the "Historian of the Strange" only in the interpretive and evaluative comments he appended to his tales.

The deliberate echoes between Historian of the Strange and Grand Historian, however, provoke the reader's curiosity, for Pu Songling's main subjects of commentary were not state affairs or eminent political figures but ghosts, fox-spirits, and abnormal human experiences—things he considered "strange." His adoption of the title "historian" was thus primarily rhetorical:[1] the title conveys the sense of comprehensiveness traditionally associated with historical writing and affirms his own authority in a field that he investigated with great, but private, passion. This particular understanding of "history" and "historian" was rooted in private forms of historiography, which had proliferated long before Pu Songling's time. (Again, we can trace this tradition to Sima Qian, whose *Records of the Historian* was first composed privately and only later accorded official status.) It is often argued that such private forms of historiography had stimulated the creation of fiction in China.[2] Indeed, two of the chief names for fiction were *waishi* ("unofficial history") and *yishi* ("left-over history"), because such works contained materials normally absent from official historical writings.

Authors of these *waishi* often labeled themselves "Waishi shi," or "Historian of an Unofficial History." But during the sixteenth and seventeenth centuries, writers increasingly took pseudonyms that indicated their specific interests more explicitly. We find authors calling themselves the Historian of Love (Qingshi shi), the Historian of the Irregular (Jishi shi), and the Historian of Illusion (Huanshi shi),[3] and anthologies entitled *A Classified History of Love* (*Qingshi leilüe*), *A Brief History of Obsession and Lunacy* (*Pidian xiaoshi*), and *The Green Window History of Women* (*Lüchuang nüshi*).[4] Like *Liaozhai*, these anthologies of stories and anecdotes are not arranged chronologically and freely mix fact and fiction; the idea of history in these works seems closer to an encyclopedic compilation of narratives past and present organized around a central theme. Yet we also find works such as Yuan Hongdao's (1568–1610) *History of Flower Arranging* (*Pingshi*) that are not even narrative. The term "history" in their titles seems only to indicate that these works are compilations on a specialized subject.[5] These examples suggest how free and elastic history as a concept or a category had become, a freedom that must have been conducive to the late Ming and early Qing experiments with fiction, in which *Liaozhai* played an important part. In a sense, "history" during this period in China, at least in certain contexts, may approach the earliest Greek meaning of *historia*—an "inquiry into" or "an investigation of."

It is in the sense of an inquiry or investigation, then, that I think we can understand Pu Songling's project. Completed over the course of thirty years, *Liaozhai* is encyclopedic in size and scope. The collection ranges from a brief item describing a symbiosis between clams and crabs in the Eastern Sea as an example of "strangeness in the natural world" to a complex and self-conscious metafiction in which the fox-heroine of the story requests that the author add her biography to his collection (see Chapter 5). Moreover, the collection consists of not only stories but also the author's preface and his commentary. Although frequently didactic, these comments never condescend to the reader. Composed in a style more ornate and difficult than the tales themselves, the comments, whether passionate, discursive, or parodic, almost always complicate the reader's interpretation of a story.

Unlike Borges's legendary Chinese encyclopedia, however, *Liaozhai*'s richness does not mean that the book thwarts all apparent logical categories. The second term in Pu Songling's self-characterization and in the title of his book (Historian of the *Strange* and Records of the *Strange*) suggests the way in which the diverse stories, comments, and preface fit together. The theme of the strange and Pu Songling's strong voice and vision keep the collection from being a completely random assemblage. In fact, we may say that the strange is the key Pu Songling offered to his readers to enter his literary world; accordingly, this concept is the focus of my interpretation of Pu Songling's work.

My focus on the strange is also necessary because most previous critics of *Liaozhai* have neglected or even denied its importance, a denial that is itself an interesting and deeply rooted impulse in the Chinese reading tradition (see Chapter 1). In the atmosphere that prevailed in the People's Republic of China beginning in the 1950's, the literature of the strange was further tainted with politically undesirable associations of superstition. Yuan Shishuo, a prominent *Liaozhai* scholar, recounts that only after the injunction "Speaking of ghosts is certain to be harmful" was lifted at the end of the Cultural Revolution did he dare turn his scholarly attention to Pu Songling's book.[6] The many publications devoted to *Liaozhai* during the 1980's attest to the renewed interest in this work both in China and abroad, but the problem of the strange still tends to be shunted aside with some discomfort.[7]

The relative silence shrouding the strange in the contemporary scholarship on *Liaozhai* becomes more glaring when we reflect that the problem of the strange long exerted a powerful fascination on writers and readers, and that the desire to record the strange played an important role in the development of Chinese fiction. Indeed, records of the strange were produced in great number throughout Chinese history, not only during the Six Dynasties when writers began to formulate the strange as a cultural category in *zhiguai* (brief accounts of anomalies) but also during the Tang when authors began to exploit the full literary potential of the strange in longer and more artfully narrated *chuanqi* (tales of the marvelous). Especially during Pu Songling's own age, previous collections of zhiguai and chuanqi were widely re-edited and reprinted, and many new collections of "strange events" were compiled and published.[8] Interest in the strange became so far-reaching that it penetrated many other fields of Ming and Qing learning, including historiography, astronomy, and medicine. The great physician Li Shizhen (1518–93), for example, ends his definitive encyclopedia of pharmaceutical natural history, *Classified Materia Medica* (*Bencao gangmu*), with an inquiry into human anomaly. He discusses multiple births, births from channels other than the vagina or the belly, transformations in sex, the metamorphosis of humans into animals or minerals, the birth of non-human offspring, and humans born from non-human parents. His concerns here—prodigies, freaks of nature, bizarre births, and metamorphosis—had long been staples of zhiguai collections. Indeed, his proof-texts are in the main culled from accounts of the strange. Li Shizhen ends his magnum opus with a passionate plea that men of learning investigate "human changes that fall outside constant principle" and not simply reject as preposterous "the boundless transformations of the universe past and present."[9]

Liaozhai contains works belonging to both zhiguai and chuanqi, the two major genres in the tradition of recording the strange. In modern times, both zhiguai and chuanqi have come to be called the "classical tale" (*wenyan xiaoshuo*) to distinguish this form of narrative written in the literary language from the now-dominant field of vernacular fiction (*tongsu xiaoshuo*). *Liaozhai* is not just the culmination of the classical tale in style, complexity, and range; it is no exaggeration to say that this collection has come to define our very notion of the genre.

The modern privileging of vernacular fiction has tended to obscure the ways in which the classical tale diverges from Western-derived models of fiction. A *Liaozhai* tale is not simply a vernacular story that happens to be written in another idiom. Unlike vernacular stories, which arguably unfold in a space clearly demarcated as fictional, *Liaozhai* tales deliberately straddle the border between fictional and historical discourse and are indeed predicated in part on the ensuing ambiguity. This ambiguity is particularly pronounced when Pu Songling provides information on sources in the fashion of a responsible historian—How are we to interpret such claims? In the eyes of some traditional critics, *Liaozhai* is "bad history" since Pu Songling could not possibly have heard or seen all that he describes (see Chapter 1). For others, he deserves praise as an historian because the facts of specific historical events and the official titles of real figures in his stories are almost always correct. We may dismiss both sorts of critics as naive readers, but because Pu Songling lays claim at least nominally to the authority of history and never completely takes refuge in purely fictional license, the credibility and accuracy of the events he describes always remain potentially at issue for his readers. This tension between factual and fictional readings of Pu Songling's work is closely related to his creation of the strange.

I employ the term "strange" as the best, but still admittedly imperfect, counterpart of three key Chinese characters, *yi* (different), *guai* (anomalous), and *qi* (marvelous). These characters are common synonyms and are frequently defined in terms of one another. Any firm distinction among them is blurred still further when they are combined together to form compounds, such as *qiguai, guaiyi,* and *qiyi*. A circular definition of guai from a Tang dictionary perfectly illustrates the interchangeability of these terms: "Anything *qiyi* and out of the ordinary is called guai."[10] Alternatively, a ghost story spoof from the Ming deliberately emphasizes the fungible nature of these terms for comic effect: the skeptical hero of the story has the style name Dayi (Enormously Strange) and the given name Qi (Marvelous).[11]

Nonetheless, the semantic ranges and connotations of each character are not completely identical. Of the three, "yi," the term that Pu Songling chose for the title of his book, is the broadest in range and most flexible in usage.[12] Its primary meaning is "difference" or "to differentiate," with the consequent implications of extraordinary, outstanding, foreign, heterodox, eccentric—whatever differs from the norm. "Guai" has the narrowest span of meanings— weird, uncanny, freakish, abnormal, unfathomable—and carries the most pejorative flavor. As the late Ming writer Feng Menglong (1574–1646) phrased it, "All in all, guai is not a pretty thing."[13] In keeping with its rather baleful connotations, guai also designates the demonic spirit of animals, plants, and inanimate things. "Qi," which has enjoyed the most consistent history as a term of aesthetic appraisal, covers the area of rare, original, fantastic, amazing, odd. Although qi is usually an index of high praise, the term is potentially negative in that it designates a deviation from the norm. As a Ming writer defending the heroic adventures recounted in a vernacular work of fictionalized history loudly protested, "Now what *I* mean by qi is not the deviant, queer, bizarre, outlandish sort of qi. . . . I mean nothing like the type of thing that shocks the common people and makes them bite their fingers in astonishment because it is un- fathomable."[14] What this writer *does* mean by qi is rather murky, and he resorts to the common argument that polarities like qi and its op- posite *zheng* (correct, orthodox) give rise to one another. It is indeed helpful to think of each of these three terms in conjunction with its most frequent polar opposite: *yi/tong* (different/same), *guai/chang* (aberrant/normative), *qi/zheng* (exceptional/canonical).

The difficulty of pinpointing a clear or adequate definition of the strange poses a question: Is the strange definable? Or is the key quality of the strange its sheer elasticity, elusiveness, and changeabil- ity? It was early recognized in China that the strangeness of a thing depended not on the thing itself but on the subjective perception of its beholder or interpreter (see Chapter 1). The strange is thus a cultural construct created and constantly renewed through writing and reading; moreover, it is a psychological effect produced through literary or artistic means.[15] In this sense, the concept of the strange differs from our notions of the supernatural, fantastic, or mar- velous, all of which are to some extent predicated on the impossibil- ity of a narrated event in the lived world outside the text. This oppo- sition between the possible and the impossible has been the basis of most contemporary Western theories of the fantastic, most notably Tzvetan Todorov's influential study. Todorov distinguishes three basic genres: the marvelous (*le merveilleux*), the fantastic (*la fantastique*), and the uncanny (*l'étrange*). If the narrated events accord with the laws of post-Enlightenment scientific common sense, we are in the realm of the uncanny; if they contradict these laws, we have entered the realm of the marvelous. Only when the reader hesitates between these two alternatives are we in the realm of the fantastic.[16] As Christine Brooke-Rose has summarized, "The basis of the fantastic is thus the ambiguity as to whether the weird event is supernatural or not."[17]

One problem with applying a Todorovian schema to the Chinese literature of the strange generally and to *Liaozhai* specifically is immediately apparent: we cannot assume that the same "laws" of commonsense reality are always operant in other cultures or during other historical periods. Li Shizhen's chapter on human anomalies and his view of the boundless transformations of the natural world reveal a standard very different from that modern science would accept as possible or from that a nineteenth-century European novella would present as "supernatural." Even so, although the bulk of *Liaozhai* tales involve ghosts, fox-spirits, gods, and immortals, quite a number are entirely free of supernatural elements. As Wai-yee Li has argued, the presence of supernatural elements does not ultimately determine the status of a narrative as either fiction or history in *Liaozhai*.[18]

Perhaps even more important, Todorov's chosen narratives can still be viewed in terms of clear-cut generic distinctions between realism and fantasy. In his prime example of *The Turn of the Screw*, the reader is invited to hesitate between two *mutually exclusive* interpretations—either the governess in the novella is mad and hallucinating, or she is actually seeing ghosts. As Todorov asserts, at the end of such a story the reader must "opt for one solution or the other."[19] But the rules are different in *Liaozhai*. Ghosts can be accepted as both psychologically induced *and* materially present, just as a sequence can be cast simultaneously as a dream *and* as a real event. As we will see, the strange often results when things are paradoxically affirmed and denied at the same time. In other words, the boundary between the strange and the normal is never fixed but is constantly altered, blurred, erased, multiplied, or redefined. In

fact, the power of the strange is sustained only because such boundaries can be endlessly manipulated.

A story from *Liaozhai* may help illuminate the deliberate blurring
of the boundaries between the real and the illusionary, which lies at
the heart of my study of Pu Songling's creation of the strange.
Entitled "Scholar Chu" ("Chu sheng"; 8.1081–85), the tale first narrates Chen's friendship with an impoverished schoolmate, Scholar
Chu. Chen is from a wealthy merchant family, but his father forces
him to leave school after discovering that his son stole money to
help with his friend's tuition. When Chen is finally able to return to
his studies after his father's death, Chu has become a teacher. To
express his gratitude to Chen, Chu volunteers to pass the civil
service examinations in Chen's place. Before the exam, he asks Chen
to spend the day with a person he introduces as his cousin Liu. As
Chen is about to follow Liu out, he suddenly feels Chu pulling him
from behind; he almost trips, but Liu quickly takes hold of his arm
and leads him away.

Chen remains at Liu's house for some time before he suddenly
realizes that the Mid-Autumn Festival is approaching. Liu invites
him on a holiday jaunt to the Royal Gardens, where a painted barge
awaits them. Once on board, Liu sends for a famous courtesan, only
newly arrived in the district, to provide entertainment. But when he
asks her to perform for the party, she mournfully sings "The Burial
Ground," an ancient funeral dirge. Chen is most displeased and
demands: "What do you mean by singing a song of death before the
living?" She apologizes and forces herself to assume a more cheerful
expression. Somewhat mollified, Chen requests her to sing a sensual
lyric of her own composition. She complies. After they moor the
boat and disembark in the garden, Chen passes through a long
covered walkway, whose walls, he notices, are covered with the
poetic inscriptions of other visitors. To mark the occasion, he takes
up his brush and records the courtesan's lyric on the wall.

It is now nearly dusk, and Chen goes home on Liu's instructions
to await his friend's return from the examinations.

Chen observed that the room was dark and unoccupied. After a brief while,
Chu came through the door, but when Chen took a careful look it wasn't

Chu after all. Just as he was hesitating, the stranger swiftly came up to him and collapsed. [Chen heard] the servants call out, "Our young master must be tired!" As they were lifting him to his feet, it suddenly dawned on him that the person who had collapsed was in fact *himself* and not somebody else. Confused, as in a dream, Chen found Scholar Chu standing by his side. Ordering the servants to retire, he asked his friend for an explanation. "Don't be alarmed when I tell you," Chu replied, "but you see, I am really a ghost." (8. 1084)

The next morning Chen attempts to contact the courtesan but learns that she has died several days earlier. Retracing his steps, the story goes,

he arrived once more at the covered walkway in the Royal Gardens. He saw that the lines he had inscribed were still there, but the ink was faint and almost illegible, as though the words were about to be effaced entirely. Only at that moment did he realize that the inscriber of the lines had actually been a disembodied soul and the authoress of the lines a ghost. (8.1084)

This final realization surely results from Chen's sober reflection on his experience, but it also leads us to reread the whole story in a different light. It appears that Chu has been a ghost throughout the story, that without Chen's knowledge he had magically switched identities with his friend to repay his extraordinary past kindness, that Liu and the courtesan who entertained Chen were also ghosts, and that the Mr. Chen being entertained during the Mid-Autumn Festival was only his disembodied soul. Just like Chen, we have been led astray by the misleading aspects of the narrative: confusing indications of time, frequent omissions of explicit subjects in sentences, and spatial disjunctions.[20] Even when Chen comes face to face with himself as other and learns that his friend is a ghost, he is still unable to comprehend what has happened to him. Amazed and not entirely convinced, he seeks external corroboration.

This corroboration, however, comes from Chen himself. His investigation ends when he discovers that he has inadvertently become the recorder of the strange in his own life. It is his own writing on the wall that most tangibly registers the crossing of boundaries in the narrative, not only between life and death but between self and other. Significantly, this wall is not the wall of an ordinary building or a room but the wall of a passageway, a transitional zone that ostensibly connects two places but seems to lead nowhere. Like the painted barge adrift on the lake, the wall itself configures his experience in limbo. The material marks of the ink on the wall have uncannily assumed the status of their writer—disembodied, elusive, in the process of dissolving entirely. This is truly phantom writing, ghostly traces momentarily suspended between presence and absence, inscribed by himself and by a double.[21] Although the narrative carefully roots Chen's experience in his subjective perception, we are not asked to wonder whether it is a figment of his imagination. The point here is that the subjectivity of Chen's vision does not cancel out the strangeness of his experience but is rather the means by which it acquires a recognizable form. But that form is by nature unstable, and the record itself is in the process of transformation.

Though brief, my reading of this story suggests a radical departure from Todorov's approach. True, "Scholar Chu" contains many elements Todorov isolates in narratives of the fantastic, such as the double, hesitation, and ambiguous language. But the expectation that the reader must inexorably choose between a supernatural cause or a rational solution is entirely absent. The narrative self-consciously acknowledges the need to supply further proof for both the character and the reader, but that proof is deliberately left ambiguous. The final image of the writing on the wall, which is *both there and not there*, graphically spells out one way in which this story, like many others in *Liaozhai,* erases the border between reality and illusion, history and fiction. One lesson may be that overly rigid classifications create false dichotomies. The recognition that such categories are complementary rather than oppositional is best summed up in a couplet from the eighteenth-century novel *The Story of the Stone* (*Shitou ji*): "Truth becomes fiction when the fiction's true, / Real becomes not-real where the unreal's real."[22] Another lesson may be that if the strange can ever be defined, it must be defined in the changing zone between history and fiction, reality and illusion.

Robert Campany proposes that in the Six Dynasties the strange may be understood as whatever arouses amazement by being "anomalous with respect to a writer's or reader's expectations."[23] Although his study hinges on the argument that the strange was self-consciously recognized to be a cultural rather than a natural category, the expectations of writers and readers in this pioneering early period were still largely engendered by their experience or knowledge of the world. The present study attempts to show how Pu Songling recreated the strange in a much later age, an age surfeited with writing, when a writer's and a reader's expectations were conditioned less by the world around them than by their familiarity with other literature. In this respect, "Scholar Chu" supplies a visual metaphor. When Chen first comes upon the garden walkway, the walls are not blank; they are already covered with the literary traces of past writers. The surface has already been converted into a series of superimposed texts. When Chen in turn adds his lines to the wall, there is nothing remarkable about his gesture, nothing to distinguish his lines from the other inscriptions; he is simply one more writer adding his experience to the lot. But upon his return, the other inscriptions serve as a stable yardstick. The implication is that *they* have not changed; only Chen's inscription, prematurely fading away, appears strange.

Metaphorically, the presence of these other inscriptions emphasizes the need for a textual context or textual contexts in studying *Liaozhai*. We need to place Pu Songling's stories in the long tradition of recording the strange, which provided him with a background of material and forced him to bring clichés alive. We need to place his stories in the context of late Ming and early Qing literati culture, both as a way of recuperating the full meaning of the stories and as a way of better understanding the culture out of which they emerged. We also need to reexamine the traditional criticism on *Liaozhai*, which forms a separate discourse and enables us to chart the changing understanding of this great work.

In the hope of interpreting *Liaozhai* in these contexts, I organize my analysis in two parts. In the first part, I trace the interpretive history of *Liaozhai* from the seventeenth to the nineteenth centuries to establish how its readers understood or explained the strange. I then closely examine Pu Songling's presentation of himself and his relation to the strange in his remarkable preface to *Liaozhai*. In the second part, which constitutes the core of the study, I turn to the tales themselves. Instead of concentrating on the ghosts and fox-spirits that have become the trademarks of *Liaozhai*, I explore three important themes that were of keen interest in sixteenth- and seventeenth-century literati culture, themes not usually associated with the collection in either the popular or the scholarly imagination. These three themes, all of which involve the crossing of fundamental boundaries in human experience, are obsession (subject/object), dislocations in gender (male/female), and the dream (illusion/reality). By focusing on these themes, I am able to circumvent the problem of the supernatural and explore Pu Songling's renewal of the strange as a literary category.

The relationship between inventing the strange and crossing boundaries is highlighted in the conclusion, in which I investigate a *Liaozhai* tale called "The Painted Wall," which echoes the story of Scholar Chu. Again, at the end of his journey the hero finds that the wall has changed—a beautiful girl portrayed on the painted wall has altered her hairstyle from that of a young maiden to that of a married woman. But this time the hero is not only the recorder of the change but also the cause of it: he has entered the wall and married the girl. When he returns to normal life, neither this world nor the boundary separating this world and the world beyond remains the same.

PART ONE

The Discourse

1　*The Discourse on the Strange*

The Master did not speak of prodigies, feats of strength,
disorder, and gods.　　　　—*The Analects of Confucius,* 7.21

"Here is that crazy scholar who didn't believe in ghosts and
spirits and who persecuted our minions when he was alive." The
King of the Ghosts glared irately at the prisoner: "You possess
five sound limbs and inborn intelligence—haven't you heard the
line 'Abundant are the virtues of ghosts and spirits'? Confucius
was a sage, but still he said: 'Revere them but keep your distance
from them!' . . . What kind of man are *you* that you alone say
we don't exist?"　　　　—Qu You, *New Tales Under the Lamplight*

"A literary work is not an object that stands by itself and that offers
the same view to each reader in each period."[1] Hans Robert Jauss's
now almost-commonplace pronouncement is given strikingly new
visual force in the standard edition of *Liaozhai's Records of the Strange,*
Zhang Youhe's collated and annotated version, which amalgamates
editions and the writings that circulated with them before the twentieth century.[2] Embedded in a welter of prefaces, colophons, dedicatory verses, interlinear glosses, and interpretive commentaries, and
crowned with a new foreword and appendix, this edition encompasses a virtual, though incomplete, history of *Liaozhai's* interpretation.[3]

This format derives directly from traditional Chinese critical discourse, which was not simply interpretive but interactive as well.
There was a snowballing effect: as a book or manuscript circulated,
readers recorded their reactions all over its pages, even between the
lines. New readers might even treat the comments of their predecessors as part of the book and comment on them accordingly.[4] In
this way, the text became the site of an ongoing dialogue not only
between the author and his readers but also between generations of
readers. A later reader thus finds it increasingly difficult to ignore

this organic process of interpretation, to screen out comment from text in reading.

Although the collation of editions, a mainstay of Chinese scholarly activity past and present, has resulted in redactions in which the amount of commentary far exceeds the amount of original text, the unusual volume of writings in Zhang's edition of *Liaozhai* is unprecedented for a collection of classical tales. It consists of three full-length commentaries, two extensive glossaries, and a mass of prefaces, colophons, and poems. These waves of literary activity attest both to *Liaozhai*'s great popularity and to the continuous printing of new editions. But these writings also reveal a strong underlying need to interpret the work.

This need to interpret *Liaozhai* is bound up with the problem of the strange posed by the tales. An understanding of what the strange represents and of the importance or value of the strange within *Liaozhai* is thus tightly intertwined with the history of the book's overall interpretation. This history began even before the collection had been completed.[5] Pu Songling's literary friends wrote two prefaces, several poems, and scattered comments for the manuscript well before it reached its final form in the early 1700's.[6] After the author's death in 1715, additional prefaces and colophons were written as the collection circulated in manuscript for fifty years. The first printed edition was published in 1766 and, not surprisingly, contributed its own influential preface and foreword. The ambitious full-length commentaries written in the first half of the nineteenth century mark another watershed.

The traditional critical discourse on *Liaozhai,* like that surrounding vernacular fiction and pornography, is on the whole apologetic and defensive; each contribution must justify anew the value of the work to a sometimes implicit, sometimes explicit, hostile interlocutor. An attentive ear thus enables us to detect elements of the negative reception of *Liaozhai* as well, even if we allow that for rhetorical purposes the defenders of the book might have altered or exaggerated their opponents' arguments.

An examination of the traditional writings surrounding *Liaozhai* uncovers three major interpretive strategies: (1) legitimating the practice of recording the strange; (2) understanding the work as an allegorical vehicle for serious self-expression; and (3) acknowledging the work as a model of stylistic brilliance and as a great work of fiction. A fourth approach, a conventional moral didacticism, drones softly through the discourse on *Liaozhai,* but with one or two exceptions, notably in funerary writings about Pu Songling, this argument seems to have been taken for granted as the most obvious line of defense and is rarely elaborated with much vigor. These approaches, all of which appeared well before the twentieth century, have profoundly shaped modern readings of the work.

In providing this selective interpretive survey, I necessarily simplify and impose order on many often contradictory and sketchy arguments. Since previous arguments are often repeated perfunctorily in later writings, I try to trace changes in emphasis rather than note mere inclusion. Finally, I have concentrated on prefaces and colophons rather than on dedicatory verses because prose writings by necessity entail exposition and argument. Dedicatory verses, in contrast, tend to be written in an altogether lighter and more bantering vein, caring more for a witty turn of phrase than for advancing an argument.

The First Wave: Legitimating the Strange

In 1679, Gao Heng (1612–97), an eminent, retired scholar-official from a prominent gentry family in Pu Songling's hometown of Zichuan and a man of eclectic interests in literature and religion, composed the first preface for *Liaozhai.*[7] Three years later in 1682, Tang Menglai (1627–98), another retired high official, a leading member of the local Zichuan gentry, and a writer of some renown, completed a second preface for the manuscript.[8] The social and literary prestige of these two men ranked among the highest in the community and extended well beyond Shandong provincial circles.[9] As personal friends of the author, who were also featured as informants or even as protagonists in several tales in the collection,[10] their prefaces offer valuable insight into the immediate circle of readers for whom *Liaozhai* was written and the social and intellectual climate from which the book emerged.

Gao and Tang's prefaces share a similar orientation: both redefine an interest in the strange in morally and intellectually acceptable terms with the aid of precedents from the Confucian classics. A corollary of their effort was to widen the boundaries of the mainstream literary and philosophical tradition to incorporate the more marginal tradition of recording the strange. To this end, they rehearse many arguments that had become almost standard by the seventeenth century in prefaces to collections of strange accounts. Tang begins by scrutinizing the concept of the strange. He argues that we cannot base our understanding of the strange on our own empirical experience because the latter is far too limited and individual powers of perception vary too greatly. What is commonly deemed strange is based on convention rather than on any identifiable qualities inherent in strangeness; conversely, familiarity blinds us to the potential strangeness that lies before us.

Now, people consider that what they see with their eyes exists, and that what they don't see, doesn't exist. They say, "This is normal," and what suddenly appears and suddenly vanishes amazes them. As for the flourishing and fading of plants, the metamorphoses of insects, which suddenly appear and suddenly vanish, this does not amaze them; only divine dragons amaze them. But the whistling of the wind, which sounds without stimulus, the currents of rivers, which move without agitation—aren't these amazing? But we are accustomed to these and are at peace with them. We are amazed only at wraiths and fox-spirits; we are not amazed at humankind.   (p. 4)[11]

Tang's contention that strangeness is a subjective rather than an objective category echoes a late third-century inquiry into the strange, Guo Pu's (276–324) influential neo-Daoist preface to the mysterious *Classic of Mountains and Seas* (*Shanhai jing*), an ancient book of geographic marvels. As Guo Pu argued: "We know not why what the world calls strange is strange; we know not why what the world does not call strange is not strange. How is this? Things are not strange in and of themselves—they must wait for me before they can be strange. Thus the strange lies within *me*—it is not that *things* are strange."[12]

Casting the strange as an epistemological problem to refute skeptics had its seeds in the Daoist parables about great and petty understanding in *Zhuangzi*. Guo Pu declares, in fact, that he took as his point of departure *Zhuangzi*'s dictum: "What human beings know is far less than what they don't know."[13] It is worth recalling here part of the famous dialogue that *Zhuangzi* uses to illustrate this point. The North Sea lectures the Yellow River:

"You can't discuss the ocean with a well frog—he's limited by the space he lives in. You can't discuss ice with a summer insect—he's bound to a single season. You can't discuss the Way with a cramped scholar—he's shackled by his doctrines. Now you have come out beyond your banks and borders and have seen the great sea—so you realize your own pettiness. From now on it will be possible to talk to you about the Great Principle."[14]

Although elsewhere *Zhuangzi* draws upon marvels to illustrate these epistemological points, Guo Pu was probably the first Chinese thinker to ask what the strange is and to ponder what makes something strange. His radical conclusion, reached through an elaborate series of double negatives, is that the strange exists only in the perceiver's mind, not in any objective reality, and that therefore "nothing is impossible."[15]

Guo Pu's and Tang Menglai's arguments will seem oddly familiar to a reader who has encountered Montaigne's celebrated essay, "Of Custom, and Not Easily Changing an Accepted Law": "These examples from strange lands are not strange if we consider what we regularly experience: how much habit stupefies our senses."[16] Like Montaigne, who developed this stance after confronting ethnographic accounts of the New World, Guo Pu was responding to the depiction of exotic lands. Not so Tang Menglai, in whose preface the conventional image of the strange is represented by the otherworldly beings in our midst rather than by the inhabitants of distant barbarian lands: "We are amazed only at wraiths and fox-spirits; we are not amazed at humankind."

But Tang's preface to *Liaozhai* represents another turn in understanding the strange. Although he borrows Guo Pu's neo-Daoist arguments, profound differences exist. Guo Pu was ultimately arguing for the veracity of the places and creatures depicted in the *Classic of Mountains and Seas* and for its practical use as an omen book and as an encyclopedia of knowledge.[17] Tang is neither confirming nor denying the factuality of books like *Liaozhai;* rather, he is contending that unless we allow a greater tolerance for the discussion of things that lie beyond empirical experience and ordinary discourse, "the beginnings and endings of the Way" are in danger of being "obscured to the world." If our curiosity is entirely suppressed, then ignorance will triumph and "what we see becomes less and less and what amazes us becomes greater and greater" (p. 4).

Tang's preface shares some of the concerns voiced in sixteenth- and seventeenth-century prefaces to both strange tales and vernacular fiction. For instance, Jiang Yingke's (1553–1605) comic preface to *Tales of Hearsay (Ertan)*, a collection of strange anecdotes, also admonishes the reader to reconsider what is really strange. Jiang mischievously selects the ear of the title as something that is not amazing because it is too commonplace: "Now an ear measures only one inch in width, twice that in length, and about three inches inside—that's just a couple of inches. And yet it can receive anywhere from a single syllable to millions of words, far too many to count. Now isn't that exceedingly odd? But no one considers it odd."[18]

Similarly, Ling Mengchu's (1580–1644) preface to his first collection of vernacular stories, *Slapping the Table in Amazement (Pai'an jingqi)* (dated 1628), closely resembles Tang's preface. Both begin with different halves of the same proverb ("To see a camel and call it a humpbacked horse"—Tang, p. 3; "To the man of little experience, everything is strange"—Ling[19]), and both demonstrate that ordinary experience is far more extraordinary than is commonly recognized.[20] The two men draw different inferences, however; Tang justifies recording otherworldly beings ("wraiths, fox-spirits, and prodigies"), whereas Ling advocates depicting "the wonders before our very eyes," by which he seems to mean the curiosities to be found in daily life.[21]

Tang insists that accounts of the strange should not be dismissed as untrue or subversive. Strange tales are valuable because they can break down the limitations of petty understanding and reason, just as Daoist parables do. His arguments, penned to an obscure manuscript with no immediate hope of publication, were presumably aimed at a small hypothetical audience of Neo-Confucian skeptics. Ling Mengchu, on the other hand, is arguing that stories of daily life can compete in interest and novelty with more fantastical and exotic accounts. This is clearly an appeal to a broad, existing reading public, one that Ling was trying to wean from what he perceived to be a considerable appetite for supernatural tales. Ling is thus distin-

guishing the intriguing and novel sense of strange from the supernatural and exotic sense; the former he tries to capture in his fiction,
the latter he vehemently rejects, at least in principle.[22]

"The Rakshas and the Sea Market" ("Luosha haishi"; 4.454–65),
one of the few *Liaozhai* tales about a voyage to a foreign country,
vividly plays out the argument that strangeness and normality lie in
the eyes of the beholder. A young Chinese merchant is blown ashore
on a strange island populated by a race of hideously deformed
people, who are in turn appalled by *his* monstrosity. A slightly more
human-looking inhabitant finally plucks up his courage and explains the native point of view: "I once heard my grandfather say
that 26,000 miles to the west lies the land of China whose inhabitants
are all of a weird physical appearance. But this was hearsay; only
today do I believe it" (4.455). Pu Songling is here mocking those
proverbial cramped scholars who refuse to believe anything that
they have not seen with their own eyes. On this isolated island, the
ordinary appearance of the Chinese merchant becomes truly extraordinary. However, the merchant quickly becomes habituated to
the sight of these monstrous natives, and he is no longer frightened
by them; indeed, he quickly learns how to profit by frightening
them. In the world of *Liaozhai,* the extraordinary is made to seem
ordinary, but the ordinary is also made to seem extraordinary.

In the first half of his preface, Tang argues that the strange is a
subjective and relative concept. In the second half, in a radical shift,
he attacks the common understanding of strangeness as anomaly
and its subsequent equation with monstrosity and evil. In his hands,
the strange is redefined exclusively in human ethical terms.

I consider that regardless of whether something is normal or abnormal,
only things that are harmful to human beings are monstrous. Thus [evil
omens like] eclipses and meteorites, "fishhawks in flight and mynah birds
nesting," rocks that can speak and the battles of dragons, cannot be considered strange. Only military and civil conscription out of season or rebellious
sons and ministers are monstrous and strange.   (p. 5)[23]

By relocating the strange to the human world and moving the
marginal to the center, Tang has diffused any potential threat that
anomaly poses to the moral order. For Tang, strangeness in the sense
of evil can exist only in the realm of human events, especially in the

political arena. In this regard, he sets the stage for the satiric demystification of the strange often found within *Liaozhai* itself.[24] At the end of the tale "Guo An" (9.1247–48), for example, it is announced that this court case is amazing not because a servant saw a ghost but because of the utter stupidity of the presiding magistrate and his miscarriage of justice.

In the other seventeenth-century preface, Gao Heng also argues that the strange is primarily a moral category with canonical roots. He begins by defining the term "strange" to explain its inclusion in the title of the book: "To say that something recorded is 'strange' clearly means that it differs from the norm" (p. 1). This definition is presented as the common understanding of strange, and indeed, judging from other examples, it seems to be so.[25] Like Tang, however, Gao seeks to demonstrate the inadequacy and even the inappropriateness of such a simple definition: by juggling a quotation from the *Book of Changes* and an audacious pun, he glosses yi (strangeness, difference) as *yi* (righteousness), one of the cardinal Confucian virtues.[26] This is possible, he declares, because "the principles of Heaven, Earth, and Man, the writings of the Six Classics, and the meanings of the sages, can be 'bound together with a single thread'" (p. 1).[27] Thus this strangeness, this difference, is not external to the proper workings of the universe and moral concerns but is incorporated within them. The potential threat that irregularity poses to order, as deviation or heterodoxy, is neutralized. The strange is no longer unfathomable, but coherent and intelligible.

Both Gao and Tang are clearly operating within what Charlotte Furth has described as "a long-standing Chinese view of cosmological pattern that sought to incorporate anomaly rather than reject the irregular as inconsistent with the harmony of natural pattern."[28] In this tradition of correlative thinking, anomalies were taken as omens manifesting Heaven's will and played a powerful role in political discourse, especially during the Han dynasty. But if we accept the argument that by the late Ming people were "beginning to question the tradition of correlative thinking which assumed that natural moral and cosmological phenomena were rendered intelligible by an underlying pattern of affinities,"[29] we can perhaps understand Gao's sophistry and Tang's brashness as efforts to reassert the old moral and political implications of anomalies in the face of the age's increasing dissatisfaction with correlative thinking.

Aware that his rhetorical conflation of strangeness and righteousness is shaky, Gao goes on to upbraid would-be critics for construing the great cultural tradition too narrowly. To this end, he refutes the staunchest attack against an interest in the strange, the statement in *The Analects of Confucius* that "the Master did not speak of prodigies, feats of strength, disorder, and gods."[30] Like many other apologists for recording the strange, Gao argues that Confucius was also the author of the canonical *Spring and Autumn Annals,* a repository of the very subjects that the Master supposedly avoided speaking of:

The narrow-minded scholars of later generations, whose pupils are as tiny as peas . . . explain away everything they haven't seen with their own eyes with the phrase "the Master didn't speak of it." Don't they know whose pen recorded [the omens of] "fishhawks in flight and meteors falling"? To blame Master Zuǫ [commentator on the *Spring and Autumn Annals*] for such errors is no different from covering one's ears and loudly declaring there is no thunder.   (p. 1)[31]

Gao also exploits other loopholes opened by contradictory remarks within *The Analects* itself to justify such Buddhist-influenced preserves of the strange as a belief in hell and the workings of karma and retribution. Modern critics may explain such textual contradictions as stemming from different strata of scriptural transmission, but for scholars such as Gao and Tang the Classics were a unified whole; any apparent contradiction arose from an inadequate understanding of the lines rather than from a problem inherent in the text. This attitude still prevailed in the seventeenth century, despite the new advances in philological studies (*kaozheng*), which were subjecting the Classics to increasingly rigorous modes of scholarship.[32]

Instead Gao and Tang prefer to resolve such contradictions in the canon by appealing to the role of the listener or reader. Gao in particular emphasizes the power of the interpretive act to activate the moral potential of a written text:

For the intelligent men of this world, even "what the Master didn't speak of" can help in the places that conventional teachings don't reach. [The strange accounts of] *The Librarian's Miscellany* [*Youyang zazu*] and *Records of the Listener* [*Yijian zhi*] can thus accomplish the same as the Six Classics. But for other types of men, even *daily* recitations of what Confucius *always* spoke of can be used to abet evil.   (p. 1)[33]

Thus, the good reader can glean enlightenment from any text; the bad reader can find a justification for evil in the most canonical of texts. What is striking in this formulation is not that esoteric or subversive texts require discerning and enlightened readers—appealing to the superior and understanding reader is a conventional move—but that bad readers can pervert a sacred text.[34] Although Gao grounds this point in historical precedent,[35] he is chipping away at the privileged authority of the Classics over other texts: moral authority is contingent not on a superior *text* but on a superior *reader*.

We thus find a merging of two seemingly unrelated and even contradictory arguments: since strangeness is a subjective perception, the morality of strange accounts ultimately depends on the reader and his interpretation of the text. This is a particularly powerful method of challenging the canon to include non-canonical texts and non-canonical traditions. But this concern with the superior reader is also symptomatic of an anxiety that *Liaozhai* will be misread. And for a book to be in danger of being misread, there must be a marked disjunction between the content and the underlying meaning that the inferior reader would miss.

Although Tang and Gao argue along similar lines, Gao's final discussion of the relationship between the strange and the fictive imagination is unique. The last in Gao's series of skeptical interlocutors reluctantly allows that strange things do occasionally occur in this world and that one can chat about them, but he bristles at taking imaginative license with them. "To allow the imagination to gallop beyond the heavens and to realize illusions in the human sphere, isn't this modeled on Qixie['s legendary book of marvels]?" (p. 2)[36] Gao's first defense is rather predictable: he cites textual precedents for indulging the imagination in Sima Qian's biographies of court jesters and the fanciful parables of *Zhuangzi*. But his next defense is more startling, for he openly calls into question the veracity of the official histories: "And is *every* record in the twenty-four histories solid [*shi*]?" (p. 2)[37] Once this point has been granted, he can logically argue that since we tolerate fictions in the histories, we ought also to tolerate fictions in other works.

Gao begs allowance for authorial inspiration and invention, "for the swift literary mind whose pen supplements the process of creation, not only by embellishing the surface but even by smelting the material" (p. 2). The allusion is to the myth of the goddess Nü Wa repairing the toppling sky with molten rock. Thus "supplement" is meant in the sense of "filling in the holes"—of placing new material where it belongs within a pre-existing structure, of mixing small doses of fiction with history. In this metaphor, literary invention bolsters and reinforces order rather than distorting and subverting it. This is not the Western image of the writer who freely imitates the Creation but rather a view of the writer as an assistant to the natural process of creation who selectively fills in gaps as needed. This image of the fictional imagination as a "rock filling in holes" culminates in the opening of the eighteenth-century novel *Story of the Stone:* the novel itself originates as a rock rejected from the celestial repair process, who becomes both the protagonist of the story and the surface upon which the story is inscribed.

But for Gao, the hard-earned license of literary invention is not to be squandered; it must be well spent in refining human beings. The polarity between exceptional and non-canonical (qi) and orthodox and canonical (*zheng*) that permeates the discourse on the strange is hereby introduced. Literary invention is qi, refining human beings is *zheng;* they are two sides of the same coin, not incompatible extremes.

The Second Wave: Self-expression and Allegory

The earliest discourse on *Liaozhai* primarily defends the tradition of recording anomalies: *Liaozhai* itself is hailed as a superior but typical example of the zhiguai genre. To this end, an attempt is made to redefine the notion of the strange and to widen the margins of mainstream literature. But the next group of writers, particularly those seeking to publish the manuscript in the fifty years following Pu Songling's death, advanced a radically different approach. These new champions of *Liaozhai* sought to distance it or even to remove it altogether from the anomalies tradition, claiming that the book was not really about the strange at all.

This tendency was reflected in the first published edition of *Liaozhai*. The prefect Zhao Qigao (d. 1766), who sponsored the publication, mentions in his foreword that he had excised forty-eight of the shorter, more insipid, and more commonplace items (p. 28). Al-

though much attention has been paid to Zhao's censorship of a
group of supposedly anti-Manchu tales, these number only a handful; the rest are standard records of anomalies in style and content:
unembellished, factual reports of strange events such as "A Freak
Melon" ("Gua yi"; 4.443), "A Passion for Snakes" ("She pi"; 1.130),
or "The Clam" ("Ge"; 9.1228).[38] Moreover, Zhao tells us he had
originally planned to publish only the tales he considered the best,
but he eventually decided to append the ones left over after his initial
selection to the end of the book. According to Allan Barr, "The tales
which were later incorporated . . . are by no means lacking in
interest, but have much more in common with the short anecdotes
recorded by other seventeenth and eighteenth century writers, and
as such, are rather unexceptional."[39] In other words, these last tales,
which tend to accentuate *Liaozhai*'s similarity to conventional collections, are relegated to the most inconspicuous place in the book
and grouped together as an afterthought.[40]

Although Zhao does acknowledge *Liaozhai*'s affiliation with the
anomalies tradition, the aim implied in his selection of tales is to
distinguish *Liaozhai* from a stereotypical image of strange accounts.
Zhao's secretary and the collator of the edition, the painter and poet
Yu Ji (1739–1823), explicitly states this idea in his preface: "Comparing it to Qixie's book of marvels or saying that it differs little from
collections of rare phenomena or strange tales is a very shallow view
and one that greatly contradicts the author's intent" (p. 6).

Pu Lide (1683–1751), Pu Songling's grandson and a keen advocate
of *Liaozhai*'s publication, makes this point even more forcefully in a
colophon to an edition that he never succeeded in publishing:

Since this book has the word "strange" in the title, someone who doesn't
know the work will assume that it must be like *The Magician's Records* [*Yu
Chu zhi*] or *Seeking the Spirits* [*Soushen ji*], or else that it's something like Su
Shi's ghost stories, randomly selected and casually prolonged, which are
told simply as material for conversation,[41] otherwise they'll say the title is
unfair. Someone who knows the work, on the other hand, will say that it
uses the supernatural to demonstrate rewards and punishments. But none of
these understand this book.[42]

In Pu Lide's scheme, the ideal reader of *Liaozhai* is not one who reads
the stories for pleasure or one who understands the work as a

didactic tract, but one who realizes that the book is an act of serious self-expression.[43]

Earlier, Gao Heng had introduced the dichotomy between *Liao-zhai*'s surface content and its underlying meaning, appealing to a superior reader capable of discerning this meaning, but he was still interested in the subject matter of the tales and the implications of the strange. In contrast, the second wave of writings on *Liaozhai* vehemently denies the importance of its content. The bizarre subject matter of the tales is dismissed as a smoke screen, one that veils not so much a concrete meaning as the presence and intention of the author.

Writers adopting this new approach interpreted the strange almost exclusively as a vehicle for the author's self-expression. *Liaozhai* is lifted into the highest reaches of the literary tradition, not by challenging the conventional boundaries of that tradition but by assimilating strange tales to the autobiographical reading conventions of the major literary genres, especially poetry. The ancient definition of poetry, "that it speaks of what is intently on the mind" (*shi yan zhi*),[44] had long been extended to other literary genres and other arts; by the late Ming and early Qing, this theory of self-expression could be applied to virtually any field of human endeavor, no matter how trivial or eccentric.

In this mode of interpretation, recording the strange was merely the means through which Pu Songling articulated "what was intently on his mind"; the very outlandishness of the material alerted the reader to the personal distress behind the work. For the reader who styled himself a knowing reader, a *zhiyin* (literally, "one who understands the tone"), the primary question was no longer "What is the strange?" or "What can we learn from the strange?" Rather, it was "Why would a man channel such extraordinary talent into a work of such a dubious genre?" Read against the background of Pu Songling's lifelong failure to realize his political and social ambitions, the strange content of *Liaozhai* was familiarized and excused. As the collator Yu Ji lamented, "He entrusted to this book all the extraordinary *qì* [energy] that otherwise had no outlet in his life. And so in the end he did not care that his accounts often involve things so weird and unorthodox that the world is shocked by them" (p. 6).[45] (This mechanistic view of qì, which here seems to mean something like creative energy, may remind the twentieth-century reader of the Freudian model of libido: if denied access to a proper outlet, it will involuntarily force its way out through some other channel.)

The promotion of *Liaozhai* as the author's self-expression probably began to take shape toward the end of Pu Songling's life. By this time, it had become clear that Pu Songling would never achieve conventional success and that *Liaozhai,* which had expanded in size and scope over the years, would be his lifework. The first written evidence of this view appears in a grave inscription commissioned by Pu Songling's family: since the normal channels were insufficient for Pu to unleash his pent-up sorrow, he "sought out the strange and composed his *Records of the Strange.* Although things in it involve the fantastic, his judgments are sober and serve to warn the people."[46] This eulogist, Zhang Yuan (1672–1756), bore a strong resemblance to the man he was eulogizing. Like Pu, he was a first-degree holder who spent most of his life failing higher examinations, the only avenue to success for intellectuals of limited means; like Pu, he was a man of literary talent forced to support himself as a tutor in a wealthy household, separated from his own family.[47] Both Pu and Zhang, then, epitomized the frustrated, public-minded literary man unable to realize his ambitions in the political, social, or literary system. This resemblance reveals not so much an uncanny correspondence between the two men as the typicality of Pu Songling's career during the Qing.[48] Yuan Shishuo's painstaking study of Pu Songling's friends and family demonstrates that this pattern applies by and large not only to Pu's childhood friends and his pupils, but even to his sons and his favorite grandson, Pu Lide.[49] The literary work of such frustrated scholars, especially if it betrayed any originality or impropriety, was invariably interpreted to fit the ancient paradigm of the worthy man who meets unjustly with failure and so vents his sorrow and disaffection in literature.[50] Zhang Yuan's eulogy introduces the self-expression theory not only because he felt sympathy and admiration for his subject, but because it was by then virtually required to confer literary value on an unusual work and to explain its emotional power.

The pervasiveness of this reading tradition ensured that a brief biography of Pu Songling would be inserted in the first published edition of *Liaozhai* and appear in the many subsequent reprints.[51] Later readers thus began their reading of the book with a strong impression of the author's personal failure. One such reader, the late Qing scholar Fang Junyi (1815–89), professes wonder that a writer of such exceptional talent chose to squander it on fantastic tales rather than employing it more fruitfully in poetry and prose essays. But the question already contained within it the answer: the choice of form and subject matter was given meaning as a desperate act. Thus Fang concludes: "This work must certainly have been written by a great man who met with failure in his time. I ache on his behalf."[52] Here we see a two-way process at work: an image of the author's life gleaned from his writing is reinforced by his biography, and this knowledge is then read back into his work.

What caused this shift in interpretation? We cannot explain it as a result of historical differences between the intellectual climate of the seventeenth century and that of the eighteenth. Seventeenth-century readers were just as prone as eighteenth-century ones to interpret problematic works as acts of self-expression. Seventeenth-century readings of the macabre and visionary poetry of Li He (791–817), for instance, reveal exactly the same impulse to locate stereotypical political motivations behind a difficult work (although in the case of Li He's poetry these explanations seem much more forced).[53] Alternatively, a famous eighteenth-century recorder of the strange, the prolific and successful Yuan Mei (1716–98), specifically forestalls such an interpretation of his work by telling the reader that the contents of his collection were gathered purely for fun, "*not* because I was moved by something."[54]

A better explanation for this shift may be found in the aging of *Liaozhai*. Often the process of interpretation follows its own pattern, one that may have less to do with a specific historical period than with the passage of time and how this alters subsequent views of a work. In this light, the reinterpretation of *Liaozhai* as a vehicle for self-expression, that is, as a plaint of personal failure and a diatribe against the failings of the age, is a highly predictable move. It is predictable not only because it was an ancient way to reclaim works that otherwise threatened the tradition, but also because the work itself had become gilded with the patina of age. To Pu Songling's senior contemporaries Gao Heng and Tang Menglai, he may have been a man of talent, but he was an insignificant figure. Moreover, when they wrote their prefaces, it was still not too late to hope for an improvement in Pu Songling's career, and the collection was much more modest in scope. For those writing later (and for critics of our times who may identify with Pu Songling's plight), the author's personal failure, which seemed merely pathetic in its own time, lent a tragic glamor and profundity to *Liaozhai*. One treats the work of a dead author differently from that of a living writer.

As the emphasis shifted from the content of *Liaozhai* to its author's intention, a general allegorical reading of the tales perhaps became inevitable. In this reading of *Liaozhai,* the evil demons and ghosts in the stories are transparent symbols of human wickedness, the bureaucratic hells of the underworld satires on corrupt human officialdom. Pu Songling was certainly cognizant of the metaphorical possibilities of the strange, a tradition that preceded the zhiguai genre and could be traced back as far as *Zhuangzi* and *Liezi,* works he particularly loved.[55] In many tales he calls attention to an allegorical reading, usually in the evaluative comments following a story, under his sobriquet Historian of the Strange. For example, in "The Painted Skin" ("Hua pi"; 1.119–24), a man who has been dallying with a beautiful woman peeps through the window one day and discovers a hideous demon using a paintbrush to touch up a human skin spread out on the couch. She lifts up the skin, and "as though shaking out a garment," drapes it over her body, transforming herself back into a beautiful woman. When he seeks to exorcise her through a Daoist charm, she flies into a rage and tears out his heart. The Historian of the Strange underlines the obvious moral allegory in his final comments to the story: "How stupid are the people of this world! Someone is obviously a demon, but people consider her beautiful" (1.123). This exact point, that beautiful appearances can conceal souls blacker than any demon's, is in fact offered in collator Yu Ji's preface as an example of how to read the strange in *Liaozhai*.[56]

Gao Heng, the author of the first seventeenth-century preface to *Liaozhai,* had already hinted that the more fanciful subject matter of the tales could be explained as *yuyan*—literally as "loaded words," a common, all-purpose Chinese figure variously translated as "allegory," "metaphor," and "parable."[57] In its broadest sense, *yuyan* designates fiction as opposed to fact. A comment to the seventeenth-century novel *The Carnal Prayer Mat* (*Rou putuan*) makes this usage quite clear: "Fiction is 'loaded words.' To say that words are loaded means they're not fact."[58] Since the term *yuyan* is employed so broadly in this period, it may be best to think of it simply as "figurative language"—something not meant to be taken as literally true that points to a larger truth.

Although Gao Heng introduced the figurative possibilities of *Liaozhai,* he was still willing to tolerate the coexistence of several levels of meaning, and he enjoyed playing with the intellectual paradoxes posed by the concept of strangeness. The lapses in logic and wide leaps in his preface reveal a refreshing lack of dogmatism. The next generation of readers, men like Yu Ji and Pu Lide, how-ever, are rigorous allegorists: they reject the literal sense altogether and retain only the figurative moral sense. By reducing a story to only one possible meaning, they eliminate *Liaozhai*'s strangeness; they try to homogenize the collection, both in terms of itself (all the stories are alike) and in terms of other works (all great literature is alike).[59]

One of the most original discussions of the interpretive problems posed by *Liaozhai* appears in a preface that has only recently come to light. Written by the philologist and official Kong Jihan (1739–89), a member of the illustrious Kong clan that traced its origins back to Confucius, this preface was preserved in Kong's collected works.[60] This preface may be seen to some extent as a bridge between the first wave of interpretation and the second, or as a compromise between the two.

For Kong, the central problem raised by *Liaozhai* is still its strangeness (yi), which he explores in terms of its related meaning, difference. He begins by setting out the common understanding of the strange: "People always consider that what runs counter to the norm and counter to nature is strange."[61] But he immediately won-ders what happens when so many tales about the strange are read collectively: "When you put together all these many piled-up stories and compare them, it's like fishing in a dried-up marsh—though every fish head is strange or different, they no longer seem strange or different."[62] When so many tales are assembled, the impression of strangeness disappears, for the tales resemble one another more than they differ.

This point repeats an earlier objection leveled at the truly voluminous twelfth-century zhiguai collection, *Records of the Listener:* "Now it is only because things that run counter to the norm and counter to nature are rare that we say they're amazing. If, however, they're too numerous to record, then we can no longer find them strange."[63] But Kong refuses to conclude that *Liaozhai* transcends strangeness or that strangeness is only relative. He continues: "Then why did the author put the word 'strange' in the title? Because it *can* be considered strange."[64]

Kong's fish-head analogy exposes the paradox that in quantity unusual things seem to lose their singularity. This leads him to introduce the opposite paradox: when ordinary things we take for granted become rare, they suddenly become strange. Kong's examples are the biographies of "singular conduct" (*duxing zhuan*) in the dynastic histories. "Transmitting biographies of 'singular conduct' in the histories began with [the historian] Fan Ye.[65] He placed them in a separate category because they differed from ordinary biographies, that is, because of their strangeness. But all the biographies of singular conduct that he transmitted display loyalty, filial piety, and virtuous principles. These are qualities present in everybody's heart; so how could they be considered strange or different?"[66] Kong resolves this contradiction, one that has profound implications for *Liaozhai,* by suggesting that in Fan Ye's time morals were so odious and rebellions so frequent that ordinary behavior deserved to be singled out. Then why, he objects, when the ethical climate had presumably improved, did later histories continue the practice of singling out ordinary morality as extraordinary?[67]

Kong is exploring the possibilities of how something can simultaneously be both strange and commonplace. For him, this paradox is the key to *Liaozhai*'s bipartite structure of meaning: "All of what *Records of the Strange* relates here are things that are seldom seen or heard; so of course people will say they're strange. But nine out of ten are allegories [*yuyan*], and if we generalize [*tong*] their meaning, then none of them are about things that people would say are strange."[68]

Kong locates the structure of allegory in the term *yuyan* itself, where *yu* is the figurative meaning and *yan* the literal meaning. The things the stories describe are strange because they are unusual, but the ethical values they convey are commonplace. Unlike his contemporaries Pu Lide and Yu Ji, Kong is not entirely willing to dismiss the literal content of the tales and concede that *Liaozhai* is not strange. Nor is he quite willing to follow his predecessor Tang Menglai and dismiss strangeness as purely subjective perception. For Kong is quite frank about the pleasure that people (including himself) take in reading about the strange, a pleasure that is not necessarily diminished by grasping the underlying moral significance. "If people don't find strange the meaning of the allegory but find strange only the words as written, it is because of people's fondness for the strange. But if this fondness for the strange is pushed to the opposite extreme [i.e., completely negating it?], then I don't know what happens to the notion of strangeness!"[69]

Kong posits two levels of reading and three kinds of readers for *Liaozhai:* the frivolous reader who sees only the obvious allure of the strange; the dogmatic reader who sees only the hidden moral or satirical meaning; and the hybrid reader who sees the surface and underlying meanings and is affected by both. The third reader in his scheme is naturally the best. Thus Kong resembles other interpreters of *Liaozhai* who attempt to prescribe an ideal reader. He concludes, however, with another paradox:

We can't know whether future readers of *Records of the Strange* will be startled at its strangeness and take delight in it. We can't know whether some will despise the allegory and grow furious or enraged at it. And likewise, we can't know whether some will comprehend the strangeness of both the allegory and the words and sigh passionately, shedding tears over it. For we see that people call strange what they find strange and don't call strange what they don't find strange. Someone might even deny that *Records of the Strange* is strange and argue instead that it is only *reading* it that is strange, thus arguing that there's nothing really strange about the work at all—but how could this be?[70]

Kong's scheme presents strangeness as an elusive concept, in constant danger of disappearing into relativity, subjectivity, or allegory. He is ambivalent about whether as a concept strangeness exists independently in the abstract or whether it must be grounded in concrete readers and reading. In the end, he seems to propose a two-tiered reading method, in which the strange is accepted as both a subjective and an objective phenomenon, and in which the surface allure of strangeness and the internal moral balance each other out.

Wang Jinfan, a contemporary of Kong's who published a rather drastically altered edition of Liaozhai in 1767, also explores some paradoxical implications of the strange.[71] Like Kong, Wang distinguishes between the content of the tales, which is admittedly strange, and their underlying morality, which is decidedly ordinary: "There are certainly strange events in this world whose underlying principle is ordinary, and extraordinary language whose intent is orthodox."[72] Nevertheless, Wang is more interested than Kong in the didactic potential of Liaozhai. Thus, rather than propose an ideal reader who perceives the author's true intentions, Wang posits two inferior extremes who are manipulated by the author, the uneducated reader and the overly sophisticated reader: the former is aroused by the satiric moral of the tales, the latter finds new delight in conventional morality. From a stock appeal to the vastness of the universe to support the claim that strange things really do exist, Wang shifts to another important topic related to the discourse on the strange: fiction making. If the principle behind an event is true, he claims, then it does not matter if the event occurred or not. In the end, he attempts to collapse the disjunction between story and message by appealing to the ancient principle that opposites become each other at their extreme: "Thus, there is nothing that is not figurative and nothing that is not real."[73]

The Third Wave: Style and the Analogy to Vernacular Fiction

The approaches introduced above may differ over the meaning and import of the strange in Liaozhai, but they basically agree that the content of the book is at stake. But the third wave, the authors of detailed, full-length commentaries on published editions of Liaozhai, circumvents this debate almost entirely. The strange is no longer a charged issue for them. What is most valuable in Liaozhai is no longer insight into the workings of the universe that it contains, the intellectual paradoxes that it poses, or the allegorical self-expression that it conceals. Instead nineteenth-century interpreters defend *Liaozhai* largely on grounds of literary style and narrative technique, and these concerns shape their entire commentary project.[74]

To summarize, because of their subjective and relativistic understanding of the strange, previous defenders of *Liaozhai* had in some way to situate the strange in the reader. For them, the strange was not an absolute value or independent quality but was realized only in the reading process, for it required interpretation and mediation. In the nineteenth-century discourse on *Liaozhai,* the concern with the strange per se evaporates; what remains is essentially an interest in the reading process itself. *Liaozhai* is now defended because its mastery of language and allusion can teach one to read other more important texts, such as the Classics and histories. Commentator Dan Minglun (1795–1853) exemplifies this new approach in his 1842 preface:

I remember that when I was losing my baby teeth, I'd come home from school and read *Liaozhai's Records of the Strange.* I couldn't bear to put it down. My father used to scold me: "How can a boy whose knowledge is still unformed like to read about ghosts, fox-spirits, and freaks!" A friend of my father's once happened to be sitting there, and he asked me why I loved this book. "Well," I replied, "all I know is I enjoy how in some places it's allusive like *The Classic of Documents,* valuable like the *Zhou Rites,* or vigorous like the *Ritual Canon,* and how in others the narrative is profound like the *Zuo Commentary, The Conversations of the States,* or *Intrigues of the Warring States.* From *Liaozhai,* I also gain insight into literary methods." When my father heard this, his wrath turned to laughter.   (p. 9)[75]

The child Dan has precociously demonstrated himself to be a "better" reader than his father by divorcing *Liaozhai's* problematic content from its brilliant literary style. Once again an obvious pleasure in the strange has been deflected onto another, subtler level of reading. To borrow Formalist terms, we may say that our child-commentator has distinguished *discourse* ("the world of the author-reader") from *story* ("the world of the characters").[76] This favoring of discourse over story characterizes the great Jin Shengtan's (1610–61) influential approach as commentator and reader of fiction and

drama.[77] Jin's annotated and amended editions of *The Water Margin*
(*Shuihu zhuan*) and *The Western Wing* (*Xixiang ji*) were so successful
that they virtually drove previous editions of these famous vernacular works off the market until the twentieth century. Scores of
readers, writers, and commentators were trained in Jin's method of
literary analysis, in which every word and every sentence were
considered deliberate and meaningful within the structure of the
work as a whole.[78]

Dan's own commentary clearly reveals that he was well schooled
in Jin Shengtan's reading methods.[79] We even begin to suspect that
Dan may have been a bit less precocious than he pretends since the
gist of his schoolboy eloquence comes directly from Jin's "Reading
Instructions for the Fifth Book of Genius" (i.e., *The Water Margin*).
Jin's edition of this novel was specifically addressed to his young son.

In the past when children read *The Water Margin,* all they learned were some
trivial episodes. Now when they read *this* edition, they'll learn some literary
methods; and they won't learn literary methods only in *The Water Margin,*
they'll also be able to detect them in books like *Intrigues of the States* and
Records of the Historian. In the past when children read books like *Intrigues*
and *Records of the Historian,* all they saw were some trivial episodes—how
absolutely ridiculous! . . . Once children gain some sense of literary methods, they'll be unable to tear themselves away from such books. *The Water
Margin* can do quite a lot for children.[80]

In fact, even Dan's recollection of his boyish love for *Liaozhai*
echoes Jin's own account of his childhood passion for *The Water
Margin,* which "he clasped to his bosom day and night."[81]

These commentators are by no means the only devotees of fiction
to ground their strong attachment to a particular work in childhood
reading experience. Wu Cheng'en, the supposed author of the fantastic novel *Journey to the West* (*Xiyou ji*), wrote in the preface to his
zhiguai collection of the youthful delight that he took in such books.

In my childhood, I loved marvelous accounts. As a pupil at the boy's
academy, whenever I sneaked off to buy unofficial histories and fiction, I
was always afraid that my father or teacher would bawl me out and confis-
cate them; so I'd read them in secret. But as I grew up, my passion became
ever more intense, the accounts ever more marvelous. By the time I was an
adult, I sought them in every way until I had accumulated a vast store.[82]

All these writers may have been influenced by the ideology of childhood in the philosophy of Li Zhi (1527–1602). In his famous essay "On the Childlike Heart" ("Tongxin shuo"), Li Zhi argued that all great literature derived from an author's "childlike heart," that is, from a mind that had not lost its original authenticity and spontaneity.[83]

The nineteenth-century commentators' debt to Jin Shengtan is essentially threefold. First, their prefaces to *Liaozhai* borrow wholesale his defense of vernacular literature—that if properly read, it can teach children, and by extension adults, the literary methods necessary to read beneath the surface of canonical texts, especially the histories.[84] Second, their commentaries adopt the literary methods and criteria Jin and his followers had developed for vernacular literature. Finally, Jin's example showed them that commentary could be as important and taxing as authorship itself.[85]

Feng Zhenluan, an important nineteenth-century commentator on *Liaozhai,* explicitly modeled himself on Jin, to whose literary prowess he attributed the very survival of the masterpieces of vernacular literature.[86] As he wrote in his 1819 "Random Remarks on Reading *Liaozhai*" ("Du *Liaozhai* zashuo"): "Jin Shengtan's commentaries on *The Water Margin* and *The Western Wing* are so insightful and cleverly worded that they constantly open the eyes and minds of later readers. This is why these works [belonging to the lowly genres] of the novel and drama have not been discarded in our own day" (p. 12).

Jin Shengtan's favoring of discourse over story provides the cornerstone for Feng's understanding of *Liaozhai.* From the beginning of his "Random Remarks," Feng emphasizes that *Liaozhai*'s aim is "to create literature" (*zuowen*), not merely "to record events" (*jishi*) (p. 9). "Anyone who reads *Liaozhai* only as stories and not as a literary work is a blockhead!" he warns (p. 12). The eighteenth-century distinction between literal and figurative readings of *Liaozhai* has given way to a distinction between literal and *literary* readings. This new literary reading is not synonymous with a purely formal reading; rather, an attention to formal features alerts the reader to the moral nuances of a text. Although this approach ultimately derived from the traditional method of combing the *Spring and Autumn Annals'* laconic text for its "subtle meaning" (*weizhi*), Feng concentrates on the stylistic techniques through which the moral nuances are uncovered rather than on the moral nuances themselves. This emphasis becomes obvious when he castigates the vogue for *Liaozhai* imitations: "Lacking *Liaozhai*'s ability, these are just stories of wraiths and fox-spirits, exaggerated accounts of strange phenomena. *Since their literary style is negligible, their purport is unintelligible*" (p. 12).

Feng makes a halfhearted attempt to defend *Liaozhai*'s strange content by echoing an old seventeenth-century argument: numerous accounts of ghosts and prodigies are also included in the histories; *Liaozhai* cannot be blamed for doing likewise. But Feng's solution is more daring: he suggests that the reader simply "take the writing itself" (p. 13).[87] It does not matter whether the strange events in a story are true or not if the writing is good. Feng has arrived at a full-fledged defense of *Liaozhai* as creative fiction.

In Feng's "Random Remarks" we encounter for the first time an explicit comparison between *Liaozhai* and the masterpieces of vernacular fiction and drama. Feng likens *Liaozhai* to *The Water Margin* and *The Western Wing* because all three works have "large structures, finely wrought ideas, extraordinary writing, and orthodox meanings" (p. 9). Unlike eighteenth-century literary claims for *Liaozhai* that assimilated the work into the autobiographical reading tradition, the nineteenth-century arguments for *Liaozhai*'s literary merit derive from analogies drawn between vernacular fiction and historical narrative. This is a great change, one that attests to the improved status of vernacular literature. In this new environment, *Liaozhai* is understood as an offspring of a genuine fictional tradition.

By the early nineteenth century, *Liaozhai* had become so identified with fiction that Feng was compelled to point out that the book records many historical events and personalities (p. 11). Compare this with original publisher Zhao Qigao's caveat that although *Liaozhai* contains some verifiable accounts, it is difficult to take most of it as "reliable history" (p. 27). The emphasis has unmistakably shifted. With the passage of more than a century and with the expansion of the readership outside Pu Songling's native Shandong province, the historical nature of many events and characters in the tales would inevitably fade and be forgotten; the fictional impression of the tales would be correspondingly enhanced. Indeed, a major task of the nineteenth-century annotators was to signal which characters and events had a basis in history and to provide necessary facts about them for the common reader. The impression of *Liaozhai*'s fictionality has accelerated with the immensely greater distance separating the modern reader from Pu Songling's world.

Feng's reading of *Liaozhai* as literature in which writing takes precedence over event obliges him both to uphold the practice of writing fiction and to defend *Liaozhai* against the charge of being bad history. The disparaging of the fictional imagination has deep roots in the Chinese tradition. Even fiction's chief defender, Jin Shengtan, argued that it is easier to write fiction than history, for in fiction the author can give free reign to his imagination, whereas in history the author is constrained by the facts.[88] Jin's insight recalls the ancient philosopher Han Fei's famous remark on representation in painting: it is easier to paint a phantom or a demon than a horse or a dog; since no one knows what a phantom looks like, the artist need not worry about painting a recognizable likeness as he would in painting familiar creatures.[89] Although this valuing of mimetic representation in painting was eclipsed quite early in China, vernacular fiction writers frequently used Han Fei's remark to attack the supernatural orientation of popular literature and to defend the focus on daily life in their own work.[90] Feng refutes this charge of reckless imagination by arguing that even when writing about phantoms, Pu Songling always conforms to the logic of the human world; he makes the incredible detailed and vivid enough to *seem* credible (p. 13).[91]

Pu Songling's use of fictional detail and dialogue lies at the heart of Ji Yun's (1724–1805) well-known complaints against *Liaozhai*. Ji, a leading scholar-official who wrote the late eighteenth-century's finest collection of strange accounts, objected to Pu's inclusion of both "short anecdotes" (*xiaoshuo*) and "narratives in the biographical style" (*zhuanji*) in a single work. In light of this complaint and the abbreviated style of his own stories, it is clear that Ji Yun's real objection to *Liaozhai* was primarily epistemological. He maintained that as varieties of historical narrative, both short anecdotes and narratives in the biographical style had to be based on plausible sources—autobiographical experience or eyewitness testimony— and not freely invented by the author, "like plot elements in a play."[92] All stories need not be true, but they must at least persuade the reader that they *might* have been seen or heard by an actual source. Thus Ji Yun complains: "Now P'u Sung-ling [Pu Songling] gives a vivid picture of the smallest details down to amorous gestures and the secrets whispered before lovers. It would be unreasonable to assume that the writer experienced these things himself; but if he was describing what happened to others, how could he have known so much?"[93]

Pu Songling's stories are too detailed and too vividly dramatized for Ji Yun to accept as based on something heard or experienced by the author himself. For Ji Yun, verisimilitude *decreases* the impression of a narrative's realness, since he understands realness as "the claim to historicity," that is, as the claim that the events in a narrative really happened.[94] It is not the strangeness of *Liaozhai* that bothers Ji Yun; rather, Pu Songling's narrative techniques too obviously betray authorial fabrication.

Feng Zhenluan defends *Liaozhai* against these charges by applying these rigid epistemological standards to the histories. Are the histories always true accounts of events? Are their sources impeccable? Or does their narrative technique also betray traces of overt fabrication? As an example of fictionalizing in the histories, Feng singles out a famous speech in the *Zuo Commentary* delivered by the assassin-retainer Chu Ni just before he smashed his head against a tree and killed himself. "Who heard the words of Chu Ni beneath the locust tree? How could Master Zuo have known them?" (p. 13) Feng's solution to this and the related problem of discrepancies between different historical accounts of the same event is once again to distinguish between discourse and story: the mode of telling a story may vary without harming the essence of the story. This example in turn helps justify Feng's assertion that he reads the *Zuo Commentary* as fiction and *Liaozhai* as the *Zuo Commentary* (p. 9).

This argument for fictional license in narrative did not originate with Feng. A letter nearly two centuries earlier from a seventeenth-century collection had cited the identical incident from the *Zuo Commentary* for the identical purpose: "As far as Ch'u Ni's [Chu Ni's] utterance is concerned, there was no one else to know what he had said, so how did Tso Ch'iu [Master Zuo] know about it?"[95] The letter's bold conclusion is to hail Master Zuo as "the progenitor of a whole line of literary lies."★ Feng accepts the definition of fiction as literary lies, but argues that "even lies must be told fully" (p. 13), that is, fleshed out with sufficient skill and logic to convince the listener. Feng's defense of lies is thus essentially the same as his defense of painting phantoms. But what is a lie? A lie is an utterance that the speaker knows is untrue. In understanding the *Liaozhai* tales as literary lies, Feng reflects another nineteenth-century view, that the ghosts and fox-spirits in *Liaozhai* are nothing but a game, a trick played by the author on the naive reader.[96] Once again, a two-tiered level of meaning is posited; an appeal is made to a superior reader aware of the discrepancy between content and intent who does not let himself be hoodwinked by the author's literary lies. In this last formulation, the strange in *Liaozhai* has finally become a purely fictional and ironic construct, one predicated on the author's and reader's mutual suspension of disbelief.

To conclude, we may also understand the development of these three interpretive approaches in terms of the circumstances behind their adoption and the context in which they were written. Pu Songling's personal friends wrote the first prefaces and dedicatory verses when his manuscript was still unfinished. Their efforts were inherently *social* in nature. They wrote to help introduce his work into society, that is, to a limited circle of like-minded readers. These established literary figures and statesmen lent their authoritative voices to an obscure and potentially suspect manuscript, supplying it with a pedigree and moral approbation.[97] To this end, they tried to carve a niche for records of the strange within the dominant literary and intellectual tradition.

The advocates of *Liaozhai*'s publication primarily constituted the second wave. They were arguing to a new class of readers, the general reading public, why people ought to read an unknown author's work. For this reason, they sought to distinguish *Liaozhai* from the plentiful collections of strange tales on the market, at-

★This questioning of the authenticity of the histories and Classics may be related to the seventeenth-century philological *kaozheng* movement. In applying more rigorous historiographical standards to canonical texts, it is possible that the philologists also contributed to an increasingly sophisticated understanding of fictional techniques. Could there be a convergence between the rise of the philology movement and the burgeoning of fiction's intellectual champions in the seventeenth century?

tempting to convince the public that something special about *this* book warranted purchase and perusal. These writers strove to elevate a mere collection of strange tales by reclassifying it as an allegorical work of self-expression, a high literary value not ordinarily associated with works of this kind. At the same time, social networks also shaped this second generation of interpreters. Pu Lide composed one of his postfaces to enlist the help of the sons of his grandfather's friend Zhu Xiang, who had expressed interest in helping him get *Liaozhai* published.[98] Yu Ji, the collator of the first published edition, wrote his preface at the behest of the publisher, the prefect Zhao Qigao, who was also his friend and employer. Yu Ji's dedicatory verse for the edition is essentially a eulogy to Zhao, who died before the book came out (pp. 37–38).

The nineteenth-century commentators who constituted the third wave were associating themselves with an already famous book. By elaborating the book's literary methods, by "scratching the author's itch," as Feng Zhenluan put it (p. 74), they hoped to win literary fame for themselves.[99] (And to some extent, they have succeeded. We remember these men today solely as commentators on *Liaozhai*.) Because a fictional tradition had been firmly established by this period, the third wave was able to transcend the problem of the book's strange content by "simply taking the writing itself."

2 The Historian of the Strange's Self-introduction

> The act of writing is a sleight of hand through which the dead hand of the past reaches over to *our* side of the border.
>
> —Marjorie Garber, *Shakespeare's Ghostwriters*

Liaozhai's Own Record

Liaozhai's Records of the Strange begins with Pu Songling's self-introduction. Scholars now agree that this 1679 preface, entitled "Liaozhai's Own Record" ("Liaozhai zizhi"), was written well before the entire collection was completed.[1] In this piece, a masterpiece of parallel prose and a model of rhetoric and allusion, Pu Songling demonstrates his remarkable ability to infuse a personal voice into the often stilted cadences of Qing formal prose. The very success of this personal and emotional stamp, however, has tended to blind readers to the extent of its rhetoric: even modern critics, for instance, have tended to read this complicated piece of writing as straight autobiography or as a reliable manifesto of the author's methods and beliefs in the tales.[2]

"Liaozhai's Own Record" is usually treated in piecemeal fashion, one section or one line extracted to represent the whole.[3] When the text of the preface is considered in its entirety, however, we discover that it traces a three-part trajectory: an opening discourse that seeks to establish the author's credibility and authority to write a "history" of the strange; a sketch of the author's origins and destiny that seeks to explain his personal affinity with the strange; and a final vignette that paints a self-portrait of the author in the very act of recording the strange.

I. "A belt of wood-lotus, a cloak of bryony"—the Lord of Three Wards was stirred and composed "Encountering Sorrow";[4] "Ox-headed demons and serpent gods"—of these the Long-Nailed Youth chanted and became obsessed. The pipes of Heaven sound of their own accord, without selecting fine tones; in this, there is precedence.*

I am but the dim flame of the autumn firefly, with which goblins jock-eyed for light; a cloud of swirling dust, jeered at by mountain ogres.** Though I lack the talent of Gan Bao, I too am fond of "seeking the spirits"; in disposition I resemble Su Shi, who enjoyed people telling ghost stories.

What I have heard, I committed to paper, and so this collection came about. After some time, like-minded men from the four directions dis-patched stories to me by post, and because "things accrue to those who love them," what I had amassed grew even more plentiful.

Indeed, within the civilized world, things may be more wondrous than in "the country of those who crop their hair"; before our very eyes are things stranger than in "the land of the flying heads."†

My excitement quickens: this madness is indeed irrepressible, and so I continually give vent to my vast feelings and don't even forbid this folly. Won't I be laughed at by serious men? Though I may have heard wild rumors at "Five Fathers Crossroads," I could still have realized some pre-

---

*The "Lord of Three Wards" was Qu Yuan's official title. Two of his poems are telescoped into one here: "Encountering Sorrow" ("Li sao") and a line from "The Mountain Spirit" ("Shan gui"): "There seems to be someone in the crease of the mountain / Wearing a cloak of wood-lotus and a belt of bryony" (*Chu ci*, p. 44). The "Long-Nailed Youth" refers to the Tang poet Li He because Li Shangyin's (813–58) biography described him as having long fingernails (*Li He shiji*, p. 358). In his preface to Li He's posthumous poetry collection, Du Mu (803–52) wrote: "Whales yawning and sea tortoises leaping, ox-headed demons and serpent gods fail to represent his wild imagination" (*Li He shiji*, p. 356). "Ox-headed demons and serpent gods" became a kenning for the fantastic. *Zhuangzi* 2.3 distinguishes "the pipes of Heaven" from the pipes of men and the pipes of Earth: "Blowing on the ten thousand things in a different way so that each can be itself—all take what they want for themselves, but who does the sounding?" (Trans. Watson, *Complete Works of Chuang Tzu*, p. 37)

**An allusion to a story about the musician Xi Kang (223–62). One night as he was playing his lute, a ghost suddenly appeared; whereupon Xi blew out the candle, saying: "I'm ashamed to jockey for light with a goblin." "A cloud of swirling dust" is adapted from *Zhuangzi* 1.1. "Heat-hazes, dust-storms, the breath which living things blow at each other" (trans. Graham, *Chuang-tzu: The Inner Chapters*, p. 42). "Jeered at by mountain ogres" alludes to an anecdote about the impoverished Liu Bolong. One day a ghost suddenly appeared and began chortling with glee over his poverty. Liu Bolong sighed: "Poverty is certainly decreed by fate, but now I am even being jeered at by an ogre!" (Li Yanshou, *Nan shi* 2: 17.482)

†Sima Qian's *Shiji* describes barbarian tribes that tattooed their bodies and cropped their hair. Duan Chengshi's *Youyang zazu* records a legendary tribe of people whose heads could sprout wings and fly away at night. At dawn the heads would return and reattach themselves to the appropriate necks.

vious causes on the "Rock of Past Lives."‡ Unbridled words cannot be rejected entirely because of their speaker!

Pu Songling begins by constructing a literary tradition and placing himself within it. The two poets named in the striking opening couplet—two of the greatest and most original in the language—are an unusual pair to claim as ancestors for a collection of stories. And yet they can be claimed. The ancient poet and courtier Qu Yuan (the Lord of Three Wards) initiated the paradigm of the virtuous man of genius, who, misprized during his lifetime, expresses his alienation in strange and intensely personal images. The allegorical poems attributed to him in the anthology *Songs of the South* (*Chu ci*), especially "Encountering Sorrow" ("Li sao"), became for later ages the essence of marvelous writing (*qi wen*), the founding works of an alternative literary tradition.[5]

The late Tang poet Li He (the Long-Nailed Youth), was viewed as the embodiment of the imagination pushed to its furthest and most dangerous extent: his poetry, it was said, "progressed from the extraordinary to the weird."[6] Li He's predilection for unearthly images and his own precocious death at twenty-six helped earn him the reputation of the Demonic Genius (*guicai*). Pu Songling's choice of epithet here, the Long-Nailed Youth, and the allusion to the chanting of "ox-headed demons and serpent gods" almost as a form of demonic possession, intensifies the macabre effect of this line. Although scholars also reinterpreted Li He's life and work to fit the Qu Yuan mold, especially during the seventeenth century, Pu Songling wrote two poems in explicit imitation of Li He, which above all reveal his fascination with the ghostliness and sensuality of Li He's imagery.[7]

More typical zhiguai predecessors are named next—Gan Bao, the Jin dynasty historian who compiled the collection *Seeking the Spirits*, and the great Song polymath Su Shi, who was said to have devel-

‡"Five Fathers Crossroads" was an ancient place-name in Chufu county, Shandong, where the *Rites* maintain Confucius was buried. The allusion is employed as an archaism to balance the "Rock of Past Lives" in the second half of the line. According to a Tang legend recorded in Yuan Jiao's *Sweet Marsh Tales* (*Ganze yao*), a Buddhist monk arranged to meet a friend twelve years after his death at a temple in Hangzhou. When the friend went to the rendezvous, he was greeted by a herdboy who identified himself as the monk's incarnation, singing: "[Behold] my former soul at the 'Rock of Past Lives' / . . . Though my body differs, my nature still persists." The "Rock of Past Lives" was a common allusion for reincarnation and predestined fate (see Wang Pijiang, *Tangren xiaoshuo*, pp. 258–59).

oped a passion for ghost stories when exiled to Huangzhou. Later in the preface Pu Songling calls his book "a sequel to *Records of the Underworld,*" the title of another famous Six Dynasties zhiguai collection.[8] By grouping Li He and Qu Yuan with these more conventional literary predecessors, Pu Songling was reaching beyond generic categories to forge a broader and more powerful fantastic tradition. Although he belittles himself as a "dim flame," "a cloud of swirling dust," on his journey into the literary past he is casting himself in exalted company.

This brief introduction is followed by Pu Songling's announcement that he derived the material for the stories from hearsay and later from written accounts sent to him by others who share his interest. This explanation for the genesis of *Liaozhai* closely echoes the Song scholar Hong Mai's preface to the second installment of his famous collection, *Records of the Listener:* "People knew of my love for the strange, and so whenever they obtained a story, they would send it to me, even from a thousand miles away, and so within five years I had obtained the same number of volumes again as my previous collection."[9] Unlike Hong Mai, however, Pu Songling was not a highly placed or prominent figure in his day, and his work was never published in his lifetime. It seems unlikely that his interest in the strange would have been well known before he wrote this preface. Rather, this equation of writing with collecting strengthens the filiation of *Liaozhai* to records of anomalies and unofficial history, genres predicated on the collection of hearsay. Although the claim that the tales were based on hearsay, especially written accounts, may be exaggerated, it cannot be dismissed. The ambiguity that the pretext of hearsay creates is of utmost importance to accounts of the strange, for the burden of truth is partially suspended: the claim becomes in some sense that the story was told, not that the events in the story occurred. Hearsay allows an appeal to an authority and an order of reality above and beyond the record itself.

Even more striking, however, is the inversion of the conventions of collecting and travel literature implicit in this formulation.[10] It is not the author-recorder who journeys to outlying lands or exotic places in search of the strange, but the stories who make the journey to him. Through this claim, Pu Songling effectively places himself in the center, with all its canonical associations of orthodoxy and authority in the Chinese historical tradition; his pivotal position is inscribed by the stories themselves, which arrive from "the four directions."[11] Once he has redrawn the boundaries so that he stands symbolically at the center rather than on the margins, he has authorized himself to tell his readers that the strange lies in a place different from that the culture conventionally assigns it.[12] "Indeed, within the civilized world, things may be more wondrous than in 'the country of those who crop their hair'; before our very eyes are things stranger than in 'the land of the flying heads.' " The cultural categories of strange and familiar, barbarian and civilized, are destabilized and inverted; the "geography of the imagination"[13] has been relocated to the here and now, shifted back to the center. The point is that the strange is not *other;* the strange resides in our midst. The strange is inseparable from *us.*[14]

For Pu Songling, the strange is inescapable in yet another more personal sense. Throughout the first part of the preface, he suggests the involuntary and compulsive nature of *Liaozhai's* composition. Like Li He's fascination with "ox-headed demons and serpent gods," which became a fatal obsession, so Pu Songling's "unbridled words" are the fruit of folly and madness: "My excitement quickens: this madness is indeed irrepressible, and so I continually give vent to my vast feelings and don't even forbid this folly." This is certainly one way of disclaiming responsibility for culturally suspect writing. But this disclaimer is disingenuous, for folly, madness, and obsession are exalted values in the late Ming cult of feeling (*qing*), whose influence permeates *Liaozhai.* And just as Pu Songling had written earlier in the preface, "The pipes of Heaven sound of their own accord, without selecting fine tones," so the stories eventually come to him, uninvited, but eagerly desired, because in the words of Ouyang Xiu (1007–72) describing his celebrated collection of inscriptions, "things accrue to those who love them."[15] The sixteenth-century preface to another zhiguai collection phrases the same idea more explicitly: "And so I secretly laughed at myself, for in fact it was the strange that sought me out, not I who sought the strange."[16] In this way, the recording of the strange is linked with obsessive collecting, a paradigm of particular resonance and popularity in the seventeenth century and a theme of great importance in many *Liaozhai* tales.[17]

Pu Songling's assertion "I could still have realized some previous causes on the 'Rock of Past Lives,'" which ends the first part of the preface, ushers in the embryonic autobiography he outlines in the next section, beginning with his birth as the reincarnation of a poor monk.

II. At the hour of my birth, my late father had a dream: a gaunt, sickly Buddhist monk, whose robe left one shoulder bare, entered the room. A plaster round as a coin was pasted on his chest. When my father awoke, I had been born, with an inky birthmark that corroborated his dream. Moreover, as a child I was frequently ailing, and when I grew up, my fate was wanting. The desolation of my courtyard resembles a monk's quarters and what "plowing with brush and ink" brings is as little as a monk's alms bowl. I often scratch my head and muse: "Could 'he who faced the wall'* have really been me in a former existence?" In fact, there must have been a deficiency in my previous karma, and so I did not reach transcendence, but was blown down by the wind, becoming in the end a flower fallen in a cesspool. How murky are the "six paths of existence!" But it cannot be said they lack coherence.

This exact motif—the dream-visitation that a father receives at the hour of his son's birth from his son's former incarnation—crops up several times in *Liaozhai* and is a common theme in Chinese folklore.[18] Moreover, the wording used here ("when he awoke, a son had been born . . .") is formulaic. We need not take this dream literally. Rather, on a symbolic level this dream excuses the author's subsequent poverty and isolation in adulthood as well as the nature of his book. The "inky birthmark" (*mo-zhi*) that corroborates the dream is itself a pun: *mo* means ink, and *zhi* (birthmark) is written not with the customary "illness" radical, but with the variant "word" radical, a character that usually means "to record," as in the book's title, "*Records* of the Strange," and even in the title of the preface itself, "Liaozhai's Own *Record*." Thus the proof-mark of his father's premonitory dream explains both the etiology of his vocation as recorder of the strange and the source of his privileged insight into such matters.

We may still wonder what Pu Songling, who is not otherwise

*The monk Bodhidarma, who founded the Chan school of Buddhism ca. the sixth century. He is said to have reached enlightenment after "facing the wall" in meditation for nine years.

known for strong Buddhist leanings, was trying to achieve here by portraying himself as the incarnation of a Buddhist monk. A letter sent to Pu Songling by his friend Gao Heng in 1692, thirteen years after both men had written their prefaces to *Liaozhai,* indicates how Pu Songling's contemporaries might have interpreted this trope.

When I read your *Records of the Strange* years ago, I didn't pay close attention. Now that I have read it carefully, I find that it far surpasses *A Compendium of Rare Beauties* [*Yanyi bian*] in novelty. . . . The postfaces to the stories move others as exhortations and warnings and show delight in your own lofty cultivation. Only now do I realize that the part in the preface about being a bodhisattva in your past life was no exaggeration.[19]

In his old age, Gao Heng explains what he sees as the significance of this reincarnation incident in Pu Songling's preface: the author is claiming that he has transcribed these strange stories out of a bodhisattva-like desire to enlighten his fellow men—an aim traditionally professed in prefaces to collections of Buddhist miracle tales. Gao Heng's words imply that he at first dismissed this unseemly boast as "exaggeration," but upon rereading the comments to the stories many years later, he became convinced that the author did indeed possess the "lofty cultivation" and compassion of a bodhisattva.

Nevertheless, Pu Songling does not remain on this lofty level of self-justification for long; he immediately returns to the present by staging for his readers the vivid but ghostly scene of the author hard at work on his collection:

III. It's just that here it is the glimmering hour of midnight as I am about to trim my failing lamp. Outside my bleak studio the wind is sighing; inside my desk is cold as ice. Piecing together patches of fox fur to make a robe, I vainly fashion a sequel to *Records of the Underworld.* Draining my winecup and grasping my brush, I complete the book of "lonely anguish."[20] How sad it is that I must express myself like this!

Alas! A chilled sparrow startled by frost clings to frigid boughs, an autumn insect mourning the moon hugs the railing for warmth. Are the only ones who know me "in the green wood and at the dark frontier"?

Spring, the year *jimo* [1679] during the reign of Kangxi

The line "Piecing together patches of fox fur to make a robe, I vainly fashion a sequel to *Records of the Underworld*" ostensibly describes the composition of the collection, but it better characterizes the method of the preface, which, like all parallel prose, is literally patched together out of snippets of allusions. The whole preface is a crazy quilt of disembodied images: the long nails of Li He and his ox-headed demons and serpent gods, the jeering goblins, the flying heads, the emaciated half-naked monk that appears in a dream. Several of the zhiguai themes that appear repeatedly in the collection are foreshadowed in the preface's allusions: premonitory dreams of rebirth and karmic retribution; dreams of encounters with the dead; the mockery of humans by otherworldly beings. The preface strives not so much to interpret or define the strange as to achieve an effect of strangeness, creating the ominous atmosphere conducive to a nightmare.

Pu Songling dated his preface spring, but we find none of the images of growth or renewal associated with this season in literature or ritual. In the Chinese calendar, spring is the first three months of the year; in the north, in Shandong, the weather would still have been bleak and wintry. Metaphorical concerns thus work together with naturalistic ones in the preface's final scene. The desolate images of ice and wind, the lamplight dimming, the *Records of the Underworld,* the dark frontier—all seem to augur death. Like the chilled sparrow clinging to frigid boughs, like the autumn insect hugging the railing for warmth, the author finds temporary refuge where he can, in the composition of his book of "lonely anguish" (*gu fen*). The ancient philosopher Han Fei coined this term as a chapter title, but it was the historian Sima Qian who first used it in his autobiographical postface to explain literature as the outpouring of suffering and indignation.[21] In the late sixteenth century, however, the philosopher Li Zhi subtly amended Sima Qian's influential theory to argue that anguish is the *only* possible source of literary creativity: "In this light, the sages of antiquity did not write unless they were anguished. For to write without anguish is like shivering without being cold or moaning without being ill; even if one did write without anguish, why would anybody read it?"[22] More important, Li Zhi explicitly introduced the reader into Sima Qian's original formulation—not only is anguish the sole legitimate motive for *writing* a work, but it is now also the sole possible reason for *reading* another's work.

Pu Songling's preface closes by posing an open-ended challenge to the reader: "Are the only ones who know me 'in the green wood and the dark frontier'?" (*Zhi wo zhe, qi zai* qinglin heisai jian *hu?*) The syntax here echoes Confucius's cry of despair in *The Analects* (14.35): "Is the only one who knows me Heaven?" (*zhi wo zhe, qi tian hu?*)[23] The same formula, "*zhi wo zhe . . . qi zai . . . hu,*" also appears in *Mencius* (3B.9), where Confucius is said to have remarked that his reputation would ultimately rest on his authorship of one book: "Will those who understand me do so through the *Spring and Autumn Annals?*" (*zhi wo zhe, qi zai* Chunqiu *hu?*)[24] But in the telescopic form of parallel prose, Pu Songling has replaced both "Heaven" and the *Annals* with yet another allusion, the phrase "the green wood and dark frontier" from the first in Du Fu's (712–70) famous poem sequence "Dreaming of Li Bo" ("Meng Li Bo"): "When your soul came, the maple wood was green yet; / When your soul returned, the frontier pass was dark with night."[25]

In the poem, the living poet Du Fu longs for the dead poet Li Bo and encounters his specter in dream; Du Fu thus presents himself as Li Bo's true friend and reader. Pu Songling's allusion might be understood as a plea: I need someone who will be my true reader just as Du Fu was for Li Bo. In that case, the line could be interpreted as a terrible prophecy: only when I am dead will I find a true reader who understands me. But in his adaptation of this couplet, Pu Songling reverses the relations governing the original poem. It is no longer the living who are the true readers of the dead writers of the past. Instead, his true readers are wraiths, disembodied spirits, inhabiting the shadowy world of the dead and of dream; it is the writer who is alive and alone, crying out for someone to understand him.

Pu Songling articulates this quest for a true friend and reader, for "one who would know him" and appreciate his talent, in several of his poems.[26] In his tales, human protagonists often find true friends and soul mates among the denizens of the underworld. The tale "Licentiate Ye" ("Ye sheng"; 1.81–85), for instance, recounts the narrative of an aspiring scholar who is so anxious to requite his one true friend and patron that he rejoins his friend and passes the exams even though he has already died. The Historian of the Strange's empassioned postface to this tale resembles "Liaozhai's Own Record" in mood and diction; one nineteenth-century commentator even reads it as Pu Songling's own covert autobiography.[27] The extraordinary achievement of the scholar in this tale provokes an outburst from the Historian of the Strange: "Could a dead man's soul really follow his true friend, forgetting in the end he was dead? Listeners may doubt it, but I deeply believe it" (1.84).

Seeing the Self as Other

It is above all the emotional intensity and the fierce literary ambition, barely masked by continuous self-deprecation, that sets "Liaozhai's Own Record" apart from most authorial prefaces to records of the strange or notation books (*biji*). In keeping with the modest status of the works they introduce, such prefaces tend to adopt a casual, even comic, tone and style. Consider Wang Shizhen's (1634–1711) preface to his *Occasional Chats North of the Pond (Chibei outan)*, a notation book that includes a section on the strange and even shares some material with *Liaozhai*. In his preface (dated 1691), Wang Shizhen, one of the most celebrated poets and officials of the age, draws an enchanting picture of his studio, filled with guests leisurely chatting on a variety of subjects. "Sometimes when we had been drinking and the moon was setting, we'd bring up events involving gods and immortals, ghosts and spirits, as material for conversation; from there we'd digress to trivia about the arts; we'd leave no subject untouched."[28] On these occasions, however, Wang Shizhen did not even bother to lift a brush himself; instead, he tells us, "Our juniors standing by recorded what was said, and as the days and months passed, their notes grew into chapters."[29] The illusion of artlessness and diffidence is complete: Wang Shizhen's book, as it were, has written itself.

What a contrast this relaxed, convivial scene makes with the picture Pu Songling draws of the author alone at midnight painfully copying his book. Throughout his preface, Pu Songling emphasizes the physical act of writing.[30] Although he too claims that his book organically grew out of the stories that he had heard or received, it is he who anxiously "commits them to paper"; it is he, as the Chinese literally reads, who self-consciously "commands his brush" (*ming bi*) to transform his collection into Literature.

Taken as a whole, Pu Songling's preface loosely belongs to a branch of Chinese autobiographical writing that Yves Hervouet has described as "the preface or the chapter of a work that the author has fashioned as a parenthesis to the rest of the work to recount his life therein."[31] In his pioneering work of 1937, Guo Dengfeng lists "the self-introduction appended to a work" (*fu yu zhuzuo de zixu*) as one of his eight categories of traditional Chinese autobiography.[32] Wu Pei-yi has recently called the "authorial self-account" "the most flexible of all subgenres" of autobiography and sees its origin in "the type of preface that the author of a book employed to introduce himself to the reading public."[33]

We can trace this tradition back to Sima Qian's self-introduction in his *Records of the Historian,* a work *Liaozhai* consciously took as its model in a number of important ways.[34] But Sima Qian placed his "self-introduction" as a postface: in undertaking to record human history from beginning to end, the Grand Historian concluded with his own life history, explaining his family genealogy and tragic mutilation as well as the motives and organization of his book.[35] "Liaozhai's Own Record," however, like most later "self-introductions," is positioned at the beginning of the work. Constructed as an entryway into the stories, Pu Songling's preface above all reveals the author's attempt to control or influence the reading of his book by fashioning himself into a lens through which the book would be refracted for his readers. This is an account of a life written in a particular context with a particular agenda: it aims not merely to explain who the author is but to explain how he came to write the book in question and, on a deeper level, how the book embodies his secret ambitions and aspirations.

Stephen Owen has argued that in traditional Chinese literature poetry (*shi*) rather than narrative became the chief medium for autobiographical self-presentation. In his view, this choice reflected the most pressing concern of traditional writers and readers: "Not how a person changed over time, but how a person could be known at all or make himself known."[36] Pu Songling's self-introduction resembles poetic autobiography in its overwhelming desire to make himself known. At the same time, the artistry of the parallel-prose form gave him an original voice that he could not find in poetry, a greater latitude for an imaginative projection of the self.

Like poetic autobiography, Pu Songling's self-introduction is not primarily narrative in thrust; we learn far more about the important events in his private life when he writes a memoir of his dead wife or recalls his late father in the preface to a book of family instructions.[37] Nor like a certain brand of Chinese autobiography does it present a formal public account of his career as though it were an official biography that happened to be written by the subject himself. "Liaozhai's Own Record" bears some resemblance to those idealized portraits of the self as recluse, such as Tao Yuanming's (365–427) "Biography of Master Five Willows" ("Wuliu xiansheng zhuan") and its countless imitations, which claim to reveal the true inner self. But recluse autobiographies after Tao Yuanming tend simply to invert the norms of official biography—they calmly present the self acting in a stereotyped private rather than public role, where private is equated with "recluse." Unlike both these types of autobiography, which tend to adopt a consistent role and present a unified voice throughout, "Liaozhai's Own Record" teems with an almost frenzied profusion of roles and voices; the author likens himself not only to historical figures like Qu Yuan and Li He, Su Shi and Gan Bao, but to "the dim light of the autumn firefly," "a cloud of swirling dust," "a flower fallen in a cesspool," a "sparrow startled by frost," "an insect mourning the moon." His self-portrait dissolves into a vortex of metaphors and allusions.

The most sustained image of himself that Pu Songling creates in the preface is his incarnation as the emaciated monk. But even this ostensibly narrative section of his self-introduction is not really narrative in intent: it depicts not a process of change, but a stasis that begins in a previous life, is confirmed at birth, and is lived out in childhood and adulthood. It purports to make manifest "the coherence" (or principle, *li*) that is in danger of being obscured by "the murkiness" of the six paths of existence. This is mythical autobiography, one that strives to display the contour of a life, not necessarily as it was but as it was imagined to be. If we accept Owen's insight that the enterprise of autobiography requires the writer to see himself as other,[38] the monk is the most prolonged case in the preface of Pu Songling viewing himself as other. Reincarnation creates a palimpsest, exposing vestiges of another self, an ancient alter ego. This feat of self-alienation may also be implied in the very notion of recording the strange, for it was understood that strangeness lies not in *things* but in *me*.

As I mentioned in the introduction, Pu Songling's alias Historian of the Strange verbally echoes Sima Qian's title Grand Historian in the *Records of the Historian*. Pu Songling's selection of this alias contains a self-conscious irony that helps undercut the authority it claims to establish, for the verbal parallels to the Grand Historian call attention to a profound difference as much as to a sameness, a difference that is itself represented in the primary meaning of yi as other. Unlike Sima Qian, who claimed descent from Zhou dynasty historians and who inherited the official position of grand historian from his father, Pu Songling invented himself as Historian of the Strange. In the first part of the preface, he strives to create a literary genealogy for himself.[39] The trope of reincarnation enables him to forge an alternative past for himself outside the bonds of family tradition (though given a de facto stamp of approval by his father's dream). But this past is conjured up entirely through sleights of hand: through analogy, metaphor, and allusion. The infant author's previous identity is verified by a likeness between the plaster pasted on the monk's chest and his own similarly placed birthmark. As he grows up, "The desolation of [his] courtyard *resembles* a monk's quarters" and "what 'plowing with brush and ink' brings is *as little as* a monk's alms bowl." Eventually he shows himself pondering his own identity, wondering who he is. He openly exposes the incongruity between the self and the role he is temporarily adopting: "I often scratch my head and muse: 'Could "he who faced the wall" really have been me in a former existence?'" But he immediately negates his question with yet another metaphor: "I did not reach transcendence, but was blown down by the wind, becoming in the end a flower fallen in a cesspool."

Pu Songling has written a highly stylized but deeply moving self-introduction that incorporates within it the idealized circumstances, motives, speaker, and audience for the tales that follow. The final tableau theatrically stages the circumstances of the collection's composition, depicting the author writing alone at midnight in his freezing studio. The motives or excuses for recording the strange take up most of the preface: there is historical precedent for doing so; he loves to do so; material abounds, and eventually stories are even sent to him; it is an uncontrollable obsession, a folly he cannot suppress; he was predestined to do so; he is stirred by "lonely anguish"; the ghosts whose history he records are the only ones who understand him. "Liaozhai's Own Record" is not a confession of sins, but it possesses the emotional intensity of such a confession.[40] The sheer overabundance of motives helps conjure up a speaker for the tales— a failed scholar who longs for literary greatness but is mocked by goblins; the incarnation of a monk who cannot achieve transcendence; the lonely writer who communes with ghosts. Throughout the preface, Pu Songling seeks to create the ideal audience for his book, to transform the "serious men" who will laugh at him and reject his "unbridled words" into sympathetic readers who will strive to understand him. His self-portrait is not a self-contained image; rather, it constantly fixes its gaze upon the viewer, building up to a final climactic question addressed directly to the reader: "Are the only ones who know me 'in the green wood and at the dark frontier'?"

The Ghostly Writer

The haunting quality of Pu Songling's self-portrait is affirmed by readers who specifically responded to the preface, particularly to the challenge posed at the end: Who will be my true reader? Yu Ji, the collator of the first printed edition of *Liaozhai,* begins his preface where Pu Songling left off, uncannily echoing the closing section of "Liaozhai's Own Record." Just as Pu Songling depicts the physical and emotional experience of writing his book, so Yu Ji recounts the scene of his first reading of the manuscript:

The Yanling mountains encircling the prefecture had high, jagged peaks, and near the prefectural building stood many ancient trees and strange rocks.[41] It was the season when the autumn winds howl and rage and when the vegetation lies sere and withered; foxes and mice scampered about even in daylight, and owls and jackals screeched at night. I sat holding the manuscript in a tiny cubicle that was dimly lit by a flickering lamp; before I had even unrolled it, a ghostly chill had already set my hair on end.   (p. 6)

In terms similar to those Pu Songling used to portray himself composing the collection, Yu Ji situates his reading at night in a cold, isolated studio beneath a dim lamp with the wind howling outside. Pu Songling had likened himself to a "chilled sparrow

startled by frost" and an "autumn insect mourning the moon." Here
Yu Ji places himself among ill-omened animals—foxes and mice
scampering by day, owls and jackals screeching at night—that in the
context seem no less metaphorical, no less descriptive, of the scene
and the writer's frame of mind. But Yu Ji has exaggerated the
disquieting mood of "Liaozhai's Own Record" into the prelude to a
horror tale. Before he has even unrolled the manuscript, "a ghostly
chill" sets his hair on end; he implies that he has encountered Pu
Songling's specter, whom he addresses in the next line: "Alas! you
too once dwelled in bright sunlight; how miserable and alone you
must have been to entrust your intent so far beyond the world!
When I had finished reading the manuscript, I grieved deeply for
this man's intent" (p. 6).[42]

Another reader, the Shandong painter Gao Fenghan (1683–1748),
who had met Pu Songling in his teens, also re-enacts the closing of
Liaozhai's preface in some dedicatory verses that he wrote for the
collection in 1723, a few years after the author's death.[43] Like Yu Ji,
he begins by setting the scene for his solitary reading of the book; it
too is a cold, dark, ominous night in late autumn.

> A volume of *Liaozhai* dissipates my loneliness;
> The lamplight turns greenish before my autumn window.
> I'm used to reading *Seeking the Spirits* and *Records of the Shades;*
> Why should I feel such pain toward *this* book?
>
> (*Liaozhai*, p. 35)

Lamplight turning greenish typically signals a ghostly visitation; as
in Yu Ji's preface, the image suggests the fleeting presence of the
author's apparition hovering over the reader of his tales. Moved by
his recollection of the author's worldly failure from their meeting
twenty years earlier, Gao Fenghan not only explicitly addresses his
ghost, but even makes a libation to appease his spirit:

> Before long the moon sets, the wind rises in the trees.
> I offer you a libation, as though you had consciousness.
> I throw myself on my pillow, blow out the candle, and bid you
>   good-bye;
> Where are you "at the dark frontier and in the green
>   wood"?
>
> (p. 35)

To Gao Fenghan, Pu Songling's own ghost is now wandering somewhere in the borderland of "the dark frontier and green wood." Now that Pu Songling is dead, he has joined the spectral world with which he had metaphorically affiliated himself in his preface. The writer of ghosts has become a ghost himself. It is this now-perfect merging of the author with his tales that so stirs the sympathy and imagination of his later readers. The sequence Gao Fenghan establishes—first reading *Liaozhai,* then grieving for the author's intent, then making a libation to his ghost, then going to bed and inquiring after the ghost's whereabouts—may suggest an attempt to incubate a dream-visitation from Pu Songling's spirit. Gao Fenghan's twice-borrowed allusion has restored the balance of Du Fu's original poem: it is once again a living man who longs to dream of a dead writer's ghost.

Thus both Yu Ji and Gao Fenghan affirm the power of the self-portrait in "Liaozhai's Own Record" and declare themselves Pu Songling's posthumous "true reader," the belated ones "who would know" him.

PART TWO

The Tales

3 *Obsession*

Without an obsession, no one is exceptional.

—Yuan Hongdao, *A History of Flower Arranging*

According to one of the apocryphal anecdotes that later sprang up around *Liaozhai* and its author, Pu Songling never passed the higher examinations because "his love of the strange had developed into an obsession."[1] As a result, when he entered the examination hall, fox-spirits and ghosts jealously crowded around to prevent him from writing about anything but them. This colorful legend continues the transformation of the author into a character in his tales that we glimpsed in the previous chapter. But it also contains an important insight: the nearly five hundred tales in the *Liaozhai* collection grew out of the author's lifelong obsession with the strange. We have seen that in his preface Pu Songling represented his fascination with the strange as an uncontrollable passion and linked his recording of strange stories with the paradigm of obsessive collecting, in which "things accrue to those who love them." Within the stories themselves, the notion of obsession and collecting is likewise a prominent theme, one translated with great art into fiction.

The Chinese Concept of Obsession

The concept of obsession, or *pi*, is an important Chinese cultural construct that after a long development reached its height during the late Ming and early Qing dynasties. A seventeenth-century diction-ary, *A Complete Mastery of Correct Characters* (*Zhengzi tong*), offers the essential Ming definition of the term: "Pi is a pathological fondness for something" (*pi, shihao zhi bing;* see Fig. 1).[2] This pathological

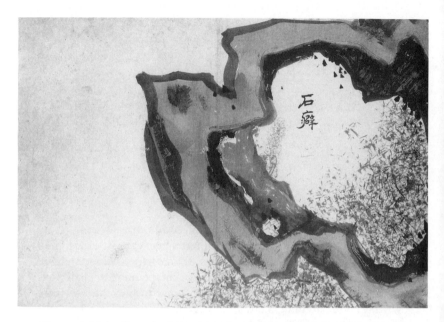

Fig. 1. An ink album-leaf painting of a rock by the seventeenth-century eccentric painter Zhu Da (Bada shanren). The painting's most unusual feature is the two characters *shi pi* ("The Rock of Obsession" or "an obsession with rocks") framed by the hollowed-out rock. The album was executed after 1659 and before 1666. ([*Shanghai bowuguan cang*] *Si gaoseng huaji,* pl. 85)

component of pi is significant: indeed a synonym for pi is sometimes "illness" or "mania" (*bing*). The medical usage of pi can be traced back to *The Classic Materia Medica (Bencao jing)* of the second century, where according to Paul Unschuld, the term *pi shi* or "indigestion" already figures as "one of the most important kinds of serious illnesses."[3] An influential early seventh-century medical book, *The Etiology and Symptomatology of All Diseases (Zhubing yuanhou lun)* offers the most detailed description of this syndrome: "If digestion stops, then the stomach will not work. When one then drinks fluid, it will be stopped from trickling and will not disperse. If this fluid then comes into contact with cold *qi* [energy], it will accumulate and form a pi. A pi is what inclines to one side between the two ribs and sometimes hurts."[4] According to a mid-eighth-century medical book, the *Secret Prescriptions of the Outer Tower* (*Waitai biyao*), a pi could even become as hard as stone and eventually develop into an abscess.[5]

From this sense of pathological blockage most likely evolved the extended meaning of obsession or addiction—something that sticks in the gut and cannot be evacuated, hence becoming habitual. When written in its alternative form with the "person" radical, rather than the "illness" radical, however, the primary meaning of *pi* becomes "leaning to one side," or "off-center."[6] An attempt to relate the meanings of both graphs (which share a phonetic element) becomes apparent in the etymology in *The Etiology and Symptomatology of All Diseases:* "A pi is what inclines [*pianpi*] between the two ribs and sometimes hurts." From this sense of one-sidedness or partiality, pi also comes to denote the individual proclivities inherent in all human nature, as in the compound *pixing* (personal taste), written with either radical. This paradoxical view of obsession as at once pathological and normative helps account for the peculiar range of behavior associated with it and for the contradictory interpretations assigned to it.

The concept of pi is not merely a matter of terminology, however: once the symptoms have been codified, this particular term need not be used for the condition to be instantly recognizable.* Nonetheless, the term is charged with a strong emotional quality and has a wide range of implicit meanings; this was particularly true during the sixteenth and seventeenth centuries when the concept of obsession had deeply penetrated all aspects of literati life. As an indication of its range of meaning, "pi" has been translated into English as addiction, compulsion, passion, mania, fondness for, weakness for, love of, fanatical devotion, craving, idiosyncracy, fetishism, and even hobby. On this level, the idea of obsession is most apparent in the pronouncements of Yuan Hongdao (1568–1610), one of the

---

*The concept of pi is associated with a cluster of words, notably *shi* (a taste for) and *hao* (a fondness for). These characters are further combined to form almost synonymous compounds, such as *pihao, pishi,* and *shihao.* One caveat: I am not employing "obsession" in the technical psychiatric sense, which stresses negative and involuntary aspects. Compare the definition of obsession in Campbell, *Psychiatric Dictionary,* p. 492: "An idea, emotion, or impulse that repetitively and insistently forces itself into consciousness, even though it may be unwelcome."

great literary and intellectual figures of his time. As he wrote in his *History of Flower Arranging* in 1599:

> If someone has something he is really obsessed about, he will be deeply immersed, intoxicated with it. He will consecrate his life and even his death to it. What time would he have for the affairs of money-grubbers and traders in official titles?
>
> When someone in antiquity who was gripped by an obsession for flowers heard tell of a rare blossom, even if it were in a deep valley or in steep mountains, he would not be afraid of stumbling and would go to it. Even in the freezing cold and the blazing heat, even if his skin were cracked and peeling or caked with mud and sweat, he would be oblivious.
>
> When a flower was about to bloom, he would move his pillow and mat and sleep alongside it to observe how the flower would go from budding to blooming to fading. Only after it lay withered on the ground would he take his leave. . . . This is what is called a *genuine* love of flowers; this is what is called *genuine* connoisseurship.
>
> But as for *my* growing flowers, merely to break up the pain of idleness and solitude—I am incapable of genuinely loving them. Only someone already dwelling at the mouth of Peach Blossom Spring could genuinely love them—how could he still be an official in this dust-stained world![7]

Rather than condemning the flower-lover as frivolous or ridiculous, or lamenting the misdirection of his energies and passion, Yuan raises an obsession with flowers to unprecedented heights, praising it as an ideal of unswerving commitment and genuine integrity incompatible with worldly success and conspicuous consumption. This idealization arises in part from his disgust at the shallow vogue for obsession in his day. For Yuan, true obsession is always a marginal activity, an act of alienation and withdrawal from conventional society. His polemic aimed at wresting obsession from the inauthentic vulgar mainstream; ironically it may have merely reinforced obsession's fashionability.

Yuan's description also implies some of the general principles of obsession. First, obsession describes a habitual fixation on a certain object or activity, rather than on a particular person, and it is particularly associated with collecting and connoisseurship. Second, it must be excessive and single-minded. Third, it is a deliberately unconventional and eccentric pose.

A Brief History of Obsession

The identification of behavior as obsessive and the attitudes toward that behavior evolved over time. Obsession first began to crystallize as a distinct concept in anecdotes about the free and unrestrained eccentrics included in the fifth-century anthology *New Tales of the World* (*Shishuo xinyu*) with corresponding overtones of eremitism and nonconformity. The spectrum of obsessions in *New Tales of the World* ranges wildly, from a fondness for funeral dirges and donkey brays to a passion for ox fights and the *Zuo Commentary*. One anecdote in the anthology even recounts an informal competition between a lover of money and a lover of wooden clogs. The lover of clogs proves himself the superior, not because of the object of his obsession, but because of his utter self-absorption in his clogs even when observers pay him a visit.[8]

It was not until the late Tang, however, that obsession was mated with connoisseurship and collecting and people began to leave written records of their obsessions. Of particular interest is a moving passage by the great ninth-century art historian Zhang Yanyuan, which lays out the basic paradigms of the fanatical connoisseur's spirit: these paradigms will be re-enacted over and over in subsequent ages.

Ever since my youth I've been a collector of rare things. . . . When there was a chance of getting something, I'd even sell my old clothes and ration simple foods. My wife, children, and servants nag and tease me, sometimes saying, "What's the point of doing such a useless thing all day long?" At which I sigh and say "If one doesn't do such useless things, then how can one take pleasure in this mortal life?" Thus my passion grows ever deeper, approaching an obsession. . . .

Only in calligraphy and painting have I not yet forgotten emotion. Intoxicated by them I forget all speech; enraptured I gaze at and examine them. . . . Does this not seem wiser, after all, than all that burning ambition and ceaseless toil when fame and profit war within one's breast?[9]

This autobiographical sketch begins by enumerating the symptoms of obsession—the utter absorption and diligence, the willingness to endure physical privation, the transcendent joy. Zhang hints at the notion of obsession as a form of individual self-expression, but his statement also becomes a defense, an apology for a private obsession, that justifies the rejection of public life. Zhang introduces the notion of obsession as compensation for worldly failure at the same time as he criticizes the fame, profit, and vain ambition underlying success. He formulates the idea that an obsession should be *useless*—something that does not contribute to official success or material wealth. In this way, obsession is linked with the tradition of the recluse in Chinese culture and the worthy gentleman who does not achieve success but instead disdains competition for power and prestige as an inferior mode of life.

Zhang's statement foreshadows the flourishing of art connoisseurship during the Song dynasty. Not only ancient masterpieces of painting and calligraphy but all sorts of antiques—bronzes, carved jades, stone engravings, and ceramics—as well as things from nature, such as rocks, flowers, and plants, became objects of collecting. With the onset of printing, the compiling of handbooks and catalogues devoted to a particular type of object came into fashion. New paradigms of eccentric collectors emerged, firmly tying the pursuit of obsession to Song literati culture. This mania for collecting culminated in one of the most notorious episodes in Chinese history, "the levy on flowers and rocks" (*huashi gang*), the mass appropriations for the collection of Huizong (r. 1100–1125), the last Northern Song emperor and an aesthete whose decadence would be blamed for the loss of the north to the Jin barbarians.

As the craze for art collecting and connoisseurship became closely associated with the notion of obsession in Song culture, an uneasiness arose that an overattachment to objects courts disaster. Zhang Yanyuan's discovery of the joys of collecting could not be replicated unequivocally by the more self-conscious Song connoisseurs. Framed by the destruction of the Five Dynasties in the mid-tenth century and the devastation of the Northern Song in the early twelfth century, three famous essays debate the dangers of obsession. These essays should be read sequentially because the later ones seem in part a response to the previous ones.

The need to justify obsessive collecting despite its potential for harm is first raised in the eleventh century in Ouyang Xiu's preface to his catalogue of epigraphy. His solution is to posit a hierarchy of value based on the kind of objects collected. He distinguishes ordinary treasures—pearls, gold, and furs—which incite conventional greed, from relics of the past, whose collection does not entail great physical risk and which supplement our understanding of history. With ordinary treasures, what counts is the power to get them; with relics of the past, what counts is the collector's taste and his whole-hearted love of them. But even compiling a catalogue does not quite set to rest Ouyang Xiu's anxieties about the future of his collection. He consoles himself in a fabricated dialogue:

Someone mocked me saying: "If a collection is large, then it will be hard to keep intact. After being assembled for a long time, it is bound to be scattered. Why are you bothering to be so painstaking?"

I replied: "It's enough that I am collecting what I love and that I will enjoy growing old among them."[10]

Ouyang Xiu's fears about the dispersal of his collection must have been prompted in part by the destruction of the great Tang estates a century or two earlier, a subject he addressed in an essay called "The Ling Stream Rocks" ("Lingxi shi ji").[11] Another connoisseur, Ye Mengde (1077–1148), reported that "Ouyang Xiu used to laugh at Li Deyu's [787–848] remark that neither his sons nor grandsons would ever give away one tree or one plant of his Pingyuan estate,"[12] for as everyone knew, the estate had been utterly destroyed.

In the next generation, Su Shi adopts another strategy to mitigate the dangers of collecting, one implicit in Ouyang Xiu's defense that what is important is the act of loving what one collects rather than the collection itself. Su Shi, too, posits a hierarchy of value, but not of the sorts of *collections* but of the sorts of *collectors*:

A gentleman may temporarily "lodge" his interest in things, but he must not "detain" his interest in things. For if he lodges his interest in things, then even trivial objects will suffice to give him joy and even "things of unearthly beauty" will not suffice to induce mania in him. If he detains his interest in things, then even trivial objects will suffice to induce mania in him, and even things of unearthly beauty will not suffice to give him joy.[13]

Su Shi draws a subtle distinction between "lodging" (*yu*) one's interest temporarily in things and "detaining" (*liu*) one's interest permanently in them. In his scheme, lodging implies viewing objects as vessels through which one fulfills oneself rather than as things that one values for their own sake. This maximizes the benign pleasures of loving things and prevents even "things of unearthly beauty" (*youwu*) from causing injury.[14] Detaining, on the other hand, implies a pathological attachment to actual things as *things*. Su Shi employs the clearly pejorative term "mania" (*bing*) rather than the more ambiguous "pi" to emphasize the harmful nature of the passions detaining engenders. He concludes that only the detaining kind of collecting brings personal and national catastrophe.

Ouyang Xiu's and Su Shi's clever arguments, however, are challenged by the poet Li Qingzhao (1081?–1149) in her autobiographical postface to the epigraphy catalogue of her husband, the antiquarian Zhao Mingcheng (1081–1129). Having survived the death of her husband, the destruction of their book collection, and the violent fall of the Northern Song dynasty, she speaks of experiencing the very disasters that Ouyang Xiu and Su Shi had most feared and warned against. She begins by echoing Ouyang Xiu's claims that epigraphy collections serve the lofty aims of redressing historiographic errors. But suddenly her tone shifts, and she attacks his privileging of scholarly collections over all others: "Alas! in the disasters that befell Wang Bo and Yuan Zai, what distinction was there between [collecting] books and paintings and [collecting] pepper?[15] Both He Qiao and Du Yu had a mania—what difference was there between an obsession with money and an obsession with the *Zuo Commentary?*[16] The reputations of such men may differ, but their delusion was one and the same."[17]

Li Qingzhao also rejects Su Shi's argument that the collector's self-control can prevent his passion from becoming pathological and thereby ward off disaster. In recounting the saga of the progressive worsening of her husband's obsession, she shows that Su Shi's distinction between "lodging" and "detaining" hangs by a thread. As Stephen Owen has pointed out, the book collecting that begins as a casual and joint pleasure for the young couple disintegrates into a nightmare of anxiety.[18] Ouyang Xiu had argued in an autobiographical essay that being encumbered by the things of office made him distressed and worried, but that being encumbered by his scholarly possessions made him detached and freed him from vexation.[19] The image of the lone woman Li Qingzhao stranded during the Jin invasion with fifteen boatloads of books that her dying husband had ordered her to protect renders the detachment posited by Ouyang Xiu and Su Shi utterly absurd.

The Late Ming Craze for Obsession

By the sixteenth century, however, most scruples or fears about the perils of obsession seem to have vanished. What is truly new in the explosion of writings in this period is the glorification of obsession, particularly in its most exaggerated form. Obsession becomes an important component of late Ming culture, in which it is linked with the new virtues of Sentiment (*qing*), Madness (*kuang*), Folly (*chi*), and Lunacy (*dian*). No longer do obsessives feel obliged to defend or apologize for their position. Although someone like the scholar-official Xie Zhaozhe (1567–1624) might caution his contemporaries that any preference, if sufficiently one-sided and extreme, should be considered "a form of illness,"[20] most of them were only too willing to contract such a pleasurable virus. Obsession had become a sine qua non, something the gentleman could not afford to do without.

As the preface to the sixteenth-century *Brief History of Obsession and Lunacy* (*Pidian xiaoshi*) puts it: "Everyone has a predilection; this gets called obsession. The signs of obsession resemble folly and madness. . . . The gentleman worries only about having no obsession."[21] Declares Yuan Hongdao: "I have observed that in this world, all those whose words are insipid and whose appearance is detestable are men without obsessions."[22] Zhang Dai (1599–1684?), a Ming loyalist, concurs: "One cannot befriend a man without obsessions, for he lacks deep emotion; nor can one befriend a man without faults, for he lacks integrity."[23] A seventeenth-century aphorism by Zhang Chao (fl. 1676–1700) clinches the indispensability of obsession on aesthetic grounds: "Flowers must have butterflies, mountains must have streams, rocks must have moss, water must have seaweed, old trees must have creepers, and people must have obsessions."[24]

The eleventh-century intellectuals had already argued that obsessions were valuable as an outlet for personal fulfillment; in the sixteenth century, obsession as a vehicle for self-expression becomes the dominant mode. The traditional Chinese understanding of the function of poetry, that it "speaks of what is intently on the mind," had long spread to the other arts, such as painting, music, and calligraphy; now this notion was extended to cover virtually any activity, no matter how preposterous. Moreover, this self-expression was no longer involuntary: it had become obligatory. Most important, the virtue of an obsession lay not in the object of devotion, not even in the act of devotion, but in self-realization. As Yuan Hongdao observes:

The chrysanthemums of Tao Yuanming, the plum blossoms of Lin Bu, the rocks of Mi Fu—people all swap stories about these men's obsessions as delightful topics of conversation and then blithely take up something as an obsession in order to amuse themselves. Alas! they are mistaken. It wasn't that Tao loved chrysanthemums, Lin loved plum blossoms, or Mi loved rocks; rather, in each case, it was the self loving the self.[25]

In this most radical equation, the boundary between subject and object has utterly dissolved. Obsession is no longer understood as a form of alterity, but as a self-reflexive act: it is not the self loving the *other,* but the self loving the *self.*

But the idealization of obsession in the sixteenth century also arose from a new evaluation of love: the fanatical attachment of a person to a particular object was interpreted as a manifestation of "that idealistic, single-minded love,"[26] "that headlong, romantic passion,"[27] known as qing. Once the relationship between someone and the object of his obsession was conceptualized as qing, it was not a difficult leap to declare that the object itself could be moved by its lover's devotion and reciprocate his feelings. Since, for the most part, the objects of obsessions were not human, this meant anthropomorphizing the object, adopting the view that animate and inanimate things alike, are capable of sentiment. As we will see, this is one of the most important developments in the theory of obsession for *Liaozhai.*

Such a position was facilitated both by the traditional Chinese animistic view of the universe and by the broader implications of qing during this period as a universal force and even as life itself.[28] For example, the main project of the seventeenth-century compendium of fact and fiction called *A Classified History of Love* is to document the power of qing over every part of the universe—from wind and lightning to rocks and trees, from animals and birds to ghosts and spirits: "The myriad things are born of qing and die of qing," comments the Historian of Qing.[29] In this scheme, the human race becomes merely one more category subject to the forces of qing.

In earlier times, an important, though not mandatory, criterion for recording an obsession was that it be strange, peculiar, incomprehensible. As a preface to *A Brief History of Obsession and Lunacy* explains: "Nowadays, no one is able to fathom the appeal that watching ox fights or hearing donkey brays held for [those in the past] who were fond of such things. That is why they are all pi."[30] A particularly idiosyncratic obsession could win someone fame in the annals of unofficial history, such as Liu Yong of the Southern Dynasties who enjoyed eating human fingernail parings or Quan Changru of the Tang who liked to eat human scabs because he said they tasted like dried fish flakes.[31] But as the fad for obsession grew during the Ming, another change began to take place: the objects of obsessions became increasingly standardized as indexes of certain virtues and personalities. By the sixteenth century, obsessions have grown noticeably less variant. Although some unusual obsessions are mentioned, such as a penchant for football or for operas about ghosts, and particularly disgusting eating habits are still listed with relish,[32] most writings now concern highly conventionalized obsessions. The most frequent are books, painting, epigraphy, calligraphy, or rocks; a particular musical instrument, plant, animal, or game; tea or wine; cleanliness; and homosexuality.[33] But even within these, the actual choices—which flower, which game—have become circumscribed and stereotyped.

By the seventeenth century, a rich tradition of lore and a corpus of specialized manuals or catalogues for the connoisseur had accumulated around virtually every standard obsession. Pu Songling appears to have incorporated research from such manuals on a number of the objects that form the focus of his obsessional tales. *Liaozhai* commentators frequently cite specialized handbooks both to explain and to praise the accuracy of Pu Songling's connoisseurship. Allan Barr has demonstrated that Pu partially derived the cricket lore introduced into the famous tale "The Cricket" ("Cuzhi"; 4.484–90) from a late Ming guide to Beijing, *A Brief Guide to Sights in the Capital* (*Dijing jingwu lüe*), which Pu abridged and wrote a new preface for.[34] According to Barr, he made use of "a number of technical details from the guidebook—the different varieties of cricket, the insect's diet" and even "borrowed some phrases wholesale" from it.[35]

The stylistic influence of catalogues and manuals is particularly evident in the unusual opening of the tale "A Strangeness of Pigeons" ("Ge yi"; 6.939–43), which abandons the biographical or autobiographical formats typical of *Liaozhai* and most classical fiction. The opening of the story is virtually indistinguishable from a catalogue: it lists the different varieties of pigeons and their locales and provides advice on their care: "The classification of pigeons is extremely complicated. Among the rarest varieties are the Earth Star of Shanxi, the Delicate Stork of Shandong, the Butterfly Wings of Guizhou, the Acrobat of Henan, and the Pointed Tips of Zhejiang. In addition, there are types like Boot Head, Polka-Dot, Big White, Married Sparrow, Spotted-Dog Eyes, and innumerable other sorts that only connoisseurs can distinguish."[36] Pu Songling explicitly acknowledges his debt to such a catalogue when he informs us that the wealthy pigeon fancier of his story strove to amass an exhaustive collection "according to the handbook" (6.839).[37] In fact, Pu Songling himself compiled two catalogues on other subjects: a rock catalogue and a flower handbook in his own hand are still extant.[38]

Narratives recounting personal experiences with the subject of a manual or a catalogue were sometimes included in such books. Such accounts may be among the most important inspirations for Pu Songling's connoisseurship tales. For instance, Ye Mengde, a Song dynasty lover of rocks, in a colophon to a famous record of a Tang estate, relates how acquiring a wonderful rock miraculously cured him of sickness.[39] The therapeutic properties of obsession are carried even further in "White Autumn Silk" ("Bai Qiulian"; 11.1482–88), a *Liaozhai* tale about a poetry-obsessed carp-maiden, whose lover's recitation of her favorite Tang poems not only cures her of illness but even revives her from the dead. Yuan Hongdao's portrait of the ideal flower-lover in his handbook on flower arranging anticipates to a remarkable degree the peony fanatic in the tale "Ge Jin"

(10.1436–44), who anxiously begins watching for peony shoots in the dead of winter and writes a hundred-line poem called "Longing for Peonies" ("Huai mudan") as he goes into debt waiting for the peonies to bloom.

As objects became associated with certain qualities and historical figures, the choice of obsession became dictated by those qualities and figures. By loving a particular object, the devotee was striving to claim allegiance to that quality or to emulate that figure. This idea can be glimpsed already in the twelfth-century preface to Du Wan's famous *Rock Catalogue of Cloudy Forest* (*Yunlin shipu*): "The Sage Confucius always said, 'The benevolent man finds joy in mountains.' The love of rocks implies 'finding joy in mountains,' for the stillness and longevity that Confucius mentioned can also be found in rocks."[40]

Thus an individual might favor rocks if he prized the moral virtues associated with rocks—benevolence, stillness, longevity, loyalty—or if he wanted to imitate the famous Song rock-lover known as Mi Fu or Mi the Lunatic (Mi Dian). Someone else, on the other hand, might feel drawn to chrysanthemums because of their association with purity and aloofness and with the recluse-poet Tao Yuanming. Although in theory the spontaneous impulse of a particular nature, in practice an obsession had become a studied act of self-cultivation. Once an object had become a fixed emblem of certain virtues, it was again an easy leap to attribute these virtues to the object itself. This again led to the anthropomorphizing of the obsessional object: the object not only symbolizes a particular virtue but also possesses that virtue and behaves accordingly.

The personification of objects is an ancient poetic trope. In the sixth-century anthology *New Songs from a Jade Terrace* (*Yutai xinyong*), for example, the attribution of sentiment and sentience to objects is a common device. Both natural objects, such as vegetation, and manufactured objects, such as mirrors, are portrayed as sharing or echoing the emotions of human beings. A typical couplet describes the grass growing over palace steps: "Fading to emerald as though it knew the season, / Holding in fragrance as though it had emotion."[41] This technique is later formulated in Chinese poetics as the overlapping of scene (*jing*) and emotion (qing): emotion is both aroused by the scene and located within it.[42] But this sort of personification differs from the personification of objects through obsession. In *New Songs from the Jade Terrace,* objects are like mirrors— they reflect the narcissistic emotions of the human world. Such objects have no separate identity or independent emotions; rather, they allegorically represent the speaker—for example, the discarded fan that symbolizes Lady Ban Jieyu's neglect by the emperor.[43]

In Yuan Hongdao's *History of Flower Arranging,* however, flowers, like human beings, experience different moods; for example, he advises fellow connoisseurs how to tell when flowers are happy or sad, drowsy or angry, so as to water them accordingly.[44] Here flowers are presented as feeling emotions of their own accord; they do not merely mirror or reinforce the emotions of a human being. Once things are seen as possessing independent emotions, they can be thought capable of responding to a specific person. Thus developed the idea that objects could find true friends or soul mates in those who love them. Zhang Chao distilled this idea into another aphorism: "If one has a single true friend in this world, one can be free of regrets. This is true not only for people, but also for things. For instance, the chrysanthemum found a true friend in Tao Yuanming . . . the flowering plum found a true friend in Lin Bu . . . and the rock found a true friend in Mi the Lunatic."[45]

The Ethereal Rock

It is this last offshoot of obsession that becomes the central theme of Pu Songling's brilliant tale "The Ethereal Rock" ("Shi Qingxu"; 11.1575–79), which narrates the friendship between a fanatical rock collector called Xing Yunfei and the rock named in the story's title.[46] One day, Xing finds a rock entangled in his fishing net. It is a fantastic rock, shaped like a miniature mountain with peaks and crannies, and it has unusual powers—whenever it is going to rain, the rock puffs tiny clouds, just like a real mountain. When word of the rock gets around, a rich local bully brazenly orders his servant to walk off with it, but it slips through the servant's fingers and falls into a river. The bully offers a substantial reward but to no avail. The rock is not recovered until the desolate Xing happens to walk by the spot and sees it lying in a suddenly transparent spot in the river. Xing keeps his recovery of the rock a secret, but one day he is visited by a mysterious old man who demands the return of "his" rock. As proof for his claim, the old man names the number of the rock's crannies (92) and reveals that in the largest crevice is carved the miniature inscription OFFERED IN WORSHIP, ETHEREAL, THE CELES-TIAL ROCK. Xing is finally granted ownership of the rock on the condition that he forfeit three years of his life. The old man then pinches together three of the crannies on the rock and tells Xing that the number of crannies (89) is now equal to the number of years he is fated to live. After more trials and tribulations—the rock is stolen by burglars, a corrupt official who wants the rock throws Xing into jail—Xing, as foretold, dies at the age of eighty-nine and is buried, according to his last wishes, with his rock. But half a year later, grave robbers steal the rock. Xing's ghost hounds the men into giving up the rock, but once again an unscrupulous official confis-cates the rock and orders a clerk to place it in his treasury. The rock twists out of his hands and smashes itself into a hundred pieces. Xing's son buries the pieces in his father's grave once and for all.

Pu Songling's comment, as Historian of the Strange, begins by raising the old fears of dangerous obsessions with beautiful things (*youwu*), but soon yields to the admiration of sentiment popularized during the late Ming:

Unearthly beauty in a thing makes it the site of calamity. In this man's desire to sacrifice his life for the rock, wasn't his folly extreme! But in the end, man and rock were together in death, so who can say the rock was "unfeeling"? There's an old saying, "A knight will die for a true friend."[47] This is no lie. If it is true even for a rock, can it be any less true for men?

The Historian of the Strange's rhetoric underscores the irony that a technically "unfeeling" rock (the phrase *wu qing* is a play on "inani-mate") displays more true feeling than most human beings, who are by definition animate and hence should "have feeling" (*you qing*).

Sentiment is not a static force in the narrative: the friendship between the hero and his rock grows and deepens, culminating in mutual self-sacrifice. The rock is an active participant in the tale. "Treasures should belong to those who love them," the proverbial saying about obsessive collectors reiterated by the divine old man in the tale, is interpreted in a new light: the object itself chooses and responds to the one who loves him. The rock flung himself into the

Fig. 2. A section from a sixteenth-century handscroll by Qiu Ying (fl. 1530–50) depicting the Song statesman Sima Guang's (1019–86) Garden for Self-Enjoyment (Dule yuan). Sima Guang designed each component of his garden in emulation of a famous historical figure. This Studio for Planting Bamboo (Zhongzhu zhai) was inspired by Wang Huizhi's proverbial obsession with bamboo. The scene depicts Wang Huizhi as a scholar who prefers the companionship of bamboo to that of human society. He is blissfully barricaded in the midst of a private bamboo thicket, which shields him from the outside world. See *Eight Dynasties of Chinese Painting,* pp. 206–9. (Courtesy of The Cleveland Museum of Art, John L. Severance Fund)

rock-lover's fishing net and entangled himself in the world of passions; the rock's desire precipitated his premature entry into the world, like the rock that becomes the human Bao Yu in *The Story of the Stone.* As the old man informs Xing, the rock surfaced three years ahead of schedule, for "he was in a hurry to display himself." And once in Xing's possession, the rock beautifies himself for his lover: the clouds that he miraculously puffs up cease when he is in anyone else's custody. Even after the rock has once more been cruelly extorted from Xing, he comes in a dream to console Xing and arranges their final reunion. Thus this tale subtly inverts the roles of object and collector: Xing becomes the object of the rock's obsession.

The philosopher Li Zhi, one of the most powerful influences behind the iconoclastic trend in late Ming thought, had explored a similar idea in a brilliant polemic called "Essay on a Scroll Painting of Square Bamboo" ("Fangzhu tujuan wen").[48] It is a radical reinterpretation of a well-known anecdote from the fifth-century *New Tales of the World*. This classified anthology detailing the wit and exploits of the Wei-Jin eccentrics enjoyed particular popularity during the sixteenth and seventeenth centuries, judging from the numerous editions and sequels to it published during this time, and it became a veritable bible for Ming and Qing fanciers of obsession.[49] The anecdote that Li Zhi drew upon concerns the love of bamboos: "Wang Hui-chih [Wang Huizhi; d. 388] was once temporarily lodging in another man's vacant house, and ordered bamboos planted. Someone asked, 'Since you're only living here temporarily, why bother?' Wang whistled and chanted poems a good while; then abruptly pointing to the bamboos, replied, 'How could I live a single day without "these gentlemen" [*ci jun*]?'"[50]

In Li Zhi's misanthropic view, Wang Huizhi preferred the companionship of "these gentlemen" to the society of humans, and the bamboos themselves recognized a kindred spirit in a man of Wang's uncommon temperament (see Fig. 2):

The one who in the past loved bamboos [Wang Huizhi] called them "gentlemen" out of love. He didn't call them gentlemen because he meant they resembled refined gentlemen; rather he was depressed and had no one to converse with—he felt that "The only ones I can associate with are the bamboos."[51] For this reason he befriended them and gave them that designation. . . . Someone said, "Wang considered bamboos as 'these gentlemen,' so the bamboos must have considered Wang as 'that gentleman.'" . . . But it wasn't the case that Wang loved bamboos—rather the bamboos loved Wang of their own accord. For when a man of Wang's mettle gazed at mountains, rivers, stones, and earth, all would have naturally grown beautiful, these gentlemen not least of all.

All things between heaven and earth have a spirit; especially these hollow gentlemen that rise straight up—could they alone be unspirited?[52] As the saying goes, "For a true friend, a knight exerts himself; for an admirer, a lady makes herself beautiful." So too these gentlemen. As soon as they encountered Wang, their distinct virtue and extraordinary energy [*qì*] would have naturally grown exhilarated; their lifelong principle of standing fast amid ice and frost would have blown away into the fluty love songs of phoenixes;[53] all must have been out of a desire to make themselves beautiful for the one who admired them. For how could they stand there so solitary, moaning in the wind for years on end, forever harboring the regret that they had no true friend?

In Li Zhi's polemic against the shallowness of the late Ming fashion for obsession, he reverses the hierarchy of object and obsessive and anthropomorphizes the bamboos by imputing to them human will and desire. He argues that every object has a *shen,* a spirit—an animate force within it—and extrapolates from this animistic view, perhaps tongue-in-cheek, that for a meaningful existence, an object, like a person, needs a true friend to love and understand him. Li cleverly imagines the scene of the bamboos' attempted seduction of Wang Huizhi through an elaborate series of puns that play on bamboo's conventional associations with integrity and steadfastness, but his anthropomorphizing of bamboo was clearly a rhetorical pose, a conceit.[54]

In "The Ethereal Rock," Pu Songling takes the ideas of Li Zhi's essay further. Carefully, with all the techniques of a novelist, he gives the intense love between an inanimate object and a man a coherent narrative shape and in so doing realizes this rhetorical stance literally. But for an inanimate rock to be fully human, it must die. The most shocking moment in the tale is when the rock smashes himself into smithereens: the valuable has been made worthless; the permanent has been destroyed. The rock is able to know love, but at the price of suffering and mortality. His obsession with Xing culminates in self-sacrifice: to demonstrate his loyalty and remain with his true friend, the rock must in the end, like a knight-errant or a virtuous widow, sabotage his own beauty and commit suicide. Only in destruction is the rock safe and buried permanently with his beloved. As in Daoist parables of crooked trees that survive because they are useless, the rock, that "thing of unearthly beauty," can only be left in peace once his material value is gone.

It is no accident that Pu Songling chose an obsession with a rock to illustrate the theme of perfect friendship: the rock was conventionally valued as a symbol of loyalty and constancy. The phrase "a rock friend" (*shi you*), for instance, signified a faithful friend and was a common poetic designation for a rock.[55] The expression "a friendship of stone" (*shi jiao*) likewise describes a friendship as strong and permanent as stone; Pu Songling himself employed this phrase in a little homily on friendship.[56] Again, as I noted earlier, it was not uncommon to locate the qualities symbolized by an object in the object's innate nature. For instance, *A Classified History of Love* argues that since love is "as strong as stone or metal," it can actually transform itself into stone or metal.[57] In "The Ethereal Rock," Pu Songling brilliantly gives these figurative expressions a concrete and literal form.[58]

By Ming times the rock had become a cult object. John Hay's study of the rock in Chinese art, *Kernels of Energy, Bones of Earth,* has revealed the extent to which the rock had assumed the stature of a cultural icon in late Imperial China. Rocks, like stories, were prized for being singular, bizarre, odd. A rock was no ordinary object; it was an objet d'art, valued not for the ingenuity and artifice of human skill but for its exquisite naturalness. An obsession with unpolished and uncarved rocks was considered refined; compared to it, a passion for jade and precious stones was merely vulgar. (During the late Ming jades were even carved to look like rough stones.[59]) Rocks were supposed to be prized only by real connoisseurs, but as Pu Songling makes clear, in a market where rocks commanded a high price, the powerful and wealthy extorted rocks for status and the ignorant chased after rocks for profit. Like Li Zhi's bamboos, who are said to detest their phony modern admirers, Pu Songling's rock could not possibly reciprocate the false love of the other collectors in the tale. It is the hero's pure and unwavering obsession amid this atmosphere of corruption that earns the rock's devotion.

The most obvious inspiration behind Pu Songling's rock-loving hero is the Song painter and calligrapher Mi Fu, whose obsession with rocks had become proverbial. Mi Fu's flamboyant brand of connoisseurship had enshrined him as the paragon of obsession and eccentricity. The numerous collections of anecdotes about Mi Fu published during the Ming attest to his great appeal.[60] The heady mixture of lunacy and sincere passion attributed to Mi Fu accorded well with the sensibility of the late Ming and can be detected in a number of Pu Songling's heroes. Xing's fanatical devotion in "The Ethereal Rock" had a precedent in the most celebrated anecdote about Mi Fu, which even figured in his official biography in the *Song History:* Mi Fu was said to have donned official garb to make obeisance to a favored rock in his collection and to have respectfully addressed it as "Older Brother Rock" (*shi xiong*) or, in a variant, as "Elder Rock" (*shi zhang*).[61]

We can be certain of Pu Songling's familiarity with at least this anecdote. Not only did stories about Mi Fu enjoy wide circulation during the seventeenth century, but a reworking of this anecdote appears in a poem by Pu Songling entitled "Elder Rock." The rock described in this poem is thought to be still standing today on the former site of the Stone Recluse Garden (Shiyin yuan), which belonged to Pu Songling's friend and employer, Bi Jiyou.[62]

> Elder Rock's inlaid sword juts up high, so high;
> He wears a turban, tablier, and sandals of straw.[63]
> Where dragon veins coil on bone, stands a mountain spirit,
> Still in a cloak of wood-lotus, in a belt of bryony.[64]
> Gong Gong hit the pillar of Heaven, and it came crashing down;
> Where one shard struck, a fold in the eastern mountains rose.[65]
> Uneven peaks like hair knots, dozens of feet tall,
> Brushed by white clouds moving through the sky.
> I ready my cap and robe and bow reverently:
> Brisk air fills my bosom, healing my grave malady.[66]

Pu Songling's poem may be read as the literary equivalent of the illustrations of Mi Fu bowing to his rock so popular in seventeenth-century art,[67] but with one important difference—it is the poet ("I") who bows to the rock in imitation of Mi Fu and finds therapeutic relief; Mi Fu himself is not depicted, as he often is in comparable poems by other writers.[68] In Pu Songling's version, the mythological description of the rock as a miniature mountain dominates the poem; the Mi Fu poet-figure has receded into the background and makes only an almost routine appearance in the closing couplet.

Compared with the description of the rock in this poem, the description of the rock in the tale is startlingly restrained and sparse. Gone are the ornate language and standard allusions of the poem: in their place is simply a brief but vivid description given when the rock first comes into view: it "was a rock barely a foot high. All four sides were intricately hollowed, with layered peaks jutting up." Further details of the rock's unearthly physical beauty—the number of crannies, the minuscule inscription bearing its name, the clouds it emits—are filled in only gradually as needed within the framework of the plot, but there are never enough details to dispel the rock's aura of mystery. The real image of the rock is left to the reader's imagination, to be inferred from the endless struggles to possess it.

Moreover, "The Ethereal Rock" does not retell any of the well-known Mi Fu anecdotes; instead it creates a new cluster of anecdotes within the heightened atmosphere of seventeenth-century obsessional culture. Pu Songling's hero does not simply imitate Mi Fu—he surpasses him, surrendering three years of his life and then risking what remains all for the rock, who in turn eclipses any previously recorded rock in history. As Feng Zhenluan exclaims: "Mi Fu bowed to a rock, but I imagine he didn't have a rock of this caliber. Niu Sengru was called a rock connoisseur, but I'll bet he never set eyes on such a rock" (*Liaozhai* 11.1575).[69] And Xing's rock is not only worshipped; invested with both demonic powers (*mojie*) and a deep humanity, he is able to respond to a true connoisseur's love as Elder Rock never could.

In addition to "Elder Rock," Pu Songling wrote two other poems expressly on rocks and, as already mentioned, compiled a brief catalogue on rocks.[70] He brilliantly incorporated the knowledge of rock lore so evident in his poems and catalogue into his tale. The rock's miraculous feat of emitting clouds, for instance, may be imaginative invention, but it plays on the traditional associations of rocks, mountains, and clouds.[71] The rock's ability to predict the weather also has a quasi-historical basis in a description of a famed mountain-shaped inkstone said to have belonged to Mi Fu: "When it is going to rain, the 'dragon pool' [in a cranny of the rock] becomes wet."[72] Giving rocks personal names likewise had a foundation in historical and contemporary practice. As a poem written on a beautiful early seventeenth-century painting of a rock proclaims: "Rocks, too, have names and sobriquets, / This rock is called Mysterious Cloud."[73] (Surely it is no coincidence that the name Pu Songling gave his rock-lover, Xing Yunfei or Moving Clouds in Flight, sounds like the name of a rock.[74]) Lastly, the history of rock collecting is notorious for epic battles between connoisseurs. These battles are scaled down in "The Ethereal Rock"; to underscore the purity of the hero's obsession, his human competitors for the rock are not true connoisseurs, and the rock is resold cheaply in the common market.

Liaozhai contains a number of wonderful tales about obsessions with flowers and musical instruments. What distinguishes "The Ethereal Rock" from these other obsessional tales is not the anthropomorphism of the object, for the heroes in *Liaozhai* frequently fall in love with the human incarnations of their obsessions. The sustained imputation of human-like behavior to the non-human (objects, plants, animals, ghosts) is a staple of the strange tale, but the ground covered by such anthropomorphism is quite broad. At one extreme, things retain their own form but are motivated by human ethics and desires; at the other extreme, things take on human form, often so convincingly that they are mistaken for people until the denouement of the tale. In the first case, there is no physical metamorphosis, and only the spirit of a thing is anthropomorphized; in the second case, metamorphosis is essential, and both spirit and form are anthropomorphized. Within any given instance of anthropomorphism, however, the ratio of thing to human is variable. Thus, although the objects of many different obsessions are anthropomorphized in *Liaozhai,* whether they seem more human or more thing-like varies enormously.

In the *Liaozhai* tales of flower obsession, the flowers primarily assume human female form in the story, although telltale clues to their floral nature are liberally provided. Part of the charm of a story about a peony-spirit like "Ge Jin" or a chrysanthemum-spirit like "Yellow Pride" ("Huang Ying"; 11.1446–52) is that the revelation the heroines are flowers rather than human beings is deferred; the tale becomes a riddle of identity, one that contemporary readers would have found enjoyable and not too difficult to unravel.[75] Pu Songling adopted a second approach in two tales of obsession with musical instruments, "Huan Niang" (7.985–90) and "The Sting" ("Ju zha"; 8.1029–34). Although the zither is the pivot of both plots, it is not anthropomorphized at all; it undergoes no metamorphosis and is given no distinct personality. It remains throughout a precious but passive object of desire.

"The Ethereal Rock" is unique in *Liaozhai* because the rock acquires a personality, an identity, a human presence, even though it remains an inanimate object. Only veiled in dream does the rock appear as a man* and speak directly, introducing himself as Shi Qingxu. Ordinarily when a rock is given a name in a catalogue or in an inscription, the character *shi* or rock follows rather than precedes the name. This is why the miniature inscription carved on the rock

---

*As Mi Fu's addressing his rock as "Older Brother" affirms, rocks were gendered as male in the Chinese imagination, just as flowers were gendered as female.

in the story reads: "Ethereal, the Celestial Rock" ("Qingxu, tian-shi"). This order, however, is reversed in the rock's self-introduction and in the story's title. Placed first rather than last, the character *shi* assumes the Chinese position of a surname. The deliberate inversion of the rock's name, then, suggests a subtle anthropomorphization. The delicate balance between the outward form of a rock and the inner soul of a man is thus encoded in this new name: "Shi" is in fact a common surname; "Qingxu" (pure and ethereal), the rock's given name, evokes his extraordinary quality of qì, for which rocks, as "kernels of energy," were prized.[76] Such a balance seems to have also been achieved in certain late Ming paintings of rocks, which, as John Hay suggests, may have been "portraying personalities as embodied in structural forms and textures."[77]

Pu Songling's rock may be fictional, but beginning in Song times numerous artists had portrayed their favorite rocks and imbued them with their own fantasies. An extraordinary handscroll painting from the early seventeenth century gives us additional insight into "The Ethereal Rock" and the cultural milieu out of which it emerged (see Fig. 3).[78] The rock in question belonged to Mi Wanzhong (1570–1628), a well-known official who adopted the sobriquet "Friend to Rocks" (You shi) and claimed descent from none other than Mi Fu himself. Contemporaries said of Mi Wanzhong that he possessed Mi Fu's obsession but not his lunacy.[79] Although Mi Wanzhong was a famous calligrapher and painter specializing in rock paintings, the handscroll was the work of his friend Wu Bin (fl. 1591–1626), a professional landscape painter and fellow rock-lover.[80] At first glance, the painting seems to belong to the "still life" genre: the rock is methodically painted, and Mi Wanzhong's descriptions are factual and meticulous, documenting the size, shape, gesture, and texture of each of its peaks. But when we gaze at the painting longer, it becomes anything but still or photographic in feel; the rock is fantastic, bizarre, unearthly, with long stalagmite-like peaks, separated by mysterious spaces. It almost seems to be moving, writhing as though on fire or blown by wind; yet it still somehow retains the solidity of stone.[81]

Most unusually, the handscroll consists of ten life-size portraits of the rock, each painted from a different angle. Such attention lavished on a single rock reminds one of an infatuated lover reveling in

此峰高一尺七寸，傍洞玲瓏，天矯玲玲，許峰玄

名之曰錦屏峰。長數寸，中峰最工，旁三峰面面玲

不識之何故。一峰高寸餘，左右數峰向背俯仰，傍一

限三尺許，三寸峰如中峰，傍出生三峰，又名峰相倚

二洪崎嶮視峰與洞內脉絡相連，疊嶂重岡三峰相

矣。若左右傍峰一斗餘，至左右傳洞而此後遠峰

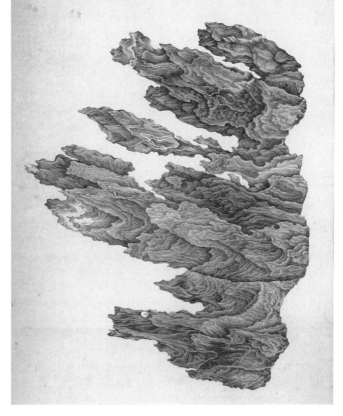

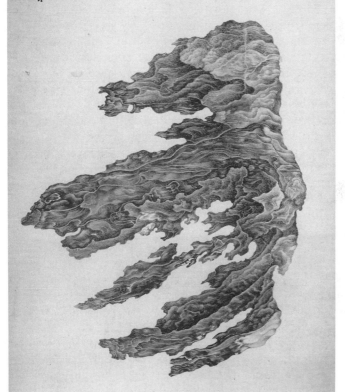

Fig. 3. A section from Wu Bin's handscroll showing two views of Mi Wanzhong's rock, with inscriptions by Mi Wanzhong dated 1610. (Reproduced with the permission of the E. & J. Frankel Gallery)

his mistress's every pose, every shift of expression. Many wonderful albums devoted to rock paintings and illustrated rock catalogues were produced during the seventeenth century; unillustrated catalogues, like Pu Songling's, were even more common.[82] The aim of a rock catalogue or album is ordinarily to record a number of exceptional examples. What we find in Wu Bin's handscroll is in essence still a rock catalogue of sorts, but one uniquely devoted to a single example, one that catalogues a single rock as though it were multiple rocks.

This compulsive repetition of the same object characterizes both Wu Bin's painting and Pu Songling's tale. One of the most striking features of "The Ethereal Rock" is that the same plot with minor variations is repeated over and over: Xing, the rock-lover, finds the rock, and someone wrests it away from him, but each time the stone contrives to return to him. This pattern of loss and recovery occurs five times, but the repetition does not become monotonous, for with each cycle, the man's display of grief at losing the rock becomes more violent; each time, his joy at regaining it becomes more profound. After each loss, the man goes to greater lengths to redeem the rock—he gives up three years of his life, mortgages his house and land, and tries repeatedly to hang himself. Even death does not break the cycle; Xing comes back as a vengeful ghost to demand the rock's return. The repetitive, cyclical nature of the story inscribes the compulsive structure of obsession: desire, possession, loss; desire, possession, loss. This repetitiveness is truly excessive, for it continues far beyond our expectations, just as Wu Bin's picture surprises the spectator with its excessive variations on the same object.

In a final, very personal inscription on the handscroll, Mi Wanzhong identifies himself as a rock-lover from birth, tracing his passion for rocks and his coming to consciousness to the same primal moment. He spent thirty years collecting rocks and won fame as a connoisseur, but this one rock, the subject of the handscroll, was the rock he had been preparing himself for and seeking all his life. So amazing was this new rock, he tell us, that upon its arrival all the rocks in his sizable collection withdrew in deference as if acknowledging their inferiority and defeat. Thus this rock is not merely the crowning jewel of his collection: it utterly effaces his collection. It *alone* is his collection.

This is perhaps the greatest parallel between Wu Bin's painting and Pu Songling's tale. In the opening to "The Ethereal Rock," the rock connoisseur Xing is introduced as someone who would spare no expense to add to his collection. And yet from the moment that he fishes up the ethereal rock (who comes of his own accord, just as we are told Mi Wanzhong's rock "crossed the river" to him),[83] no other rock is ever mentioned again. Xing's rock collection no longer exists for him once he gives himself up to this rock. His collection simply disappears from the text, just as Mi Wanzhong's painstaking assemblage of rocks is displaced from the scene. Xing, like Mi Wanzhong, becomes uniquely obsessed with a single rock. Both Pu Songling and the painter Wu Bin seem to have captured the identical truth about obsession when idealized to its furthest extent.[84]

The late Ming sensibility that shaped both Pu Songling's and Wu Bin's representations of obsession was powerful enough to transform medical discourse. By the late sixteenth century, "pi" no longer retains much force as a medical term; this sense has been almost completely eclipsed by the extended meaning of "obsession" or "addiction."[85] In his encyclopedic Classified Materia Medica, Li Shizhen addresses obsession in a single entry on a drug called a pishi, or pi stone: "There are people who concentrate on something until it becomes an obsession [pi]. When this develops into an illness, knots in their bowels will solidify and form a stone."[86] Li's medical understanding of pi springs from the extended notion of obsession and presumes a psychological rather than somatic etiology: single-minded concentration on something obstructs the digestion, and this obstruction may harden into stone. In this very interesting move, Li reconciles the old medical definition of pi with the now-predominant cultural understanding of it.

Li Shizhen's main interest lies in the problem of how obstructions within the body can turn to stone. He cites other known examples of petrifaction, including meteors, kidney stones, fossils, and Buddhist relics. This is so in each case, he explains, because "vital energy" (jingqi) has solidified.[87] But this traditional theory is too vague to satisfy him. To account for the petrifaction of human flesh, he draws on the Ming theory of the overwhelming power of single-minded passion.[88] As evidence, he cites an amazing story about a Persian who broke into an ancient tomb. "The Persian saw that all the skin and muscles [of the corpse] had disintegrated; all that remained was a heart hard as stone. He sawed it down the middle and found a landscape inside resembling a painting. On one side was a girl leaning out over a railing and gazing fixedly in the distance. In fact, this girl must have had an obsessive love of landscape for her to be recomposed in this fashion."[89] The picture formed inside the petrified heart records her fatal history. The girl's obsession with the landscape has literally etched itself into her heart, the seat of consciousness, figuring herself into this stone landscape. In fact, certain rocks, like marble, were indeed prized for the painting-like landscapes that could be glimpsed in them, natural pictures that John Hay has called "mountainscapes in marble."[90] In transmuting to stone, this heart has outlasted the organic process of decay, recording for posterity the obsession responsible for the metamorphosis.

Li Shizhen's entry concludes with a final prescription that follows the principle of curing like with like: a dissolved pi stone taken orally will cure a "blocked gullet" (yege), a condition whose symptoms include the inability to ingest food, vomiting, and constipation. Such a stone would be obtained, his final case suggests, among the cremated ashes of someone who had died from knots in the bowels.[91] A stone thus becomes at once the perfect symbol of obsession, the somatic result of obsession, and the cure for obsession. We have come full circle to Pu Songling's "Ethereal Rock" in which only the destruction of the rock can dissolve the rock-lover's obsession and bring peace.

Addiction and Satire

Although the rock-lover in "The Ethereal Rock" is disparaged by the Historian of the Strange for being "foolish" in his devotion, this is clearly not intended as a real rebuke. The admiring tone adopted in the final comment accords with the late Ming glorification of folly and sentiment that trumpeted the excesses of obsession as the highest form of self-expression.

In a number of other tales, however, Pu Songling parts company with the late Ming cult of feeling to expose the dark underside of obsession. In these tales of addiction, obsession is stripped of its glamor to reveal its potential to inflict human misery. *Liaozhai* paints devastating portraits of addictions to gambling, sex, alcohol, geomancy, and chess that are emphatically not idealized or applauded. These more conventional moral tales, on the whole, emphasize the consequences of immoderate indulgence and the loss of self-control. For instance, in "The Gambling Charm" ("Du fu"; 3.419–21), a chronic gambler loses his house and land in a game and, even after winning them back with the aid of a Daoist amulet, cannot bring himself to quit. Only after the amulet suddenly vanishes into thin air does he come to his senses and withdraw from the game. In case the point has not been driven home clearly enough, the Historian of the Strange appends a lengthy sermon to the story lamenting the evils of gambling, which begins: "Of all things on earth that destroy households, nothing is swifter than gambling; of all things on earth that wreck virtue, nothing is worse than gambling" (3.420). But even in the case of gambling, a subject that he evidently felt very strongly about, Pu Songling cannot resist including another tale, "Ren Xiu" (11.1473–75), in which a gambling addict's fatal weakness for dice ironically provides the very means through which ghosts restore his stolen family fortune.

In *Five-fold Miscellany* (*Wu za zu*), Xie Zhaozhe lists famous figures of the past whose deaths were caused by uncontrollable addictions, and dryly observes that "although life and death are both important, that which someone loves can be more important to him than life itself."[92] Pu Songling vividly translates this notion into fiction when his addicts not only forfeit their lives in this world for what they crave but also do the same again in the next. Even death cannot break the title character in "The Chess Ghost" ("Qi gui"; 4.532–34) or "The Alcoholic" ("Jiu kuang"; 4.583–88) of their addictions. Forgetting that he is dead, the alcoholic gets drunk as usual and kicks up a ruckus in hell until he is finally fished out of a foul, knife-infested stream. This explains the ferocious hangover that he faces upon waking the next morning back among the living, but it still does not cure him of his alcoholism, and he is soon marched back to hell for good.

In the more moving story, "The Chess Ghost," a young scholar's uncontrollable passion for chess leads to his father's death; he himself is taken off to the purgatory of hungry ghosts as punishment. On his way to redeem himself by drafting an official inscription for the underworld authorities, he happens to pass by living men playing a chess game in the open air. He joins the game and, glued to the spot, loses every match until the deadline has passed and he has forfeited any further chance for rebirth. Comments the Historian of the Strange: "When he glimpsed a chessboard, he cared no more about death; once he was dead, he glimpsed a chessboard and cared no more about life. Isn't it the case that his desire to play was greater than his desire to live? But to be as obsessed as this and *still* be unable to score even one great move!" (4.533)

It is difficult to determine what saddens the Historian of the Strange more—the chess ghost's dooming himself to damnation for eternity or his inferior skills at the game. It goes against the grain of the late Ming idealization of obsession for a man to fail so miserably at what he sincerely loves; in fact, foolishness and talent should go hand in hand. In "A Bao" (2.233–39), the Historian of the Strange defends foolishness on precisely those grounds: "If one's nature is 'foolish,' then one's resolve will be firm: thus those who are foolish in their love of books are sure to excel in composition, and those who are foolishly devoted to the arts are bound to have excellent technique, whereas those people who make no progress and achieve nothing are always those who claim that they are not foolish" (2.239).[93]

Although the privileging of foolishness and single-mindedness enabled obsession to be idealized as a vehicle for self-expression in the first place, such excessive behavior also becomes an irresistible target for social satire. The comic possibilities of the subject are already discernible in Mi Fu's official biography in the *Song History,* where the anecdote about him bowing to the rock is reported as a current joke.[94] In fact, this anecdote also circulated with an additional punchline that completely undercut its seriousness. Someone is said to have asked Mi Fu whether he had really bowed to a rock, to which he slowly replied: "How could I have bowed to a rock?—I merely saluted it."

Both modes of treating obsession—glorification and satire—coexist in the writings of certain authors and even in certain books during the late Ming. Feng Menglong preaches the gospel of obsession and folly in his commentary to *A Classified History of Love,* but makes these same traits the butt of jokes in his *Survey of Talk New and Old* (*Gujin tan'gai*). The prefaces to *A Brief History of Obsession and Lunacy* advance solemn claims for the moral virtues of obsession, but most of the anecdotes in the book are quite funny and are clearly constructed as jokes; the comments also tend to maximize the humor by coining ludicrous epithets or pairing incompatible cravings. In *Liaozhai,* too, although certain stories treat obsession extremely seriously, it is also lampooned, even sometimes within the same story. The hero of the tale "Huang Jiulang" (3.316–23), for example, has a fixed penchant for homosexuality ("the obsession with rent sleeves").[95] His love affair with a fox-boy is narrated fairly sympathetically since he manifests all the symptoms of the sincere love-fanatic and refuses to give up the boy even at the cost of his own life. But the story starts to slip into comedy when as a reward for his devotion he is "converted" to heterosexuality in his next incarnation. At the end of the story, in another, more abrupt change of tone, the Historian of the Strange indulges himself in an amazingly arcane and rather hostile parody in parallel prose on homosexual practices. The piece's scholastic, punning wit hinges on the contrast between its erudite style and obscene content.

In "A Strangeness of Pigeons," the wealthy pigeon fancier Zhang Youliang, who boasts of the finest pigeon collection in Shandong, pampers his birds with all the attentiveness of a mother caring for her baby. Because of his exquisite devotion, he is honored with a visit from the pigeon god, who presents him with a pair of snow-white pigeons. These and their offspring become the gems of his collection. Sometime later, a friend of his father's, a high official, inquires about his pigeons. Assuming that the official is a fellow connoisseur and hoping to get into his good graces, Zhang sends him, after much agonizing, a pair of the snow-white pigeons. Later he meets the official, but to his chagrin the official says not a word about the pigeons.

Unable to contain himself, Zhang blurted out: "And how were the pigeons?"

"Nice and plump," replied the official.

"You don't mean you *cooked* them?" asked Zhang, alarmed.

"Why, yes."

"But those were no ordinary pigeons . . . !" cried Zhang in shock. The official reflected for a moment. "Well, they didn't *taste* especially out of the ordinary." (6.841)

The joke is beautifully constructed with comic pauses and a slow buildup to the punchline as the pigeon fancier realizes that his worst fears have come true. The story ends sadly when the remaining snow-white pigeons desert Zhang for betraying them; in remorse, he gives away the rest of his collection. Once again, an obsession ends with dispersal and loss. The Historian of the Strange reprimands Zhang for trying to curry favor with an official but defends his passion: "We can see that gods and spirits are angered by greed but not by foolishness" (6.842).

Two short anecdotes appended to the comment are closer to jokes than to stories; they are essentially variations on the joke told in "A Strangeness of Pigeons." In the second anecdote, a monk, a fanatical tea connoisseur, entertains a high official with his second-best grade of tea. Since the official does not react, the monk, conscience-stricken, assumes he must be a true connoisseur and immediately offers him his best grade of tea. When a response is still not forthcoming, the monk breathlessly asks him what he thought of the tea. "It was hot," is the answer. These secondary items reinforce a comic rather than tragic reading of the main tale. As a final authorial comment explicitly points out: "These two anecdotes are funny in the same way as Master Zhang presenting his pigeons" (6.843).

A version of the pigeon joke in *A Brief History of Obsession and Lunacy* concerns the famous calligrapher Wang Xizhi, who was said to love geese because their sinuous necks inspired the curves of his brush strokes.[96] Knowing of his passion, a friend invites Wang to view a remarkable goose raised by his old nurse in the countryside. Upon hearing that the famous calligrapher is coming to visit, however, the old lady slaughters the goose and cooks it in order to have some delicacy to serve him. A joke about a beloved animal being eaten appears as early as *New Tales of the World* of the fifth century in which the grand marshal Wang Yan maliciously slaughters and consumes the Prince of Pengcheng's favorite ox.[97] It is not hard to understand why this kind of joke was common: it makes fun of both parties at once.

The satire in "A Strangeness of Pigeons" is double-edged but unmistakable: the aficionado is lampooned for his overfastidiousness and consequent misreading of other people, and the unappreciative philistine is ridiculed for his boorishness. When the targets of satire are less obvious, however, the tales become correspondingly more ambiguous. In the tales "Yellow Pride" ("Huang Ying") and "The Bookworm" ("Shu chi"; 11.1453–58), the spirits of the objects themselves seem to take pleasure in debunking their stereotyped associations, to the shock and alarm of their devotees.

In "Yellow Pride," Ma, a poor and austere chrysanthemum connoisseur, unknowingly befriends brother and sister chrysanthemum-spirits, who are the descendents of that most famous lover of chrysanthemums, the recluse-poet Tao Yuanming. (Chrysanthemums had become so identified with this poet by the Ming that in one anecdote a scholar hosting a chrysanthemum-viewing party in his garden cautioned his tipsy guests to take care lest they step on "Tao Yuanming."[98]) To Ma's horror, the brother and sister do not share his eremitic tastes and set up a profitable chrysanthemum business, trading on their phenomenal horticultural skills. After Ma marries the sister, Yellow Pride, he valiantly tries to hold onto his poverty and spiritual purity in the face of his bride's commercial wealth, but after some ludicrous maneuvering, is forced to live in the comfortable style she prefers.

Most important, Ma's obsession with chrysanthemums is not the fashionable pseudo-connoisseurship that Yuan Hongdao and Li Zhi attacked. Ma faithfully adheres to all the rules of idealized obsession, and the chrysanthemums duly love him back. But these rules are themselves called into question and mocked in this story. As befits the true connoisseur, Ma is steadfast in refusing to profit from the buying and selling of the things that he loves. He clearly prides himself on being a pure-minded recluse, a latter-day Tao Yuanming. But Ma's obdurate poverty and eremitism in the face of his improved financial circumstances are ridiculed as priggishness and affectation, most notably by his wife, the chrysanthemum-spirit, the very one who ought to understand these virtues best.

The paradoxically materialist behavior of the chrysanthemum-spirits becomes even more striking when we consider that in his poetry Pu Songling professed to be a chrysanthemum-lover in much the same conventional terms as his protagonist Ma. The first couplet of his poem "Admiring Chrysanthemums in Sun Shengzuo's Studio, the Tenth Month" ("Shiyue Sun Shengzuo zhaizhong shang ju") reads: "My old love of chrysanthemums has become an obsession, / To seek a lovely variety I'd travel a thousand miles."[99] The couplet closely echoes the opening description of Ma in "Yellow Pride": "Whenever he heard of a lovely variety, he would travel a thousand miles to buy it" (11.1446). Although the language is extremely conventional in both cases, Pu Songling does not employ this exact wording in any other poem on flowers or in any of his other obsessional tales in *Liaozhai*. In a consecutive poem entitled "Drinking at Night and Composing Another Verse" ("Ye yin zaifu"), Pu Songling likewise praises chrysanthemums in a model couplet that he could easily have attributed to Ma: "Literary groups delight in pouring the Sage's wine; / Worldly faces are shamed before the recluse flowers."[100] In light of these poems, Pu Songling's flouting of the chrysanthemum stereotype in "Yellow Pride" may come close to a mild form of self-satire.

In *Liaozhai*, although vulgarity is derided, poverty is decidedly not glamorized.[101] Pu Songling, as the son of a scholar turned merchant, tends to be concerned with the material well-being of his heroes. More often than not, the intrusion of the strange into the world of the hero vastly improves his finances: the satisfaction of one desire (love) leads to the satisfaction of other desires (fortune and career).[102] Business dealings are described in surprising detail, and the most lovely heroines often prove to be the most hardheaded businesswomen. Despite Ma's resistance, this pattern basically prevails in "Yellow Pride."

On the other hand, it is hard to avoid the impression that the commercialization of seventeenth-century society is also being mocked here or at least milked for its comic possibilities. The implication is that if Tao Yuanming himself somehow came back to earth in this late day and age, he too would turn his back on poetry and earn a fortune raising chrysanthemums instead. Underlying this fable of the industrious chrysanthemums is a subtext: the opening of that most famous of Tao Yuanming's poems, "Drinking Wine," no. 4 ("Yin jiu"):

> I built my cottage in the realm of men,
> And yet there is no noise [*xuan*] of horse and cart.
> You ask me, "How can this be so?"
> "When the mind is distant the place is naturally remote."
> I pick chrysanthemums beneath the eastern hedge.[103]

When Ma first learns of his friend Tao's proposal to sell chrysanthemums, he specifically alludes to this poem to dissuade him: "If you follow this plan, you will be converting your *eastern hedge* into a bazaar and profaning your chrysanthemums" (11.1447). Although Tao defends himself that it is not vulgar to make an honest living selling flowers, sure enough, before long the quiet refuge in the poem has been turned into a marketplace: "Crowds gathered outside T'ao's [Tao's] house, and the place was as noisy [*xuan*] and busy as the market. . . . [Ma] saw that the street was filled with people and carts loaded with chrysanthemums" (11.1447).[104] With the profits from the chrysanthemum business, Tao Yuanming's thatched cottage is torn down, and a palatial residence is built in its place. The Historian of the Strange carefully refrains from commenting on any of the controversial points in the story and merely praises the one obvious similarity between Tao the chrysanthemum and Tao Yuanming—insouciant drunkenness: "To die of drunkenness after spending a carefree life, though deplored by the world, need not be an unhappy ending" (11.1452).[105] He deliberately seems to leave open to the reader's interpretation the extent and scope of the tale's satire.

An underlying strain of self-satire is also discernible in the portrait of the impecunious scholar in "The Bookworm." Pu Songling seems to harbor a secret sympathy and affection for his bookish hero, Lang. In his naiveté and stubbornness, Lang carries to absurdity the philosopher Li Zhi's call to preserve one's "childlike heart" (*tongzi xin*), the supposed wellspring of spontaneity, authenticity, and literary creation.[106] Lang loves the books in his ancestral library with an almost-blind devotion, refusing to part with even a single volume despite his poverty. He is no true connoisseur or scholar, however, for no one book appears more or less valuable to him than any other. Although he spends every waking moment studying, he does not know how to read between the lines or interpret what he reads; he takes everything literally and consequently never passes the exams.

Just as Tao Yuanming's poetry underlies the chrysanthemum story, so too in this tale there is a subtext: the "Exhortation to Study" ("Quanxue pian"), a pedantic poem "extolling the glory of scholarship" composed by the Northern Song emperor Zhenzong (r. 997–1022), which enjoyed particularly wide currency in the cheap popular primers of the sixteenth and seventeenth centuries.[107] This poem, which Lang's father had hung in an honored position by his desk, is a blueprint for the plot: the bookworm believes it will come true exactly as written, and as so often in *Liaozhai,* it miraculously does. The poem's most important line for the story is: "Regret not that you have no fine maid; / In books are girls with cheeks smooth as jade [*yan ruyu*]."[108] Sure enough, one day he happens to open volume eight of the *Han History;* there between the pages is a paper-cut of a beautiful woman. Beneath his ardent gaze, she comes to life and introduces herself as Miss Jadesmooth Cheek (Yan Ruyu), explaining dryly that she has been moved by his devotion: "I'm afraid there will never again be anyone like you who so profoundly believes the ancients" (11.1454). The bookworm is a fool because he cannot distinguish figurative and literal levels of meaning. Because he so profoundly believes obvious lies to be the truth, they come true after all. But in their coming true, he paradoxically learns that they were lies.

Although the bookworm is admired in the story for his sentimentality, naiveté, and childlike heart, all cardinal virtues in the late Ming cult of feeling, he is also ridiculed mercilessly for taking them to excess. Lang's total immersion in books has kept him so ignorant that even at the age of thirty-three he is completely unaware of the facts of life. Ironically, it is the spirit of the book, Jadesmooth Cheek herself, who forces him to stop reading and introduces him to the pleasures of gaming, music, and the bedroom arts, because as she tells him, "the reason you're not successful is simply because you're always studying" (11.1454). She even urges him to get rid of his library before it is too late; he refuses in horror: "But this is your native land, and my entire life! How can you suggest such a thing!" (11.1456) In fact, the book-spirit turns out to be the catalyst for the library's destruction, which paradoxically instigates Lang's worldly success. Under the pretext of searching for the beautiful demon, the district magistrate torches Lang's library, repeating, as the Historian of the Strange suggests, the trauma of the First Qin Emperor's burning of the books. Once again, obsession results in the destruction of the loved object and the dispersal of a collection. We are back to the poet Li Qingzhao contemplating the destruction of her husband's library.

But Lang's very different response to this catastrophe forces us to recognize that the world and official success are also being mocked. When Lang's library goes up in smoke, so does his foolishness. His passion for books is transformed into a passion for revenge. His career takes off only after he turns his back on reading and scholarship and forsakes the cardinal rule of the "Exhortation to Study"— "My boy, to achieve life's reward / just face the window and study hard." As soon as he realizes that the words of the ancients are lies, he swiftly passes the *jinshi* exam, becomes governor of his enemy's native province, and wreaks his revenge.

4 *Dislocations in Gender*

I was a girl for seventeen years and a boy for twelve years more.
A thousand glances took me in, which one saw the truth?
Only now do I know for sure,
You can't trust your eyes to tell girl from boy.

—Xu Wei, "Maid Mulan"

The Human Prodigy

The most disturbing tale in *Liaozhai* to the twentieth-century reader, and one that is therefore never anthologized and rarely discussed, is "The Human Prodigy" ("Renyao"), translated here in its entirety:[1]

Mr. Ma Wanbao, a native of Dongchang, was wild and unrestrained. His wife, née Tian, was also uninhibited and amorously inclined, and they were a devoted couple. A young woman came to lodge at the house of the old woman[2] who lived next door, saying that she had run away from home on account of her parents-in-law's abuse. Her needlework was exceptionally skillful, and she began to do things for the old woman, who was pleased and kept her on. After several days, the girl announced that she knew how to administer nightly massages that could cure feminine ailments. The old woman came often to Ma's house and boasted of the girl's skills, but Tian never paid much attention.

One day, Ma spied the girl through a chink in the wall. She was around eighteen or nineteen years old and rather charming, and he secretly took a fancy to her. He plotted in private with his wife for her to feign illness and summon the girl. The old woman paid a visit first and, after making inquiries at Tian's bedside, said to her: "Since you've called for the girl, she'll come. But she's afraid of meeting men, so don't let your old man in."

"What can I do? My house isn't very large, and he often goes in and out." She brooded for a moment and then said: "My uncle in the West Village has invited him for a drink tonight. I'll just tell him not to come back. It will be very easy." The old woman agreed to this and left.

Tian suggested to her husband that they use the ruse of "switching the flag of Zhao for the flag of Han." He laughed and took her up on it.

When it grew dark, the old woman led the girl in and asked: "Is your old man coming back tonight?"

"He won't be back," said Tian.

"Perfect," said the girl happily.

After a few more words the old woman left them. Tian lit a candle, pulled down the quilt, and had the girl climb into bed. Then she herself undressed and put out the candle. All of a sudden, she said: "I almost forgot, the kitchen door is still open. I'd better close it to keep the dogs from stealing anything." So she climbed out of bed, opened the door, and changed places with her husband.

Ma tiptoed in. He climbed into bed and lay down with his head on the girl's pillow. In a trembling voice, the girl said: "I am going to cure you of what ails you." She whispered suggestively to Ma, but he did not reply. The girl then stroked his belly, until little by little she reached the area below his navel. She rested her hand, then suddenly probed his privates, which leaped up at the touch of her wrist. The girl's horror was no different from that of someone who realizes he's caught a snake or a scorpion by mistake. She rushed to her feet, meaning to escape, but Ma stopped her. He placed his hand between her legs and got a fistful of a pounding stick; here, too, was a mighty instrument.

Ma was greatly shocked and called for some light. His wife, supposing that the affair had backfired, lit a candle and hurried in, hoping to smooth things over. Instead she saw the girl on her knees pleading for her life. Embarrassed and afraid, she hastily withdrew.

In reply to Ma's questions, the "girl" said that he was Wang Double Joy of Gucheng. His older brother, Big Joy, was a disciple of Sang Chong's and so had been able to teach him the arts of female impersonation.

"How many people have you debauched?" asked Ma.

"Only sixteen. I haven't been in the business on my own very long." Ma knew that such an offense was a capital crime and considered handing Double Joy over to the authorities. But Double Joy's beauty aroused his pity, and so he tied Double Joy's hands behind his back and castrated him. The blood spurted out, and Double Joy fell into unconsciousness.

After a short time he revived. Ma lay him on the bed, covered him with a quilt and warned him: "I will heal you with medicines, but when your scars have healed, you must serve me for the rest of your life. If not, the matter will be exposed and you can expect no pardon." Double Joy acquiesced to his terms.

The next day, when the old woman came by, Ma deceived her: "She is Wang Double Lass, the daughter of a distant cousin. She was driven away from her husband's household because of natural sterility. We first learned about this last night when she told us her circumstances. She suddenly felt a little unwell, and so I am going to buy medicine for her and ask her family for permission to keep her here as a companion for my wife." The old woman went into the bedchamber to take a look and saw that Double Joy's complexion was ashen. She went up to the bed and asked what was the matter. "My sex has swelled up violently. I'm afraid I may have a terrible infection," said Double Joy. The old woman believed her and went away.

Ma fed Double Joy medicinal broth and applied powdered medicine to his wound, and in due time he recovered. At night, Ma always had Double Joy sleep with him. In the morning, Double Joy would rise and serve Tian by fetching water from the well, mending and sewing, washing and sweeping, and tending the fire, exactly like a maidservant.

Before long, Sang Chong was arrested and put to death, and seven of his gang were also publicly executed. Only Double Joy evaded the net of the law. Public notices were posted advertising for their arrest. All the villagers secretly had suspicions about Double Joy and got a group of village women to probe Double Joy's genitals through his clothing; only then were their doubts put to rest.

From then on, Double Joy was grateful to Ma and served him for the rest of his days. When he died, he was buried alongside the Ma family cemetery west of the city, whose traces may still be found there today.   (12.1711–13)

"The Human Prodigy" can be read to a fascinating degree as a companion piece to Balzac's tale "Sarrasine" (1830), which has acquired a new life from Roland Barthes's innovative study *S/Z* (1970). I do not mean, however, that Pu Songling's tale is a mirror image or negation of "Sarrasine," for that would imply that these two historically and culturally unrelated stories share the same terms of discourse, which could thus be negated. Rather, there is an odd and illuminating symmetry between the two: the plots of "The Human Prodigy" and "Sarrasine" are uncannily parallel but radically different. "Sarrasine" is a nested narrative, a story within a story that the narrator recites to satisfy a curious young woman he wishes to seduce. A French sculptor, Sarrasine, falls passionately in love with a beautiful Italian soprano, La Zambinella. When at last he discovers that he has been duped and that Zambinella is not a woman but a castrato, Sarrasine attempts to murder him/her, but it is Sarrasine who is assassinated instead. The narrator's stratagem likewise backfires: the young woman is so disturbed by this story that she reneges on her implicit promise to grant him a night of love.

In an essay on *S/Z,* Barbara Johnson argues that "Sarrasine" "is . . . in a way a study of difference—a subversive and unsettling formulation of the question of sexual difference."[3] "The Human Prodigy" offers a similarly unsettling formulation of the same question. It, too, is a tale of a man who falls unwittingly for a female impersonator; castration and deception are likewise the key to this tale, but the terms are reversed: This is a story not of love tragically thwarted but of sexual power usurped.

Double-crossing, in both senses of the word, is the key to the plot of "The Human Prodigy." Double Joy masquerades as a woman and persuades the old woman of his female identity, not only by his girlish appearance but also by his fine needlework, feminine work par excellence. The old woman is the patsy—her main function in the narrative is to hear and spread lies she believes to be truth. Double Joy's self-advertised ability to give nightly massages to cure feminine ailments is, on first reading, a warning, and in retrospect, a transparent euphemism. But in laying his trap, Double Joy is ignorant that another, more powerful predator is laying a trap for him.[4] Ma's scheme is even more complicated: his wife feigns illness, lies to the old woman and girl about her husband's return, and finally implements the great ruse—"the switching of the flag of Zhao for the flag of Han," a historical allusion to a third-century B.C. military stratagem.[5] This conjugal switching of identities (female to male) matches Double Joy's switch of identity (male to female), which is to become permanent. Finally, the successful deception of the entire village results in the unexpectedly peaceful denouement of the tale.

The Chinese language, with its lack of gender pronouns or genderized endings, is ideally suited to stories about ambiguous sexuality. Since gender markers are not required, awkward constructions such as him/her or a definitive gender assignment can be avoided, something impossible to do in English. The narrator is required to lie less, to strew fewer "snares," to employ Barthes's term. Instead, a vagueness of language can mask the uncertainty of gender. In "The Human Prodigy," the narrator's only direct lie is to call Double Joy a "girl" in the first part of the tale. This lie is essential to the shocking revelation of the "girl's" true sex and the comedy of the unwitting double male seduction.

Once Double Joy's sex is unmasked, the narrator is no longer obliged to deceive the reader. In the Chinese original of this tale, after Double Joy is castrated, the narrator carefully avoids any direct linguistic reference to Double Joy's gender. Instead, the burden of covering up the truth is shifted to the story's protagonists. The lies Ma and Double Joy tell the old woman hinge on double entendres that stick as closely as possible to the truth. For example, Double Joy diagnoses his ailment as a violent swelling and infection of the genitals. Ma explains that Double Joy was rejected by her family for "natural sterility," or *tian an;* this Chinese term is commonly applied to men to mean something like "natural eunuch."[6] Ma's fabrication is a practical and farseeing one, capable of explaining any future irregularities in Double Joy such as the lack of menses. These loaded explanations are ironic, for they secretly disclose the truth of the castration. The reader understands the truth these lies convey, something the unsuspecting old woman cannot perceive.

Structurally, this tale divides into two parts. The first half sets up the elaborate three-way seduction scene, which culminates in the revelation of the transvestite's true sex and his castration. The second half sketches the positive consequences of this castration. Thus the pivot of the story is the act of castration, unlike "Sarrasine," where the turning point is the revelation of "being-castrated" rather than any actual surgical procedure. According to Barthes, Balzac's tale "hinges on a structural artifice . . . making the search for truth (hermeneutic structure) into the search for castration (symbolic structure)."[7] In "The Human Prodigy," the important thing is not a search for truth and revelation but a search for rehabilitation and order.

Thus what cuts the narrative in two (the castration) is also the story's key symbolic structure. The castration is presented as a symbolic death and rebirth: Double Joy's blood is shed, and he faints. This is both a premonition of and a substitution for the execution that befalls his fellow conspirators, and it leads to his new identity and renaming as Double Lass. Like an initiation rite, the castration allows Double Joy to pass from his old state of outlaw to a new state of acceptance into the community. From the point of view of Ma and the law, the human prodigy's crime was that outward reality did not conform to the inward reality. Ma's action can thus be seen as a perverse Confucian "rectification of names." The prodigious has been cut off from the human prodigy; what remains is merely the human being.

What the lover of "the human prodigy" discovers in his paramour is not absence, as in "Sarrasine," but an unexpected presence. It is the lover himself who castrates the beautiful impersonator, an act that allows Ma to fulfill his desires; the castration paradoxically leads to the preservation of life and long-term sexual union rather than to death and the frustration of desire. This castration does not make its victim "an accursed creature," "a phantasmagoria," as it does in the case of Balzac's eunuch; rather, it is the means for Double Joy's reintegration into normal human society—as a concubine, he becomes a permanent member of the family and is even buried by the family tomb. The "monster" is domesticated.

Balzac's tale never mentions the word "castration"—it is always broken off, a blank in the text. This taboo does not operate in Pu Songling's tale, which straightforwardly depicts the castration and the accompanying loss of blood. Such forthright descriptions of this most disturbing act are also found elsewhere in *Liaozhai* and are not at all uncommon in the work of other seventeenth-century Chinese authors, possibly due to the high visibility and power of eunuchs during the late Ming.[8] Unlike "Sarrasine," then, it is not castration or transvestism that is dangerous in "The Human Prodigy" but male predatoriness masked in female guise. This point is made more clearly in another *Liaozhai* tale, "The Male Concubine" ("Nan qie"; 11.1530–31), in which a scholar purchases a young concubine, "whose skin was as lustrous as jade" (11.1530), only to find to his chagrin that she is actually a boy. The scholar is dismayed not at the boy's violation of sexual norms but at being swindled. This problem is easily solved when a friend whose tastes are more catholic enthusiastically volunteers to take the boy off the scholar's hands and refunds the purchase price in full. As a vulnerable and defenseless minor, the transvestite boy is not perceived as a danger or a threat. The substitution of a passive sexuality for Double Joy's active sexuality reduces him to the same category of harmless male concubine.

In traditional Chinese literature we virtually never find the nested-narrative structure employed so skillfully in "Sarrasine."[9] "The Human Prodigy" is not embedded in an overarching story; rather, in keeping with the conventions of historical discourse employed by the classical tale, Pu Songling's narrative is set off from and framed by the authorial commentary that follows it. In his comments on "The Human Prodigy," the Historian of the Strange singles out the castration episode and assigns it a political meaning: "It can be said that Ma Wanbao was good at making use of people. Children like to play with crabs, but they fear the claws, so they break them off and keep the crabs as pets. Alas! If one has grasped this meaning, one can rule the world!" (12:1713)

The comments of the Historian of the Strange are often considered to be moral or didactic in essence. But as we can see in this example, his commentary can be as twisted and disorienting as the story it purports to interpret. This sardonic finale continues the process enacted in the story itself of playing against our expectations: the tale does not so much deplore Double Joy's transgression of boundaries as praise Ma's ingenious restoration of them.

Such a political interpretation is less startling than it might seem at first glance. The Historian of the Strange is here drawing on the historiographic tradition of interpreting anomalies such as dislocations in gender as heavenly signs that something is morally out of whack in the political cosmos. This mode of interpretation is implicitly encoded in the very title of the story. The Chinese term *renyao* (human prodigy) originally denoted any human physical anomaly or freak. It was first employed in the philosophical writings of *Xunzi* (third c. B.C.), where it designated "human prodigies or portents" as implicitly opposed to "heavenly prodigies or portents" (*tianyao*).[10] Alongside this general meaning of human freak or monster, the term came to acquire an additional, more specialized usage: an impersonator of a member of the opposite sex.[11] It was first used in this sense in the *History of the Southern Dynasties* (*Nan shi*) to criticize a woman named Lou Cheng who for years masqueraded as a man and held official post. The historians considered her an evil omen of a subsequent rebellion, for in their words, "you cannot have yin acting as yang."[12] Their interpretation follows the tradition of meticulously correlating irregularities in gender with specific political disasters. Although, as John Henderson has argued, the tradition of correlative thinking may have declined by the seventeenth century,[13] it was still commonly drawn upon, perhaps as a form of deliberate archaism, to explain anomalies in Ming and Qing records of the strange.

The Historian of the Strange's comment also shifts the narrative to another level, that of allegory, by turning this flesh-and-blood tale of sexual one-upmanship into an ironic parable of how to wield

political and military power. This last twist is slyly anticipated by
the historical allusion to "switching the flag of Zhao for the flag
of Han" used within the story to describe the couple's seduction
scheme. Feng Zhenluan, one of *Liaozhai*'s early nineteenth-century
commentators, conveniently explains and re-historicizes the Historian of the Strange's final metaphor of the crab claws: "That Cao
Cao ruled the world and was able to make others his subjects is the
same meaning as breaking off the claws and keeping crabs as pets"
(12.1713).[14]

This gloss makes explicit the correlation between state and gender
hierarchy underlying the resolution of this tale. Ma diffuses the
threat the transvestite poses to the social and political order by
forcing him to assume permanently the subordinate roles of female
and servant. In so doing, Ma proves himself a model master and is
rewarded with an unusual concubine for himself and a hardworking
maidservant for his wife. Through their shrewd exploitation of a
fluke, the couple gains services they could not otherwise have af-
forded and even illicitly parallel the imperial household in having
their own personal eunuch. For his part, Double Joy is privately
converted into a grateful subject and is rewarded with a natural
death and a proper burial, rather than public disgrace and a painful
execution.

But the seriousness of this interpretation is called into question by
the Historian of the Strange himself. Although the historian's commentary seems to possess an authority above and beyond the story,
this structural hierarchy, which privileges commentary over tale,
also allows the author to take great liberties and lead his readers
astray by turning commentary into parody. In fact, commentary in
Ming and Qing informal writings frequently plays a comic or parodic role.[15] The clearest example of this tendency is a jokebook entitled *Comic Encomia* (*Xiao zan*), compiled by a well-known late Ming
educator and official, Zhao Nanxing (1550–1628).[16] His pseudo-
serious comments appended to standard jokes tend to poke fun at a
subject on the pretext of praising it, as in the following joke about a
shrewish wife:

A man was being beaten by his wife. In desperation he darted under the bed.
"Come out at once!" said his wife. The man replied: "When a man of spirit
says he won't come out, he certainly won't come out!"

The encomium says: "I often hear about henpecked husbands whose bones turn to water when they see their wives, like snakes that go limp upon hearing a crane squawk. Now this man was still able to dart under the bed and even dared to refuse to come out. Wasn't he indeed a hero!"[17]

The suspicion that the Historian of the Strange is likewise having fun in "The Human Prodigy" at the reader's expense is further aroused by the repetition of the reptilian metaphor that, along with the shared language of military strategy, helps bridge the customary disjunction in tone between comment and tale. The proverbial "crab claws" that children tear off for pleasure echo Double Joy's horror at suddenly discovering "a snake or a scorpion" in bed.[18] Both analogies vividly convey the point that a penis out of place is dangerous, but because the images are so comic (reminiscent as well of the humorous "snake that goes limp" in the shrew joke), they also seem to caution us against taking the political moral of the tale completely at face value. It is very possible that, as in *Comic Encomia,* the commentary here is in part reinforcing the ribaldry of the story under the very guise of deflating it.

The Female Body Transformed

We can better understand the allure of the disguised phallus in the Ming-Qing imagination when we discover that the transformation of the female body was perceived quite differently. The metamorphosis of a woman into a man is the subject of a single terse and unembellished anecdote in *Liaozhai:*

In Mudu township in Suzhou, a daughter of a commoner was sitting in a courtyard one night when a meteor suddenly struck her on the forehead. She fell down in a dead faint. Her elderly parents, who had no sons but only this one daughter, cried out grievously and rushed to save her. In due time she revived and announced with a smile: "I am now a man!" They examined her and indeed it was true. Her family did not consider her a prodigy but secretly rejoiced at their abrupt acquisition of a son. Amazing! This event occurred in the year *dinghai* [1707]. (8.1060)

The obvious key to Pu Songling's story is that the family has no sons: thus both the girl and her parents welcome her change in sex and do not treat it as prodigious. Although the transformation is attributed to external intervention, as in certain tales of miracles, the transformation appears to have been triggered above all by human will and desire.

As Charlotte Furth notes, accounts of women who underwent changes in sex crop up frequently in Ming and Qing notation books, including Wang Shizhen's *Occasional Chats North of the Pond;* ten such cases are even recorded in a draft of the Qing dynastic history. In her words: "The narratives constructed around these events show a common set of themes. . . . There are rejected brides; but families gain a son. There is a new, auspicious name, and a happy ending, especially if the stock theme of heirless parents figures in. The event is not explained or described, but presented as rebirth mediated by some extraordinary power."[19]

Alongside these other narratives, Pu Songling's account of this change in sex does not seem at all "amazing," as he exclaims, but unusually tame and stereotyped compared with other crossings of gender boundaries that he developed into full-fledged stories in *Liaozhai.* By presenting this incident without much narrative embroidery in the zhiguai manner of a report or a case history, complete with date, he may have been striving primarily to increase the impression of the event's historical veracity. Perhaps because, as Furth so astutely observes, Ming and Qing accounts of females transformed into males "were marked by a total suppression of the sexual in favor of the social,"[20] this particular story did not excite Pu Songling's imagination to the same extent as the male-to-female shift of "The Human Prodigy."

The uniformly positive response in all these accounts toward women who metamorphose into men, however, appears to be a later Ming and Qing development. Entries in *Seeking the Spirits* culled from "The Five Phases Treatise" of the *Han History* reveal that a transformation of *either* sex was originally correlated with a dangerous imbalance in the forces of yin and yang, and hence interpreted as an evil portent. For example:

During the thirteenth year of the reign of Prince Xiang of Wei, a woman metamorphosed into a man. He was given a wife, who bore one son. As Jing Fang [77–37 B.C.] wrote in his commentary to the *Book of Changes:* "When a woman metamorphoses into a man, this means that yin is thriving and a base person is on the throne; when a man metamorphoses into a woman, this means that yin has prevailed over yang, and it is responsible for the fall [of the dynasty]." Someone else wrote: "When a man metamorphoses into a woman, punishment by castration is excessive; when a woman metamorphoses into a man, a woman is controlling the government."[21]

A comparison with Galenic medical explanations of sex changes helps shed light on the radical interpretive shift in Chinese accounts of such phenomena.[22] *Des monstres et prodiges,* a medical book by the famous French physician Amboise Paré first published in 1573, includes a fascinating chapter on women who metamorphose into men ("Histoires Memorables de Certaines Femmes Qui Sont Degenerées en Hommes"). Paré contends that shifts in gender are exclusively one-way; it is possible only for women to become men, not the reverse: "We therefore never find in any true story that any man ever became a woman, because Nature tends always toward that which is most perfect, and not, on the contrary, to perform in such a way that what is perfect should become imperfect."[23]

Although Chinese historiographic, medical, and anecdotal sources report cases of men who metamorphosed into women, there are equally powerful asymmetries at work in the Chinese context. The early cosmological and political interpretations are always one-sided: sex changes are invariably blamed on an excess of yin, on a disorder in the female principle, regardless of the direction of the change. In Ming and Qing accounts, however, the asymmetry in interpretation swings in the reverse direction. The metamorphosis of women into men now becomes a matter for rejoicing, whereas men who become women are at best tolerated, if not punished, by the authorities. Thus we discover a new social and moral one-sidedness. Abstract and increasingly archaic cosmological principles are outweighed by the practical advantages of being a man. No longer a manifestation of profound disorder in the public realm, the metamorphosis of a woman into a man becomes redefined as an essentially filial act within the private confines of the family.[24]

This shift is explicitly encoded in a late Ming encyclopedia of dream interpretations, He Dongru's (1527–1637) *Arcane Explanations to the Forest of Dreams (Menglin xuanjie),*[25] which assigns a purely beneficial value to yang and a purely malevolent one to yin. To dream that one has been transformed into a woman is thus diagnosed as "inauspicious" (*xiong*) and augurs a yin-induced calamity or disease for the dreamer. To dream that one witnesses someone else being transformed into a woman predicts failure. In contrast, dreams in which a woman is transformed into a man are hailed as "highly auspicious" (*daji*) and augur success in every endeavor.[26]

Certain late Qing accounts explain more explicitly the powerful fantasy of a family without sons gaining an heir through the sudden miraculous transformation of a daughter. In "The Amazing Case of a Woman Who Turned into a Man" ("Nü bian nan an"), which is dated to 1782 but is included in a collection of retold case histories published in 1919,[27] the underlying power of human desire to effect sex changes is overt. The motivation of the girl is supplied (she is trying to escape marriage into a family with an unusually cruel mother-in-law) as is the planting of the suggestion (her mother tells her that instead of praying to heaven for death, she would do better to pray for a change in sex). Another account of a woman who became a man, in Li Qingchen's *Drunk on Tea's Strange Accounts* (*Zuicha zhiguai;* preface dated 1892), is noteworthy because it describes the bodily growth of the male sexual organ, judiciously glossed over in earlier accounts, and also because the author's pedantic comment so clearly articulates the ideology only implicit in previous versions:

Doesn't this girl resemble [the filial woman warrior] Mulan going off to battle? How sincere was her will! For if you are sincere, you can reach Heaven, especially if your sincerity arises from filial piety. How could Heaven not take pity on you? How clever is the Creator to be able to transform a woman into a man! But, in fact, she accomplished her will by trusting to her filial piety. If it weren't for her filial piety, then she would merely be a human prodigy and would deserve no praise.[28]

Thus, as we will find in the case of female cross-dressers who merely pass for men, in the final analysis the ethical motivation for a female's change in sex ultimately determines whether she is classified as a human prodigy or as an exemplary woman.

The Transformation of Sang Chong

Accounts of seduction by men supposedly disguised as women appeared in Chinese literature long before Pu Songling's "Human

Prodigy" and indeed are part of international folklore.[29] An anecdote in a thirteenth-century Southern Song miscellany, *New Tales from a Green Window* (*Lüchuang xinhua*), presents this fantasy as a case of biological hermaphroditism. A maidservant, suitably named Companion of Joy (Banxi),* feigns nightmares and frightens her young mistress, Miss Zhang, into inviting her into bed. Once in bed, Companion of Joy offers to instruct her innocent mistress in her upcoming nuptial duties. "Though I am a woman," she explains, "both forms are present in me. When I encounter a woman, I assume a male form; when I encounter a male, then I become a woman again."[30] Miss Zhang proves a talented pupil. When their liaison is eventually discovered, the false maidservant is arrested and exiled. A later Yuan embellishment, however, allows Companion of Joy to escape and concludes on an oddly practical note: "I have recorded this to let others know that they cannot be too careful in examining their maidservants."[31] Both versions concur, however, in positing a premeditated seduction scheme based on deception and interpret the assumption of male sexuality as a willful act.

The maidservant's self-description is virtually identical to one of the three types of hermaphrodites later classified by Li Shizhen's *Classified Materia Medica* in his discussion of human reproductive anomalies: "There is one type that is female when it meets a male, and male when it meets a female."[32] This description also resembles what Wendy O'Flaherty has called "the alternating androgyne (male for a period of time, female for a period of time)" found in Indian myths.[33] A Chinese vernacular story about a hermaphrodite nun by the late Ming writer Ling Mengchu is more forthcoming about the actual mechanics of this condition. The nun can retract her male organs inside her body. It is only thanks to the perspicacity and perseverance of the official investigating the case that her secret is divulged. He devises a test in which her genital area is painted with oil and a dog is induced to lick it. Unable to withstand the yang heat generated by the friction of the dog's tongue, the nun's male organs emerge, and she is duly executed by the authorities.[34]

Pu Songling's tale was directly inspired by a notorious court case known as "The Case of the Human Prodigy" ("Renyao gongan"),

*Note the parallelism with Double Joy or Erxi and the clever choice of "Ban" (companion), which is also a pun for "half and half."

which reportedly came to trial in Beijing during the Chenghua reign period (1465–87) of the Ming dynasty. The interest aroused by this sensational case was considerable and persisted for several centuries, as the number of accounts in Ming and Qing sources attest. The case was even the basis for the prologue of a vernacular story entitled "Two Brothers of Different Sex" ("Liu Xiaoguan cixiong xiongdi") published by Feng Menglong.[35] The most detailed account of the case appears in *Gengsi bian,* a Ming notation book whose author, Lu Can (1494–1551), claims to have transcribed it from a copy of official documents found at a friend's house.[36]

According to Lu Can's report, which consists of an official memorial to the throne and the emperor's reply, the case was brought against a female impersonator named Sang Chong, the leader of a gang of vagabond men who dressed as women with bound feet, made their living plying female trades such as sewing, and abused their disguise to gain unlawful sexual access to women of good families. The willing they seduced; the unwilling they drugged and raped. For fear of damaging their reputation, however, none of the women informed on their seducers. Sang Chong was finally apprehended when a man, smitten by Sang Chong's feminine charms, stole into his room to seduce him. When he was unable to repel the man's advances, Sang Chong's secret was uncovered and reported. Taken into custody and interrogated, Sang Chong confessed and implicated seven other female impersonators said to be his disciples. The throne recommended that he be put to death by slow slicing for committing a crime akin to the "ten perversities" and for injuring popular mores. Orders were issued for the seven other transvestites to be rounded up and sent to Beijing for a similar fate. Lu Can's account does not, however, indicate whether the authorities were successful in capturing them all.[37]

Pu Songling clearly assumed his readers' familiarity with the case, for he added no explanation of his reference to Sang Chong and his gang. Pu Songling probably had access to one or more written accounts of the case since Wang Big Joy (Daxi), the older brother and initiator of Double Joy into the art of impersonation, was the name of one of the seven gang members listed in the *Gengsi bian* report and two other accounts.[38] But Pu Songling's original twist on the Sang Chong case—the castration of the transvestite and his conversion into a male concubine—may, as Charlotte Furth suggests, have been inspired by another famous sixteenth-century case in which a man named Li Liangyu, who had set up housekeeping with his male lover, actually metamorphosed into a female when his testicles withdrew into his body and became a vagina.[39] Pu Songling's alternative explanation for the change is also featured in a parodic short story by the seventeenth-century writer Li Yu in which a young man castrates himself out of love for his male partner, thereby transforming himself into an exemplary woman, a veritable "Male Mother Mencius."[40]

Pu Songling's substitution of a premeditated seduction scheme involving the collaboration of the wife, rather than a straightforward rape to unmask the impersonator, resembles three other accounts of the Sang Chong case in Ming notation books; however, these all employ a variant graph for Sang Chong's given name and have the female impersonator passing himself off as a widow.[41] Of these, Huang Wei's (*jinshi* 1490) sketch of the seduction subplot is the earliest and comes closest to Pu Songling's version:

There was a certain licentiate who fancied widows and was determined to have her [Sang Chong]. So he got his wife to pretend she was his younger sister and bribed an old woman of the neighborhood to go and invite the widow. When she arrived, the licentiate secretly cautioned his wife to open the door just before getting into bed as though she were going out to the toilet. His wife did as she was instructed. The licentiate rushed in and put out the candle. The widow screamed, but the man grabbed her by the throat and forced himself on her, and lo and behold, she turned out to be a man.[42]

Pu Songling has worked out the comedy of unwitting double male seduction in much more detail than this or any other account of the case; his construction of events is more piquant and dramatic, and he fleshes out the embryonic plot of the notation books into a tightly woven and gripping story. The narration's control of point of view is particularly deft, beginning with Ma's erotically charged glimpse of Double Joy through a chink in the wall and continuing with Tian's embarrassed candle-lit view of Double Joy on his knees pleading for his life, the widow's sickbed observation of Double Joy's ashen complexion, and the village women's tactile "verification" of Double Joy's womanhood.

Most significant, in Pu Songling's treatment, names and figures mentioned in earlier records have been developed into full-fledged characters. Only his version makes switching places the wife's idea and promotes the old neighbor woman into a crucial figure in the deception. This is significant because as Barthes observes of "Sarrasine": "The symbolic field is not that of the biological sexes; it is that of castration: of *castrating/castrated, active/passive*. It is in this field, and not in that of the biological sexes, that the characters in the story are pertinently distributed."[43] So, too, in "The Human Prodigy" the four characters can be arrayed into two opposing camps that are not strictly biological: Ma and his wife, Tian, in the castrating camp and Double Joy and the old woman in the castrated camp. Tian, who like her husband is "uninhibited and amorously inclined," is the agent who sets the possibility of castration in motion. She thinks of the ruse, she feigns illness, she cleverly lies to the old woman and the girl. Her active role in the plot differs radically from the powerlessness of the female victims in accounts of the case who are either drugged senseless or effectively gagged by fear for their reputations. Yet, although Tian benefits from her cooperation by acquiring a slave, she still ends up the sexual loser. Once Double Joy enters their household, we are told, "Ma always had Double Joy sleep with him" (12.1713). In their ménage à trois, Tian is "odd man out." In contrast, Double Joy starts out in the powerful castrating camp—combining a man's mobility with a woman's free access to the inner quarters, he cuckolds husbands and robs women of their virtue. In the end, however, he survives only by passively enduring the attack of the village women, whose groping for his genitals corroborates his utter powerlessness, his already "being-castrated." And yet it is not impossible that we are meant to suppose that even in his unorthodox guise Double Joy achieved the sexual fulfillment ultimately denied to Tian.

As Mircea Eliade has observed about the decadent nineteenth-century European writers' treatment of androgynes, the Chinese writers on female impersonators or hermaphrodites in both anecdotal and fictional literature were concerned "not with a wholeness resulting from the fusion of the sexes, but with a superabundance of erotic possibilities."[44] Sang Chong himself is presented as phenomenally virile—the *Gengsi bian* account, for example, has him confessing to having debauched 182 women. (Double Joy, who admits not having been in the business very long, has managed only sixteen.) Ling Mengchu's hermaphrodite nun keeps a record book of her partners' names and nineteen handkerchiefs stained with the blood of the virgins she has deflowered; after her execution the nun's naked body is exhibited, much to the amusement of the onlookers, who comment not on her anatomical deficiency but on its overgenerosity. Yuan Mei best sums up this erotic fantasy of sexual difference in his account of an eighteenth-century successor to Sang Chong who declares: "I have tasted bliss hitherto unknown in this human world. Why should I regret to die?"[45]

Although clearly prey to the erotic fascination surrounding female impersonators, in "The Human Prodigy" Pu Songling is less interested in the erotic per se than in sex as a symbol of power. As we have seen, the subject of "The Human Prodigy" is not so much the transgression of boundaries as the ingenious and productive reinstatement of them. But, paradoxically, this reordering is accomplished only through the most extreme and inexorable crossing of gender boundaries.

All other accounts of the Sang Chong case end with the unmasking and public execution of the human prodigy, the conventional resolution of the dangerous imbalance created by dislocations in gender. Pu Songling's tale, however, resolves this contradiction by adding a second part to the tale. Similar efforts can be observed in other Ming and Qing works, but the method each author employed differs. In the two seventeenth-century vernacular stories, "Two Brothers of Different Sex" and Ling Mengchu's account of the hermaphrodite nun, a compensatory symmetry in narrative structure rectifies the imbalance: each piece consists of a short prologue story and a long story as its main body. The comic prologue of "Two Brothers of Different Sex" portrays Sang's sexual initiation into female impersonation to offset the main story of a young woman who innocently masquerades as a man.[46] Ling Mengchu's main story likewise includes an additional man disguised as a nun to compensate for the loss of a nun disguised as a man. "Two Brothers of Different Sex" expresses this symmetry in explicit moral terms: the man in the prologue impersonates a woman for base purposes (seduction and rape) and is punished by an ignominious death; the woman in the main story dresses as a man for moral purposes (filial piety) and is rewarded with a good marriage. As the storyteller explicitly tells the reader: "Just now I've told you about a man made up as a woman to harm popular mores. Now I'll tell you the main story about a woman who dresses as a man but who is both chaste and filial."[47]

In "The Human Prodigy," the symmetry is enacted within the confines of the narrative itself. In another brief *Liaozhai* tale, "A Boy Bears Sons" ("Nan sheng zi"; 8.1037), a similar sort of neutralizing effect is established in the symmetrical relationship between the main item and the Historian of the Strange's comment. A short while before the rebellion of Wu Sangui, a catamite belonging to a Fujian military commanding officer named Yang Fu suddenly conceived. When the pregnancy came to term, the boy dreamed that a god gave him a caesarean. Upon awakening, he is flanked by twin baby boys and discovers a scar on his ribs, proof of the birth. As if to compensate for this excess of yang, the twin boys are given names that attempt to recuperate the imperiled yin-yang balance, "Heaven Bestows" and "Earth Bestows."[48] The Historian of the Strange's comment, unusually long in proportion to the main anecdote, recounts Yang Fu's death at the hands of Governor Cai of Fujian and interprets the prodigious birth of Yang's twin sons as a portent of his murder:

Now Yang's wife, who was brave and resourceful, was suspicious of Cai and tried to prevent Yang from going to see him, but Yang wouldn't listen. In tears, his wife escorted him on his way. Upon her return, she called together the various fellow officers, donned armor, took up weapons, and waited for news. Not long thereafter she learned that her husband had been beheaded, and she proceeded to launch a counterattack against Cai. Cai was in a panic and didn't know what to do. Fortunately, his guards held fast; the attackers could not overcome them and departed. Only after they had gone a considerable distance did Cai rush out in martial attire and his band of soldiers raise a great hue and cry. People passed around the story, considering it a joke. Several years later the rebels finally surrendered. Before long Cai suddenly died. Right before his demise, he and his attendants saw Yang come in, holding a weapon. (8.1037)

The inauspicious sexual imbalance initiated by Yang's male lover giving birth is matched, as it were, in the story incorporated in the comment, by the virility of Yang's wife. She not only dons armor and bears weapons, she also convokes and leads other officers in an attack on her husband's murderer, Governor Cai. Her martial prowess is enhanced by the contrast with Cai's cowardice and subsequent ridicule. The virtuous woman warrior succeeds in unmanning the craven governor. This loss of face symbolically leads to his downfall and prepares the way for Yang's posthumous revenge. In retrospect we find that the passive catamite who assumes the female role of bearing children can perhaps be balanced only by a "manly" woman of unusual martial power.[49]

Heroes Among Women

In the *Fivefold Miscellany,* Xie Zhaozhe quips that although many women have masqueraded as men, the female impersonation in the Sang Chong case is something new.[50] He undoubtedly had in mind the long literary tradition in China regarding women disguised as men. Within this tradition two coexisting branches can be distinguished. Early historiography, steeped in the theory of cosmological correspondences, is hostile to male impersonators, regardless of their motives. The romance, on the other hand (as represented by ballads, chantefables, plays, and fiction), treats women who masquerade as men as virtuous and even heroic figures. Filial piety, blood vengeance, requital of true friendship, and the desire to serve the state are all acceptable motives. But even within the parameters of the historiographic tradition, female impersonation like that of Sang Chong is dealt with as a capital crime, and male impersonation seems, at worst, a misdemeanor, punishable with ridicule and disgrace.

As with transformations of sex, the interpretation of cross-dressing as a dangerous anomaly can be traced back to the copious Six Dynasties discourse on the strange. For example, an item in the present edition of *Seeking the Spirits* taken from "The Five Phases Treatise" of the *Jin History,* interprets women wearing elements of masculine attire and the concomitant breakdown of gender distinctions as an evil portent for the unlawful and tyrannical female rule of Empress Jia (256–300): "The distinction between men and women is an important matter to the state, and so dress and ornaments differ according to regulations. Nowadays women are using weapons as ornaments; in fact, this is prodigious in the extreme. Following this, the Empress Jia affair ensued."[51]

In a similar vein, let us reconsider the biography of the woman Lou Cheng recorded in the *History of the Southern Dynasties,* which I discussed earlier in this chapter as a locus classicus for the term "human prodigy." Disguised as a man, Lou Cheng served in moderately high official positions during the Qi dynasty. When her secret was finally divulged, the emperor ordered her to don woman's attire and leave office. The early Tang historians who compiled the *History of the Southern Dynasties* appended Lou Cheng's tiny biography as an explanation for a series of rebellions. Because of the correspondence drawn between violations of gender hierarchy and uprisings against the state, as in the case of women wearing masculine weapon-shaped ornaments, she is evaluated as an evil portent: "This was a human prodigy. Yin's desire to be yang cannot be realized; hence the matter will [always] come to light. [The rebellions] of Jingze, Yaoguang, Xianda, and [Cui] Huijing were all fulfillments [of this inauspicious omen]."[52]

And yet, the historians' position is slightly more complicated, for they also interject a rhetorical question, cast in Lou Cheng's own voice, that suggests a more sympathetic, almost tragic view of her predicament: "Isn't it a shame to possess such skills and still be obliged to resume the identity of an old woman?" Of course, the historians promptly answer in the negative: "This was a human prodigy." But Lou Cheng's fate and that of a handful of male impersonators like her, stirred the imagination of subsequent readers. Lou Cheng's biography was culled from the official history and copied in the human prodigy section of the tenth-century anthology *Taiping guangji,* where it must have been read for entertainment, especially during the sixteenth and seventeenth centuries when reprints of the collection circulated widely.[53] In fact, Lou Cheng's name invariably appears on the numerous lists of women who passed as men featured in Ming and Qing notation books. Significantly, in such works as the *Fivefold Miscellany* and Chu Renhuo's (1630–1705) *Useless Gourd Collection (Jianhu ji),* she and women like her are no longer viewed negatively as human prodigies but are praised as "extraordinary persons" (*yiren*) or "heroes among women" (*nüzhong zhangfu*).[54]

This last, rather elastic sobriquet, which enjoyed particularly wide currency during the late Ming and early Qing, describes a woman who adheres to a lofty masculine code of honor but preserves her female chastity.[55]

As such, by the late Ming, Lou Cheng could easily be grouped with the heroic cross-dressers of the romantic tradition, such as the famous woman-warrior Mulan, who was immortalized in two separate anonymous ballads (*yuefu*), one dated possibly as early as the Southern Dynasties, another dated to the Tang. Out of deep filial piety, Mulan donned male clothing and joined the army in her aged father's place. After a spectacular military career, however, she returned home and voluntarily resumed a female identity.[56] The eponymous heroine of the Tang tale "Xie Xiao'e" is another famous case. Xiao'e disguised herself as a man for several years in order to avenge the murders of her father and husband. After accomplishing her mission, she shaved her head and became a nun. The author, Li Gongzuo (ca. 770–850), does not censor her for violating gender norms; on the contrary, he is explicit about having recorded the tale to commemorate her extraordinary *female* virtue:

A gentleman says: "She never wavered in her resolve and eventually avenged the deaths of her father and her husband—that is loyalty; she mixed with menials and yet never betrayed her sex—that is chastity. And loyalty and chastity are the maximum virtues that can be expected of women. . . . I have written this story of Xiao'e to commemorate her virtue. In doing so I am only following the principle of praising good deeds laid down by the author of the *Spring and Autumn Annals* [i.e., Confucius]."[57]

Indeed, in accordance with this judgment, the official *New Tang History* (*Xin Tang shu*) included a short biography of Xiao'e in the "exemplary women" (*lienü*) section.[58]

Thus instead of being labeled human prodigies, Xie Xiao'e and Mulan qualify as exemplary women. It seems to have been allowable, even admirable, to masquerade as a man for virtuous motives as long as the shift was temporary. Once the desired ends had been accomplished, the impersonator had to resume a female identity; otherwise her motives for cross-dressing would be revealed simply as yin's forbidden desire to appropriate yang's privileges. Although Lou Cheng may have entertained permissible motives for her cross-dressing (serving the state), she sought to alter her status permanently. Such an ambition may have contributed to her initial evaluation as a human prodigy. Nevertheless, once the romantic approach toward male impersonators had become prevalent, Lou Cheng, too, was rehabilitated as "a hero among women."

By Pu Songling's time, then, the historiographic and romantic traditions of the female cross-dresser seem to have merged. *Liaozhai* includes two stories about exemplary women who impersonate men: "Miss Yan" ("Yanshi"; 6.766–69), whose heroine disguises herself as a man to pass the examinations and serve in office, resembles the Lou Cheng type; the heroine in "Shang Sanguan" (3.373–75), who dresses as a boy to kill her father's murderer, fits the mold of Xie Xiao'e.[59]

Miss Yan, an intelligent girl of unusual precocity, is educated by her father, who regrets that the family's "female scholar" cannot "cap her hair like a man when she comes of age" (6.766). After both her parents' death, she marries another orphan, a handsome and witty young man, who unfortunately has no head whatsoever for scholarship. Although Miss Yan patiently tutors him, he still utterly lacks the wherewithal to pass the examinations. The inversion between the abilities of husband and wife is marked in the "praise and blame" conventions of traditional historiography, which evolved from meticulously interpreting the laconic wording of the *Spring and Autumn Annals* to yield moral judgments. In this vein, although Pu Songling's tale begins with the husband, his name is omitted as a sign of disapproval—he is simply called "a certain young scholar from an impoverished family in Shuntian" in contrast to his wife, who, though introduced second, is honored with a name to commemorate her virtue: Miss Yan (Yanshi).[60]

The couple, however, share an unusually amicable relationship despite (or ironically even because of) their apparent mismatch. Consider the marital quarrel that sparks Miss Yan's resolve to assume a male identity and compete in the examinations herself after her husband repeatedly fails them:

His reputation was at a nadir, and he couldn't even provide for their food. He felt so desolate that he started to cry.

"You aren't a man!" scolded Miss Yan. "You're betraying your cap of manhood! If you'd let me change my hairbuns for a hat, I'd pick up an official post with ease!" Her husband had been feeling miserable and disappointed. Hearing his wife's words, he glared at her and burst out angrily: "A person in the women's quarters like you, who's never been to the examination hall, thinks that winning rank and reputation is as simple as fetching water and making plain rice porridge in the kitchen! If you had a hat on your head, I'm afraid you'd be just like me!"   (6.767)

But here, at the height of this quarrel, the mood suddenly shifts, and instead of coming to blows, the couple starts to tease each other:

"Don't get so angry," she said with a laugh. "I ask your permission to switch my clothes and take your place at the next examination session. If I fail like you, then I'll never again dare to slight the gentlemen of this world!" Her husband in turn laughed and replied: "You don't know how bitter the flavor is. It really is fitting that I give you permission to taste it. But I'm afraid that if anyone sees through you, I'll become the laughingstock of the village."

"I'm not joking," said Miss Yan. "You once told me that your family has a house in the north. Let me follow you there dressed as a man and pretend to be your younger brother. You were in swaddling clothes when you left; who will know the difference?"   (6.767–68)

The ease and lightheartedness of Miss Yan's assumption of male identity is facilitated by the narrative's recurrent emphasis on the socially constructed outward symbols of masculinity and femininity—"the cap of manhood" versus the feminine coiffure.[61] Because attention is shifted away from any innate biological sexual differences, altering one's sexual identity becomes as simple as changing one's hat and clothes. Unlike Double Joy, who confesses to having studied "the art of female impersonation" from his brother, a disciple of the master transvestite, Sang Chong,[62] Miss Yan's transformation is seemingly effortless and instantaneous. The situation resembles nothing so much as an actress pantomiming a quick change of costume, which would suffice to turn her into a man on the traditional Chinese stage.[63] Thus after Miss Yan's husband agrees to her scheme, she "went into the bedroom and emerged in male garb. 'How do I look?' she asked. 'Will I do as a boy?' In her husband's eyes, she seemed the spitting image of a handsome young man" (6.768). Although her question seems almost coquettish as she poses in private before her husband's gaze, Miss Yan manages to pull off the impossible in the public, masculine sphere. She passes the *jinshi* exam in no time and is made censor of Henan province; eventually she even receives a noble title that is posthumously conferred on her husband's parents. Having proven her point and provided for their future, she voluntarily retires right before the fall of the Ming and resumes female dress; the couple lives happily ever after.

The Historian of the Strange's sarcastic remarks continue the process of inversion enacted in the tale itself: "That parents-in-law should be granted honorary titles through their daughter-in-law can be called amazing! But what age has ever lacked censors who were women? Women who actually were censors, however, have been few. All those wearing scholar's hats in this world who call themselves men ought to die of shame!" (6.769) Once again sexual difference is represented by ceremonial headgear, but here it is given a rhetorical twist. Precisely because the story illustrates how easily outward symbols of masculinity can be put on and taken off, scholars are reminded that they cannot (like Miss Yan's ineffectual husband) rely on symbols alone to make them men.

In a unique way, this tale also creates a comic inversion of the standard "scholar-beauty" romance (*caizi jiaren*), with Miss Yan assuming the scholar role and her husband assuming that of the beauty. (In fact, only the husband's handsome looks are described; Miss Yan is never physically described at all.) As in more conventional romances, the narrative highlights the couple's relationship rather than the scholar's official career. Miss Yan's meteoric rise through the examinations and ten years in office is compressed into a mere two lines, for the tale is concerned mainly with Miss Yan's smooth transition from woman to man and then back again to woman. Miss Yan's cross-dressing and the inversion between husband and wife (though Miss Yan is still technically subordinate to her husband as his "younger brother") are not treated as prodigious either in the tale or in the Historian of the Strange's comment,[64] for in addition to her masculine talent, Miss Yan possesses the requisite womanly virtues, most notably chastity. She is first and foremost a helpmeet to her husband: she tutors him unstintingly; she is faithful to him and in the end unjealously buys him a concubine because she is infertile. The double standard between the sexes that persists despite their inversion of roles is even the butt of a joke between husband and wife. Says Miss Yan to her husband after presenting him with the concubine: "People who make an illustrious career generally buy concubines to wait upon them. I was an official for ten years, but I'm still on my own. Why do you have the good fortune to enjoy such a beauty?" Replies her husband: "Go ahead and take thirty handsome men as concubines if you wish, like that princess of the Southern Dynasties" (6.769).[65] In that she combines the best qualities of both sexes, Miss Yan seems to come closest to representing an androgynous ideal in *Liaozhai*.

The lightheartedness of "Miss Yan" contrasts sharply with the tragic tone of "Shang Sanguan." This story seems to have particularly fascinated Pu Songling, for he not only wrote it up as a *Liaozhai* tale, but he also expanded it into a lengthy vernacular play, *The Cold and the Dark (Hansen qu)*, and even composed a poem called "The Ballad of a Swordswoman" ("Xianü xing") on a similar theme.[66] Although the tale is narrated with icy detachment and precision, the Historian of the Strange gives reign to his emotions in an empassioned panegyric to Sanguan's virtues. In the tale, the father of a sixteen-year-old virgin, Shang Sanguan, is openly beaten to death by the servants of the rich village bully. After her brothers' attempts to obtain justice through the corrupt legal system fail, Sanguan refuses to go through with her impending marriage and runs away from home. About six months later, the bully holds a birthday party and hires two young male entertainers. One of them takes the bully's fancy and retires with him for the night. A few hours later, the servants discover that the bully has been beheaded and that the entertainer has hung himself. The entertainer turns out to be Shang Sanguan, who had dressed as a boy to avenge her father's death and then committed suicide. One of the men hired to watch over the bodies tries to violate her corpse, but he mysteriously falls down dead, bleeding, as though struck. His death is attributed to the divine power of the corpse, who even posthumously manages to preserve her chastity.

As in "Miss Yan," a moral inversion between the sexes contrasts Sanguan's masculine resolve to avenge her father's death at any cost with her elder brothers' effeminate weakness and dillydallying. Although in the tale itself this inversion is only implicit, the Historian of the Strange comments directly upon it: "The Shang brothers' ignorance of the existence of a female assassin-retainer in the family

shows what kind of men they were" (3.375).[67] Pu Songling's vernacular play makes this point even more explicitly: "She surpassed
in every way the men of this world."[68] Sanguan's impersonation of
the young actor should be another manifestation of the sexual inversion in this tale. But ironically, she never seems as feminine as when
she masquerades as a boy named Jade ("whose face and bearing were
like those of a fine maiden" [3.373]) or as masculine as when as a
young lady she bitterly admonishes her elder brothers. The narrative exploits the ambiguous erotic charms of a girlish boy (or boyish
girl) during the party by depicting the drunken bully's arousal,[69] but
instead of the farcical revelation beneath the covers that we find in
"The Human Prodigy" or "The Male Concubine," a veil is significantly drawn over the final bedroom scene.

The strangeness and power of "Shang Sanguan" are increased by
gaps in the narrative and the corresponding abruptness of the action.
The reader learns virtually nothing of Sanguan's life during the six
months of her absence or of how she learned that her father's enemy
was fond of attractive boys and managed to be hired for his birthday
celebration. She reappears as suddenly as she disappears. The with-
holding of crucial information, which creates these gaps in the
action, is effected through sudden shifts in point of view. Most
important, after the young singing-boy Jade has retired for the night
with the bully and locked the door of his bedroom, the focus shifts
to the household servants. Their attention is attracted by strange
noises and silences until they are led to discover the corpses:

After some time, the servants heard a squawking noise emanating from the
bedroom. One of the servants went to take a peep and saw that the room
was pitch-black and utterly still. He was about to turn on his heel, when
suddenly there was a terrible thud, like some heavy dangling object whose
cord had snapped. He quickly asked what was going on, but there was no
reply. He called out to the group of servants to break down the door and
they discovered their master's head sundered from his body; Jade had hung
himself, and the severed rope had fallen to the ground. Between the edges of
the beams, the remnants of the rope were still faintly visible.   (3.374)[70]

The murder itself has been narrated obliquely; in commentator Dan
Minglun's words, "The author has used only 'empty' [*xu*] strokes"
(3.374).

木蘭遺像

商丘人父病不能從軍為有
司所苦木蘭代父戍邊十二年人
不知其為女也或云姓花
父名孤弧此魏時人有缺
曰木蘭罕見咬兒

Fig. 4. Woodblock illustration of Mulan cross-dressed as a soldier from the *Catalogue of Peerless Historical Figures* (*Nanling wushuang pu*, preface dated 1690). To create a visual image of a woman cross-dressing as a man, the early Qing illustrator Jin Guliang has added tiny bound feet to Mulan's martial attire. (*Zhongguo gudai banhua congkan* 4: 427)

These gaps in the narrative match the telltale gap in Sanguan's sexual identity. When the servants move the young actor's corpse into the courtyard, they notice to their amazement that "his socks and shoes felt empty, as if there were no feet inside. They took them off and found a pair of white silk slippers as tiny as hooks, for this was in fact a girl" (3.374). The revelation of female identity has been displaced from the genitals to the feet. Significantly, the identical process of revelation occurs as well in "Miss Yan." To convince her incredulous aunt that she is not a man, Miss Yan pulls off her boots and displays her bound feet; the gaps in her boots have been stuffed with cotton wool. In contrast to headgear, the socially constructed symbols of gender manipulated with such skill in the story, bound feet, those man-made fetishes that had become the locus of the erotic imagination in late Imperial China, are transformed into a *natural* and *immutable* proof of true femininity.[71] This ultimate test of feminine sexuality sharply contrasts with the purely genital and in fact *alterable* evidence of Sang Chong or Double Joy's masculinity* (see Fig. 4).[72]

The Grotesque Woman

In *Liaozhai,* women need not, however, dress as men to be considered "heroes among women"; several tales recount the exploits of women who, like Shang Sanguan, modeled themselves on the assassin-retainers of the histories or the knight-errants of Tang dynasty tales, figures Pu Songling passionately admired. In the tale "Woman Qiao" ("Qiao nü"; 9.1283–87), a grotesquely ugly widow requites the true friendship of Meng, the only man who ever looked upon her and was delighted with what he saw. Unlike other *Liaozhai* heroines such as Miss Yan who voluntarily transgress conventional gender boundaries, Qiao is forced, as it were, out of the female sex, indeed almost out of the human race, by her physical disfigurement. She is succinctly but graphically described as "dark and ugly, with one pit-like, yawning nostril, and also lame in one foot" (9.1283). As she herself declares as she rejects Meng's offer of

---

*It is hard to resist explaining the allure of bound feet in Freudian terms as representations of the female genitals—as mutilated appendages with *something missing.*

remarriage, forbidden to her in the Qing cult of chaste widowhood: "My ugliness and deformity are such that I do not even resemble a human being. The only thing I can trust to is my virtue. If I now serve two husbands, then what will be left for you?" (9.1283)[73]

Although none of *Liaozhai*'s commentators note the resemblance, Qiao must have been at least partially inspired by a character in the famous *Biographies of Exemplary Women (Lienü zhuan)*, the monstrously ugly Zhongli Chun who ultimately became queen of Qi. "She had a mortar-shaped head and sunken eyes, long fingers and big joints, a turned-up nose and a swollen throat, a thick neck and sparse hair. She was stooped at the waist with a protruding bust; her skin was as dark as if it had been varnished."[74] The ugliness that makes Zhongli Chun an outcast gives her, like Qiao, a privileged moral vision and a remarkable degree of freedom from conventional restraints on her sex. Zhongli Chun succeeds in gaining an interview with the king by audaciously offering herself to him in marriage and teaching him her magic powers of invisibility. Through her frank Confucian admonishments against the king's misrule, she helps bring peace and prosperity to the land.

The obvious lesson of this didactic story—that beauty and ugliness are only skin-deep—also plainly underlies "Woman Qiao"; Pu Songling, however, has added the new and important theme of selfless friendship between man and woman. Although the same kind of excessiveness that marks the hagiographic tale is at work in "Woman Qiao," the setting has been transposed to a humbler rural world. The ethical significance of the two stories remains similar, but the problems in "Woman Qiao" have been scaled down from those of the preservation of the state to the preservation of the family. Pu Songling has returned to the local disputes and petty villainy that he knew best.

After Meng's premature death, the village hoodlums help themselves to his land and property, knowing his orphan son is powerless to stop them. Everyone turns a blind eye, except woman Qiao. Despite ridicule and intimidation, she steps outside the feminine sphere of hearth and home to demand publicly that the authorities redress this injustice to a man who was no kin to her. Commentator He Shouqi makes explicit the extent to which this unseemly mode of behavior violated traditional gender norms: "Even if we say that her indignation came from a sense of morality, her later course of action seems not to have been fitting conduct for a woman" (*Liao-zhai* 9.1287). After her efforts finally meet with success, however, she brings Meng's orphan up in an exemplary fashion, without allowing herself or her own son to profit in the slightest. Like Shang Sanguan, her heroic spirit is powerful enough to preserve her chastity posthumously and ensures that her corpse is buried in her late husband's plot rather than beside her soulmate Meng's grave.

It is through her steadfast chastity that Qiao proves her worthiness to be a member of the female sex despite her physical deformity and unwomanly behavior. Her selfless requital of the man who valued her, however, wins her honorary membership in the male sex. Although in her conduct she seems a perfect fusion of both the exemplary woman and the exemplary man, her high-mindedness is still ultimately evaluated as male. Exclaims the Historian of the Strange: "To be moved by a true friend and to devote yourself to him—this is the conduct of a principled man. How could a mere woman know how to act with such greatness? Had she met Jiufang Gao, he would directly have seen she was a male" (9.1286).

Jiufang Gao, the proverbial judge of horseflesh in *Liezi,* understood a horse's true spirit but ignored its outer appearance and gender. When the king complained that a horse Jiufang Gao had recommended as a bay mare was actually a black stallion, he was told: "What Gao observes is the innate mechanism. He takes the pith and forgets the husk; he stays with the interior and forgets the exterior."[75] As Jiufang Gao predicted, the horse indeed turned out to be a magnificent specimen. *Liaozhai* annotator He Yin spells out the direct implications of this allusion here: " 'He would directly have seen she was a male' means that she was of such exceptional mettle that she could be taken for a male even though she was a female. This has the same sense as 'a hero among women' " (9.1286). In *Liaozhai,* masculinity has thus become re-evaluated as an essentially *moral* quality, one that women, as well as men, can achieve through self-cultivation and right conduct.

The Shrew

Within the moral and social universe of *Liaozhai,* the antithesis of the hero among women is the shrew. Yenna Wu has amply documented the great popularity of the shrew in seventeenth-century

Chinese literature, both classical and vernacular, and has traced the history of this theme in earlier writings. Wu has also isolated the distinctive characteristics of the Chinese shrew: she is typically childless, jealous, and murderously violent.[76] Pu Songling's interest in the theme of the shrew has received much attention. It was above all "Jiang Cheng" (6.854–64), the *Liaozhai* tale about the taming of a shrew, and Pu Songling's vernacular play based on this tale that led Hu Shi to attribute the authorship of the novel *Marriage Destinies to Awaken the World* (*Xingshi yinyuan zhuan*) to Pu Songling.[77] This theory, however, has been generally discredited. As Wu has persuasively demonstrated, no concrete proof connects Pu Songling and this novel, and the theme of the shrew was too widespread in the seventeenth century to constitute a solid piece of evidence.[78]

What is perhaps less well known, however, is the extent to which the theme of the shrew permeates Pu Songling's work. It is by no means restricted to only a few of the more famous *Liaozhai* tales such as "Jiang Cheng" or "Ma Jiefu" (6.721–36). In many tales the shrew is central to the story; in others she is merely a tangential and lightly sketched figure, as though shrews were always lurking about and Pu Songling elected to develop only some of them into full-fledged characters. In addition, he wrote two comic prose pieces on shrews: "The Classic of Henpecked Husbands" ("Papo jingshu") and "A Sequel to the Harmony Sutra" ("Miaoyin jing xuyan"), which he appended to the *Liaozhai* tale "Ma Jiefu."[79] Finally, the shrew is featured in several of his vernacular plays.

The figure of the shrew, then, is not in itself strange or unusual. As the Historian of the Strange comments bitterly after "Jiang Cheng": "Nine out of ten wives are shrews" (6.863). Wu argues that the appeal of the shrew in seventeenth-century literature lay primarily in the comic inversion of the marital roles between the sexes.[80] As we have already seen in such tales as "Miss Yan," Pu Songling was certainly fascinated by such marital inversions; to make the theme of the shrew sufficiently novel and intriguing, however, he was also obliged to add other elements or to devise new angles.[81] In several *Liaozhai* tales, the taming of the shrew becomes purely a woman's affair; the husband, whether cowed or enraged by his shrewish wife, is almost extraneous to the plot. In these cases, the emphasis is not so much the inversion between the two sexes as the opposition and reversal within a single sex.

For instance, in the tale "Woman Shao" ("Shao nü"; 7.883–94), a vicious and jealous virago who engineers the deaths of two of her husband's concubines is finally won over by the patient martyrdom of a co-wife who saves her life. In "The Concubine Who Beat up Robbers" ("Qie ji zei"; 4.507–8), a pretty concubine meekly endures the physical abuse inflicted by the jealous principal wife but easily thrashes a band of robbers that breaks into the family compound. When the concubine reveals to the amazed family that she was trained in martial arts by her father, a famous master, but has accepted the principal wife's torture as her fate, the wife is so stunned and ashamed that, in the metaphor of the Historian of the Strange, she "is transformed from a hawk into a dove" (4.508). In "Shan Hu" (10.1409–16), a long tale that Pu Songling also developed into a vernacular play, the shrew reforms not because she is swayed by the moral example of a virtuous woman but because she gets a taste of her own medicine. A mother-in-law who drives away a daughter-in-law meets her match in her son's second wife. The shrewishness of the second wife causes the mother-in-law to realize the errors of her ways, and in the end both women reform.

Pu Songling's most original reversal of the stereotypical plot, however, is his invention of what can be called the "benign shrew." Although in character the benign shrew mostly resembles her sister viragoes—she is vituperative and violent, though significantly not barren—her cumulative effect is radically different: she paradoxically brings blessing rather than disaster to a household. In "Princess Yunluo" ("Yunluo gongzhu"; 9.1264–75), the princess, a goddess, has two sons by a human lover. With divine prescience she realizes that her younger son, Keqi, is thoroughly evil and insists as a safeguard that he be betrothed to a girl who will only be born four years later. Keqi bears out the princess's prediction: he is violent and dissolute: a gambler, a thief, an unfilial son, and a jealous brother. In his violation of family hierarchy, he is in fact the male equivalent of a shrew. The princess's remedy turns out to be to fight fire with fire. After Keqi's wife has born him a son, she proves to be a terrible shrew who attacks him with a knife and throws him out of the house. When she at last consents to take him back, he reforms and they prosper. As the Historian of the Strange wryly comments on this unorthodox solution: "A shrewish wife and a jealous woman are like abscesses against the bone that terminate only with death—

aren't they poisonous? Now arsenic and wolfsbane are the best poisons on earth. If one can use them, they'll effect a great cure that ginseng and immortal fungus [*lingzhi*] can't match. Yet who but a goddess with penetrating vision would dare dose her children with toxic medicine?" (9.1273)

The hero among women and the shrew provide a key for understanding the limits of gender in *Liaozhai*. Although both types transgress gender boundaries, the hero among women violates social norms to accomplish a goal that itself embodies the highest social ideals. She exhibits a degree of personal integrity and morality considered highly untypical of her sex. Her transgression of boundaries poses no threat to the greater social order. Her exploits demand a greater respect for the female sex, but as such she can be contained under the old rubric "exemplary woman" or treated as an honorary male. In contrast, the shrew is a justification for and a vindication of the most misogynist views of women. She may be dominant, but she is not in the least masculine. She does not behave like a man, for her misrule embodies an exaggeration and intensification of all the worst and quintessentially feminine traits in Chinese thinking. She is not so much *un*feminine as *hyper*feminine. Xie Zhaozhe sums up this misogynist stance in the *Fivefold Miscellany*: "Generally speaking, a woman's feminine nature has not a single fine quality: she is jealous, stingy, obstinate, lazy, stupid, ignorant, tyrannical, quick-tempered, suspicious, gullible, petty, superstitious, ghost-ridden, and lovesick; but of these, jealousy is the worst."[82]

And yet, Pu Songling's innovation of the benign shrew suggests that at least in an imperfect society the division between the shrew and the hero among women may not be absolute. In another story that takes its name from its heroine, "Qiu Daniang" (10.1391–1403), the vociferous and assertive Qiu Daniang, recently widowed, is recalled to her younger brother's home through the machinations of the family's archenemy, who hopes that the increased family strife she is sure to provoke will accelerate the downfall of the household. Instead, in a brilliant reversal, her shrewish disposition proves to be the family's salvation. Goaded into action against a common enemy, the sharp-tongued Qiu Daniang takes public action and succeeds in saving her brother's household; as a reward she even wins for herself and her son an uncustomary one-third of her maiden family's property. At the same time, she retains her widow chastity. The shrew, therefore, has been reborn as a "hero among women" by putting to productive use the very qualities that made her a shrew in the first place.[83] The two traditions of female transgression of gender boundaries have here merged into one.

5 Dream

> How magnificent are dreams! If dreams did not exist, the
> universe would be so ordinary and not at all wondrous. And
> wouldn't that be tragic?
>
> —Dong Yue, "Charter for a Dream Society"

> Dream can create what does not exist; dream can invent what
> has never been imagined. Dream is what does not come true; if
> it comes true, it is not a dream. If we dream and it is a dream,
> then illusion has become real; if we dream and it is not a dream,
> then reality is even more an illusion.
>
> —The Historian of Love, *A Classified History of Love*

Pu Songling's Dream

Significantly, the only story in which Pu Songling casts himself as
the hero of a strange adventure is cast as an autobiographical dream.
Although Pu Songling introduces himself as a first-person narrator
in a number of tales, in keeping with his self-styled role as Historian
of the Strange, he appears merely as an eyewitness, listener, or
recorder; he does not play a direct part in the unfolding of the story.[1]
"The Goddess of Flowers" ("Jiang Fei"; 6.739–47), in contrast,
narrates a dream said to have occurred in the spring of 1683 when Pu
Songling was living in Chuoran tang (Spacious Hall), the residence
of his employer and friend, Bi Jiyou. One day after wandering in
Bi's exquisite garden, he dreams that he is suddenly summoned by
two beautiful emissaries to the luxurious dwelling of the Goddess of
Flowers.[2] After feasting him with wine, the Goddess courteously
requests him to draft an official "call to arms" to incite the flowers in
battle against the incursions of the wind. Surrounded by beauties
who prepare the writing materials, he composes the draft with
uncharacteristic speed. It meets with the Goddess's unqualified approval. Upon awakening, he recalls the experience vividly but can

remember only about half of his composition. The remainder (and greater bulk) of the tale is devoted to the comic text of the dream summons, which he wrote in elaborate parallel prose and, we are told, completed on waking.[3]

A lengthy narrative poem written earlier by Pu Songling in 1671 titled "Describing a Dream in Eighty Rhymes, Written for a Friend" ("Wei youren xiemeng bashi yun") bears comparison with "The Goddess of Flowers." It, too, depicts a dream journey of the author's. In this poem, which is composed in the ornate allusive style that characterizes erotic trysts with divine women in the Chinese poetic tradition, the author is also summoned to the sumptuous mansion of a mysterious Beauty, where he attends a banquet and is entertained by her ladies. The poem's sequence of events virtually replicates that of the tale, and the almost identical expression—"the tinkling of jade girdle pendants"—that signals the advent of the Goddess of Flowers in the tale introduces the Beauty in the poem.[4] But, unlike the tale, the poem climaxes with the consummation of the dreamer's desire for the divine woman. Then, after a tearful parting, he awakens to find that it was only a dream: "I was just hesitating at the crossroads / when I awoke and laughed at what nonsense it was."[5]

In "The Goddess of Flowers," the poem's sexual climax is displaced by the eroticized act of writing, which in itself brings the fulfillment of desire:

All the ladies busied themselves, to wipe the table and dust my seat, grind the ink and moisten the brush. One young girl, with her hair dangling down, folded over the paper for me, holding it steady beneath my wrist. And I, who usually write so slowly, this one time felt my thoughts pour forth like rushing waves. (6.740)[6]

Moreover, the tale, no less than the poem, is a transparent allegory of desire, for it is portrayed as a seasonal "spring dream" (*chun meng*), set into motion by the stroll in the flowering garden. The garden is privileged as a paramount site of erotic desire, not only in Ming and Qing romantic fiction and drama but also in *The Forest of Dreams,* the most comprehensive handbook on dream interpretation from the period.[7] The personification of flowers as beautiful women who manifest themselves to their true admirers is likewise a favorite

topic in Ming and Qing sentimental writings and is taken to wonderful lengths in several other tales about amorous liaisons between
flower-spirits and literary men in *Liaozhai*.[8] Here, however, literary
ambition displaces sexual desire in the extemporaneous theme the
Goddess assigns Pu Songling (in mock imitation of an imperial
court audience) at which he performs so brilliantly.[9] In the tale,
unlike the erotic poem, the dream experience is not simply dismissed at the end as "nonsense." Instead, the text of the summons is
introduced, ostensibly to verify the dream, but its travesty of the
solemn regulations of parallel prose and its exuberant word games
associate the tale's dream experience all the more closely with laughter and play.

"The Goddess of Flowers" is also the only tale in the *Liaozhai*
collection in which the story acts as a preface to another text.[10] The
narrative is subordinated to the set piece, serving essentially as a
gloss to explain the context and genesis of the dream summons's
composition. This binary structure, however, is among the most
common ways of portraying the relationship between dream and
literary creativity and is indeed employed in several poems inspired
by dreams, or even partially composed in dream and reconstructed
upon waking, found in Pu Songling's collected work.[11] Thus, a
quatrain entitled "Recording a Dream" ("Zhi meng") written in
1708 is prefaced with a brief prose account of a dream that unfolds in
a deserted garden in early spring:

On the night before the Lantern Festival, I dreamt that I was strolling alone
amid pavilions in a garden. The new moon was just rising; the willow
branches were hanging down in threads. I leaned against a bridge, and the
dew felt cold as autumn. A line [*or* Lines] suddenly came to me, and so I
have recorded it [them] and completed the poem.

The quatrain then recapitulates and describes this dream scene in
verse:

> The Milky Way is high and bright, the willows level with the
>   bridge;
> By the dull sheen of the moon, it seems even lonelier.
> Nobody deep in the courtyard, the night is clear and cold;
> Where the wind blows, a scent floats out in the darkness.[12]

The poem is a highly conventional rendering of a night scene, but coupled with the preface, the lines do exude an eerie dreaminess. Their oneiric origin makes these lines worth recording; the preface transforms the poem into something out of the ordinary. The preface structure of "The Goddess of Flowers" is also reminiscent of "Liaozhai's Own Record," which sets forth the author's reasons for composing the collection and which ends by depicting him in the act of writing. Indeed, as if in recognition of this affinity, the first published edition of *Liaozhai* placed "The Goddess of Flowers" last, where it could be read as a rhetorical conclusion, echoing the book's beginning.[13] But the solitary writer of the preface "completing his book of lonely anguish" at a "desk cold as ice" has given way to the amorous dreamer of "The Goddess of Flowers," who, surrounded by beautiful women, musters all his literary skill and erudition to compose a playful parody about flowers. As commentator Dan Minglun points out: "He's presented with pen and paper in the palace, but he only gets them from the Goddess of Flowers; he only gets them in dream. It seems as though he's boasting, but he's actually mocking himself" (*Liaozhai* 6.740).

Late Ming Interest in Dreams

"The Goddess of Flowers" is one of eighty-odd tales in *Liaozhai* that involve dreams; about twenty-five of these take the dream as a major subject. It is evident, from these tales and from his poetry, that Pu Songling both inherited the rich Chinese literary tradition regarding dreams and shared the extraordinary late Ming, early Qing fascination with dreams.

The dream was a staple theme of zhiguai and chuanqi from the inception of these genres. For example, the fourth-century *Seeking the Spirits* devotes a full chapter to dream, as does the ninth-century *Librarian's Miscellany*. The tenth-century imperial anthology *Taiping guangji* includes no less than seven chapters of dream tales; the twelfth-century *Records of the Listener* contains a striking proportion of entries recording dreams and their interpretations. Ming compendia with a romantic orientation such as *A Classified History of Love, The Green Window History of Women,* and *A Compendium of Rare Beauties* feature chapters on dream tales; several of the most influential Tang chuanqi included in the widely read sixteenth-century anthology *The Magician's Records* involve dreams.[14] Many Ming and Qing notation books with a penchant for the strange include significant entries on dreams.[15] Thus, in concentrating on the dream in *Liaozhai,* Pu Songling was clearly following the thematic conventions of the classical tale, conventions reinforced by the many reprints and new anthologies of classical fiction on the market. This seems particularly true when we reflect that of the very small number of tales in *Liaozhai* that retell earlier written stories, three are outright imitations of Tang dream narratives.*[16]

At the same time, *Liaozhai*'s preoccupation with dream was part of a contemporary cultural phenomenon—the surge of interest in the dream among literati circles during the sixteenth and seventeenth centuries, which was expressed not only in drama and fiction (both classical and vernacular), but also in scholarly treatises and compendia, informal essays, autobiographical writings, poetry, and even paintings and woodblock illustrations (see Fig. 5). A representative sampling of scholarship would include Chen Shiyuan's dense *Treatise on Dream Interpretation (Mengzhen yizhi)*, the playwright Zhang Fengyi's (1527–1613) *Classified Investigation into Dream Interpretation (Mengzhan leikao)*,[17] and He Dongru's *Forest of Dreams*. In the essay form are Dong Yue's (1620–86) fervent expositions on the creative possibilities of dreaming, and in the novel, his experimental *Supplement to Journey to the West (Xiyou bu)*, which is couched entirely as a dream; all reveal his lifelong obsession with dream.[18] A number of late Ming and early Qing intellectuals left records of their dreams in their literary works;[19] Dong Yue's friend Huang Zhouxing even published his dream diary.[20] In the drama, we have Tang Xianzu's (1550–1616) phenomenally influential quartet *The Four Dreams of Linchuan (Linchuan simeng)*, especially his masterpiece, *The Peony Pavilion (Mudan ting)*; in poetry, works by Wang Yangming, Xu Wei, Yuan Hongdao, Tang Xianzu, Dong Yue, Pu Songling's friends Gao Heng and Zhu Xiang, as well as Pu Songling himself;[21] and in painting, Tang Yin's (1470–1523) "Dreaming of Immortality in a

---

*By "imitation," I mean rewriting an original work in the same genre so as to express the imitator's own style and concerns while still preserving a recognizable likeness to the original. An "adaptation," on the other hand, involves the transposition of the original work to another medium or genre.

Fig. 5. One of the loveliest of all woodblock dream illustrations by the famous artist Chen Hongshou (1598–1652). This scene from *The Western Wing* depicts the hero of the play fast asleep on a mat, dreaming of an amorous encounter with his beloved Yingying in a garden. In contrast to most woodblock illustrations of dreams, here the dream bubble is solidly filled, while the space occupied by the sleeper seems empty. The result is to reverse the viewer's impression of which scene seems real and which scene illusion. The illustration originally belonged to the *Zhang Shenzhi xiansheng zheng Bei xixiang miben* edition of the play. (*Zhongguo banhua shi tulu*, p. 839)

Thatched Cottage"; and Li Rihua's (1565–1635) "Rivers and Mountains in My Dream."[22]

The late Ming scholarly works that gathered and classified earlier oneiric materials must have contributed to this growing output of original writings on dream and in turn been stimulated by them. In the work of Dong Yue, who probably carried the literary experimentation with dream conventions furthest, both modes, historical synthesis and literary invention, closely coexist. At the same time, even that ostensibly practical manual on dream interpretation *The Forest of Dreams* includes contemporary stories to illustrate specific interpretations and at least once draws a comparison with Tang Xianzu's *Peony Pavilion*.[23] Like other late Ming thematic compendia such as *A Classified History of Love* (with which it bears a certain affinity), parts of *The Forest of Dreams* could have easily been read for entertainment, as well as for practical instruction or scholarly erudition.

The late Ming emphasis on synthesizing earlier dream materials is exemplified by Chen Shiyuan's *Treatise on Dream Interpretation,* which was composed some time after 1562 and reprinted in abridged form in He Dongru's *Forest of Dreams* (preface dated 1636).[24] Chen's treatise is a concise yet encyclopedic history of the dream placed in a loose theoretical framework. This work is invaluable for the study of the literary dream in China because it is unusually well argued and identifies its sources. Organized thematically rather than chronologically, Chen's treatise testifies to the astonishing breadth and complexity of the written corpus on dreams available to educated readers by the late Ming. In addition to the Classics, histories, and Buddhist and Taoist canons, he quarries sources as diverse as medical books, poetry criticism, anecdotes, prefaces, and both zhiguai and chuanqi. As is also evident in Li Shizhen's contemporaneous *Classified Materia Medica,* which draws on zhiguai and chuanqi, these genres, which we now usually label "fiction," were still valued as a legitimate source of human knowledge during the Ming and well into the Qing.

Chen's work also reveals that we cannot speak of a single Chinese oneiric tradition; rather, several powerful, potentially contradictory traditions coexist and overlap. Of these, Chen singles out two major approaches to the dream: as prophecy (*zhao*) and as illusion (*huan*). The first holds that dreams predict the future and thus reveal the workings of fate. As Chen Shiyuan puts it: "A dream is a mirror that reflects the journey of the spirit into the future."[25] The second approach treats the dream as a means to question the boundaries between illusion and reality. Both approaches share an understanding of dreams as a possible means of communication either between parallel worlds (e.g., the dead and the living, the divine and the human) or simply with anyone for whom ordinary avenues of communication are blocked.

In his treatise, Chen Shiyuan illustrates the stances of these two polar approaches by staging a debate between two allegorized spokesmen. Venerable Emptiness (Zongkong sheng) argues in Buddhist terms, but following a long tradition of Chinese skepticism, that since dreams are merely illusion, "like dew, lightning, foam, and shadow," they have no predictive function and hence need no interpretation.[26] The Master of the Subtle (Tongwei zhuren) counters that since not only apocryphal records and anecdotes but even the Confucian classics and official histories are filled with prophetic dreams, dreams must be taken seriously and interpreted. Not surprisingly, the Master of the Subtle wins in the end, allowing the Confucian scholar Chen Shiyuan to complete his book in peace. Chen's championship of the prognostic function of dreams, however, does not prevent him from drawing freely on the illusory associations of the dream, especially in his preface, where he credits the initial inspiration for his project to a dream, and in the book's rhetorical conclusion: "In writing this treatise, am I dreaming or awake? Since I am not awake, I must be dreaming. If later gentlemen attempt to read my treatise, they will realize that these are all my past dreams."[27] In the end he suggests that his whole project, despite its rigor, may ultimately be an illusion.

Nevertheless, each of the viewpoints represented in the debate between Venerable Emptiness and the Master of the Subtle involves a separate problem that must at least be obliquely addressed within a dream text. The French scholar Roger Caillois has written that "there are two types of problems concerning dreams that have always puzzled men's minds. One problem concerns the actual meaning or significance of the dream; the other, the relationship between the dream and the waking world, or one might say, the degree of reality that one may attribute to the dream."[28] For stories in which dreams reveal the future, the basic questions are hermeneutic. What does the dream mean? How should it be interpreted? Is the interpretation correct? The meaning of the dream may be immediately transparent to the dreamer, or the dream may be an oracle or a riddle that must be decoded to uncover its secret. In the illusory dream tale, on the other hand, the key problem is not what the dream *means,* but what the dream *is.* This type of story raises ontological and even epistemological questions. How can we adjudicate between dreaming and waking, illusion and reality? Can the veracity of the dream experience ever be determined? Here the narrative interest in a story lies not in testing the correctness of a specific interpretation but in depicting the vividness and complexity of the dream experience measured against the shock of awakening.

In a prophetic dream account, the dream itself is presented baldly, as a fact; neither the dreamer nor the interpreter ever questions that it is a dream. The dream may be portrayed in a dramatized scene or, more commonly, merely summarized. Upon awakening, the dreamer may even transcribe his dream, so that it literally becomes a written text ready for interpretation. The dreamer may then interpret the dream himself, or he may seek the aid of another—an acquaintance or a professional dream-interpreter. In its simplest form, the prophetic dream tale has a tripartite narrative structure: the dream (portrayed or related); the interpretation (by the dreamer or another); the outcome (the fulfillment of the interpretation).

In the Chinese literary tradition, prophetic dreams tend to be the subject of short zhiguai-type anecdotes, and illusory dreams are usually narrated as longer chuanqi-type tales. But this rule is by no means absolute. A prophetic dream can embellish the plot of a more complex story, as in the *Liaozhai* tale "Poetry Solves a Crime" ("Shi yan"; 8.1135–37) in which a man falsely accused of murder dreams the name of the official who will acquit him. Conversely, an elaborate dream narrative can also have a prophetic significance, as in the *Liaozhai* tale "A Dream of Wolves" ("Meng lang"; 8.1052–56), where a dream journey to hell is transcribed by the dreamer, interpreted, and fulfilled.

The Interpretation of Dreams

What prompts someone to record a dream in written or visual form is not identical with what causes someone to dream or even to relate a dream. Only practical manuals (like parts of *The Forest of Dreams*), which aim to teach the symbolic vocabulary and techniques of dream interpretation, are concerned primarily with standard dreams.[29] Most other varieties of Chinese literature record dreams because they are exceptional or strange, that is, because they *differ* in some striking way from ordinary dreams.[30] It may be the dream itself that is considered extraordinary and thus warrants transcribing. Alternatively, a particularly ingenious interpretation or unexpected outcome may make a dream worth recounting.

Thus, when the main subject of a tale or anecdote is a prophetic dream, the focus tends to be displaced from the dream itself onto the interpretation and its fulfillment. A story about the famous dream interpreter Zhou Xuan included in his biography in the *Record of the Three Kingdoms* (*Sanguo zhi*) illustrates this point cleverly:

> Someone once asked Zhou Xuan to interpret a dream in which he had seen a straw dog. "You will obtain food and drink," said Xuan. Another day the same man again asked Xuan about a dream in which he had seen a straw dog. "You will fall from a carriage and break your foot," said Xuan. Another day the man once again asked Xuan about a dream in which he had seen a straw dog. "A fire will break out," said Xuan.
>
> "None of my three questions were about real dreams," said the man. "How is it that all of your interpretations came true?"
>
> "The gods prompted you to utter those things, and so they were no different from real dreams."[31]

Although the dream interpreter modestly credits his interlocutor with divine inspiration, what this anecdote proves most of all is the amazing skill of the interpreter, who is able not only to interpret three identical dreams in completely different ways but also to interpret false dreams as successfully as real ones. The dream content itself has become almost irrelevant, a mere pretext for interpretation.[32]

Chen Shiyuan's treatise offers three general techniques for interpreting prophetic dreams that have close counterparts with modes expounded by the Hellenist Artemidorus in his famous second-century A.D. manual of dream interpretation, the *Oneirocritica*.[33] Chen calls his first technique *zhixie,* the direct or, to use Artemidorus's term, the "theorematic" mode, in which the interpretation of the dream corresponds to the literal content of the dream. What is seen in the dream is the meaning of the dream; the dream will be fulfilled exactly as dreamed: no transposition or translation is necessary. The second and most varied technique Chen calls *bixiang,* the symbolic or, in Artemidorus's parlance, the "allegoric" mode. This interpretive strategy assumes that the dream vision does not signify itself but a hidden meaning. Thus two levels come into being in allegoric dream interpretation: the literal level of meaning is discarded, and a figurative level prevails and determines the outcome. Chen's last category is called *fanji* or, to borrow Artemidorus's term once again, the "antithetical" mode, in which one first interprets the dream theorematically and then reverses that meaning. In other words, the fulfillment of the dream prophecy will be the opposite of what was seen in the dream.

Knowing which interpretive mode to adopt in a given case thus becomes the key to successful dream interpretation.[34] Understandably, the amateur dream-interpreter in literature often finds himself unequal to this difficult task. Duped by the ambiguous possibilities of dream language, by the very surfeit of significance, the dreamer in several *Liaozhai* tales chooses the wrong oneirocritic technique and misinterprets his own dream. As a result, the unexpected outcome of the dream becomes the punchline of a joke told at his expense.

In one such *Liaozhai* anecdote, an ambitious young scholar dreams he is addressed as "Lord of the Five Black Sheepskins" ("Wugu dafu"; 3.427).[35] He is overjoyed, for he instantly assumes the dream is an auspicious omen meaning that he will achieve high office. The scholar has interpreted his dream allegorically, by reference to a well-known historical allusion to the official title of a Spring and Autumn period statesman.[36] No overt explanation is provided in the narrative for the scholar's interpretive rationale, however, because the anecdote's humor requires that the allusion and its meaning be as self-evident to the reader as they are to the scholar himself.[37]

Some time later the scholar is set upon by bandits, who strip him of every stitch of clothing and then shut him up in an empty room. Since it is winter and bitterly cold, the scholar gropes around in the dark for something to cover his body with. Luckily he finds a couple of sheepskins and thereby manages to avoid freezing to death. In the morning light, when he discovers that there are exactly five sheepskins, he bursts out laughing at the trick the gods have played on him.

The scholar's eagerness to achieve office and the conventional use of historical allusions have led him to misread his dream. Rather than coming true figuratively as he had hoped, the dream comes true literally. The scholar does indeed merit the epithet Lord of the Five Black Sheepskins, but under the circumstances, in which he is left with literally nothing but five sheepskins, it becomes a title of ridicule rather than of honor. The scholar's error had been to interpret his dream allegorically rather than theorematically, and therein lies the twist that inspired the anecdote. But curiously, the scholar does eventually pass the exams and becomes a local magistrate. The allegoric prediction of official success turns out to have had merit after all.

A similar misinterpretation of dreams is at work in another humorous *Liaozhai* anecdote called "The Ox That Flew Away" ("Niu fei"; 9.1237). A man buys an ox that is quite healthy. One night he dreams that the ox sprouts wings and flies away. He believes this to be an inauspicious omen and fears that the ox will die. Once again, the dreamer interprets his dream allegorically, but this time, reflecting the dreamer's lack of education, no verbal wit or erudite allusions are involved. The association between the dream image and its interpretation is simple: flying away symbolizes loss and probably death. But as is often the case in such anecdotes, the more obvious the interpretation, the easier it is to be led astray.

At this juncture, the man tries to outmaneuver his dream:

He led the ox to market and sold it at a loss. He wrapped the money from the sale in a kerchief and tied it around his shoulder. When he was about halfway home, he spotted a falcon feasting on the remains of a hare. The falcon seemed quite tame when he approached, so he tied the kerchief around his thigh and put the falcon on his shoulder. The falcon flapped its wings a few times. As soon as the man relaxed his grasp a little, the falcon flew away, carrying the kerchief [and the money] with it. (9.1237)

Once again, the joke is that the dream prediction, with some modification, has come true theorematically rather than allegorically. The money the man received for the ox does almost literally sprout wings and vanish into thin air. The hybrid dream image of a flying ox is comical in itself, confusing as it does the categories of aerial bird and earthbound beast. But the chief irony here, as a gleeful authorial comment points out, is that by misinterpreting his dream, the man himself becomes the agent for its unexpected fulfillment. "Although this was fated, if the man had accepted his dream, and hadn't been so anxious to stave off a loss, then how could a four-legged beast have suddenly flown away?" (9.1237)

In these two examples, dreamers miscalculate by interpreting their dreams allegorically rather than literally, and this error makes them the butt of rather gentle mockery. The antithetical mode of dream interpretation, however, lends itself to more savage satire in *Liaozhai*. In "The God of Mount Tai" ("Yue Shen"; 9.1209), the misinterpretation proves fatal. An official dreams that he is summoned by an irate God of Mount Tai (one of the lords of hell), but luckily a man standing by the god's side intervenes on his behalf. Upon awakening, the official considers the dream to be an evil omen and goes to pray at the God of Mount Tai's temple. On his way out, he notices a doctor in a neighboring medicine shop who is the spitting image of the man in his dream. Upon reaching home, the official falls violently ill. Naturally, he sends at once for this doctor on the assumption that having helped him in the dream, the doctor will save his life.[38] Instead, the opposite occurs. The official dies just a few hours later after swallowing medicine prescribed by the doctor.

A tongue-in-cheek authorial caveat proposes a divine conspiracy to drum up business in hell to explain the official's fatal misinterpretation and makes explicit the social satire against incompetent doctors so common in Ming and Qing literature that is the real point of this joke: "Someone said: 'King Yama [the king of hell] and the Lord of Mount Tai dispatch eighteen thousand male and female attendants daily, who are sent all over the world to be physicians and witch doctors. They're called *Soul-Lurers*.' Medicine takers cannot afford to be negligent!" (9.1209)[39]

Allegorical dreams that rely on transparent symbolism for satiric purposes also appear in *Liaozhai* without a comic twist of misinterpretation. In such cases, much of the narrative emphasis is thrown back onto the dream itself, which must be substantial enough to sustain the increased allegorical weight placed upon it. The finest example is the often-anthologized tale "A Dream of Wolves," which bitterly criticizes corrupt officials and their clerks. A man finds himself in the underworld, where he is taken to the official residence of his son the magistrate. To his horror, he sees that the courtyard is piled high with bones, and the building itself is swarming with wolves, including one carrying a human corpse in its mouth. Suddenly two divinities clad in gold armor burst in and arrest his son, who falls to the ground and turns into a ferocious tiger. Rather than cutting off the tiger's head, however, they merely knock out his fangs as a warning, telling him they'll return for him the following year. The tiger's roar awakens the terrified man. Deeply distraught, he makes a record of his dream and sends the text to his son, urging him to reform before it is too late. Despite corroborating proof of the dream's veracity (the son's front teeth had coincidentally been knocked out by his horse on the very night of his father's dream), the son scoffs at his father's nightmare and continues his evil ways, until at last the remainder of the dream comes true. Even in this story, however, the dream is fulfilled in an unexpected way—at the appointed time, the son's head is cut off by bandits, but divinities mischievously reattach his head backwards and he becomes an outcast from the human race.

In this case, there is no need for the father to interpret the dream because the meaning of its imagery is immediately clear to him, as well as to his scornful son. Corrupt officials and their clerks were traditionally likened to tigers and wolves because they ruthlessly preyed on the people and grew fat from human suffering. As the Historian of the Strange alerts us, this analogy had long been incorporated into common parlance: "I lament that all the tiger officials and wolf clerks in the world are exactly like this" (9.1055). The dream imagery in this tale is both so transparent and so powerful because it is the concrete realization of a proverbial expression. Thus, we find a distinct similarity between dream symbolism, which derives from figurative expressions in *Liaozhai,* and one of Pu Songling's most common mechanisms for generating fantasy, the literal realization of metaphoric language. Through this device, Pu Songling restores the shock of immediacy to a dead metaphor, reinvesting language itself with a new strangeness. Although the metaphoric made literal in *Liaozhai* often produces the comic effect that Bergson pointed out in his famous essay on laughter,[40] the effect in "A Dream of Wolves" is rather one of horror and outrage because the most monstrous implications of an expression dulled by habit and familiarity can no longer be ignored. Modern readers may be reminded of Lu Xun's madman who, detecting the secret words "Eat People" between the lines of ancient texts, determined that the old society was based entirely on cannibalism. The madman is a madman precisely because he can no longer differentiate figurative and literal levels of discourse.[41]

In "A Dream of Wolves," the dream itself has become a didactic fable, and the father's journey to the underworld is portrayed as a coherent narrative. The real emphasis is placed on the entire idea being signified (the voraciousness of corrupt officials and clerks) rather than on each individual signifier and its order of appearance (the pile of bones, the wolves, the tiger). But in stories in which the symbolism of dream images is more cryptic, allegorical interpretation must operate on different principles. The dream symbols cannot simply be interpreted by drawing an analogy between the image and the idea signified. Instead, each image is treated as a discrete unit that is first deciphered on its own; only then, as in an algebraic equation, are the pieces reassembled in the proper sequence to obtain the entire meaning of the dream.

This distinction comes out most clearly in the oneirocritical technique that Chen Shiyuan calls "xizi jiemeng" ("analyzing characters to explain a dream") or "cezi," which Roberto Ong has translated as "ideographic analysis."[42] Here the dream images are discrete semantic units that form a seemingly nonsensical utterance. Pieced together in the correct sequence, these individual units form a Chinese character that inscribes the secret meaning of the dream. It is also possible to use this method to produce, one by one, a string of characters to create a phrase that contains the dream's meaning.[43] Ideographic analysis is the Chinese equivalent of the anagram, a method favored by Artemidorus, in which the letters of a word are scrambled and reassembled to produce a new word that contains the true meaning of the dream. In both hermeneutic techniques, a word or a character contains entirely within itself a cryptic meaning, unrelated to its ordinary sense, that is brought to light by the manipulation of its component parts.

Ideographic analysis is used as well in Chinese etymology, the form of divination known as glyphomancy, and riddles. But there is

an important distinction. In etymology and divination, the interpreter begins with an intact character, which he then dismantles and
recombines to find new meanings. In dreams and riddles, on the
other hand, the interpreter confronts a disassembled character and
must put the pieces back together in the correct order to arrive at the
appropriate meaning. The two processes are mirror images.[44]

In dream literature, ideographic analysis is often applied to proper
names. Pu Songling draws on this technique in "Poetry Solves a
Crime." A murderer frames a certain Mr. Wu by leaving a fan
inscribed with Wu's name at the scene of the crime. Languishing in
prison, Wu dreams that a god answers his prayers and tells him not
to worry: "You won't die. Earlier you met with the inauspicious
outside; now you will meet with the auspicious inside [nangri *waibian xiong,* muxia *libian ji*]." The solution to this enigmatic utterance, however, is delayed until the end of the story, after Wu has
been acquitted through the brilliant detective work of the official
reviewing the case, the famous writer Zhou Lianggong (1612–72):
"Only then did Wu realize that the 'auspicious inside' (the graph for
'auspicious' 吉 enclosed in the graph for 'border' 冂) spelled the
character for 'Zhou' 周" (8.1137).[45]

The dream interpretation in this story is clearly a minor touch, a
rhetorical embellishment designed to enhance the prestige of Zhou
Lianggong, whom Pu Songling deeply admired, judging from the
Historian of the Strange's extravagant praise of his acuity.[46] Since
Zhou Lianggong authored a book on ideographic analysis in dream
and divination, *A Sense of Words (Zi chu),* Pu Songling may have
inserted the cryptic dream of Zhou's name in sly homage to this
interest.[47] Whatever the case may be, the irony of the story is that
interpreting this dream riddle is far less difficult than understanding
how Zhou solved the crime. Indeed, even after Wu has grasped the
significance of his dream, he remains mystified by Zhou's deductive
process. The mystery is finally cleared up for the reader when Zhou
explains himself, Sherlock Holmes fashion, to a select audience of
local Watsons. Upon reading that the crime had occurred on a cold
and rainy night, he suspected that the fan had been planted by
the murderer. Why would anyone drop a fan by accident in such
weather? The poem inscribed on the fan rang a bell—he recalled
seeing a poem in an identical tone and style written on the wall of an

inn in the district. He then called in the innkeeper, who referred him to the poet, who referred him to the calligrapher, who referred him to the man who had commissioned the fan—the true murderer. The deciphering of the divinely inspired dream utterance in this story thus becomes far less of a tour de force than the rational solving of the murder itself.

Dream interpretation plays a more pivotal role in cracking a sensational crime in "The Ferrymen of Laolong" ("Laolong xianghu"; 12.1610–14). Zhu Hongzuo, a new official reviewing the cases of some one hundred missing persons in Guangdong, is unable to turn up a single clue. Deeply concerned, he makes a written appeal to the local city god, who dutifully appears to him in a dream and announces: "Snow trails at the temples, clouds form on the horizon, wood floats on the water, a door is set on a wall" (12.1610). Zhu is unable to make sense of these four phrases, but after wrestling with this dream conundrum all night, he triumphantly arrives at the correct solution: " 'Snow trails' means old [*lao*]; 'clouds form' means dragon [*long*]; 'wood on the water' is a ferry [*xiang*]; 'door on a wall' is a portal [*hu*]. It must be 'the ferrymen of Laolong' [*Laolong xianghu*]!" (12.1610)[48] The hermeneutic technique that Zhu uses to decipher the riddle is not predicated on the physical structure of characters as in ideographic analysis; instead, through semantic circumlocution, each four-character cluster describes a single character, which is then joined with the others to form the four-character solution.

Pu Songling's tale was based on a notorious case of 1689 brought against a gang of thieves who were passing themselves off as ferrymen at Laolong Ford. They would drug traveling merchants, cut open their bellies, stuff them with stones, and then fling the heavy corpses overboard and make off with the goods and money. This way, the bodies were never found. Zhu Hongzuo, the father of Pu Songling's friend and enthusiastic reader Zhu Xiang (1670–1707), solved the case.[49] Remarkably, both Zhu Hongzuo's written appeal to the city god and a detailed public announcement commemorating Zhu's handling of the case are still extant.[50] The *Liaozhai* tale adheres closely to the events as described in the public announcement but reorders them to create suspense; the identity of the murderers is revealed only at the end.[51] The public announcement does indeed credit Zhu's solution of the mystery to a dream sent by the city god in response to his written appeal: "In consideration of Zhu's sincerity and devotion, the god then appeared to him in a dream, from which Zhu learned that the murderers were the 'ferrymen of Laolong'" (12.1613). But the document does not specify what form the dream took. The cryptic form of the dream utterance and its interpretation in the *Liaozhai* version of the case were thus most probably an embellishment added to heighten the mystery and to dramatize Zhu Hongzuo's intelligence and commitment to ferreting out the truth.

Both "Poetry Solves a Crime" and "The Ferrymen of Laolong" continue the tradition of the famous Tang crime tale, "Xie Xiao'e," in which the dream and its interpretation are the essence of the story. The dream conundrum in this case also conceals the names of the unknown assailants who have murdered Xiao'e's father and husband. She jots down the incomprehensible phrases on a piece of paper and shows them to everyone she meets: "A monkey inside a carriage, and the grass east of the gate, / walking across the wheat, and a husband for one day."[52] The difficulty of unraveling this riddle is such that she meets with no success for several years. In the end it is, fittingly, Li Gongzuo, the narrator and purported author of this tale, who decodes the dream text. His lengthy ideographic interpretation solves the mystery of the murderer's names in what is the true climax of the story:

If you omit the top and bottom strokes from the word for carriage 車, you would have the character *shen* 申. Moreover, monkey is the symbol for the hour of *shen*. If you add the character for gate 門 under the grass radical and the character for east 東 inside the gate, you would have the character *lan* 蘭 .... "To walk through the wheat" is to walk across the field 田 and that also indicates the character *shen*, which is the character for field with the vertical stroke prolonged at both ends 申. As to "husband for one day," you will have the character *chun* 春 if you add the character for one 一 on top of the character for husband 夫 and place the character for day 日 underneath it (一 + 夫 + 日 = 春). It is obvious, therefore that Shen Lan killed your father and Shen Chun killed your husband.[53]

It is no coincidence that so many interpretations of dreams occur in crime case tales, for crime fiction always requires the deciphering of a mystery and a reconstruction of the truth. Indeed Albert Hutter has drawn an analogy between Western detective fiction and dream interpretation in that both "involve the transformation of a fragmented and incomplete set of events into a more ordered and complete understanding."[54] The unraveling of a dream conundrum is such an effective way to highlight the solution to a murder in Chinese crime case literature that it becomes something of a cliché.[55] One *Liaozhai* crime tale, "Rouge" ("Yanzhi"; 10.1367–80), even cleverly takes advantage of the literary convention that crimes are solved by divinely sent dreams. Shi Runzhang (1619–83), the official reviewing the murder case, fakes a dream to try and trick the murderer into identifying himself. He has the suspects rounded up and taken to the temple of the city god, where he sternly informs them that the god had informed him in dream that the murderer is one of them. When the murderer still refuses to confess, Shi takes his psychological manipulation one step further and, after having the suspects stripped to the waist, tells them that the god himself will make a mark on the murderer's back. Unbeknownst to the suspects, he had earlier had the walls of the temple smeared with ashes. When the real murderer presses his back against the ash-covered wall to avoid being identified, he plays right into Shi's hands and incriminates himself. Thus, as in the dream of the straw dog discussed earlier but from a completely different angle, false dreams are proven to be as efficacious as real ones. Once again this brilliant solution rebounds to the glory of the official, who in this case was the examiner who granted Pu Songling the licentiate degree and for whom Pu professed his sincerest admiration in a long note appended to the story.[56] As in the case of "Poetry Solves a Crime," conventional ideas of the strange are deflated: the shrewdness and zeal of the presiding official are shown to be far more amazing and unexpected than any divinely inspired dream or feat of oneiromancy.

But the strangest and most sinister dream account is one for which there is no interpretation. In the tale "Tiny Coffins" ("Xiao guan"; 8.1139–40), a ferryman has a recurrent dream in which someone tells him that a man with a bamboo trunk will come to hire his boat. He is to charge him a thousand pieces of gold; if the man refuses to pay, he is to show him three unknown characters (8.1139): [illegible]. The ferryman has no idea what these characters mean, but they turn out to be an efficacious charm: when the man with the bamboo trunk comes to hire the boat and refuses to pay the preposterous fare, the ferryman writes the three characters in the palm of the man's hand. The man instantly vanishes.[57] The ferryman opens the trunk and finds thousands of tiny coffins, each filled with a single drop of blood. The coffins are interpreted retrospectively in the story as an omen for a bloody uprising that ensued; but although the ferryman shows the enigmatic characters far and wide, they are never deciphered. The dream, then, acts like a parenthesis to the appearance of the coffins. No solution to the dream characters is forthcoming because they usher in a larger mystery: the uncanny correspondence between the number of tiny coffins and the number of people slain in the uprising and its bloody suppression.

Dream and Experience

A long intellectual tradition in China explores the difficulty of adjudicating between dreaming and waking states and accords an objective reality to dream experiences. As A. C. Graham describes the extended treatment of this theme in *Liezi,* a philosophical Taoist text of the fourth century A.D.: "Perception and dreaming are given equal weight. If waking experience is no more real than dreams, then dreams are as real as waking experience. We perceive when a thing makes contact with the body, dream when it makes contact with the mind, and there is nothing to choose between one experience and another."[58]

Although it may be, in the end, impossible to distinguish between dream and reality, Chinese philosophers have attempted to come up with a viable solution to the problem. The famous parable of Zhuangzi, who "didn't know if he was Chuang Chou [Zhuang Zhou] who had dreamed he was a butterfly, or a butterfly dreaming he was Chuang Chou" is a good example. The point of the parable seems to be that the distinction between waking and dreaming is indeterminable, but the final line, which is often omitted in the retelling, moves to resolve the dilemma: "Between Chuang Chou and a butterfly there must be *some* distinction! This is called the Transformation of Things!"[59]

The overriding need for a practical solution is the point of a legal case in *Liezi*. A man shoots a deer and buries the carcass. When he later forgets where he buried it, he decides that he must have dreamed the whole thing. A second man, overhearing the first man relating the story to his wife, discovers the location of the deer and claims it as his own. When the first man learns of this, he demands his deer back. Unable to resolve their dispute, the two men go to court:

The case was referred to the Chief Justice, who said: "If in the first place you really did catch the deer, you are wrong to say you were dreaming. If you really dreamed that you caught it, you are wrong to say it actually happened. The other man really did take your deer, yet contests your right to it. His wife also says that he recognized it in his dream as another man's deer, yet denies the existence of the man who caught it. Now all I know is that here we have the deer. I suggest you divide it between you."

It was reported to the Lord of Cheng, who said: "Alas! Is the Chief Justice going to dream that he has divided someone's deer?"

The Prime Minister was consulted. He said: "It is beyond me to distinguish dreaming and not dreaming. If you want to distinguish dreaming from waking, you will have to call in the Yellow Emperor or Confucius. Now that we have lost the Yellow Emperor and Confucius, who is to distinguish them? For the present we may as well trust the decision of the Chief Justice."[60]

Although it is acknowledged that this legal impasse, complicated *ad absurdum,* cannot be definitively untangled, after an appeal to a higher authority the Solomonic ruling of the Chief Justice is accepted as the best workable compromise.

The dream tale tends to try to resolve the unresolvable by proving the material reality of the dream experience. To this end, all manner of proofs are supplied in *Liaozhai,* ranging from physical objects brought back from the dream world, such as bracelets or rings, to more ambiguous evidence, such as literary compositions recalled upon waking or nocturnal emissions staining the bedclothes. In one *Liaozhai* tale, proof even arrives in the form of an infant said to be the fruit of the hero's oneiric liaison with an immortal woman; appropriately, the child is named "Meng xian," or "Dreaming an Immortal" (3.344). But even uncanny coincidences between events in the dream and events in waking life may be used to verify the dream's reality.

On rare occasions, the dilemma may be solved in the opposite fashion, by proving that the dreamer was not dreaming at all. In "The Palace of Heaven" ("Tiangong"; 9.1278–82), the handsome young hero is the victim of a ruse meant to persuade him that he has had an erotic dream adventure in Heaven. Later, he discovers that he had been illicitly smuggled into the harem of the most nefarious official of the Ming court for the pleasure of his ladies. The secret procurers have taken advantage of oneiric conventions in which dream is a shuttle between one world and another. The hero is drugged and transported in his sleep, so that he awakens in an underground grotto under the illusion he is dreaming; only much later does he reawaken in his own bed under the illusion that he is awaking for the first time. But as it is beyond mortal powers to simulate the temporal condensation of a dream, when the hero learns he has been gone not a single night but three months, he becomes convinced that it was no dream and runs away to escape the official's revenge.[61]

In general, however, dreaming and waking seem to partake equally of reality in *Liaozhai*. The distinction between the two is often presented as a matter of form rather than of substance. For example, in "Yingning" (2.147–59), the human hero dreams that a ghost, his wife's aunt, comes to thank him for reburying her bones. But when he awakens and tells his dream to his wife, a fox-spirit, she explains: "Oh, I saw her last night and cautioned her not to startle you" (2.158). We infer that on her mission to their household, the ghost had appeared plainly to the fox-wife but had deliberately assumed the cover of dream to visit the hero. Whether an experience is deemed a dream or not, then, also depends upon the sender and the receiver.

In certain other *Liaozhai* tales, it seems almost as if a transformative membrane hangs between the dream world and the waking world. Something may take one shape in a dream and another in ordinary life, but still be considered two facets of the same reality. In "Princess of the Lilies" ("Lianhua gongzhu"; 5.673–77), for example, the bee-princess and the inhabitants of her bee-kingdom assume human form in the hero's dream but revert to their apian form when he awakens to the sound of their buzzing. Likewise, only in dream does the rock collector in "The Ethereal Rock" ever apprehend his beloved rock in human guise.

By Pu Songling's day, the lack of distinction between dream and waking as a sharply focused philosophical or religious idea seems to have faded; it had become instead a literary conceit, metaphoric shorthand for a whole range of issues. Pu Songling manages to revitalize the old dream formulas in *Liaozhai* by playing games with them. One of his favorite ways of restoring the amazement an overused trope once aroused is to invert it, a tactic he applies to the cliché of the *lebenstraum*. The tale "Liansuo" (3.331–37) culminates in the dramatic resurrection of the ghostly heroine, dead for twenty years. In an unusually open instance of closure in *Liaozhai*,[62] the story ends abruptly with the heroine telling her lover: "These past twenty years seem just like a dream" (3.337). The conceit that "life is but a dream" has been replaced by the notion that "death is but a dream," now replete with all the elegiac associations of dream as a metaphor for a vanished past.[63]

Dream and the Emotions

One of the most influential Chinese theories of dream causation holds that dreams are the product of the thoughts, emotions, and memories of waking life. This theory has tended to evoke the most enthusiasm from scholars seeking Freudian psychological insights in Chinese dream literature.[64] It should be borne in mind, however, that thought and emotion are themselves cultural and historical constructs and are conceptualized differently in different societies. In traditional China, the heart was understood as the site of both mental and emotional processes, and thinking and feeling were not diametrically opposed concepts.

Chinese thought has long recognized the power of the mental and emotional faculties to affect the human body, a concept Paul Unschuld has described as "the seamless linking of the psychic with the somatic." According to Unschuld, "It was known that the various emotions . . . were directly anchored in the biological organism and could also influence it. Excessive anger, it was recognized, eventually led to liver damage; fear strained the kidneys. Conversely, this biological integration of emotions also meant that what initially is a purely somatic effect . . . can also cause psychic disorders."[65] In one theory of dream causation described by Chen Shiyuan, dreams of a particular emotion may diagnose the condition of its corresponding organ. Thus he writes: "If the qì [energy] in your liver is replete [*sheng*], you will dream of anger; if the qì in your kidneys is replete, you will dream of fear."[66]

An anecdote from the fifth-century *New Tales of the World* introduces some important insights into the relationship among dream, illness, and the workings of the mind:

When Wei Chieh was a young lad with his hair in tufts, he asked Yüeh Kuang about dreams.

Yüeh said, "They're thoughts."

Wei continued, "But dreams occur when body and spirit aren't in contact. How can they be thoughts?"

Yüeh replied, "They're the result of causes. No one's ever dreamed of entering a rat hole riding in a carriage, or of eating an iron pestle after pulverizing it, because in both cases there have never been any such thoughts or causes."

On the surface, Yue's (Yüeh) argument is straightforward: dreams are made up of our thoughts and must have plausible causes. But the anecdote does not end here; it proceeds to introduce a new theme about the causal relationship between thinking and illness.

Wei pondered over what was meant by "causes" for days without coming to any understanding, and eventually became ill. Yüeh, hearing of it, made a point of ordering his carriage and going to visit him, and thereupon proceeded to make a detailed explanation of "causes" for Wei's benefit. Wei immediately began to recover a little. Sighing, Yüeh remarked, "In this lad's breast there will never be any incurable sickness."[67]

Just as dreams are induced by the mind, so illness may be induced by certain types of thinking. In demonstrating how potent and dangerous thoughts can be, this anecdote illustrates the extent to which mental processes can affect the body and influence material reality. The precocious Wei falls ill because he is unable to think through Yue's novel theory of dreams; a detailed explanation produces an immediate improvement in the boy's health. As soon as the troublesome thoughts are dispelled, the body responds.

By Ming times, however, with the increased prominence of the concept of qing (sentiment), greater weight seems to have been placed on the purely affective dimensions of the dream. For example, the categories "dreams of longing" (*simeng*), "dreams of memory" (*jixiang*), and "meditational dreams" (*yijing*) found in early typologies are collapsed into the single category "overflow of feeling" (*qingyi*) in Chen Shiyuan's list.[68] This theory of dreams and its implications about the power of desire are staples of fiction and drama. In such literature, excessive emotion—love, anger, grief— often produces illness, which, left unappeased, not infrequently results in death. For example, Li Ping'er literally dies of anger after the indirect murder of her baby in the novel *Jin Ping Mei*. Du Liniang, the heroine of the play *The Peony Pavilion*, dies from a desire conceived in dream; the force of this desire is eventually sufficient to bring her back to life.

Unmarried lovers in *Liaozhai* frequently fall ill from desire; this illness also serves the covert purpose of coercing parents to agree to their children's wishes. If love is sufficiently sincere and strong, however, dream itself may take over the role of matchmaker. In such cases, dreams not only are provoked by desire but become the means of permanently fulfilling that desire. In "Wang Gui'an" (12.1632–37), a man falls passionately in love with a girl at first sight but is unable to trace her name or whereabouts. One night, he dreams that he finds himself in a village along the banks of a river and enters a beautiful garden, whose poetic scenery is itself the harbinger of an erotic encounter. He comes to a tree in full bloom, whose very name—"nocturnal union" (*yehe*)—encodes his desire, in front of what looks like the women's quarters. A girl emerges and, to his unexpected delight, turns out to be his beloved. Just as he is about to embrace her, her father returns and he awakens. Although every detail of the dream still seems as vivid "as though it were before his eyes," he keeps it to himself "fearing that if he told anyone about it, he'd destroy this beautiful dream" (12.1633). This precaution proves effective, because about a year later he finds himself in a scene whose every detail, including the tree, replicates his dream. Although he hesitates, fearing that it is again a dream, he does find the girl, exactly as in the dream, and wins her by telling her how his dream has been corroborated. After a number of setbacks, the two lovers are finally married.

In "Ji Sheng" (12.1638–44), the only tale presented as a sequel to another tale in the collection, the son of the couple in "Wang Gui'an" falls ill with longing for his lovely cousin; another beautiful girl takes advantage of his indisposition and offers herself to him in a shared erotic dream. The lucky boy, truly an extraordinary dreamer, winds up marrying them both. A final note to the story emphasizes that the thread linking this tale with the one before it is the dream romance: "That the fine matches of father and son both resulted from dreams is an amazing thing. For this reason, I have recorded them both" (12.1644).

Dreams of desire may also suddenly give way to nightmares of anxiety in *Liaozhai*, as in the tale "A Gentleman from Fengyang" ("Fengyang shiren"; 2.187–90). There are several Tang versions of this tale, but Pu Songling's narrative reworking is most closely indebted to "Dugu Xiashu."[69] In this version, a merchant returning from a long sojourn abroad is prevented from reaching home by nightfall and takes shelter in a deserted temple. It is a bright moonlit night, and he has just lain down when a bunch of rowdy merrymakers suddenly enters and begins having a party. To his amazement, the merchant sees his wife among them and then hears her sing a drinking song. Unable to restrain his jealousy, he throws a tile at the company. As soon as it hits the ground, everyone vanishes, including his wife. The next morning, upon arriving home, the merchant finds his wife, not dead as he had feared, but still in bed asleep. She awakens and tells him the nightmare she has just had, which coincides exactly with the scene he had witnessed and disrupted in the temple.

As Allan Barr has pointed out in an excellent close reading, Pu Songling's most important revision of the Tang tale is to shift the point of view from the husband to the wife.[70] But this change in focus also inspires Pu Songling's second crucial innovation, the compression of the anonymous band of revelers into a single powerful female figure. Pu Songling's version begins with a prose rendering of the classic poetic trope of a woman longing for her absent husband, her desire intensified by moonlight.

One night, as she was getting into bed, the moonlight rippled through the gauze curtains, and the pain of separation flooded her breast. Just as she was tossing back and forth, a beautiful lady with a pearl headdress and a crimson robe pushed aside the curtains and came in. "Don't you want to see your husband?" she asked, with a smile. (2.187)

The dream, instigated by the beautiful lady, has begun without explicit indication. She takes the wife on a journey into the moonlight to meet her husband, who appears riding on a white donkey. But the lady maliciously destroys this longed-for reunion. Under the pretext of feting the couple's reunion, she seduces the husband. The beautiful lady is both the wife's double and her rival, the embodiment of the dual nature of her desire and her fears.

The double motif is entrusted to a recurrent image—a pair of shoes, the essence of female sexual identity in the Chinese imagination. The shoe (*xie*) is sometimes punned with a homonym meaning union (*xie*) to symbolize marriage in dream interpretations.[71] Unable to match the lady's swift pace, the wife loses her shoes. This is the first sign that the promised reunion will be forfeited because the wife is not the lady's equal. Refusing to let the wife turn back to retrieve them, the lady lends the wife her own slippers, who discovers that they fit perfectly and speed her along as though she were flying. But when they meet the husband, the lady reclaims her slippers and with them, it turns out, the wife's eagerly anticipated night of love with her husband. As the three sit drinking together in the moonlight, the lady brazenly "entwines her slipper-clad feet" with those of the husband in an explicit gesture of seduction (2.188).[72] She sings provocatively of a woman's longing for her lover and her resentment at being left alone, emotions that rightfully belong to the wife. Such a song, which in all the Tang versions of the tale was sung by the wife, has been stolen by the beautiful lady and cruelly used to enflame the wife's husband.[73]

The man, who is now drunk, succumbs to the lady's charms, and they retire together for the night, abandoning the wife anew. Unable to find her way back home and beside herself with jealousy, the miserable wife eavesdrops beneath the window on the couple's lovemaking. In the ultimate act of betrayal, she "hears her husband describe in complete detail the positions that she would always assume when the two of them were making love" (2.189). The double has utterly usurped her dream.[74]

Just when the devastated wife is considering putting an end to herself, her younger brother suddenly appears. After hearing his sister's account of her grievances, he hurls a rock through the window, taking over the husband's role in the Tang tale. "Oh no! Your husband's head has been smashed!" cries a voice from within (2.189). When the wife tearfully reproaches her brother for killing her husband, he savagely turns on her and pushes her to the ground. Only then does she awake and discover it was all a nightmare.

The next day, however, her husband does arrive home riding on a white donkey just as in the dream. The clear psychological origins of this dream do not in the end vitiate its prognostic potential. The playwright Zhang Fengyi attempts to theorize this connection between the workings of the mind and the prediction of the future in his preface to *A Classified Investigation into Dream Interpretation:* "Dream is the motive [*ji*] of the mind, the sign of movement, the anticipation of auspiciousness and inauspiciousness. The mind starts from motive and motive is signified in dream; there are good and bad motives, just as dreams are distinguished as auspicious and inauspicious."[75] By comparing experiences, husband and wife discover that not only the two of them but also the wife's younger brother shared the same dream. In a twist of one-upmanship, Pu Songling has restored the uncanniness to this familiar tale by transforming the original two-way dream into an unprecedented three-way dream.

Liaozhai commentator Dan Minglun acknowledges that the dream is a projection of the woman's own desires and anxieties, but he considers this normal and not at all strange. To him the three-way dream is bizarre: " 'Longing and intense anxiety'; 'the pain of parting flooding her breast'—everything encountered in the dream was born of thought and transformed into illusion. Such things are a matter of course and are nothing to be amazed at. But a dream shared by three people with the white donkey to prove it—now, *that* is really strange!" (2.190)

Dreams of encounters with ghosts are also sometimes understood to arise from the mental and emotional state of the dreamer. But this recognition of the psychological etiology of ghostly dreams does not rule out the material reality of ghosts. Chen Shiyuan's explanation of how vengeful ghosts provoke dreams combines a firm belief in the existence of ghosts with shrewd insight into how the workings of the mind affect dreams. He argues that the subject matter of a nightmare comes from one's own perturbed emotional state and that ghosts take advantage of this.[76] Nor is Chen alone in espousing this view. The late Ming scholar Shen Defu (1578–1642) explains the origins of a nightmare with exactly the same logic: "In the end, if you lose your mind, ghosts and gods may take the opportunity to humiliate you."[77]

In *Liaozhai,* which only occasionally ventures into the realm of horror,[78] ghosts frequent dreams less for vengeance and more for the sake of great friendship or love. "A Dream of Parting" ("Meng bie"; 3.405–6) tells the story of a newly dead soul who appears in a dream to take leave of his closest friend. The tale illustrates the profundity of their friendship, not so much by the spectral notification as by the friend's utter conviction of the veracity of his dream. Without pausing to make inquiries, he puts on mourning clothes and hastens to his friend's house, who, as indicated by the dream, had indeed just died.

"A Dream of Parting," which Pu Songling wrote to commemorate the relationship between a great-uncle and his dearest friend, reenacts a conventional trope of devoted friendship. The most famous exemplar is the friendship between Fan Juqing and Zhang Yuanbo recorded in the *History of the Latter Han.* Juqing dreamed that Yuanbo had died, but, despite all due haste, was unable to arrive in time for the funeral. The burial was delayed, however, because, miraculously enough, the coffin thwarted all efforts to place it in the grave until Juqing arrived.[79] The final comment to "A Dream of Parting" expresses admiration that a modern friendship could recreate the proverbial devotion of Fan Juqing and Zhang Yuanbo: "Alas! In friendship, the ancients trusted each other in life and death just like this. The story that Yuanbo's funeral chariot waited until Juqing arrived could not have been false!" (3.405) This comment in turn recalls the Historian of the Strange's passionate outburst at the end of the tale "Licentiate Ye": "Could the soul of a dead man follow his true friend, forgetting in the end that he was dead? Listeners may be skeptical, but I deeply believe it!" (1.84)

As I have previously mentioned, a considerable number of tales in *Liaozhai* testify to the extremely high value the author placed on a friendship that transcended death. Two poems by Pu Songling that record dreams suggest that the affirmation of belief in the comments to "A Dream of Parting" and "Licentiate Ye" might be more than rhetorical. The first poem is an elegy entitled "Dreaming of Wang

Rushui" ("Meng Rushui"), written in 1702. Pu Songling felt deeply indebted to his friend Wang Rushui because Wang had helped him pay for his mother's burial during a famine year, even though Wang was not wealthy. (A poem written in 1685 describes Pu's shame and regret that he was still not in a position to repay the money, even though Wang Rushui was himself in real financial need.[80]) The moving preface to the elegy recounts how a dream encounter with his friend's ghost dissolved his writer's block and enabled him at last to discharge his emotional debt by completing the elegy:

After Rushui recovered from his illness, I didn't go to see him for half a year. On the nineteenth day of the eighth month, I was returning from Jimen when I heard that he had again taken ill. I made a detour, intending to hold his hand, but by the time I reached his gate, he had already passed away. I went inside and wept for him and then set out on my way. I wanted to compose a funeral dirge for him, but even after a long time, it was still incomplete. Three days after the Double Yang festival, I suddenly dreamed that Rushui came and we met just as we had all our lives. He smiled and said: *"Why are you taking so long with what you intend to give me?"* In a flash, I remembered he was dead. Holding him, I burst into tears and awoke. Alas! how sad it is![81]

A poem written in 1711, just four years before Pu Songling's own death, is even closer in spirit to "A Dream of Parting." This poem commemorates the death of the poet and official Wang Shizhen, one of the most famous literary men of his day, with whom Pu Songling enjoyed a slight friendship. The poem's lengthy title doubles as a preface: "On the last night of the fifth month, I dreamed that Mr. Yuyang (Wang Shizhen) honored me with a visit; I didn't know that he had already passed away several days earlier" ("Wuyue huiri, ye meng Yuyang xiansheng wangguo, bu zhi ershi yi sun binke shuri yi").

A huge discrepancy in social status and literary fame separated Pu Songling and Wang Shizhen during their lifetimes. In fact, although they were from roughly the same vicinity in Shandong, they seem to have met only once. Wang Shizhen penned some favorable comments on drafts of Pu Songling's poems and a number of *Liaozhai* stories and even wrote a dedicatory poem for the collection, but he apparently declined to write a preface for it. The two men did correspond, but only Pu Songling seems to have cared enough to preserve his poems and letters to Wang.[82] It seems reasonable to suppose that the friendship between the obscure Pu and the celebrated Wang was essentially one-sided. The poetic evidence suggests that this elusive friendship had great emotional significance for Pu Songling. By casting his final dream of Wang Shizhen in the literary mold of the ghost who takes leave of his friend in dream, Pu Songling finds the long-awaited proof of Wang Shizhen's true friendship. At the same time, he affirms that their friendship will transcend death by carving out a central position for himself in the elegy:

> Last night I still dreamed of Yuyang [Wang Shizhen],
> Never expecting he'd already ridden the clouds to Heaven!
>   . . . . .
> You bid adieu to an old man in decline; surely before long,
> Our souls will swear an eternal oath.[83]

Both these strands—the emotional power of dreams and a friendship that transcends death—are magically woven together in the *Liaozhai* tale "Becoming an Immortal" ("Cheng xian"; 1.87–94).[84] The story begins with two friends, Zhou and Cheng, swearing an oath of friendship. Since Cheng is poor, Zhou supports him and his family. Cheng, for his part, goes to extraordinary lengths to get Zhou released after he has been imprisoned and sentenced to death on trumped-up charges. Disillusioned with a world in which the innocent are persecuted by rich bullies and corrupt officials, Cheng decides to go off in quest of immortality. Zhou declines to accompany him but continues to support Cheng's family in his absence.

This detailed and convincing picture of ordinary life with its ruinous lawsuits and loyal friendships provides the necessary backdrop for the magical Daoist adventures of the second half of the story.[85] At the core of the tale are three dreams. But on closer inspection these are not really dreams; they are dream parables that partake of reality and that collapse the boundaries between dream and waking, illusion and reality, engineered by Cheng the Immortal when he returns to enlighten his deluded friend Zhou.

In the first dream, Zhou dreams that Cheng is lying naked on top of him and suffocating him. When he awakens, he discovers that he is lying in Cheng's bed and that he has somehow entered Cheng's body. Cheng himself has vanished. But what has occurred to Zhou under the vague guise of dream persists even after awakening. Nor is this Zhou's solipsistic fantasy: his own brother is so completely convinced that he is Cheng, not Zhou, that he forbids him access to his own wife. When Zhou sees his reflection in a mirror, he cries out, "Mr. Cheng is here, but where have *I* gone?" (1.90) Zhou has no alternative but to embark on a quest to regain his true self that leads him to Cheng and the mountains of immortality. Zhou's profound loss of identity and lack of self-knowledge culminates when he comes face to face with his real self in Cheng's body and does not realize who he is. "How strange!" he exclaims. "How could I have gazed upon my own face and not recognized myself!" (1.91)

By switching identities with Zhou in this erotically tinged dream, Cheng has, as in certain Indian myths of illusory doubles, shaken Zhou's "confidence in the uniqueness and solidity of his waking persona."[86] This profound disorientation is the first prerequisite for Zhou's future enlightenment. But even after Zhou has regained his original identity (once again, through a quasi dream), he is still bound by his emotional attachment to his wife. To persuade him to withdraw from the world once and for all, Cheng resorts to yet another magic dream. Zhou finds that he has returned home with Cheng "in no time" and that he is able to float over the wall of his family compound through sheer volition. He licks a hole in the paper window of the women's quarters and peeps through it, only to find that his adored young wife is cuckolding him with the servant. Zhou and Cheng burst into the room, behead the adulteress, and strew her entrails over a tree in a violent, misogynist scene that would not be out of place in the outlaw world of *The Water Margin*.

Suddenly Zhou awakens and finds himself back on a couch in the mountains. Convinced that he has had a terrible nightmare, he cries out: "Queer dreams one after another are so terrifying!" (1.92) But Cheng shatters even this certainty by displaying the bloody knife and interpreting the dream for him: "What's a dream you consider real, and what's real you consider a dream!" (1.91)[87] And indeed, upon returning home a second time, this time at a normal pace, the dream proves to be true: Zhou's wife has, in fact, been brutally murdered. At long last, now that his final emotional tie to the world has been severed, Zhou reaches enlightenment, "as if suddenly waking from a dream" (1.93) and goes off to become an immortal, joining Cheng for eternity. Theirs has now become quite literally "a friendship that transcends death."

In the end, however, this kaleidoscope of dreams, awakenings, illusory tricks, and proofs of reality negates itself. Although the conventions for portraying the temporal and spatial differences between a dream journey and a real journey are carefully followed on Zhou's two trips home, the distinction between the two journeys becomes irrelevant. We can no longer distinguish where dream begins and reality leaves off. This is perhaps the point of the story: the philosophical and religious trappings of the dream as enlightenment have become a pure game of words and images. Any potentially serious message is belied by the story's conclusion. It ends not with Zhou's metaphoric awakening, not even with his final reunion with Cheng, but with a shining image, one that illustrates not so much the transformative power of Daoist alchemy as the strength of worldly desire and mundane dreams: Zhou sends to his remaining family members "a fingernail the length of two fingers" that turns everything it touches into gold (1.94).

Dream and Fictionality

A number of modern scholars have remarked upon the uneasy acceptance of a genuine notion of fictionality in the Chinese literary tradition, a problem that I broached in Chapter 1 with regard to the interpretive history of *Liaozhai*.[88] I believe that it may be possible to see in the writings of a number of seventeenth-century authors, commentators, and publishers an attempt to work out a new understanding of fiction and drama as a special sort of discourse with its own rules and properties. One of the chief attractions of the dream for writers like Pu Songling and his contemporaries was that it allowed them to explore their interest in the paradoxical nature of fiction—If fiction, like dream, is by definition "illusory," "unreal" (*huan*), in what sense may it be understood to exist?

The ontological status of literary characters seems to have posed the general problem of fictionality in the most compelling way.[89]

These issues are raised in an interesting letter written by the seventeenth-century publisher Wang Qi:

Mr. Wang Suidong [Siren] once said: "There are no lies in this world." He meant that as soon as you tell a lie, it comes to be an accepted matter. For instance, Tang Xianzu's dream plays are, for the most part, made up; but when he writes that Miss Du Liniang dreams of Scholar Liu and dies, hasn't she already come into existence? When he writes that Miss Huo Xiaoyu meets the Yellow-robed Knight and is reunited with her lover, hasn't the Yellow-robed Knight already come into existence? Yes, indeed, "there are no lies in this world!"

The fiction and drama of today are all lies. . . . With the characters in the best of them, it's like hearing them with your own ears and seeing them with your own eyes, like sitting side by side and talking face to face, so that it seems if you call them, they'll come out, or if you summon them, they'll get up, so that if they laugh, there's actually sound, and if they weep, there are actually tears. Readers today only realize how wonderful they are, but don't realize they are all lies. How remarkable that literary technique can reach such heights![90]

Wang is arguing here, I believe, that there is no important difference between real characters and fictional ones; once fictional characters are created and enter the public domain, they take on a real existence in the minds of readers. Because the affective power of the unreal can be so strong in great literary works, such as *The Peony Pavilion* and *The Purple Hairpin* (*Zichai ji*), readers enter into an intimate relationship with fictional characters and willingly take them as real.[91] The paradoxical implication to be drawn from his letter, therefore, is that the best fiction and drama can be considered "lies that are not lies."

In her first-rate study of nonsense, Susan Stewart argues that "the distinguishing characteristic of the fiction is its reversibility, its status as a form of play that both is and is not in the world, that both counts and does not count." By reversibility, she refers to the commonsense idea that fictive events are retractable because they "can be taken back by saying 'This is just a story' or 'I was just joking' "[92]— or, we could add, by saying "It was just a dream." Wang Qi's letter arrives at an understanding of fiction that comes remarkably close to at least part of Stewart's definition as something that "both is and is not in the world." But Wang Qi does so by *denying* the reversibility of fiction, at least from the reader's point of view. In his formulation, once fictional characters or events have been created, they *cannot* be retracted or taken back. They *do* count because they have entered the world of their readers and are no longer exclusively controlled by the author who invented them. [93]

The deliberate denial of the reversibility of fictional language forms a pattern in many *Liaozhai* tales, a pattern that calls attention to the fictional nature of these tales by exaggerating the difference between the way language works in the text and in everyday life. There is a continual blurring of literal and figurative truth in *Liaozhai,* and fibs, metaphors, and jests—like dreams—tend to come true. Regardless of a character's intention in a *Liaozhai* story, no statement can be taken back or made not to count, for once it has been articulated, it inevitably assumes a momentum of its own. [94] In "Playing at Hanging" ("Xi yi"; 6.876), for example, a practical joker bets his friends that he can get a young woman riding by to smile. He rushes over to her shouting "I'm going to die!" and then pretends to hang himself. He wins the bet, for the woman does grant him a smile, but when his friends get over their mirth, they discover that he has hung himself to death by mistake. Joking can be a very perilous act in *Liaozhai.*

Pu Songling's most "foolish" heroes (themselves often the irresistible targets of practical jokes) seem completely unaware that a distinction even exists between figurative and literal language or that, depending on the speaker and the context, alternative interpretive modes ought to be applied. They are the fools of the popular adage "Don't tell a dream to a fool [because he'll think it's true]." And yet paradoxically, it is this blind refusal to distinguish truth and lies that converts lies into truth and makes practical jokes backfire on their perpetrators. In the tale "Yingning," for example, one such foolish hero falls dangerously ill with longing for a mysterious girl whose identity and whereabouts are unknown to him. Fearing for the boy's health, his cousin knowingly deceives him, telling him that the girl is their maternal cousin and that she lives in the mountains thirty *li* to the southwest. The gullible boy believes him and journeys to the uninhabited region specified by his cousin. But lo and behold his naiveté is rewarded: in a tiny village, he finds the object of his desire, who does turn out to be the adopted daughter of his maternal aunt. Although the girl proves to be a fox-spirit and the aunt is a ghost, this does not affect the inadvertent truth of the cousin's falsehood. In the fantastic world of *Liaozhai* there are no real lies, because a lie comes true as soon as it is believed.

In the tale "The Great Sage Equal to Heaven" ("Qitian dasheng"; 11.1459–63), which describes the Fujian cult of Sun Wukong, the monkey king from the novel and play *Journey to the West (Xiyou ji)*, Pu Songling broaches the ambiguous status of fictional characters within the context of the worship of heroes popularized by novels and plays, a genuine phenomenon in China during his day.[95] A morally upright merchant from Shandong traveling in Fujian enters a temple and is flabbergasted to discover that the statue of the deity inside has the head of a monkey. "Sun Wukong is nothing but a parable [*yuyan*] invented by [the novelist] old Qiu,"[96] he objects. "How can people sincerely believe in him? If he really is a god, then let me be struck down by spears or lightning!" (11.1459) The rest of this tale predictably recounts the skeptical merchant's conversion to the cult, for what god can ever let such a challenge go unmet in literature?[97] Stricken by one painful ailment after another, the merchant is unrelenting until his brother falls ill and dies. Proof of the god's existence is provided in oneiric form, when the merchant is summoned to a dream audience with the Simian Sage, who agrees to pull strings in the underworld and bring his brother back to life if the merchant will become his disciple. Sure enough, when the merchant awakens, the corpse in the coffin has revived, and the merchant becomes a fervent devotee to the god. But, unlike a conventional conversion narrative, the story does not conclude on this note. A second encounter that befalls the merchant is far more in keeping with the playful spirit of the monkey's character in *Journey to the West*. In a dream-like sequence, the merchant meets the monkey king traveling incognito and, as though he had actually entered a scene in the novel, is wafted up to the Palace of Heaven and back again by means of the monkey king's trademark magic of the cloud-trapeze.

In his final comment, the Historian of the Strange offers an alternative rejoinder to the merchant's original question:

A gentleman once passed by a temple and painted a mandolin on the wall. By the time he came to the spot again, the spiritual power [*ling*] of this mandolin was renowned, and incense was being burned there nonstop. Certainly it isn't necessary for someone [like Sun Wukong] to actually exist in this world: if people believe someone to be powerful, then he will be powerful for them. Why is this? When the human mind is fixed on something, the spirits will appear.

In the case of merchant Sheng's moral rectitude, it was fitting that he receive the god's blessing, but how could a monkey really keep "an embroidery needle in his ear" or be able "to transform all the hairs on his body?"[98] How could he possibly "perform a cloud-somersault" and ascend the azure sky? In the end Sheng was deluded, which means that what he perceived wasn't real at all. (11.1462)

Because the merchant no longer believed that the monkey king was merely "a parable invented by old Qiu," however, the monkey becomes "real" for him—through the ambiguous proof of a dream and through a flight of fancy that imitates a work of fiction. Although the last lines of the comment express the Confucian scholar's typical condescension toward popular cults, the story itself illustrates that spiritual power depends not on the actual existence of a god or a fictional character but on the illusory strength of human belief and desire.

The power of fictional characters is self-consciously explored through the medium of a shared dream in a fascinating piece narrated in the first person by a woman named Qian Yi (1671–?). The piece was appended to her annotated edition of Tang Xianzu's play, *Wu Wushan's Three Wives' Combined Commentary to The Peony Pavilion* (*Wu Wushan sanfu heping Mudan ting*), first printed in 1694.[99] It is New Year's Eve, and the woodblocks for her edition have finally been proofread and printed. Upon a small table in the courtyard, Qian Yi places a bound volume of her edition alongside a vase with a branch of flowering plum. She then sets up a spirit tablet to Du Liniang, the play's famous heroine, and makes a New Year's offering to her. Qian Yi's husband, Wu Wushan (1647?–after 1697), who collaborated on the edition with her, bursts out laughing:

"What a great fool you are! According to Tang Xianzu's own writ, Liniang is a fictitious name. If there's no such person, on what grounds are you making an offering to her?"

"Even so," she retorts, "what the 'breath of the Great Clod' lodges in becomes powerful [*ling*]—so spirits may possess a mere rock, and divinities inhabit a mere tree. The Goddess of the Xiang River in the song of Qu Yuan and the Nymph of Mount Wu in the rhapsody of Song Yu might well have been fictitious at first, but afterwards many shrines were dedicated to them all the same.[100] How can you and I determine whether Liniang exists or not?"[101]

Qian Yi is advancing two related arguments here, neither one complete. The first, drawing on an allusion from *Zhuangzi,* argues that if even inanimate objects can be suffused with a divine spirit, why can't the same be true of fictional characters?[102] In the second, she argues that even if an author announces his work is fictional, his readers still have the freedom to appropriate his creations and worship them as they please. Here she seems to echo the publisher Wang Qi's point that once an author introduces fictional characters into the public domain, they may take on an independent existence of their own in the lives of his readers.

Although Qian Yi's husband gallantly acknowledges himself to be in the wrong, the sketchiness of her arguments requires additional proof. That night both husband and wife have the same dream: they find themselves at Flowering Plum Shrine and come upon a small pavilion surrounded by peonies in full bloom. A woman of dazzling beauty emerges, whom they take to be Du Liniang. But though Qian Yi presses her to reveal her name, she merely smiles and refuses to speak. A great wind comes up, the scene is suddenly obscured by a shower of peony petals, and they awaken.

This dream weaves in obvious allusions and recurrent symbols from the original play—for example, Du Liniang's first dream of her lover also ends in a shower of flower petals, and she is later reunited as a ghost with him at Flowering Plum Shrine. But most important, Qian Yi's initial gesture of placing a sprig of flowering plum in a vase as an offering to Du Liniang's spirit and the shower of petals that concludes her dream re-enact a central scene from the play. In Scene 27, the nun-custodian of Flowering Plum Shrine, where Du Liniang's remains are buried, places a sprig of flowering plum in a vase to appease her spirit. Returning as a ghost, Du Liniang is indeed moved by the offering and scatters flower petals on the altar to show her appreciation.[103] Thus having restaged the opening of this scene in "real life" to consecrate her book, Qian Yi receives Du Liniang's appreciation for her devotion in a dream.

For her husband, however, the dream serves the same ostensible purpose as the dream in "The Great Sage Equal to Heaven": it converts a skeptic into a believer. Wu Wushan interprets the amazing coincidence of the shared dream as a direct rejoinder to the couple's earlier debate. Drawing an analogy from yet another literary work, the Six Dynasties collection *Seeking the Spirits,* he renounces his former skepticism: "In the past when Ruan Zhan argued that ghosts don't exist, a ghost appeared to him; so such a person as Du Liniang must indeed exist."[104] But the ambiguous nature of this proof is itself represented in the dream scene: Du Liniang steadfastly refuses to admit her identity outright, but merely smiles and turns away, for as both dreamers understood, the question of fictionality can never be definitively resolved.

It is no accident that both Qian Yi and the publisher Wang Qi drew their examples of fictional characters from the drama. During the seventeenth century, the problem of how historically accurate or how inventive a play ought to be was the subject of fierce debate. Proponents of the view that playwrights should enjoy full imaginative license because drama was fundamentally a fictional medium often compared the play to a dream and the audience to dreamers to point out the essentially unreal nature of both the theater and the dream. As Li Yu, the famous seventeenth-century playwright and drama critic, wrote in his essay "Discriminate Fiction from Fact" ("Shen xushi"), "Anyone who reads chuanqi drama and must check where the story came from and where the characters lived is a 'fool relating a dream.' One need not respond to him."[105]

Arguing along similar lines,[106] the late Ming scholar Xie Zhaozhe compared a dreamer swayed by auspicious or inauspicious dreams to a spectator affected by the tragic or triumphant moments in a play. Professing himself the greatest skeptic of all about dreams, he drew the following analogy: "The theater resembles a dream; parting and reunion, sorrow and joy, are not real emotions; wealth and honor, poverty and dishonor, are not real states. In such a fashion, the world also passes before our eyes."[107]

Xie Zhaozhe's triple analogy equating the illusory spectacle of dream, drama, and life is given substance in the *Liaozhai* tale "Mr.

Gu" ("Gu sheng"; 8.1154–55). In this tale (assigned the wonderful Edwardian title "A Singular Case of Ophthalmia" in Herbert Giles's translation),[108] dream becomes a drama of life projected against the screen of the eyelids, on the possible model, I imagine, of the Chinese shadow-puppet theater.[109] Mr. Gu, who is staying at an inn, is suffering from a painful eye inflammation with an unusual symptom: whenever he closes his eyes, he sees the buildings of a large and enticing mansion. By deliberately concentrating his gaze, he "suddenly feels his body enter the mansion," where an opera performance is being staged. In contrast to earlier Chinese dream parables of enlightenment such as the Tang "Tale of the Pillow" ("Zhenzhong ji") in which the hero lives out the plot of his own life in the dream world, here Mr. Gu, exactly like a spectator at a play, witnesses an allegorized version of Life passing, without really participating in it.

The allegory unfolds in two phases. On his first trip, Mr. Gu comes upon a room crawling with gurgling babies; he is then invited by a handsome young prince to watch an opera performance. The opera chosen is entitled "The Blessings of the Borderguard of Hua," an allusion to a passage in *Zhuangzi*. Since these blessings are long life, much wealth, and many sons, the title suggests that this play represents the desires of youth.[110] But after only three acts, Mr. Gu is unfortunately awakened by the innkeeper and finds himself once more lying in his bed in the inn. When he is finally alone again and able to close his eyes in peace, he comes upon the same room in the mansion, but it is now overrun with hunchbacked old crones who hiss menacingly at him. The seventh act of the opera is almost over, and the performance is soon completed. The now long-bearded and elderly prince chooses a second opera, "Peng Zu Takes a Wife." The reference to Peng Zu, the Chinese Methuselah, unmistakably associates this play with old age. One act of the opera seems to be the equivalent of a decade, and some seventy years have elapsed between Mr. Gu's first and second visits. As so often in *Liaozhai*, a common figurative expression has been realized literally: time has indeed passed "in the blink of an eye!"[111]

This narrative attempts to dissolve the boundaries separating dream and reality. Although dreams commonly unfold in *Liaozhai* without being explicitly introduced as such, the end of the dream is usually signaled by the character's realization that he has been dreaming. Although nowhere in the story are we told Mr. Gu is experiencing a dream or a hallucination,[112] a number of clues do suggest this. After Mr. Gu awakens the first time to find himself lying in his bed, "he realizes that he had never left the inn." Moreover, his final awakening plays on the traditional Chinese dream theory that the physical environment of the sleeper may affect the content of his dream.[113] Thus what Mr. Gu hears as gongs ringing at the end of the second opera in the other world turns out to be the clamor of dogs licking an old oil drum in the inn.[114]

And yet this seamless connection between the world of the inn and the world of the mansion does not necessarily vitiate the supposed "reality" of Mr. Gu's vision. Mr. Gu's eye ailment is treated by the prince's doctor in the other world; when he awakens, he discovers he has indeed been cured. Yet even this evidence of his experience's reality can equally prove that it was an illusion, if interpreted according to the traditional medical theory that dreams can be induced by pathological imbalances within the body and even perform a therapeutic function.[115] After Mr. Gu's "singular case of ophthalmia" has been cured, to his infinite regret he is never able to glimpse the tantalizing mansion again.

Mr. Gu's experience resembles that of watching a play in which actions unfold outside one's control. What makes this story so arresting is that the dream has become independent of the dreamer, and this independence seems above all to prove the reality of the characters in his dream. Significantly, the central conceit in this story appears as well in Ming and Qing jokebooks: "A man dreamed that he had gone to a banquet at which an opera was to be performed. He had just taken his seat, when he was woken up by his wife. He began swearing at her. Retorted his wife: 'Oh, quit swearing! If you hurry back to sleep, the opera won't be even halfway through yet!' "[116] Although the same logic governs this joke and the *Liaozhai* tale— the temporal condensation of dreams, the common desire to return to an interrupted dream—the results are quite different. The joke, told from a skeptical point of view, perfectly illustrates the old warning "Don't relate a dream to a fool." The joke is funny because both husband and wife stupidly behave as though the dream opera were real. But in the tale, because Mr. Gu realizes the fantasy

Fig. 6. Huang Yingcheng's woodblock illustration of a successful first-place graduate's prophetic dream. The scholar dozing off over his books on the right reappears in the dream bubble on the left, holding a placard clearly inscribed with the characters *zhuangyuan* (first-place graduate). (*Ming zhuangyuan tu kao, juan* 1)

ridiculed in the joke, the effect is no longer comic but strange and haunting.

In another, oddly similar *Liaozhai* anecdote called "Senior Licentiate Zhang" ("Zhang gongshi"; 9.1189), an old village schoolmaster is lying in bed ill. Suddenly, he sees a tiny man clad in a scholar's costume like an actor climb out from his heart and begin to sing an opera in the refined *kunshan* mode. The name and home town chanted in the performer's self-introduction are the same as the schoolmaster's, and the plot of the play corresponds to the events of his own life. After four acts, the performer recites a poem and abruptly disappears, leaving the schoolmaster with only vague memories of the performance he had just witnessed.[117] Although not explicitly labeled a dream, this spectacle of an autobiographical play performed by a miniature double perfectly expresses what Wendy O'Flaherty has called "the peculiar ambiguity of the experience of a dream in which the dreamer sees himself simultaneously as subject and object."[118] The story's conceit resembles nothing so much as those Ming and Qing woodblock illustrations that represent a dream as a cartoon-like bubble spiraling out from the dreamer's head and depict him at once as sleeper and actor (see Fig. 6).[119] What makes this brief story so uncanny is that the difference among life, dream, and dramatic performance has entirely vanished.

A Fox Dream

"A Fox Dream" ("Hu meng"; 5.618–22) is the only explicitly self-referential tale in the *Liaozhai* collection. Although other stories acknowledge their relationship to actual events and historical personages or to other literary texts such as Tang tales of the marvelous,[120] only "A Fox Dream" announces itself as written specifically in response to a previous *Liaozhai* tale. The unusual self-consciousness of this story seems designed to call attention to itself as a fictional construct and to problematize the question of fictionality and authorship in the collection. (See Appendix, pp. 211–16, for a full translation of this story.)

In meticulous keeping with "the conventions governing the zhiguai genre, according to which the text is taken as a report and the author as a recorder of actual events,"[121] the protagonist of the tale, one Bi Yi'an, is introduced as a personal friend of the author's and as the nephew of his employer, Bi Jiyou. The modern *Liaozhai* expert Yuan Shishuo has been unable to locate anyone with the sobriquet Bi Yi'an in the Bi family genealogy, but is inclined to believe he existed because many other patently fictional stories in *Liaozhai* feature Pu Songling's friends or contemporary figures.[122] Some scholars go beyond Yuan Shishuo and treat this as a story for which we have a known informant and date of composition.[123] Allan Barr points out that the story makes a number of jokes at Bi Yi'an's expense and tentatively suggests that it might possibly have been "a joint venture" between Pu Songling and his friend.[124] Although Pu Songling may have elected to use an obscure sobriquet for his friend to keep his identity an inside joke, it is nonetheless ironically appropriate for the story that Bi Yi'an cannot be definitively identified as a "real" figure any more than can a fictional character.

Bi Yi'an's professed desire to meet a fictional character from another *Liaozhai* tale, the charming fox-maiden Blue Phoenix (Qingfeng), sets this new tale in motion.

My friend Bi Yi'an . . . once paid a visit for some reason to the villa of his uncle, the district magistrate, and retired upstairs. It was said that the building had long been haunted by foxes. Now whenever Bi read my "Biography of Blue Phoenix" ["Qingfeng"; 1.112–18], his heart always went out to her and he regretted that he couldn't meet her even once. So he sat upstairs, lost in deep contemplation and longing for her. (5.618)

A similar yearning to meet fictional types is recalled by Pu Songling's friend Gao Heng, the author of the first preface to *Liaozhai,* in the preamble to his biography of a modern knight-errant: "As a boy, I was fond of reading books of Tang tales; I longed day and night to meet swordsmen and heroes."[125] In the *Liaozhai* tale "The Bookworm" (discussed at the end of Chapter 3), this childish wish to meet the characters in books is literally granted to the hero. Between the pages of a history tome, the bookworm finds a paper-cut of a beautiful woman, who springs to life under his fervent gaze, ironically becoming his unorthodox tutor in every sphere *but* books.

A reader's desire to meet fictional characters is played out in dream in both Qian Yi's account of her offering to Du Liniang and in Pu Songling's tale "A Fox Dream." But Qian Yi's dream narrative is related in a rather rudimentary fashion; her story really becomes complicated only when interpreted in light of the original play and its relationship with the *Three Wives* edition. In contrast, Pu Songling's narrative proliferates so many layers of nested dreams that it becomes almost as impossible to untangle them as it is to tease apart the question of what is real and what is illusion. Like a series of expanding double negatives, the layers of dream in this story seem to be continually erasing themselves. The story's structure mimics the kinds of negative logical paradoxes that so frequently appear in the Chinese discourse on dream, such as this statement from He Dongru's 1636 preface to *The Forest of Dreams:* "From this we know that what is not not illusion is not not real. If it is not not real, then it is not illusion; if it is not not illusion, then it is not real."[126]

The narrative complexity of "A Fox Dream" becomes apparent when we compare it with "Mr. Gu." Even though Pu Songling also attempts to blur the boundaries between dream and waking in "Mr. Gu," the narrative structure he employs still reproduces the dichotomy: the story can still be discussed in terms of the world of the inn and the world of the prince's mansion and in terms of the categories dream and reality. But in "A Fox Dream" we are given no stable frame of reference to represent the waking state; we are left with no standard at all in the tale against which to measure reality. The tale is like an onion whose layers can be peeled back without ever revealing a hard core. There is no final awakening and no final resolution.

Bi's first encounter with a fox-spirit is couched in highly ambiguous terms: "By the time he returned to his studio, it was growing dark. Since it was summertime and the weather extremely hot, he made up his bed facing the door. Someone shook him out of his sleep. He awoke and looked up, and there was a woman past forty but who still retained her charms." The woman immediately introduces herself: "I am a vixen. Having received the honor of your deepest thoughts, I was secretly moved to accept you" (5.618). Although the narrator informs us that Bi "awoke," by acknowledging that her appearance is a result of Bi's innermost thoughts, the fox-spirit indicates that Bi's ardent desire to meet a fox has caused her to materialize, and that this is a dream of the "overflow of feeling" or "meditational" variety catalogued in traditional typologies. Although Bi may have merely *dreamed* that he awoke, this sudden reversal has the force of a lie told by the narrator to deceive the reader. The effect is to transform the historian-narrator, who claims to be "a recorder of actual events," into a "fictive narrator," one, who in Stewart's words, "doesn't have to stand behind what he says—he can change the rules of the game, undercutting the reader's assumptions."[127]

After repelling his misplaced advances on the grounds that she is a bit too old for him, the fox-matron offers to fix him up with her young daughter: "Tomorrow night let no one remain in your chamber, and she will come to you." True to her word, the fox-matron reappears the next night with her exceptionally beautiful daughter in tow, and Bi's passion for foxes is finally gratified: he leads the fox-maiden through the bed curtains "where all the intimacies ensued. When the act was over, she laughed and said: 'Mr. Plump weighs so much, it's too much for any woman to bear!' And she left before it was light" (5.618).

If we consider Bi's first encounter with the fox-matron to be a dream, then we must consider his two following nights with her daughter a continuation of the same dream, for Bi does not awaken from it again. On the third night, Bi then enters a dream within a dream: "Bi waited for the fox-maiden as arranged, but as she didn't come for quite some time, he began to grow sleepy. Scarcely had he laid his head upon the table, then she suddenly appeared, saying, 'Forgive me for having kept you waiting so long'" (5.619).

The fox-maiden takes him to meet her three sisters, who hold a celebratory banquet in his honor. The riotous scene that ensues reinforces the impression that it is a dream through Alice-in-Wonderland distortions in volume, distance, weight, and texture. The mischievous fox sisters vie with one another to trick Bi into drinking more and more liquor from increasingly bawdy cups—a hair-bun cover that turns out to be a huge lotus leaf; a rouge box that is really a large basin; a silky, lotus-shaped cup that proves to be a lady's slipper.[128] These magical sleights of hand in this nested dream create further layers of illusion; nothing really is what it claims to be.

The ludic quality of the story's narrative frame is mirrored in the content of the nested narratives that constitute the dream. Unlike the many other *Liaozhai* tales that are so tightly constructed that no one word or image is superfluous, "A Fox Dream" is very digressive, with one scene only loosely connected to the next. The central plot of Bi's love affair with the fox-maiden is rather insubstantial and pro forma, subordinated to a series of vignettes, all of which revolve around teasing and game playing, including chess. The various drinking games at the banquet flaunt their status as games that can be arbitrarily overturned by continually transgressing or altering the rules.[129] Emblematic of this are the drinking vessels offered to Bi, which continually shift their shapes. As another example, when the youngest fox-sister arrives holding a cat, the company decides to pass around a chopstick so that "whoever is holding it when the cat meows will drink as forfeit" (5.620). Only after Bi has been forced to drink several large goblets in a row does he discover he has been tricked; the little girl has deliberately been making the cat meow whenever the chopstick reaches him.

After Bi leaves the banquet, he finally awakens again:

In the end, it had been a dream. And yet, he was still intoxicated, and the smell of wine was still strong. He thought this extraordinary. That evening the fox-maiden came to him asking, "So you didn't die of drunkenness last night?"

"I suspected it was a dream," said Bi. The girl smiled. "My sisters took cover in dream because they feared you were a wild carouser. Actually, it was no dream." (5.621)

Until the fox-maiden reappears, we are unsure which layer of the dream Bi has woken from. But her resolution is utterly paradoxical. "It was both a dream and not a dream," she explains, echoing the publisher Wang Qi's implied definition of fiction as "a lie that is not a lie." By pointing out that this embedded dream "was no dream," however, she also implicitly identifies the continuing overarching dream and herself as well as part of reality. This convoluted argument is maintained throughout the narrative until several years later the fox-maiden is obliged to break off her affair with Bi because she has been appointed to the post of "flower and bird emissary" by the goddess the Queen Mother of the West.

It is ironic that Pu Songling nevertheless entitles his story "A Fox Dream," a title that should have privileged authority above and beyond the narrative. In fact, the title itself betrays the story's ambiguity and tendency to undercut itself, for "fox" (*hu*) can be read as a pun for "nonsense" or "confusion" (*hu*), suggesting that it, too, may be discounted. Even so, the title puts readers in a double bind because they seemingly cannot agree at once with the premise of the tale (that it was not a dream) and with the title (that it was a dream). After puzzling over the story's logical conundrums, He Shouqi, one of *Liaozhai*'s nineteenth-century commentators, finally reached this stalemate: "A fox-spirit is already illusion, so a fox dream is even more illusion, but to consider it not a dream is the most illusory thing of all. There's a saying 'If there's a dream in a dream, then it was never a dream.' Was it a dream or not? I cannot decide" (*Liaozhai* 5.622). Commentator Dan Minglun, on the other hand, arrives at a more sophisticated reading by reveling in the negative logical propositions that the story's structure engenders:

It all came about from Bi's having read "The Biography of Blue Phoenix" and longing for her; so when he encountered the girl it was a dream. The banquet and congratulations were entrusted to another dream, but later Bi considered it wasn't a dream. So he wasn't dreaming, and yet it was a dream; he was dreaming, and yet it wasn't a dream. How was it not a dream? How was it *not* not a dream? How was it *not* not not a dream? When Bi related his dream, he realized that he had been dreaming, but that it wasn't a dream. Liaozhai recorded Bi's dream, but said that it wasn't a dream, so it was *not* not not a dream.   (5.622)

At any rate, the fox-maiden's interpretation is suspect, for the testimony of a character within a dream is insufficient proof of a dream's reality. It is not impossible for a dream to be interpreted or even denied within a dream. This phenomenon was pointed out as early as *Zhuangzi:* "When one is dreaming one does not know it is a dream and in one's dream one may even try to interpret one's dream."[130] Another *Liaozhai* tale, "Princess of the Lilies," blatantly exploits the possibility of false reassurance in dream. The hero of the story fears, rightly as it turns out, that his wedding night is a dream and tries to take his bride's physical measurements as a precautionary proof. His bride laughs at his foolishness: "I am plainly here with you—how could it be a dream?" Replies her husband: "I've been duped by dreams many times before, so I'm taking a detailed inventory" (5.675). Since this story is an imitation of the famous Tang dream tale "The Governor of the Southern Branch," the hero's fear that he is dreaming and his vain attempts to corroborate this are a sly allusion to the reader's familiarity with the plot: we know he will awaken to find that his illustrious career and felicitous marriage were nothing but a dream, his glorious kingdom nothing but an insect's nest.

But in "A Fox Dream," which treats all dream conventions as a literary joke, the ending is by no means a foregone conclusion. The story does not close with Bi's awakening or enlightenment; instead it loops back to its beginning:

> She sat dispiritedly for quite some time and then asked: "How do you think I compare with Blue Phoenix?"
>
> "You probably surpass her," he replied.
>
> "I was ashamed that I fell short of her. You and Liaozhai have a literary friendship. If you would be so kind as to trouble him to write a short biography of me, then one thousand years hence there may still be one who loves and remembers me as you do."
>
> On the nineteenth day of the first month, in the twenty-first year of Kangxi's reign [1683],[131] Master Bi and I stayed together in [his family's] Spacious Hall, and he told me this strange tale in detail. I said: "Liaozhai's pen and ink would be glorified by such a vixen," and so I recorded it. (5.621–22)

Here Pu Songling presents his own witty solution to the problem of fictional characters: it is not the author who creates his characters, but the characters themselves who insist on being created or recreated through the mediation of his readers. Just as in "Mr. Gu," where the dream becomes independent of the dreamer, the premise of "A Fox Dream" is that narratives can unfold outside the author's explicit control. This is highlighted by dwelling on a relationship that is always implicit but usually suppressed in a story, namely, the relationship between the reader and the story's characters. We are reminded of Qian Yi's debate with her husband when she asserted a reader's right to ignore the author's instructions and to worship a fictional character as real. And just as Qian Yi makes an offering to Du Liniang to demonstrate her faith and devotion, so the fox-maiden hopes that a thousand years hence there will still be someone who loves and remembers her through reading the tale.[132] What was argued in the first case from the viewpoint of a reader of fiction is being argued in the second case from the viewpoint of a fictional character. The discourse on fictionality has been carried from *outside* the original work of fiction to *within* it. "A Fox Dream" has become a fiction *about* fiction.

By inserting himself in the narrative as the real biographer of a fictional character, Pu Songling creates a twisted parallel with the sixteenth-century philosopher Li Zhi's invention of a fictional biographer to be the author of his own autobiography. Li Zhi's biographer is given a transparently allegorical name that puns on its own fictionality, Kong Ruogu (Vacuous as a Hollow), and like "A Fox Dream" the piece ends on a circular note with Li Zhi's request that Kong write his "biography."[133] Although this biography is not at all comic in spirit, Li Zhi, like Pu Songling, is travestying the conventions of historical discourse, parodying the attempt to prove authenticity in a text. The effect in both cases, by self-consciously blurring the boundaries between biographer and subject, author and informant, is not to undermine but to enhance the creative role of the author in the compositional process.

We have seen throughout this chapter how Pu Songling attempts to blur the boundaries separating dream and waking, illusion and reality. In "A Fox Dream" this is taken one step further, and this play between the boundaries of fiction and reality is enacted by blurring the boundaries of the discourse itself. The two frames of reference that ordinarily represent reality in *Liaozhai*—the state of waking and historical discourse—cancel themselves out. The embedded dream narrative has leaked into the frame that ordinarily sets it apart, collapsing the separation between real life and literary text and perhaps in the end pointing to the shared fictive nature of life, dream, and text.

Conclusion: The Painted Wall

> We all know that dream is illusion, but we don't realize painting
> is even more an illusion. Dream is form without shadow;
> painting is shadow without form. . . . But if one doesn't
> consider such things illusion, then illusion will become real.
> —*Wu Wushan's Three Wives' Combined Commentary
> to The Peony Pavilion*

Crossing Boundaries

Some readers consider "The Painted Wall" ("Hua bi"; 1.14–17)
simply another variety of dream narrative in *Liaozhai*.[1] I single it out
here as a conclusion because it provides the greatest insight into the
complex play with boundaries that helps engender the strange in
Liaozhai. Like much of Pu Songling's best work, this tale's tightness
of construction and precision of language result in a rich profusion
of layers. Three major leaps in the narrative, each contingent on the
preceding one, forcibly lead the reader to the final, jolting resolution. The tale begins:

Meng Longtan of Jiangxi was sojourning in the capital along with Zhu, a
second-degree graduate. By chance they happened to pass through a Buddhist temple, none of whose buildings or rooms were very spacious and
which were deserted except for an old monk temporarily residing there.
When he caught sight of the visitors, he respectfully adjusted his robe, went
to greet them, and then led them on a tour of the temple. In the main hall
stood a statue of Lord Zhi, the Zen monk. Two walls were covered with
paintings of such exceptionally wondrous skill that the figures seemed alive.
On the eastern wall, in a painting of the Celestial Maiden scattering flowers,
was a girl with her hair in two childish tufts. She was holding a flower and
smiling; her cherry lips seemed about to move; her liquid gaze about to
flow. Zhu fixed his eyes upon her for a long time until unconsciously his
spirit wavered, his will was snatched away, and in a daze, he fell into deep
contemplation. Suddenly his body floated up as though he were riding on a
cloud, and he went into the wall.

This is the first leap, which Feng Zhenluan's commentary explains as "longing leads to deep contemplation, illusion turns into reality" (*Liaozhai* 1.14). From the narrator's sly description of the painting, which relies on a preponderance of modals (*xu ci*), such as "*seemed* alive," "*about* to move," and from the intensity of Zhu's response to the girl's portrait, couched in the language of love at first sight, we suspect that she will step down from the painting.[2] Such an expected development is supported by the number of Chinese legends in which paintings and statues come to life. In another *Liaozhai* tale called "The Painted Horse" ("Hua ma"; 8.1028), for instance, the spirit of the picture, an equine "painting demon" (*hua yao*), comes alive and enters the real world: his astonished human rider eventually traces the origin of this extraordinary horse to a scroll painting by the Yuan master Zhao Mengfu. In the Tang tale "Zhu Ao," a man (also surnamed Zhu) follows a girl into a temple and discovers that she has vanished into a painting. Following this experience, he is haunted by debilitating erotic dreams of this "painting demon"; only after several attempts does a prominent Daoist succeed in exorcising her for good.[3] These expectations are thwarted in "The Painted Wall"; rather than the painting springing to life, it is Zhu who enters the painting. The narrative itself anticipates this reversal in its opening description of the painted image gazing at the viewer, rather than the viewer gazing at the image.

Once inside the fresco, Zhu sees a large complex of halls and pavilions and realizes that he is no longer in the human world. As he mingles in the crowd surrounding an old monk preaching a Buddhist sermon, he feels a slight tug on his robe—it is the smiling girl with her hair in tufts. She waves the flower in her hand and beckons him inside a deserted chamber where they blissfully consummate their passion. After two days have passed, the girl's companions get wind of the secret affair and come along with her to meet the young man. "When a little boy has grown quite big in your belly, will you still be wearing your hair uncombed like a virgin?" they tease her. The group persuades her to go through the married woman's ceremony of putting up her hair and then, still giggling, leaves the lovers alone again.

Zhu looked at the girl. With her tresses piled up like clouds and some phoenix-like coils dangling, she was even more bewitching than when she had worn her hair in tufts. There was not a soul around, and slowly they entered into intimate embraces. The scent of orchid and musk inflamed their hearts, but their pleasure had not yet reached its height. Suddenly, they heard the heavy thud of leather boots and the clanging of chains and then the sound of uproar and heated discussion. The girl leaped up startled, and the two surreptitiously peered outside. They saw a gold-armored envoy, with a face black as lacquer, holding chains and brandishing a hammer, surrounded by a group of maidens. "Is everyone here yet?" asked the envoy.

"We're all here," they replied.

"If there's anyone hiding someone from the world of men, let her publicly confess, don't let her be sorry!" said the envoy.

"There's no one here," they replied again in one accord. The envoy turned around and peered eagle-like around him, as though he were going to make a search. The girl grew deathly afraid, her face turning ashen. In a panic, she told Zhu: "Quick, hide under the bed!" Then she opened a small door on the wall and abruptly darted away. Zhu crouched under the bed, not even daring to breathe. Suddenly, he heard the sound of boots come into the room and then go out again. Before long, the clamor gradually receded into the distance, and he calmed down somewhat, but there were still people coming and going and talking outside the door. Having been constrained for so long, Zhu felt his ears buzzing and his eyes on fire. The situation was almost unendurable, but all he could do was quietly strain his ears for the girl's return, for in the end he could no longer remember from where he came.

Their lovemaking has suddenly turned into a nightmare. During the raid the girl escapes through "a small door in the wall," leaving Zhu entirely alone. This last detail is particularly interesting: when the girl vanishes behind this second "wall," Zhu is left stranded in the dark, unable to see anything at all. Deprived of his gaze, the very thing that had propelled him into the painting, he is forced to rely on his sense of hearing alone: "All he could do was quietly strain his ears for the girl's return, for in the end he could no longer remember from where he came." It is as though another wall has been built inside the wall that Zhu has entered, and he is now imprisoned in a blind intermediate zone between the two worlds inside and outside the mural. Since the outside world has already receded in his memory, his only thought in this moment of crisis is to rejoin the newly acquainted world of the painting.

Up until this point the narrative has consistently focused on Zhu, on his sensations and perceptions. This careful control of point of view convinces the reader that Zhu's experience in the painting is a subjective and private experience; indeed, Zhu's entry into the painting is represented literally as "mental flight"—desire and contemplation waft him into the wall "as though he were riding on a cloud." The detailed narration of events through the sounds overheard by Zhu during the raid and the depiction of his extreme physical discomfort bring the reader's identification with Zhu to a height. The reader, who has followed him into the painting and then into the secret realm within the painting, is now painfully suspended in limbo along with him. To prolong this suspense, the narrative abruptly resorts to a flashback. Accompanying this change in narrative sequence is a radical shift in point of view as the story returns to Zhu's friend Meng and the place that Zhu can no longer remember:

All this time, Meng Longtan was in the temple, and when in a flash Zhu disappeared, he wondered about it and asked the monk. The monk laughed and said: "He's gone to hear Buddhist doctrine expounded."
   "Where?" asked Meng.
   "Oh, not far away."

The old monk's ironic double-talk reveals that he alone knows Zhu's whereabouts. Meng is still completely in the dark, and his ignorance and anxiety become the second impulse of the narrative. Although we have been told what has happened to Zhu in his absence, this new motif leads the story back to the ground where Meng stands.

After a while, the monk flicked the wall with his finger and called out: "Donor Zhu,[4] why are you taking so long to come back?" Just then Meng saw that in the painting on the wall was a portrait of Zhu, standing stock-still and cocking his ear as though he were listening for something. Again the monk called out: "Your companion has been waiting for you for some time!" And suddenly Zhu floated down from the wall and stood there paralyzed and leaden-hearted, his eyes bulging and his legs trembling.

This second leap in the narrative is even more shocking than Zhu's entry into the wall. His subjective presence in the painting is suddenly witnessed by an objective observer, Meng. The painted wall, which for Zhu had been a point of entry into another world, has for Meng become a transparent screen through which he glimpses his friend flattened into a two-dimensional figure, trapped in the painting.[5] The description of Zhu's pose in the portrait, "standing stock-still and cocking his ear as though he were listening for something," can thus be interpreted from two angles. On the one hand, stranded in the intermediate zone, Zhu retains solely his power of hearing and can hear not only sound from inside the painting but also sound from the outside world—the monk flicking the wall. On the other hand, his friend Meng can hear nothing within the painting but has recourse only to his sight. In contrast to the vividly rendered noise and movement that Zhu perceives in the painting, the exaggerated listening pose of his portrait emphasizes the silence and stillness of the painting when viewed from the world below.

Only when Zhu has returned to the human world can he and his astonished friend communicate. The narrative backtracks again briefly to explain Zhu's last moments in the painting: "In fact, Zhu had been crouching under the bed when he heard a banging like thunder, and so he had gone out of the room to listen." Zhu, Meng, and the monk then take one final look at the painted wall: "They all looked up at the girl holding a flower: her coiled tresses were piled on top of her head and no longer hung down in tufts."

This is the final turn of the screw—all three men witness visible proof of Zhu's experiences in the painting: the change in the flower girl's hairstyle. In the strangest moment in the tale, the reader realizes that the girl's surrender of her maidenhead to Zhu is now inscribed in the painting.[6] In this last erotic twist, illusion has merged with reality. Like Oscar Wilde's novel *The Picture of Dorian Gray,* these tales are unnerving because time and experience are reflected inside a painting that should by all rights enshrine permanence and immutability. "Zhu in alarm bowed to the old monk and asked him the reason for all this. The monk gave a chuckle. 'Illusion arises from oneself; how could I explain it to you?' Zhu, oppressed by melancholy and Meng, stricken with shock, got to their feet, went down the stairs, and departed."

Illusion That Is Not Illusion

In a hilly suburb west of Beijing stands the Buddhist temple Fahai si. Built under Ming imperial patronage in 1439–44, the interior of this temple is covered with well-preserved frescoes of extraordinary

Fig. 7. Detail from a Ming wall painting in the Beijing Fahai temple of a celestial maiden holding a flower, her hair hanging down in tufts. (*Beijing Fahai si Mingdai bihua*, pl. 29)

quality. Behind the central door, at the end of a series of deities portrayed on the left section of the back wall, is a celestial maiden delicately holding a flower between two fingers, her hair hanging down in tufts. She is smiling gently and seems to gaze directly at us (see Fig. 7). To her left stand a heavenly queen and two attendant ladies, their hair piled on top of their heads in elaborate coiffures. To their left is a ferocious-looking heavenly king, heavily clad in armor (see Fig. 8). Although as far as we know Pu Songling never visited this particular temple, the Fahai si fresco gives a sense of how strongly the iconography of Buddhist wall paintings must have stimulated his imagination. With the exception of the monk (dis-

Fig. 8. The group of figures in the Ming painting on the left side of the back wall of the Beijing Fahai temple. (Drawing by Wu Hung)

cussed below), all the major Buddhist character types in the tale are present in this configuration: the seductive maiden beckoning with her flower, her elegant companions with their well-dressed hair, and the terrifying figures of celestial authority. Peering into the semi-darkness as the figures gradually emerge, we can almost visualize how the contemplation of such dazzling images sets the story into motion.

The spatial and temporal disjunction between the human world and the painting resembles that of dream and waking. The scale of the human world is magnified in the looking glass of the painting.[7] The small and deserted buildings of the real monastery are transformed into a large and bustling complex in the painted world. As in the condensation of dream time, a few minutes in the human world are the equivalent of more than two days in the immortal realm of the painting. Finally, the faint noise of a finger flicked against the wall from the human side resounds like thunder inside the painting. The temporal discrepancy between the human world and the painting is negated in the final frozen image of the girl's coiled tresses. But when viewed by Zhu in the temple, this same image also emphasizes the now-unbridgeable gulf separating the two lovers.

It is no accident that this tale about the power of illusion focuses on a painting, for like dream, painting had long symbolized the blurring of the boundaries between the real and the unreal. As the Song scholar Hong Mai wryly observed in his notation book, *Miscellaneous Jottings from Rong Studio (Rongzhai suibi):*

Beholders of the lovely vistas in this world inevitably pronounce them to be "like paintings," and so people have said, "The scenery is like a painting," "Scenery is Heaven unrolling a painting," or *"My body is in a painting."* Wondrously skillful paintings that connoisseurs sigh over endlessly, on the other hand, are always deemed "utterly real." . . . Treating the real as unreal and treating the unreal as real are both misguided positions. But so many things in life are of this sort.[8]

The viewer's sensation upon beholding a great work of art that "my body is in a painting" is realized literally in this tale, although it is Zhu's carnal desire for the girl that propels his body into the fresco rather than his aesthetic sensibilities.

The modern scholar Zhang Shaokang has demonstrated that this rhetorical tendency to liken paintings to real scenes and real scenes to paintings was noted from the Tang through at least the Ming.[9] Despite the dominance of literati aesthetic values in the Ming and Qing art world, which disparaged formal likeness and illusionism in painting, for writers of the period, painting continued to symbolize illusion that seemed more real than reality itself. This contradictory position is taken one step further in seventeenth-century commentaries to vernacular fiction: vividly rendered scenes are routinely praised for being "utterly real like a painting" (*bizhen ru hua*) or simply "like a painting" (*ru hua*). The 1632 preface to Ling Meng-chu's second installment of *Slapping the Table in Amazement* goes so

far as to defend the new realism of the vernacular story by drawing
on legends about the magical illusionism of ancient paintings:

This passage in *Records of Broad Learning* has always lingered in my mind:
"After Liu Bao painted *The Drought*, those who saw it felt hot; after he
painted *The Northern Wind*, those who saw it felt cold."[10] I have privately
wondered how a painting that was not real could do this, but I could still say
that people looking at it made it so. But what about lightning and thunder
cracking the wall after [Zhang] Sengyou had painted in the eye pupils of the
dragons? What about the five dragons painted by Wu Daozi in the inner hall
that would give off mist whenever it rained?[11] In these cases, it's not possible
to treat the paintings as real [*zhen*], but if one says they're fictional [*yan*],
well, aren't they superior to what's real?[12]

The suggestion here that the illusion of painting (and by extension
the illusion of fiction) represents something superior to reality itself
points to an underlying theme in "The Painted Wall": the contemplation of religious images as a means of reaching transcendence. As in several other *Liaozhai* tales, the imaginary journey in
"The Painted Wall" is linked to the process of enlightenment. The
old monk, who has magically supervised Zhu's experience of illusion, alone knows of Zhu's mental flight and calls him back to the
temple. But who is this old monk? Isn't it likely that he and the old
monk expounding Buddhist doctrine in the painting are one and the
same? As soon as this question arises, however, we realize that there
are not merely two monks in the story, but three. In the same temple
as the murals stands a statue of Lord Zhi (Zhi gong), a "crazy" Chan
(Zen) Buddhist monk of the Southern Dynasties who came to be
worshipped as a bodhisattva.[13] Although the statue is mentioned
only in passing, the hint is enough to suggest that the temple is
dedicated to Lord Zhi and that he controls everything happening in
the temple. Besides, the strong Chan Buddhist flavor of the monk's
last pronouncement is unmistakable. Both the monk in the hall and
the monk in the painting can be interpreted as manifestations of
Lord Zhi. A bodhisattva coming to earth to enlighten suffering
human beings is an established motif in Chinese religious folklore
and indeed is explicitly mentioned at the end of the tale by the
Historian of the Strange.

Rather than creating a religious parable in this story, however, Pu

Songling explores the paradox implicit in the conventional Buddhist wisdom that the phenomenological world is no more than illusion. If the superior mind views everything, both real and unreal, with indifference, then any idea of illusion is eliminated as well. On the other hand, to be guided beyond illusion, images must first be conjured up, and the more seductive and puzzling the images are, the more shattering and profound enlightenment will be. But in "The Painted Wall," image, though perhaps illusory, proves more powerful than religious realization.

Zhu misses all five chances at sudden enlightenment in the story. Each is described in highly symbolic language: (1) Zhu's mental and physical crisis during the raid ("having been constrained for so long, Zhu felt his ears buzzing and his eyes on fire"); (2) the clap of thunder; (3) his state of shock and loss on his return to the human world; (4) the change in the painting; and (5) the old monk's pronouncement "Illusion arises from oneself." Throughout the narrative, the forces of religion and illusion battle one another. This conflict is inherent in the image of the painted wall itself. "Facing the wall" (*mian bi*), as Zhu and Meng do at the beginning and the end of the story, is a set phrase for Chan Buddhist meditation.[14] But in this tale, the wall is covered with images so dazzling that self-realization and enlightenment ultimately pale in comparison. The story ends by telling us that "Zhu, oppressed by melancholy, and Meng, stricken with shock, got to their feet, went down the stairs, and departed." This signals a victory for image or illusion, for Zhu's melancholy at the monk's final words arises from the change in the girl in the painting. This is something seemingly beyond the power of the individual imagination or the conventional magic of a bodhisattva. The painted wall is thus "an illusion that is not an illusion" and follows the same paradoxical logic of the strange discovered in previous chapters: the dream that is not a dream and the lie that is not a lie.

In his final remarks to "The Painted Wall," the Historian of the Strange appears to support the monk's rational position: " 'Illusion arises from oneself'—this saying seems to be the truth. If a man has a lustful mind, then filthy scenes will arise; if a man has a filthy mind, then terrifying scenes will arise. When a bodhisattva instructs the ignorant, a thousand illusions are created at once, but all are set in motion by the human mind itself." The key to these remarks is the phrase "*seems* to be the truth" (*lei you dao*), which raises the possibility that this platitude may not be the entire truth.

The second half of the comment bears out this suspicion: "The monk was a bit too keen to see results.[15] But it's a pity that upon hearing his words, Zhu did not reach enlightenment, unfasten his hair, and withdraw to the mountains." Zhu does not withdraw to the mountains; his heart is too entangled with his illusions, illusions powerful enough to withstand simple rationalization or religious truth.

The Historian of the Strange's double-edged understanding of Zhu's predicament forcefully reminds us of a symbolic passage from the preface to *Liaozhai* in which Pu Songling describes himself: "I often scratch my head and muse: 'Could "he who faced the wall" have really been me in a former existence?' In fact, there must have been a deficiency in my previous karma, and so I did not reach transcendence, but was blown down by the wind, becoming in the end a flower fallen in a cesspool." Like his protagonist Zhu, Pu Songling excuses himself for not withdrawing to the mountains, despite his disappointment and self-awareness. Like Zhu, he is entangled in the power of image and illusion that defies rationalization. But out of this love of illusion he created the strange tales of the *Liaozhai* collection.

Making the Strange Legible

It is fitting to end this inquiry into *Liaozhai*'s vision of the strange with the image of the painted wall. A wall by definition is a boundary that demarcates two distinct zones, one inside and one outside. And yet, as Glen Dudbridge has pointed out, a boundary not only "defines the separation of autonomous regions, but also their point of contact."[16] The painted wall perfectly embodies this dual nature of the boundary—as a suddenly permeable membrane, it becomes the point of entry that allows Zhu to cross over into the properly separate realm of the painting, but when Zhu returns to the human world, once again through the wall, it reverts to a solid barrier dividing the two lovers forever.

Keith McMahon has called attention to the importance of the wall as a romantic topos in seventeenth-century vernacular fiction. Reminding us that as early as the *Book of Odes* and *Mencius* the phrase "jumping over the wall" signified an illicit affair, he singles out the erotic image of "a gap or breach in the wall" as setting up a classic seduction scenario.[17] In a society that practiced or at least preached the seclusion of women, walls specifically defined an interior female space forbidden to male outsiders.[18] Thus, any crack in a wall is potentially exciting and potentially invites transgression. In a number of tales in *Liaozhai,* the wall also operates in this sense—for instance, in "The Human Prodigy," as soon as Ma catches a glimpse of the runaway "girl" next door through a chink in the wall, he begins to hatch his seduction scheme. But the world of *Liaozhai* differs from the world of vernacular fiction in that openings in a wall need not already exist; they can simply materialize in response to the hero's desire and imagination. In "Jin Se" (12.1682–89), a young scholar bent on suicide spies a pretty ghost peering out from a cliff deep in the mountains. Upon his demand, a door magically opens in the smooth surface of the cliff wall to let him in.[19] "The Painted Wall" takes this principle one step further. When Zhu catches sight of the girl's image literally embedded in a wall, he does not jump over the wall or cross through any apparent breach in it—he enters the wall itself.[20]

Once inside the painted wall, however, Zhu enters another secret and forbidden interior space (the deserted chamber), whose boundary is defined by another wall through which the girl flees when she abruptly opens a hidden door in it. This second boundary too is explicitly double-sided because it acts simultaneously as a barrier imprisoning Zhu and as a conduit of escape for the girl. The presence of this new boundary, however, wipes out the memory of the old boundary for Zhu, and he can no longer remember where he belongs. Zhu's incarceration in this wall within a wall, in this world within a world, thus suggests another important property of boundaries in *Liaozhai*—their ability to proliferate and in their proliferation to efface at least temporarily the previously existing ones. It could be argued that all boundaries in *Liaozhai* implicitly contain within them further boundaries, just as all worlds implicitly nestle within them other worlds.[21]

This tendency for conceptual as well as spatial boundaries to multiply and erase themselves is brilliantly exploited in "Zhang Aduan" (5.627–31). The ghost-heroine in this tale falls ill with a serious ailment. At her sick bed, her human lover learns that she is terrified of something called a *jian*. "What are *jian?*" he asks, mystified. He is told: "When people die, they become ghosts; when ghosts die, they become *jian*. Ghosts fear *jian* just as people fear ghosts" (5.629). Although Pu Songling derived the category of *jian* from the practice of inscribing this character as an amulet to exorcise ghosts, in his hands it takes on a completely new cast.[22] By constructing an additional boundary distinguishing ghosts from *jian*, the old boundary separating the living from the dead is effectively superseded and erased. The boundaries have been redrawn so as to absorb the conventional category of the anomalous rather than to exclude it; at least, the demarcation of a new periphery increases the territory that can properly be said to belong to the center. In recognition of this shift, the ghost-heroine paradoxically dies a second death, and as a marker of her new human status, her bones are reburied with "the rites of a living person."[23]

The motif of reburial as a way to redraw boundaries and accord human status to the category of the non-human is also at work in "The Ethereal Rock." When the rock is buried the first time in the rock-lover's tomb, it is in accordance with the deceased's last wishes, as a precious object that belonged to him. But when the broken pieces of rock are buried a second time, it is on terms of equality with Xing: in willfully sacrificing itself for love, the rock has earned a final resting place for its remains in accordance with *its* last wishes. Symbolically then, the second burial marks the rock's trajectory from object to subject. The last boundary separating the rock and the rock-lover has been superseded and erased when they are joined forever in death.

As a physical as well as conceptual boundary, however, the painted wall itself can register a transformation of conventionally fixed categories. It is no ordinary blank wall, but a wall covered with images; like the text of the story itself, it is "a surface replete with significance."[24] Thus Zhu's anomalous state of being in the painting is inscribed on the wall when he is suddenly reduced to an image of himself as viewed from the world below. But this sign is only temporary; it disappears as soon as he returns to the human realm. Most important is the final and lasting image of the girl's coiled tresses on the wall, a signal that the boundaries between painting and life have not only been crossed and recrossed but also visibly changed.

The example of "The Painted Wall" alerts us that the strange (or the effect of the strange) is often produced in *Liaozhai* through the perception that conventional boundaries and categories have somehow been bent or altered even after the normal order of things has seemingly been restored. Hence the repeated emphasis on "proving" the dream that we observed in the previous chapter or Pu Songling's own "inky birthmark" that corroborates his father's dream in his self-introduction. But the need to provide some tangible sign of changing boundaries in a story is by no means restricted to dream narratives. It is one of the most powerful impulses in *Liaozhai*.

In "Zhicheng" (11.1511–15), a scholar finds himself lying drunk in a boat on Lake Dongting that has been temporarily borrowed by water divinities. Ignorant of his existence, one of the young goddesses in attendance stands beside him, and he gives way to his desire to bite the tiny stockinged foot that she unwittingly presents him. Much later in the story, long after the divinities have vanished and he has disembarked, he meets up once again with the goddess from the boat, who is wearing the same exquisite shoes and stockings fixed in his memory. To his amazement, the imprint left by his toothmarks can still be glimpsed through her stocking. Like the image of the girl's coiled tresses in "The Painted Wall," the mark of this cicatrix, which is inherently sexual in nature, bears witness to the frequent intersection of the strange and the erotic in *Liaozhai*.[25] "The Human Prodigy" twists this idea still further, for the strangeness that erupts from the permanent disturbance of gender categories in the story is ultimately marked by absence rather than presence. The tangible sign that sexual boundaries have indeed been crossed and altered is the lacuna left by the prodigy's castrated genitals, which is revealed through the probings of the village women. The ambiguous nature of this proof, however, points to the gap between signifier and signified that lies at the heart of this tale. It is the burial alongside the family tomb ("whose traces may still be found there today") befitting the prodigy's new status as concubine that closes this gap by ritually finalizing the change.

The self-reflexive tendency to physically record the strange within a narrative of the strange is particularly striking in "Gong the Immortal" ("Gong xian"; 7.895–901). In this tale, a scholar and his lover are secretly given refuge in an alternative world magically enclosed within a Daoist's sleeve.* After making love, the scholar says to his beloved: "Our extraordinary destiny today must absolutely not go unrecorded." The two lovers compose matching couplets to commemorate the miraculous occasion and inscribe them on the wall of the room inside. After the lovers part and the scholar emerges from the sanctuary of the sleeve, the Daoist takes off his robe and turns it inside out: Peering at the lining, the scholar can just make out the faint traces of characters "as tiny as lice" (7.898).[26] This startling metaphor, which yokes together such seemingly incompatible categories as lice and writing, establishes a necessary point of reference for the drastic shift in scale of the worlds inside and outside the sleeve.[27] At the same time, this figure of speech emphasizes the singular "inside-out" quality of the lovers' experience in the other world, for of course it is lice, not humans and their written traces, that properly inhabit the inner recesses of a garment. In this tale, as in "The Painted Wall," it is the character's re-viewing of a sign previously recorded in the narrative—miniaturized in the one, flattened in the other—that results in the perception that boundaries have indeed been crossed and indelibly altered. *It is this rereading that makes the strange legible.*

Liaozhai's repeated insistence on "proving" the strange within a narrative clearly takes off from the claims to historicity assumed in zhiguai and chuanqi. A conscientious attention to proving a strange occurrence, usually through uncanny correspondences, is indeed a constant throughout the Chinese literature of the strange. It is ultimately aimed at persuading the reader that something strange has taken place in the story; thus, we may think of it as part of an overall rhetoric of verification. In this respect, we can better appreciate the innovation of "A Fox Dream," which seems deliberately to refrain from providing any concrete sign in the story that could verify the nested dreams' reality. Instead, it is the narrative itself, which the author agrees to record at the end of the tale, that becomes a circular

*The sleeve is the Chinese equivalent of the pocket.

proof-mark of the strange. Here, in this extreme case, the disjunction between the proof of the strange and the writing of the strange has entirely disappeared. By dissolving the boundaries between narrative and discourse, life and text, this story points to the profoundly hybrid nature of the strange as a literary category perched between history and fiction.

As I stated in the introduction to this book, the strange as a literary category cannot be pinned down in a fixed definition or resolved once and for all but must constantly be renewed. Narratives of the strange resemble pornography in a way: just as it is notoriously easy for sexual description in literature to become monotonous and therefore lose its eroticism, its power to arouse, so it is easy for the strange to become so conventional, so predictable, that it loses its strangeness, its power to arouse amazement. When the strange becomes ossified, it is in imminent danger of disappearing altogether. Robert Campany has argued that the early Six Dynasties zhiguai writers created the strange as a new and exciting cultural category through the act of writing in common about it. Only later authors "who inherited and developed the genre," he points out, "can be accurately described as 'finding' the strange" as an already established and pre-existent category.[28] By the late Ming and early Qing, earlier zhiguai and chuanqi collections were being reprinted on a wide scale, and contemporary collections were being copiously produced; accounts of the strange inevitably began to lose their sense of novelty and to seem stereotyped both in their thematic range and literary expression.[29] Thus, even if it were still recognized that strangeness was a matter of subjective perception rather than objectively rooted in things themselves, as Guo Pu had first argued during the Six Dynasties, the strange in these works had de facto become inseparable from certain themes and certain modes of expression. The problem of the strange not appearing new or different in such literature clearly helped fuel the seventeenth-century arguments on behalf of vernacular fiction discussed in Chapter 1—the point has been reached where stories of everyday reality in everyday language are stranger than so-called "records of the strange."

The ongoing discussion has tried to show how Pu Songling continually renewed the category of the strange in his work by manipulating boundaries in many different senses. Above all Pu

Songling was working within and against the boundaries established by previous literature of the strange. The tales in *Liaozhai* could be perceived as new or different, ergo strange, because they were unfolding against a normative set of conventions and expectations developed from the vast corpus of strange accounts. Divergence is possible only when there is something to diverge from. It becomes strange for a man to enter a painting when we are prepared from reading other tales for the painting to come to life; it becomes strange for a female impersonator to be castrated and live out his days in peace when knowledge of the court case leads us to expect that he will be publicly exposed and executed. Although it could be argued that any great work in a genre defines itself by positioning itself within certain recognizable parameters and by pushing or rearranging these parameters to reshape the genre itself,[30] the need for literature of the strange to perennially arouse amazement and thwart the reader's expectations makes this process especially fundamental for a work like *Liaozhai*.

On the deepest level, the strange may take shape in *Liaozhai* through the crossing of boundaries inherent in language itself. At the end of "Gong the Immortal," the Historian of the Strange explicitly calls our attention to the literal realization of metaphor that, as in so many cases in *Liaozhai,* underlies the entire story: " 'A universe in a sleeve' is just a figurative expression [*yuyan*] of the ancients. Surely it couldn't really exist? Otherwise, how marvelous it would be!" (7.900)[31] He goes on to imagine a paradise in the sleeve, a world in which people would marry, bear children, and grow old in peace, a world with no examinations, in which even the fleas and lice in the sleeve's lining would be the microscopic equivalents of the dogs and chickens in that most famous Utopia, the Peach Blossom Spring.[32] But we could push this analogy of "a universe in a sleeve" still further: the blurring of the boundaries between literal and figurative language in *Liaozhai* results in our renewed understanding of the infinite possibilities of language enclosed in the miniature space of a text.[33] Like the universe itself, which in Chinese cosmology is considered to be in a constant state of flux and transformation, the strange and the language through which it is made legible are infinitely elastic, infinitely protean, in *Liaozhai*.

Appendix

Appendix: Translations

The Ethereal Rock (Shi Qingxu; 11.1575–79)

Xing Yunfei, a native of Shuntian, was a lover of rocks. Whenever he saw a fine rock, he never begrudged a high price. He once happened to be fishing in the river when something caught in his net. As the net began to grow heavy, he drew it out, and there was a rock barely a foot high. All four sides were intricately hollowed, with layered peaks jutting up. He was as delighted as someone who has received a rare treasure. After he got home, he had a piece of dark sandalwood carved into a stand for the rock and placed it on his desk. Whenever it was going to rain, the rock would puff out clouds; from a distance it looked as though it were stuffed with new cotton wool.

A rich bully called at his door and asked to see the rock. As soon as he clapped eyes on it, he handed it over to his muscular servant, then whipped his horse, and galloped straight away. Xing was helpless: all he could do was stamp his foot in sorrow and rage. Meanwhile, the servant carried the rock until he reached the banks of a river. Tired, he was just resting his arms on the railing of the bridge when he suddenly lost his grip, and the rock toppled into the river. When the bully learned of this, he flew into a temper and whipped the servant; then he brought out gold to hire skilled swimmers, who then tried a hundred different ways to find it. But in the end the rock was not located, and the bully posted a reward notice and went away. From then on, seekers of the rock daily filled the river, but no one ever found it.

Some time later, Xing went to the spot where the rock had fallen in. Looking out at the current, he sighed deeply. All of a sudden he noticed that the river had turned transparent and that the rock was still lying in the water. Xing was overjoyed. Stripping off his clothes, he dove into the water and emerged cradling the rock in his arms. Once he got home, he didn't dare set the rock in the main hall, but instead cleansed his inner chamber to receive it.

One day, an old man knocked on his gate and asked permission to see the rock. Xing made the excuse that it had been lost long ago. The old man smiled and asked: "Can't I at least come in?" So Xing invited him into the house to prove that the rock wasn't there. But when they got inside, the rock was once again displayed on the desk. Xing was speechless with shock. The old man patted the rock and said: "This is an heirloom that belongs to my family. It's been lost for a long time, but now I see it's here after all. Since I've found it, please give it back to me." Xing was really hard-pressed and began to argue with him over who was the owner of the rock. The old man smiled and said: "What proof do you have that he belongs to *you?*" Xing could not reply. "Well, *I* definitely recognize him," said the old man. "He has 92 crannies altogether and in the largest crevice are seven characters that read: OFFERED IN WORSHIP: ETHEREAL, THE CE-LESTIAL ROCK.

Xing inspected it closely, and in the crevice were indeed tiny characters fine as grains of rice. Only by squinting as hard as possible could he make them out. He then counted the crannies, and they numbered exactly as the old man had said. Xing had no way of refuting him. Still, he held onto the rock without giving it up. The old man smiled and then addressed the rock: "It's up to you to decide whom you belong to." He joined his hands politely and went out. Xing escorted him beyond the gate. When he returned, the rock had disappeared.

Xing raced after the old man, who was strolling at a leisurely pace and had not gone far. Xing ran over and tugged at his sleeve, begging him to give back the rock. "Amazing!" said the old man. "How could a rock almost a foot high be hidden in my sleeve?" Xing realized he was a god, and tried to forcibly drag him back home. Then he prostrated himself before the old man and implored him. "Does the rock really belong to you or to me?" asked the old man.

"It really belongs to you, but I beg you to surrender what you love."

"In that case," said the man, "the rock is certainly there." Xing went into his chamber and found the rock already back in its former place. "The treasures of the world should belong to those who love them," said the old man. "I do indeed rejoice that this rock can choose his own master. But he was in a hurry to display himself and emerged too early so that his demonic power has not yet been eradicated. I was actually going to take him away and wait three more years before I presented him to you. If you wish to keep him, you must forfeit three years of your life; only then can he remain with you forever. Are you willing?"

"I am."

The old man then used two fingers to pinch together one of the rock's crannies, which was soft like clay and closed up with the touch of his hand. After closing three of the crannies, he stopped and said: "The number of crannies on this rock now equals the years of your life." The old man then said good-bye and prepared to leave. Xing desperately tried to detain him, but he was adamant. Xing then asked his name, but he refused to say and departed.

A little more than a year later, Xing had to go away from home on business. That night robbers broke into his house; nothing was stolen except for the rock. When Xing returned, he was stricken with grief over his loss and wanted to die. Though he made a thorough investigation and offered a reward, not the slightest clue turned up.

Several years later, he went by chance to the Baoguo temple. He noticed someone selling rocks and there discovered his old possession among the wares. He identified the rock as his, but the seller refused to acknowledge his claim, so the two of them took the rock to the local magistrate. "What evidence do you have that the rock is yours?" the magistrate asked the rock seller. The man was able to recite the number of crannies, but when Xing challenged him by asking if there was anything else, he was silent. Xing then mentioned the seven-character inscription in the crevice as well as the three fingermarks. He was thus proven to be the rock's true owner. The magistrate was going to flog the rock seller, but the merchant insisted that he had bought it in the market for twenty pieces of gold and so he was released.

When Xing got the rock home, he wrapped it in brocade cloth and hid it in a casket. He would only take it out from time to time to admire it, and even then he would burn rare incense beforehand.

There was a certain government minister who offered to buy the rock for 100 pieces of gold. "I wouldn't exchange it even for 10,000 pieces of gold," said Xing. Furious, the minister plotted to implicate him on a trumped-up charge. Xing was arrested and had to mortgage his land and property to cover his expenses. The minister sent someone to hint at what he desired to Xing's son, who then communicated it to his father. Xing said he would rather die and be buried along with the rock, but in secret, his wife and son contrived to present the rock to the minister. Only after he had been released from prison did Xing discover what they had done. He cursed his wife and beat his son and tried repeatedly to hang himself, but a member of the household always discovered him and saved him in time.

One night he dreamed that a man came to him and said: "I am Mr. Ethereal Stone." He cautioned Xing not to be sad, explaining: "I'll only be parted from you for about a year. Next year on the twentieth day of the eighth month, you may go to the Haidai gate just before daybreak and redeem me for two strings of cash." Xing was overjoyed at receiving this dream and carefully made a note of the date.

Meanwhile, since the rock had entered the official's household, it had ceased its miraculous puffing of clouds, and in due course the official no longer valued it very highly. The next year the official was discharged from his post on account of some wrongdoing and sentenced to death. Xing went to the Haidai gate on the appointed day. It turned out that a member of the official's household who had stolen the rock had come out to sell it, and so Xing bought it for two strings of cash and brought it home.

When Xing reached the age of 89, he prepared his coffin and funerary garments and also instructed his son that the rock must be buried along with him. After his death, his son respected his last wishes and interred the rock in his tomb.

About half a year later, grave robbers broke open his tomb and stole the rock. His son learned of this, but there was no one he could question. Several days later, he was on the road with his servant, when he suddenly saw two men run toward him, stumbling and dripping with sweat. Staring up at the sky, they threw themselves to the ground and pleaded: "Mr. Xing, don't hound us! We did take your rock, but we got only four ounces of silver for it!"[1] Xing's son and his servant tied up the two men and hauled them off to the magistrate. The moment the two men were interrogated, they confessed. When asked what had happened to the rock, it turned out they had sold it to a family by the name of Gong. When the rock arrived in court, the magistrate found that he enjoyed toying with it. He conceived a desire for it and ordered it placed in his treasury. But as one of his clerks picked up the rock, it suddenly fell to the ground and smashed into a hundred pieces. Everyone present turned pale. The magistrate had the two grave robbers severely flogged and then sentenced them to death.[2] Xing's son gathered up the shattered pieces and buried them again in his father's tomb.

The Historian of the Strange remarks: "Unearthly beauty in a thing makes it the site of calamity. In this man's desire to sacrifice his life for the rock, wasn't his folly extreme! But in the end, man and rock were together in death, so who can say the rock was unfeeling? There's an old saying 'A knight will die for a true friend.' This is no lie. If it is true even for a rock, can it be any less true for men?"

Miss Yan (Yanshi; 6.766–69)

A certain young scholar from an impoverished family in Shuntian followed his father south to Luoyang to avoid a famine year at home. He was such a dunce by nature that although he was already seventeen he still could not write a composition. Yet he was handsome and winning, capable of witty repartee, and gifted at calligraphy. No one who met him realized he had nothing of substance inside.

Before long, his parents died in succession, and he was left an orphan completely on his own. He found work teaching schoolboys in the Luorui region. At that time there was an orphaned girl in the village by the name of Miss Yan, the daughter of a renowned scholar. From childhood, she had displayed precocious intelligence. When her father was still alive, he taught her how to read, and she was able to commit anything to memory at a single glance. In her early teens, she studied poetry composition from her father. "There is a female scholar in this family," he used to say. "What a pity she can't simply cap her hair like a man when she comes of age." He doted on his daughter and cherished high hopes of finding her a distinguished husband. After her father's death, her mother held fast to this ambition. But three years later, Miss Yan was still unbetrothed when her mother too passed away. Some urged the girl to marry a fine gentleman, and although the girl had consented, she had not yet taken any steps in that direction.

It so happened that a neighbor woman came over and struck up a conversation with the girl. The neighbor had with her some embroidery thread wrapped in a piece of paper with calligraphy on it. The girl unfolded the paper to have a look, and it turned out to be a letter in the hand of the young man from Shuntian, which he had sent to the neighbor's husband. The girl perused the letter several times and became enamored of it. The neighbor detected the girl's feelings and whispered: "He's a very charming and handsome young man, an orphan like yourself. He's the same age too. If you're interested, I can ask my man to arrange the match." The girl remained silent, but her eyes were filled with longing.

The neighbor went home and told her husband, who had long been on good terms with the young man. When the neighbor's husband mentioned the match to the young man, he was overjoyed. He had a gold bracelet[3] left him by his mother, which he presented as a betrothal gift. The couple set a date, went through the marriage ceremony, and were as happy together as fish are in water. But when the girl examined his essays, she said, smiling: "You and your writing seem like two entirely different people. If you go on in this vein, when will you ever be able to establish yourself?" Day and night she urged him to devote himself to his studies, as strict as a teacher or a concerned friend. As dusk fell, she would trim the candle, go over to the desk, and first begin chanting by herself to set a model for her husband. Only when they had heard the third watch would they stop. After more than a year like this, the young man's essays had improved somewhat, but when he sat for the examinations he failed again. His reputation was at a nadir, and he couldn't even provide for their food. He felt so desolate that he started to cry.

"You aren't a man!" scolded Miss Yan. "You're betraying your cap of manhood! If you'd let me change my hairbuns for a hat, I'd pick up an official post with ease!" Her husband was feeling miserable and disappointed. Hearing his wife's words, he glared at her and burst out angrily: "A person in the women's quarters like you, who's never been to the examination hall, thinks that winning rank and reputation is as simple as fetching water and making plain rice porridge in the kitchen! If you had a hat on your head, I'm afraid you'd be just like me!"

"Don't get so angry," she said with a laugh. "I ask your permission to switch my clothes and take your place at the next examination session. If I fail like you, then I'll never again dare to slight the gentlemen of this world!" Her husband in turn laughed and replied: "You don't know how bitter the flavor is. It really is fitting that I give you permission to taste it. But I'm afraid that if anyone sees through you, I'll become the laughingstock of the village."

"I'm not joking," said Miss Yan. "You once told me that your family has an old house in the north. Let me follow you there dressed as a man and pretend to be your younger brother. You were in swaddling clothes when you left; who will know the difference?" Her husband acquiesced to the plan. The girl went into the bedroom and emerged in male garb. "How do I look?" she asked. "Will I do as a boy?" In her husband's eyes, she seemed the spitting image of a handsome young man. He was delighted and went off to make his farewells in the village. Some friends presented him with a small sum of money, with which he purchased an emaciated donkey. The couple returned to Shuntian, Miss Yan riding on the donkey.

An older cousin of the young man's was still living there and was overjoyed when he set eyes on a pair of cousins as refined as the jade ornaments on a scholar's hat. He looked after them from dawn to dusk. When he also observed how late into the night they labored at their studies, he cherished them twice as much. He hired a little servant boy, who still cropped his hair in childish fashion, to tend to their needs, but they always sent him away after dark.

Whenever anyone from the village came to pay respects, the elder brother would emerge alone to receive them, while the younger brother put down the curtain and simply went on studying. Even after they had lived there for half a year, hardly anyone had ever seen the younger's face. If a visitor requested to meet the younger, the elder always declined on his behalf. But anyone who read the younger brother's writings was stunned by their brilliance. If some visitor forced his way in and confronted the younger brother, he would make a single bow and escape. The visitor, however, attracted by the youth's elegant appearance, only admired him all the more.

From then on the younger brother's reputation became the talk of the district. Old and honorable gentry families vied to secure him as a son-in-law who would marry into his wife's family. But whenever the cousin tried to bring up the matter, the younger brother would burst out laughing. If his cousin forced the issue a second time, then he would say: "I've set my ambitions on empyrean heights; until I pass the highest examination, I shall not marry."

When it was time for the education commissioner to administer the examinations, both brothers went together. The elder brother once again failed, but the younger, having passed first on the list for the licentiate degree, went on to sit for the prefectural examinations and passed fourth in all of Shuntian prefecture. The next year he passed the *jinshi* exam, and was appointed magistrate of Tongcheng, where he achieved a distinguished record. Before long he was promoted to censor in charge of the circuit of Henan and became as wealthy as a prince or a lord. Then he begged leave to retire on the grounds of illness and was granted permission to return home.

Would-be protegés jammed his gate, but he firmly declined to take any of them on. From the time he became a licentiate until he became famous and distinguished, he never spoke of taking a wife. Everyone thought this peculiar. After he returned to his village, he gradually purchased a number of maidservants. Some people suspected he was having an illicit affair with them, but when his cousin's wife investigated the matter, it turned out there was nothing at all improper in their relations.

Before long, the Ming dynasty fell, and the empire was engulfed in chaos. Miss Yan then said to the cousin's wife: "Let me tell you the truth: I'm really the wife of my 'elder brother.' Because my husband was a weakling and couldn't make a name for himself, in a fit of pique I decided to do it myself. I've been deeply afraid that rumors would circulate, causing the emperor to summon me for questioning, and I'd become the laughingstock of the nation." The cousin's wife refused to believe her, so Miss Yan pulled off her boots and displayed her feet. Astounded, the cousin's wife looked inside the boots and discovered they were wadded with old cotton.

After that Miss Yan arranged for her husband to assume her titles, shut her door, and secluded herself as a woman. But since throughout her whole life she was unable to conceive a child, she purchased a concubine for her husband from her own funds. "People who make an illustrious career generally buy concubines to wait upon them. I was an official for ten years, but I'm still on my own. Why do you have the good fortune to enjoy such a beauty?" Replied her husband: "Go ahead and take thirty handsome men as concubines if you wish, like that princess of the Southern Dynasties." And this circulated as a joke. During Miss Yan's tenure in office, the emperor had showered her husband's parents with honorary titles. When the local gentry came to pay their respects, they honored Miss Yan's husband with the courtesies due a censor. He in turn was ashamed of having inherited his wife's titles and was satisfied to be treated like a licentiate. It is said that he never once went out in a sedan chair with a canopy like that of a high official.

The Historian of the Strange remarks: "That parents-in-law should be granted honorary titles through their daughter-in-law can be called amazing! But what age has ever lacked censors who were women? Women who actually were censors, however, have been few. All those wearing scholar's hats in this world who call themselves men ought to die of shame!"

A Fox Dream (Humeng; 5.618–22)

My friend Bi Yi'an was an unrestrained romantic, above the crowd and content in himself. He cut a rather fleshy figure and sported a heavy beard, being well known among the literati. He once paid a visit for some reason to the villa of his uncle, the district magistrate, and retired upstairs. It was said that the building had long been haunted by foxes. Now whenever Bi had read my "Biography of Blue Phoenix," his heart always went out to her, and he regretted that he couldn't meet her even once. So he sat upstairs, lost in deep contemplation and longing for her. By the time he returned to his studio, it was growing dark. Since it was summertime and the weather extremely hot, he made up his bed facing the door.

Someone shook him out of his sleep. He awoke and looked up, and there was a woman past forty but who still retained her charms. Startled, Bi asked who she might be. She smiled and said: "I'm a vixen. Having received the honor of your deepest thoughts, I was secretly moved to accept you." Bi was delighted to hear this and made some ribaldries toward her. The woman laughed and said: "I'm afraid I'm a little too old for you. Even if you don't despise me, I'd be ashamed myself. I have a young daughter of fifteen who can serve as your wife. Tomorrow night let no one remain in your bedchamber, and she will come to you." With that, she departed.

When the next night fell, he burned incense and sat up waiting. As she had promised, the woman led in her daughter whose manner was refined and winning, without equal in the entire world. "Master Bi and you were predestined for each other," said the woman to her daughter, "so you must remain with him. Tomorrow morning, come home early. Don't be too greedy for sleep." Bi took her hand and led her through the bed curtains where all the intimacies ensued. When the act was over, she laughed and said: "Mr. Plump weighs such a lot, it's too much for any woman to bear!" And she left before it was light.

The next evening she appeared unattended and told him: "My sisters wish to congratulate the groom. Tomorrow let us go together." He inquired where they would go, and she replied: "My eldest sister is playing hostess. It's not too far from here." So the next night Bi waited for her as arranged, but since she didn't come for quite some time he began to grow sleepy. Scarcely had he laid his head upon the table than she suddenly appeared, saying, "I'm sorry to have kept you waiting so long." She took his hand and led the way. Soon they reached a large courtyard. They mounted directly to the first building, and he saw candles and lanterns glittering like stars.

Before long their hostess came out. She was about twenty, and though casually attired, exceedingly beautiful. After she had gestured politely and congratulated him, they were about to proceed to the banquet when a maid entered and announced: "The Second Lady is here." He saw a young lady between eighteen and nineteen years old enter grinning: "So my little sister has lost her cherry! I hope the groom was to her liking!" The girl rapped her shoulder with her fan and turned up the whites of her eyes. "I remember when we were children," said the Second Lady, "and we would wrestle with each other for sport. You were so afraid of a person tickling your ribs that if I even blew on my fingers from afar you'd go into hysterics. And you got so cross at me and said I'd marry a tiny prince from the land of the pygmies. I told you that someday you'd marry a bearded man whose whiskers would prick your little mouth. Today I see it's come true." The Eldest Lady laughed: "I wouldn't blame our sister for showing you her temper. Even with her new husband at her side, you've certainly lost no time in teasing her!" Soon she was urging them to be seated according to rank, and the banquet was in full swing.

Suddenly a little girl appeared with a cat in her arms. She couldn't have been more than eleven or twelve—why, her downy feathers weren't even dry yet—but her seductive beauty pierced right to the bone. The Eldest Lady spoke up: "Does our little sister also want to see her brother-in-law? There's no place for you." So she pulled her onto her lap and fed her tidbits. After a while she transferred her to the Second Lady's lap saying: "You're crushing my thighs and making them smart!"

"You're too big," complained the Second Lady. "Why, you must weigh three thousand pounds! I'm too delicate and weak to bear it. You wanted to see our brother-in-law. Since he's strong and manly, let him hold you on his more than ample lap." And she took the little girl and placed her on Bi's lap.

Sitting on his lap, she was fragrant and soft and so light that it felt as though nobody were there. Bi embraced her and they drank from the same glass. "Don't drink too much, little maid," said the Eldest Lady. "If you get drunk, you'll misbehave, and I'm afraid our brother-in-law will laugh at you." The little girl giggled and toyed with her cat, who meowed. The Eldest Lady said: "You still haven't gotten rid of her? You're still carrying around that bag of fleas and lice?"

"Let's use the feline for a drinking game," said the Second Lady. "We'll pass around a chopstick, and whoever is holding it when the cat meows will drink a forfeit."

The group followed her suggestion. But whenever the chopstick reached Bi, the cat always meowed. Bi drank heartily and downed several large goblets in succession before he realized that the little girl had been deliberately making the cat meow. They all laughed uproariously. Finally, the Second Lady said: "Little sister, go home and go to sleep. You're crushing our brother-in-law to death, and I'm afraid the Third Lady will blame *us* for it." The little girl left then, still carrying the cat.

Seeing that Bi was a good drinker, the Eldest Lady took off her hairbun cover, which she filled with wine and offered to him. It looked as though the cover could hold only a pint, but when he drank it seemed as much as several gallons. When it was empty, he examined it and discovered it was really a lotus leaf.

The Second Lady also wished to drink with him. Bi excused himself on the grounds that he could drink no more. The Second Lady then produced a rouge box a little larger than a pellet into which she poured out the wine and toasted him: "Since you can drink no more, just have this one for sentiment's sake." It looked to Bi as though it could be drained in one sip, but he took a hundred sips, and it was still never empty. The girl by his side exchanged the box for a tiny lotus cup, saying: "Don't let yourself be tricked by that wicked woman!" She placed the box on the table and it turned out to be a huge basin. "What business is it of yours?" said the Second Lady. "He's been your lover for just three days, and already you're so love struck!" Bi took the cup and instantly emptied it into his mouth. In his grasp it felt silky and soft. He looked again, and it was no glass but a silk slipper padded and decorated with marvelous skill. The Second Lady snatched it away and scolded: "Crafty Maid! When did you steal my slipper? No wonder my feet are icy cold!" And she rose and went inside to change her shoes. The girl arranged with Bi that he should leave the feast and make his farewells. She escorted him out of the village but had him return home alone.

Suddenly, he awoke. In the end, it had been a dream. And yet, he was still intoxicated, and the smell of wine was still strong. He thought this extraordinary. That evening the fox-maiden came to him and asked: "So you didn't die of drunkenness last night?"

"I had suspected it was a dream," said Bi.

The girl smiled. "My sisters appeared to you in dream because they feared you were a wild carouser. Actually, it was no dream."

Whenever the girl played chess with Bi, he always lost. "You're so addicted to this," said the girl with a smile, "that I considered you must be a player with great moves. But now I see you're just rather average." Bi begged her to instruct him, but she replied: "Chess is an art that depends on one's own self-realization. How can I assist you? If you soak it up gradually, morning and night, perhaps there will be a change." After several months, Bi felt that he had made a little progress. The girl tested him, then told him, laughing, "Not yet, not yet." But when Bi went to play with his former chess partners, everyone could feel the difference, and all marveled at it.

As a person, Bi was frank and honest and unable to keep anything buried inside, and so he let news of the girl's existence slip out. The girl learned of this and chided him: "No wonder my colleagues don't associate with wild scholars! I told you to be careful so many times, how could you do this to me?" She was about to go off in a huff, but Bi hastily apologized for his faults, and the girl was somewhat mollified. But from that day on she came less often.

Several years went by. One night she came, and they sat on a bench facing each other. He wanted to play chess with her, but she wouldn't play; he want to lie with her, but she wouldn't lie down. She sat dispiritedly for quite some time and then asked: "How do you think I compare with Blue Phoenix?"

"You probably surpass her," he said.

"I was ashamed that I fell short of her. You and Liaozhai have a literary friendship. If you would be so kind as to trouble him to write a short biography of me, then one thousand years hence there may still be one who loves and remembers me as you do."

"I've long harbored this ambition," said Bi, "but because of your past instructions, I kept it secret."

"In the past I did instruct you to keep quiet. But now that we're going to part, why should I still inhibit you?"

"Where are you going?" he asked.

"My little sister and I have been sought by the Queen Mother of the West to fill the office of 'flower and bird emissary.' I won't be able to come to you anymore. There was once someone in my older sister's generation who had an affair with your cousin. Before she left, she had borne him two daughters; today they are still unbetrothed. You and I are fortunate to have no such entanglements."

Bi implored her for some words of advice. "Keep calm and com-

mit few errors" was her reply. Then she arose and took his hand.
"Please see me off," she said. After nearly a mile, she let go of his
hand and wept. "If both of us have the intent, perhaps we'll meet
again." And with that, she departed.

On the nineteenth day of the first month, in the twenty-first year
of Emperor Kangxi's reign [1683], Master Bi and I stayed together
in Spacious Hall, and he told me this strange tale in detail. I said:
"Liaozhai's pen and ink would be glorified by such a vixen," and so I
recorded it.

The Painted Wall (Hua bi; 1.14–17)

Meng Longtan of Jiangxi was sojourning in the capital along with
Zhu, a second-degree graduate. By chance they happened to pass
through a Buddhist temple, none of whose buildings or rooms were
very spacious and which were deserted except for an old monk
temporarily residing there. When he saw the visitors, he respectfully
adjusted his robe, went to greet them, and then led them on a tour of
the temple. In the main hall was carved a statue of Lord Zhi, the Zen
monk. Two walls were covered with paintings of such exceptionally
wondrous skill that the figures seemed alive. On the eastern wall, in
a painting of the Celestial Maiden scattering flowers, was a girl with
her hair in two childish tufts. She was holding a flower and smiling;
her cherry lips seemed about to move; her liquid gaze about to flow.
Zhu fixed his eyes upon her for a long time until unconsciously his
spirit wavered, his will was snatched away, and in a daze, he fell into
deep contemplation. Suddenly his body floated up, as though he
were riding on a cloud, and he went into the wall.

He saw many layers of halls and pavilions and realized he was no
longer in the human world. An old monk was seated preaching a
Buddhist sermon surrounded by a large crowd of monks watching
him, and Zhu mingled among them. In a little while, it seemed
as though someone were secretly tugging at his robe. He turned
around, and there was the girl with her hair in tufts. She smiled at
him and walked away. He followed after her. She passed through a
winding balustrade and entered a small chamber. Zhu hesitated
outside, not daring to come in. The girl turned her head and, raising
the flower in her hand, waved it back and forth beckoning him

inside. Only then did he hasten in. Since the chamber was deserted, he immediately embraced her. She didn't offer much resistance, and so he made love to her. When they were finished, she closed the door and left, warning him not even to so much as cough and saying she'd come again that night. This went on for two days.

The girl's companions got wind of what was going on and came along with her to find the young man. "When a little boy has grown quite big in your belly, will you still be wearing your hair uncombed like a virgin?" they teased her. They presented her with hair ornaments and earrings and persuaded her to go through the married woman's ceremony of putting up her hair. The girl bashfully kept silent throughout. Finally, one girl piped up: "Sisters, we'd better not stay too long, lest a certain person be unhappy." The group giggled and went away.

Zhu looked at the girl. With her tresses piled up like clouds and some phoenix-like coils dangling, she was even more bewitching than when she had worn her hair in tufts. There was not a soul around, and slowly they entered into intimate embraces. The scent of orchid and musk inflamed their hearts, but their pleasure had not yet reached its height. Suddenly, they heard the heavy thud of leather boots and the clanging of chains and then the sound of uproar and heated discussion. The girl leaped up startled, and the two surreptitiously peered outside. They saw a gold-armored envoy, with a face black as lacquer, holding chains and brandishing a hammer, surrounded by a group of maidens. "Is everyone here yet?" asked the envoy.

"We're all here," they replied.

"If there's anyone hiding someone from the world of men, let her publicly confess; don't let her be sorry!" said the envoy.

"There's no one here," they replied again in one accord. The envoy turned around and peered eagle-like around him, as though he were going to make a search. The girl grew deathly afraid, her face turning ashen. In a panic, she told Zhu: "Quick, hide under the bed!" Then she opened a small door on the wall and abruptly darted away. Zhu crouched under the bed, not even daring to breathe. Suddenly, he heard the sound of boots come into the room and then go out again. Before long, the clamor gradually receded into the distance, and he calmed down somewhat, but there were still people coming and going and talking outside the door. Having been constrained for so long, Zhu felt his ears buzzing and his eyes on fire. The situation was almost unendurable, but all he could do was quietly strain his ears for the girl's return, for in the end he could no longer remember from where he came.

All this time, Meng Longtan was in the temple, and when in a flash Zhu disappeared, he wondered about it and asked the monk. The monk laughed and said: "He's gone to hear Buddhist doctrine expounded."

"Where?" asked Meng.

"Oh, not far away."

After a while, the monk flicked the wall with his finger and called out: "Donor Zhu, why are you taking so long to come back?" Just then Meng saw that in the painting on the wall was a portrait of Zhu, standing stock-still and cocking his ear as though he were listening for something. Again the monk called out: "Your companion has been waiting for you for some time!" And suddenly Zhu floated down from the wall and stood there paralyzed and leaden-hearted, his eyes bulging and his legs trembling. Meng was greatly shocked but calmly asked him what had happened. In fact, Zhu had been crouching under the bed when he heard a banging like thunder, and so he had gone out of the room to listen.

They all looked up at the girl holding a flower: her coiled tresses were piled on top of her head and no longer hung down in tufts. Zhu in alarm bowed to the old monk and asked him the reason for all this. The monk gave a chuckle. "Illusion arises from oneself; how could I explain it to you?" Zhu, oppressed by melancholy, and Meng, stricken with shock, got to their feet, went down the stairs, and departed.

The Historian of the Strange remarks: " 'Illusion arises from oneself'—this saying seems to be the truth. If a man has a lustful mind, then filthy scenes will arise; if a man has a filthy mind, then terrifying scenes will arise. When a bodhisattva instructs the ignorant, a thousand illusions are created at once, but all are set in motion by the human mind itself. The monk was a bit too keen to see results. But it's a pity that upon hearing his words, Zhu did not reach enlightenment, unfasten his hair, and withdraw to the mountains."

Reference Matter

Notes

For complete author names, titles, and publication data for the works cited here in short form, see the Selected Bibliography, pp. 283–300. For the abbreviations used here, see p. xiii.

Introduction

1. On Pu Songling's rhetorical uses of the historian's mode, see W. Y. Li's superb study in "Rhetoric of Fantasy," chap. 1.

2. See, e.g., DeWoskin, "Six Dynasties *chih-kuai* and the Birth of Fiction"; and Plaks, "Toward a Critical Theory."

3. See Barr, "Pu Songling and *Liaozhai*," p. 217. Qingshi shi was employed by Feng Menglong, Jishi shi by Huang Zhouxing, and Huanshi shi by Xu Yao. The last two are examples of several such pseudonyms in Zhang Chao's late seventeenth-century anthology *Yu Chu xinzhi*.

4. In this context, it is interesting that an early working title for *Liaozhai* is believed to have been *A History of Foxes and Ghosts* (*Hugui shi*) and that a Yongzheng manuscript of *Liaozhai* discovered in the 1960's but published only in 1991 bears the title *A History of the Strange* (*Yi shi*).

5. Compare the fate of *jing*, the term for "classic," which by Song times had come to designate any handbook, manual, or how-to book, as in *Ge jing* (The pigeon handbook) or *Cuzhi jing* (The cricket manual).

6. Yuan Shishuo, *Pu Songling xinkao*, p. 1.

7. Some notable exceptions are Togura Hidemi, "*Ryōsai shii*"; and Maeno Naoaki, *Chūgoku shōsetsu shikō*.

8. Until recently, most scholars accepted Lu Xun's pronouncement that *Liaozhai* represented a sudden revival of Six Dynasties zhiguai and Tang chuanqi. Barr ("Pu Songling and *Liaozhai*," pp. 196–215) has convincingly

demonstrated that the period 1500–1700 was particularly active for the reprinting of earlier compendia and the publishing of new collections.

9. Li Shizhen, *Bencao gangmu* 6: 5.112–16. According to *DMB*, p. 861, *Classified Materia Medica,* first printed in 1593, went through at least eight reprintings during the seventeenth century. We know that Pu Songling was familiar with Li Shizhen's work: he compiled a brief pharmacopoeia entitled *Prescriptions for Evil Influences* (*Yaosui shu*), whose prescriptions were adapted from *Classified Materia Medica.* See Pu Songling's preface dated 1707, "*Yaosui shu* xu," *PSLJ* 1: 61; for the text of the pharmacopoeia, see Pu Songling, *Liaozhai yiwen jizhu,* pp. 160–90.

10. *Yiqie jing yinyi,* compiled by the Buddhist monk Xuanying, *juan* 6; cited in Li Jianguo, *Tangqian zhiguai xiaoshuo shi,* p. 12.

11. Qu You, "The Regulator of the Ultimate Void" ("Taixu sikong zhuan"), in *Jiandeng xinhua,* p. 91.

12. In his survey of the book titles of Six Dynasties zhiguai, Campany ("Chinese Accounts of the Strange," p. 190) notes that the term "yi" appears with the greatest frequency, "appearing in no less than seventeen titles."

13. Feng Menglong, preamble to the "Guaidan" (fantastic) section in his *Gujin tan'gai* 1: 2.1. Several of the other classifications in this compendium also involve aspects of the strange, such as "Huangtang" (the absurd), "Yaoyi" (the demonic), and "Lingji" (the miraculous).

14. Xu Ruhan, "Preface to *The Extraordinary Adventures of Heroes Banding Together*" ("*Yunhe qizong* xu"), in Huang Lin and Han Tongwen, *Zhongguo lidai xiaoshuo lun* 1: 212. The novel in question, which has the alternative title of *A Tale of Heroes and Martyrs* (*Yinglie zhuan*), depicts the founding of the Ming dynasty.

15. In this last respect, my formulation of the strange bears some similarities to Freud's idea of the uncanny (*unheimlich*), but with the important stipulation that in *Liaozhai* the strange does not necessarily, indeed rarely, involve feelings of fear, horror, or dread.

16. Todorov, *The Fantastic,* p. 25. In his introduction to *Classical Chinese Tales,* K. Kao has attempted to apply the categories of the supernatural and the fantastic to Six Dynasties zhiguai and Tang chuanqi: "Some of the tales here may be considered as belonging to the category of the *supernatural* in that they represent phenomena that exist beyond the observable world or occurrences that apparently transcend the laws of nature; while other tales are *fantastic* because their stories involve what is supranormal or so highly extraordinary as to become unnatural, though not necessarily supernatural" (pp. 2–3). Kao's supernatural corresponds to Todorov's marvelous, his fantastic to Todorov's uncanny; he offers no equivalent of Todorov's ambiguous fantastic. Kao's clumsy distinction does not illuminate his material

very well, and he soon switches to a more helpful one based on the presence of an "esthetic of presentation" (p. 22) and the degree of "literary processing" (p. 26).

17. Brooke-Rose, *A Rhetoric of the Unreal,* p. 63.

18. W. Y. Li, "Rhetoric of Fantasy," p. 9.

19. Todorov, *The Fantastic,* p. 41.

20. The temporal confusion and omission of explicit subjects are somewhat less apparent in my retelling of the story because to be intelligible English requires more specific indications than does Classical Chinese.

21. I have been influenced here by Marjorie Garber's work on the relationship between ghosts and writing in *Shakespeare's Ghostwriters.*

22. Trans. Hawkes, *Story of the Stone* 1: 55. The novel is better known in English under the title *Dream of the Red Chamber.*

23. Campany, "Chinese Accounts of the Strange," p. 335.

Chapter 1

EPIGRAPHS: Trans. D. C. Lau, *The Analects,* p. 88 (slightly modified); Qu You, "The Regulator of the Ultimate Void" ("Taixu sikong zhuan"), in *Jiandeng xinhua,* p. 92.

1. Jauss, "Literary History as a Challenge to Literary Theory," in *Toward an Aesthetic of Reception,* p. 21.

2. *Liaozhai zhiyi huijiao huizhu huiping ben.* Zhang did modify the traditional format of the editions that he collated, for example, by moving long prefatory remarks to the end of a tale, by inserting marginalia into the text, and by eliminating the dotting traditionally used to underline favorite passages (see his "Appendix," p. 1728).

3. It is incomplete both because Zhang overlooked certain materials and because editors naturally choose writings that promote rather than ignore or disparage the work to which they are attached.

4. For example, at the end of the *Liaozhai* tale "Liansuo" (3.337), Feng Zhenluan responds to a comment by the famous seventeenth-century writer Wang Shizhen and even speculates that Wang abridged the ending of the story. Of course, no one edition had all the comments a single text might accumulate through time.

5. Opinion varies as to how much of the collection had been completed by 1679, the year Pu Songling wrote his own preface to *Liaozhai,* but the old view that the collection was almost complete when the preface was written has been effectively discredited. Instead, scholars now assume the collection was written over a period of some thirty years. For a detailed discussion of the debate, see Barr, "Textual Transmission." For a represen-

tative presentation of the old view, see Průšek, "*Liao-chai chih-i* by P'u Sung-ling: An Inquiry into the Circumstances Under Which the Collection Arose," reprinted in his *Chinese History and Literature,* pp. 92–108. For a bibliography of *Liaozhai* editions and critical studies, see Fujita Yūken and Yagi Akiyoshi, *Ryōsai kenkyū bunken yōran;* and Sasakura Kazuhiro's update, "Bunken mokuroku."

6. See Barr, "Textual Transmission," pp. 542–43, for a summary of the debate on the date of completion.

7. See Yuan Shishuo's *Pu Songling xinkao,* pp. 100–120, for a discussion of this very interesting figure. Gao Heng (*jinshi* 1643) served both the Ming and the Qing dynasties, reaching as high as examining editor in the Imperial Library (*bishuyuan jiantao*). He appears to have shared Pu's orientation toward the cult of sentiment and his interest in popular fiction and drama. Like Pu, he composed vernacular plays (*liqu*). If the attribution is correct, Gao also wrote a long and fascinating colophon attached to a copy of Pu Songling's erotic ballad "The Pleasures of Marriage" ("Qinse le") preserved at Keiō University. The ballad recounts a young girl's initiation into marriage. The colophon fervently defends it along with such masterpieces of erotic fiction as *Jin Ping Mei.* For an expurgated version of Pu's ballad under the alternative title "Guiyan qinsheng," see Pu Songling, *Liaozhai yiwen jizhu,* pp. 57–67. See Yuan Shishuo, *Pu Songling xinkao,* pp. 115–18, for a full transcription of this important colophon, which does not appear in Gao Heng's collected writings (*Qiyunge ji*).

8. See Yuan Shishuo, *Pu Songling xinkao,* pp. 121–47, for a biographical sketch of Tang Menglai (*jinshi* 1649), who also served as examining editor in the Imperial Library and was a close friend of Gao Heng's. Tang took a personal interest in the strange. A miscellaneous section (*zaji*) in Tang's literary collection (*Zhihetang ji, juan* 12) contains records of anomalies, often explained and rationalized; the *zhuan* section (*juan* 6) has a running authorial commentary by The Historian of the Old (Jiushi shi).

9. Both Gao and Tang were among the chief editors of the 1687 Zichuan gazetteer, and their writings are liberally included in it and in the 1743 gazetteer. They are also heavily represented in Lu Jianzeng's mid-eighteenth-century anthology *Guochao Shanzuo shichao.* Two selections from Tang's works appear in Zhang Chao's *Zhaodai congshu,* compiled ca. 1700; Gao Heng is featured in Wang Zhuo's *Jin shishuo,* which collects anecdotes of seventeenth-century literati.

10. Gao Heng is named as the informant of "The Monkey Spirit" ("Hou Jingshan"; 5.693); he is also mentioned in "Shang xian" (5.691), a sober account in which Gao's nephew falls ill while traveling, and they consult a fox-spirit shamaness. See Yuan Shishuo, *Pu Songling xinkao,* p. 112. Tang

Menglai is featured as the protagonist of two anecdotes involving divinities: "The Clay Demon" ("Ni gui"; 3.403) and "The God of Hail" ("Bao shen"; 1.51). As Yuan Shishuo (*Pu Songling xinkao*, pp. 121–22) notes, Pu's comments on these tales cast Tang in a highly flattering light.

11. My translation. Giles translates Tang's preface in its entirety (with a few errors) in *Strange Stories*, pp. xvii–ix.

12. *Shanhai jing jiaozhu*, p. 478. For a complete translation of this preface, see Chen Hsiao-chie et al., *Shan hai ching*, pp. 387–90.

13. Cited by Guo Pu in his preface (*Shanhai jing jiaozhu*, p. 478), quoting the "Autumn Floods" ("Qiu shui") chapter of *Zhuangzi* (p. 42).

14. Watson, *Complete Works of Chuang Tzu*, pp. 176–77.

15. Guo Pu's preface, *Shanhai jing jiaozhu*, p. 478.

16. Montaigne, *Complete Essays*, p. 78. In "It Is Folly to Measure the True and False by Our Own Capacity," Montaigne cites Cicero in support of this epistemological position: "The mind becomes accustomed to things by the habitual sight of them and neither wonders nor inquires about the things it sees all the time" (p. 133).

17. For an account of the early use of *Shanhai jing*, see Wu Hung, *Wu Liang Shrine*, p. 83.

18. "*Ertan yin*," in Wang Tonggui, *Ertan*. Wang Tonggui subsequently published an expanded version under the title *Ertan leizeng*. Jiang Yingke, a friend of Yuan Hongdao's and a member of the Grape Society (Putao she), compiled several collections of jokes and anecdotes. For a short introduction to Jiang's life and work, see Barr, "Pu Songling and *Liaozhai*," pp. 210–13.

19. For Ling Mengchu's preface (under his pseudonym Jikongguan zhuren, or The Master Who Has Reached a View of Emptiness), see Huang Lin and Han Tongwen, *Zhongguo lidai xiaoshuo lun* 1: 256.

20. In the *Liaozhai* tale "Jiaona," a fox uses the second half of the proverb to tease his human friend: "You really are 'a man of little experience, to whom everything is strange!'" (1.59)

21. Huang Lin and Han Tongwen, *Zhongguo lidai xiaoshuo lun* 1: 256. Note that Ling Mengchu's understanding of the new orientation of vernacular fiction is close to Congreve's definition of the novel in his preface to *Incognita* (1691): "Novels are of a more familiar nature; come near us, and represent to us intrigues in practice, delight us with accidents and odd events, but not such as are wholly unusual or unpresidented, such which not being so distant from our belief bring also the pleasure near us" (*Shorter Novels: Jacobean and Restoration*, p. 241).

22. His stories are not entirely free of "supernatural" elements, despite his claims to the contrary. See, e.g., Ling Mengchu, *Pai'an jingqi chuke*, no. 14.

23. Tang's arguments bear a striking resemblance to those advanced in Yu Wenlong's preface to his *Shiyi bian*. This compilation gathers together accounts of the strange from the dynastic histories, thus creating an *orthodox* zhiguai collection. The eighteenth-century editors of the *Siku quanshu* catalogue (*Siku quanshu zongmu*, p. 582) still complain that Yu was unconcerned with prognostication or scholarly issues: "All one can see is his love of the strange."

24. W. Y. Li ("Rhetoric of Fantasy," pp. 53–54) argues that in *Liaozhai*, "The demystification of the supernatural often involves a playful twist to the question 'what is really strange.'"

25. The imperially commissioned *Kangxi Dictionary* (1: 1728), completed in 1716, provides essentially the same definition for *yi:* "*Yi* means to differ from the norm." Interestingly, this dictionary omits the common political meaning of *yi* as rebellion or heterodoxy.

26. Gao's rather forced play on words and quotations taken out of context pivots on *yi* (difference) and its antonym *tong* (sameness).

27. The phrase "bound together with a single thread" is quoted from *The Analects* 15.3 (see D. C. Lau trans., p. 132).

28. Furth, "Androgynous Males and Deficient Females," p. 7.

29. Ibid., p. 8. Furth is summarizing the thesis of Henderson's *Development and Decline of Chinese Cosmology*. See Willard Peterson's modification of this view in his review of Henderson's book, *HJAS* 46.2 (Dec. 1986): 657–73.

30. This line has been the subject of much debate and is consistently refuted in prefaces to later collections of strange accounts. Qian Zhongshu (*Guanzhui bian* 4: 1252–55) reconstructs the Jin dynasty discussion, the period during which zhiguai emerged as a genre and the problem of the strange came to the fore. He demonstrates that this line was variously interpreted to account for different beliefs. Thus, one writer argued that Confucius's failure to speak of gods does not mean they do not exist; it simply meant that Confucius did not *elect* to talk about them. The statement was even taken to corroborate the existence of spirits, since the other parallel terms in the phrase, such as "strength" and "disorder," did unquestionably exist. Qian demonstrates that differences in belief coexisted in the same period and that an individual could reject one aspect of the "supernatural" but accept another. For example, the skeptic Wang Chong (27–97) of the Han refuted the belief in ghosts but subscribed to the belief in animal spirits.

31. "Fishhawks and meteors" are omens recorded in the *Spring and Autumn Annals* under the sixteenth year of Duke Xi (Xi Gong). The *Zuo Commentary* explains them as signs that Duke Xiang of Song would even-

tually fail. The *Zuo Commentary* is a lengthy narrative interpretation of the *Spring and Autumn Annals,* which fills in the historical details and spells out the moral lessons supposedly implied by the *Annals'* laconic entries.

32. For an account of this movement, see Elman, *From Philosophy to Philology.*

33. These two works are famous collections of strange accounts. The *Librarian's Miscellany (Youyang zazu)* was compiled by the Tang imperial librarian Duan Chengshi (ca. 800–863). In his preface, Gao calls the book by the subtitle of the section on marvels, "Nuogao" (a form of address for the spirits). *Records of the Listener* is the translation for Hong Mai's (1123–1202) massive compilation of strange reports, *Yijian zhi,* that Valerie Hansen employs in *The Changing Gods of Medieval China.* Yijian is the name of a mythological listener in *Liezi.*

34. The preface to *Yanyi bian,* one of the most widely read Ming romantic anthologies, argues the identical point. The preface assures us that even though Confucius summed up the *Odes* as "swerving not from the right path" (*Analects* 2.2; D. C. Lau trans., p. 63), if you have "someone not good at reading the *Odes,* he'll simply indulge himself in the lustful verses and immediately forget they're meant for moral instruction" ("*Yanyi bian* xu"). The preface is dubiously attributed to Tang Xianzu (1550–1616). In Tang's play *The Peony Pavilion (Mudan ting)* reading the *Odes* does indeed arouse the heroine's sexual desires.

In a letter from Gao Heng to Pu Songling, which Yuan Shishuo dates to 1692, Gao praises *Liaozhai* as "more original and vastly superior to *Yanyi bian.*" It seems probable that Gao Heng would have been familiar with *Yanyi bian's* preface when he wrote his preface for *Liaozhai* in 1679. Gao Heng's letter is attached to an old manuscript called *Liaozhai shiwen ji* (A collection of Liaozhai's poetry and prose) preserved at Zhongshan University in Guangzhou. For the text and dating of this letter, see Yuan Shishuo, *Pu Songling xinkao,* pp. 110–11.

35. For example, Wang Mang used the *Rites of Zhou (Zhou li)* to legitimate his usurpation of the Han throne.

36. Qixie appears in *Zhuangzi* (1.1) as either the name of the author of a collection of marvels or as the title of a collection of marvels. Scholars are divided on this issue; in later literature "Qixie" is treated both as a book title and as an author's name. Li Jianguo (*Tangqian zhiguai xiaoshuo shi,* p. 10) points out the fallacy of taking an allegorical figure like Qixie as a historical figure or his collection as an actual book.

The discourse on the strange frequently employs Qixie as a kenning for strange accounts, usually with the overtones of nonsense or tall tales. A number of strange accounts billed themselves as sequels or updates of *Qixie;*

the best known is Yuan Mei's (1716–98) *The New Qixie* (*Xin Qixie*), the alternative title to his collection, *What the Master Didn't Speak Of* (*Zi bu yu*).

37. The Ming bibliophile Hu Yinglin (1551–1602) had made the identical observation a century earlier: "But surely not everything recorded in reliable histories is solid" (*Shaoshi shanfang bicong*, p. 483). As early as the Northern Song, the Neo-Confucian philosophers Cheng Hao (1032–85) and Cheng Yi (1033–1107) (*Er Cheng ji*, 1: 20.266) had asserted that events in the *Zuo zhuan* were not entirely credible.

38. According to Barr ("Textual Transmission," p. 533), "Only a handful of tales are likely to have been censored purely for political reasons."

39. Ibid.

40. In the last slot in the collection, a position of much significance because it carries the force of a conclusion, Zhao inserted Pu Songling's own dream narrative, "The Goddess of Flowers" ("Jiang Fei"). I discuss this story in Chapter 5.

41. The passage refers to these books as "the collections of Yu Chu and Gan Bao." Yu Chu was a Western Han magician (*fangshi*) credited with writing an early book of *xiaoshuo*, a term later understood as fiction. The book is no longer extant. In recognition of his legendary association with fiction, the title *Yu Chu zhi* was given to a widely read Ming anthology of Tang chuanqi. Gan Bao (fl. 320), a Jin dynasty historian, compiled *Soushen ji*, a famous record of anomalies. Su Shi (1037–1101), poet, official, scholar, painter and arguably the most famous figure of the Song dynasty, acquired a reputation as a lover of ghost stories in later times. He compiled a collection of strange anecdotes, which was later given the title *Su Shi's Forest of Anecdotes* (*Dongpo zhilin*). See *Siku quanshu zongmu*, p. 1037.

42. "Postface Written on the Zhu edition of *Liaozhai zhiyi*" ("Shu Liaozhai zhiyi Zhu ke juanhou"). The edition was never published, and the manuscript is not extant (Barr, "Textual Transmission," pp. 521–24). The colophon survives in Pu Lide's *Donggu wenji, juan* 2. I am grateful to Yuan Shishuo for lending me a photocopy of this work. See also Yuan, *Pu Songling xinkao*, p. 232, for a partial citation and discussion of the text. Pu Lide also wrote another postface dated 1741, which was included in the first published edition of *Liaozhai* (for this text, see *Liaozhai*, p. 32). The thrust of this postface resembles that of the Zhu postface, but it is somewhat more modest and subdued in tone.

43. Pu Lide claimed that his grandfather's friend Zhu Xiang (1670–1707), who added a dedicatory poem to *Liaozhai* the year before his death, was this ideal reader. Zhu Xiang befriended Pu Songling during the 1690's. As Yuan Shishuo (*Pu Songling xinkao*, pp. 220–43) reconstructs the friendship from their correspondence and poetry, it is clear that Zhu was a great

enthusiast of *Liaozhai* and went to great lengths to obtain an up-to-date and perfect copy of the manuscript. But Pu Lide is our only source for the view that Zhu Xiang read *Liaozhai* primarily as a work of self-expression. In fact, we know that Zhu Xiang himself had great interest in the strange. *Liaozhai* twice cites a now-lost work by Zhu entitled *Records of Hearsay* (*Erlu*), and Zhu was clearly Pu Songling's informant for two additional stories (see Barr, "Textual Transmission," p. 522).

Pu Lide lacked the means to publish *Liaozhai* himself and was evidently trying to enlist the help of Zhu Xiang's sons in the project when he wrote this colophon. It is not surprising in this context that he would praise their father as his grandfather's ideal reader. But it is also probable that Pu Lide was attributing to Zhu Xiang his own feelings about the book, for they sound remarkably close to the views he expressed without reference to Zhu Xiang in his other postface to *Liaozhai* (p. 32). We should exercise caution, I believe, in taking Pu Lide's characterization of Zhu Xiang's views at face value.

44. The quotation is from the famous Mao preface to the *Book of Odes*. The translation is Owen's (*Traditional Chinese Poetry*, p. 63).

45. Another eighteenth-century colophon represents the composition of *Liaozhai* as a physical necessity: "The *qi* knotted up and filled his chest until he had no recourse but to write this book" (colophon by the pseudonymous Nancun, ca. 1723, p. 31).

46. "Mr. Pu Liuquan's Grave Inscription" ("Liuquan Pu xiansheng mubiao"), *PSLJ* 2: 1814.

47. For a biography of Zhang Yuan and the circumstances under which he came to write the grave inscription, see Yuan Shishuo, *Pu Songling xinkao*, pp. 269–74. Unlike Pu Songling, Zhang Yuan did eventually pass the provincial exams and receive the *juren* degree, but by this time (1725), he was already in his fifties. When he wrote the grave inscription for Pu some ten years earlier, he had not yet passed the provincial exam.

48. Pu Songling was born in 1640 just four years before the Manchu conquest of China established the Qing dynasty, in a small village in Zichuan county outside the city of Ji'nan in Shandong province. Born into a family of reduced means, to a father who had reluctantly abandoned hopes of a scholarly career to earn his living as a merchant, Pu Songling made a brilliant start by passing first on the list of graduates for the licentiate degree in Ji'nan prefecture at the age of eighteen. Such a degree granted him scholar status, but to be eligible for even a minor post in the state bureaucracy he needed to pass the far more competitive provincial examinations. Despite repeated attempts, he never succeeded. With the exception of a one-year stint as a private secretary to a magistrate friend in Jiangsu province during

1670–71, he seems to have passed his entire life within the confines of his native county. He managed to support himself and his family by serving as a resident tutor for wealthy gentry families in the area, most notably for the congenial Bi household where he spent the years from 1679 to 1709. He died in relative obscurity in 1715 after having received the honorary degree of senior licentiate (*gongsheng*), but as far as we know, without seeing any of his works published. For detailed and up-to-date studies of Pu Songling's life, see Barr, "Pu Songling and *Liaozhai*," pp. 105–91; Yuan Shishuo, *Pu Songling xinkao;* and Ma Ruifang, *Pu Songling pingzhuan.*

49. See Yuan Shishuo, *Pu Songling xinkao,* esp. pp. 3–25, 244–62.

50. This paradigm springs from the legend of the poet Qu Yuan (340–278 B.C.), loyal minister of King Huai of Chu. After being unjustly slandered, Qu Yuan was exiled to the wilderness of the south, where he expressed his anguish in poetry and eventually drowned himself. Readers interpreting *Liaozhai* as self-expression frequently compared it to Qu Yuan's poetry.

51. *Liaozhai,* p. 4. The biography was copied from the Zichuan local gazetteer, probably the edition of 1743. In his 1825 glossary to *Liaozhai,* Lü Zhan'en even annotated this biography as an integral part of the book.

52. *Collected Sayings from Dream Garden* (*Mengyuan congshuo*), reprinted in *ZL,* p. 365. Fang would not have known that Pu Songling did in fact leave a sizable collection of poetry and prose, for these circulated little and were published rather late.

53. For instance, the famous intellectual Wang Siren (1576–1646) explained away the weirdness of Li He's verse as the result of political frustration: "Since [Li] He was filled with 'lonely anguish' [*gu fen*] at not meeting with a proper fate, he wrote words that were spat out from his heart, and they became more sublime each day" (*Li He shiji,* p. 365).

54. "Preface to *Zi bu yu*" ("*Zi bu yu xu*"), in Yuan Mei, *Xiaocang shanfang shiwen ji* 28.1767. It is very possible that Yuan Mei was deliberately reacting against the extravagant eighteenth-century claims for *Liaozhai* as a product of self-expression. Yuan Mei's disclaimer follows almost directly his critique of Pu Songling's work: "*Liaozhai's Records of the Strange* is especially fine, but I wish it weren't so verbose!"

55. We know that Pu Songling was an avid reader of *Zhuangzi* and *Liezi.* In the preface to his lost anthology, *Excerpts from Zhuangzi and Liezi* (*Zhuang-Lie xuanlüe*), he writes: "The extraordinary writing of the past stops with *Zhuangzi* and *Liezi.* . . . I have always loved these books" (*PSLJ* 1: 54).

56. "Alas! There are indeed in this world people who look splendid on the surface [*fusheng beise*], appearing to belong to the human race. But if

you penetrate their disguise, they are far worse than ghosts and monsters; jackals and tigers would be hard pressed to emulate them!" (p. 6) The Historian of the Strange employs one of the same phrases, an allusion to the *Odes*, in his tale "Confidence Men" ("Nian yang"; 4.564): "But confidence men who prey on travelers, are these not worse than ghosts or monsters?"

57. The term *yuyan* is more often translated as "lodged words," as in the IC entry on *yuyan* (p. 946). The term originated in *Zhuangzi* to denote a specific rhetorical device: "Imputed words [*yuyan*] . . . are like persons brought in from outside for the purpose of exposition" (trans. Watson, *Complete Works of Chuang Tzu*, p. 303). Watson explains "imputed words" as "words put into the mouth of historical or fictional persons to make them more compelling." For *yuyan* as allegory, see Plaks, "Allegory," pp. 163–68; as metaphor, see Owen, *Traditional Chinese Poetry*, p. 61.

58. Postface to chap. 8. The comment is cautioning the reader to take the hero's grafting of a dog's member onto his own figuratively rather than literally. Compare Patrick Hanan's (*The Carnal Prayer Mat*, p. 131) translation of this passage: "Fiction is parable and as such, its content is obviously not factual."

59. Pu Lide ("Shu *Liaozhai zhiyi* Zhu ke juanhou," in *Donggu wenji, juan* 2) argued that *Liaozhai* resembled Qu Yuan's poetry, *Zhuangzi*'s parables, Sima Qian's biographies of the jesters, and Han Yu's allegorical "Biography of My Brush" ("Mao Ying zhuan"): "What they expressed was not the same, but their reasons for expressing themselves were the same."

60. For a transcription of the preface and a biographical sketch of Kong, see Li Xin, "Jieshao Kong Jihan." Li cites the opinion that Kong Jihan is the Kong Meixi mentioned in the first chapter of *Story of the Stone*.

61. Ibid., p. 349.

62. Ibid., pp. 349–50.

63. Chen Zhensun (fl. 1211–49), *Records from the Straightforward Studio* (*Zhizhai shulu jieti*); this excerpt is reprinted in *Yijian zhi* 4: 1821–22.

64. *PSLK* 4: 350.

65. Kong uses the appellation Fan Zhuan. I have been unable to find another such usage, but from the context, it must designate Fan Ye, the historian who compiled *History of the Latter Han* (*Hou Han shu*).

66. *PSLK* 4: 350.

67. Wang Jinfan (*Liaozhai* 7.967), another eighteenth-century editor of *Liaozhai*, is bothered by the inclusion of a straightforward morality tale, "Fourth Sister Hu" ("Hu Sijie"), in which goodness and talent triumph over snobbery and cruelty. As he comments, probably sarcastically, under the name Ziyuan: "This book records the strange. But something like the Fourth Sister affair happens the world over—how can it be considered

strange? Could it be that at the time Liaozhai was wielding his pen the customs of the world were still a bit better?"

68. *PSLK* 4: 350. *Tong,* here translated as "generalize," could also be translated as "comprehend."

69. Ibid.

70. Ibid.

71. Wang freely abridged and revised the tales and then rearranged them thematically. His edition never enjoyed the wide readership of Zhao Qigao's 1766 edition, and few copies survive. Zhang Youhe omitted it entirely from his variorum edition because it had been so liberally altered. Yuan Shishuo (*Pu Songling xinkao,* pp. 409–32) has emphatically reconfirmed the inferiority of this edition.

72. Wang Jinfan's "Preface to *Extracts from Liaozhai*" ("*Liaozhai zhiyi zhaichao* xu"), in *ZL,* p. 384.

73. Ibid.

74. On the history, sources, and techniques of traditional fiction criticism, see Rolston, *How to Read the Chinese Novel.*

75. For a biographical sketch of Dan Minglun and a discussion of his commentary, see Sun Yizhen, "Ping Dan Minglun."

76. This is Ellen Widmer's (*Margins of Utopia,* p. 90) summary of Todorov's redaction of the Russian Formalists.

77. Ibid.

78. "In writing a composition, there must not be one sentence or [even] one word which is brought in at random" (trans. J. Wang, *Chin Sheng-t'an,* p. 40). For other discussions of Jin's methods, see Irwin, *Evolution of a Chinese Novel;* Widmer, *Margins of Utopia;* and Rolston, *How to Read the Chinese Novel.* Jin's method is thought to derive most directly from the analysis of formal essays, but it amalgamated many different forms of commentary and criticism.

79. For example, Dan Minglun treats *Liaozhai* as a unified work and tries to uncover the hidden significance of the placement of the first and last stories in the collection. In the Zhao edition that he worked with, "Examination for the Post of City God" ("Kao chenghuang") came first and "The Goddess of Flowers" came last; see his comments at *Liaozhai* 1.3 and 2.746. For a good example of Jin's influence on Dan's analysis of a particular story, see his elaborate comment to "Wang Gui'an," 12.1637.

80. *Shuihu zhuan huiping ben* 1: 22.

81. Trans. J. Wang, *Chin Sheng-t'an,* p. 26.

82. "Preface to *Yu's Tripods*" ("*Yuding zhi* xu") in Huang Lin and Han Tongwen, *Zhongguo lidai xiaoshuo lun* 1: 122. According to the editors, this book is lost and only the preface survives in a posthumous collection of Wu Cheng'en's writings.

83. Li Zhi, *Fen shu*, pp. 98–99.

84. He Tongwen's 1837 "Preface to the Annotated *Liaozhai*" ("Zhu *Liaozhai zhiyi* xu") in Huang Lin and Han Tongwen, *Zhongguo lidai xiaoshuo lun* 1: 565–68), contends that since *Liaozhai* is composed in the allusive literary language, it is even *better* suited than vernacular fiction as a pedagogic manual for the classics and histories.

85. In Jin's case, commentary turned into authorship because he freely altered the text he was working on. In *The Water Margin*, he chopped off the last fifty chapters or so and wrote an entirely new ending. Fortunately, the *Liaozhai* commentators did not follow his example in this regard.

86. On several occasions, Feng Zhenluan explicitly cites Jin in his commentary. Following an ingenious description of a mosquito hunt in "The Miniature Hunting Dog" ("Xiao liegou"), he exclaims: "If Jin Shengtan had seen this, he'd have poured himself a huge cup of wine and said: 'Isn't this delightful?'" (4.529) Regarding the tale "Wang Gui'an," Feng remarks: "As [Jin] Shengtan said: 'If the writing isn't dangerous, it isn't felicitous.' This is extremely dangerous and extremely felicitous!" (4.1635)

87. Even this argument is not new. Mei Dingzuo (1549–1618; *DMB*, pp. 1057–59) defended his compilation of poetry by ghosts, *Caigui ji*, on essentially the same grounds: "It's exactly like Su Shi's wanting people to tell ghost stories—why in the world double-check them? Just consider such things as literary writing and be done!" (untitled preamble following the table of contents to the 1605 edition)

88. "Reading Instructions for the Fifth Book of Genius" ("*Diwu caizi shu dufa*"), in *Shuihu zhuan huiping ben*, p. 16. Jin defines history as "literature that conveys events" (*yi wen yun shi*); fiction as "literature that invents events" (*yi wen sheng shi*).

89. Bush and Shih translate the original anecdote from *Han Fei* in *Early Chinese Texts on Painting*, p. 24:

There was a retainer painting for the King of Ch'i, whom the King of Ch'i asked: "What is most difficult in painting?" He replied: "Dogs and horses are most difficult." "What is easiest?" He replied: "Demons and goblins are easiest. Since dogs and horses are things known by man, visible before us the day through, they cannot be completely simulated and thus are difficult. Demons and goblins are without form, and not visible before us, hence they are easy."

90. For two seventeenth-century examples, see Ling Menchu's "Organizing Principles" ("Fanli") to *Pai'an jingqi chuke* and Li Yu's essay "Against Absurdity" ("Jie huangtang") in his *Xianqing outan* 7: 18.

91. Feng paraphrased the charge as "Nothing is easier to tell of than a phantom; nothing is harder to tell of than a tiger" (*Liaozhai*, p. 13). He may well have had in mind Jin Shengtan's praise of the realism of Wu Song's fight with the tiger in *The Water Margin*.

92. Sheng Shiyan's 1793 colophon to the *No Harm in Listening* (*Guwang ting*) installment of Ji Yun's *Yuewei caotang biji* 18.18; also in *ZL*, pp. 604–6. Ji Yun's genres correspond to what we now usually call zhiguai and chuanqi. See Barr, "Pu Songling and *Liaozhai*," pp. 192–93, for a discussion of the historical inaccuracy of Ji Yun's pronouncement. The idea that mixing these two genres constituted a breach in decorum seems to have been of eighteenth-century origin. In my opinion, the separation of long and short narratives in the first published edition of *Liaozhai*, which placed zhiguai items at the end, may reflect this eighteenth-century taste.

93. Lu Xun, *Brief History of Chinese Fiction*, p. 262.

94. For a similar epistemological controversy in the history of English literature, see McKeon, in *Origins of the English Novel*, p. 53. "In 17th century prose narrative, verisimilitude and the claim to historicity are incompatible and competitive . . . expressions of that epistemological revolution."

95. Trans. Ellen Widmer, "*Hsi-yu cheng-tao shu* in the Context of Wang Ch'i's Publishing Enterprise," p. 45. The letter was written by Wang Qi and published in his first letter collection, *Chidu xinyu*, in 1663.

96. The view that Pu Songling "used ghosts as a game" appears in Liu Yushu's (Liu Qingyuan's) miscellaneous notes, *Commonplace Conversations* (*Chang tan*): "Someone said: 'Pu Songling must have had legions of ghosts and foxes in his breast.' I say that Pu Songling was the only one without a single ghost or fox in his breast. Don't let him fool you!" (See the relevant excerpts, based on a 1900 edition, in *ZL*, pp. 614–15.) For the fictional understanding of *Liaozhai* that these remarks imply, see Maeno Naoaki, *Chūgoku shōsetsu shikō*, pp. 348–49. According to Maeno, *Chang tan* was written "about one hundred years after Pu Songling."

97. Here I would also include Wang Shizhen, who declined Pu Songling's request to write a preface to *Liaozhai* but contributed a dedicatory quatrain and a number of evaluative comments.

98. See *n*43 to this chapter.

99. The same expression appears in He Tongwen's 1837 preface to *Liaozhai* (Huang Lin and Han Tongwen, *Zhongguo lidai xiaoshuo lun* 1: 566). I suspect it was a common metaphor for commentary.

Chapter 2

EPIGRAPH: Garber, *Shakespeare's Ghostwriters*, p. xiv.

1. See Chapter 1, n5. The text of "Liaozhai's Own Record" appears immediately after the table of contents in Zhang Youhe's edition and is paginated separately, pp. 1–3. I acknowledge a stylistic debt to Giles, who translates the preface in *Strange Stories*, pp. xii–xiii.

2. For a representative interpretation, see Huang Lin and Han Tongwen's analysis of Pu Songling's preface in *Zhongguo lidai xiaoshuo lun* 1: 360–65.

3. In particular, modern critics usually single out this line: "Draining my winecup and grasping my brush, I complete the book of 'lonely anguish.' How sad it is that I must express myself like this!" They then compare it with a couplet extracted from a 1671 poem entitled "Stirred by Anguish" ("Gan fen"): "New stories are added to *Records of the Listener.* / A gallon of wine cannot wash away my grievous sorrow" (*PSLJ* 1: 476).

4. These are poetic and exotic plants, literary allusions in Pu Songling's day rather than references to any real vegetation. Bao Yu makes this point in a wonderful discussion in chap. 17 of *The Story of the Stone:* "A lot of these rare plants are mentioned in *Li Sao* and *Wen xuan.* . . . Of course, after all these centuries nobody *really knows what all those names stand for.* They apply them quite arbitrarily to whatever seem to fit the description" (my italics; trans. Hawkes, 1: 340).

5. The very concept of strangeness as a desirable literary quality may initially have emerged to legitimate the originality of the *Songs of the South* and its deviance from the Confucian canon as represented by the *Book of Odes.* See Liu Xie's (465–520) chapter "Evaluating the Sao" ("Bian sao"), *Wenxin diaolong xuanzhu,* pp. 41–49, which names "Li sao" as the paradigm of "marvelous writing." The chapter lists four qualities that differentiate "Li sao" from the canon: "outlandish diction" (*guiyi zhi ci*), "weird discourse" (*jueguai zhi tan*), "obscenity" (*huangyin zhi yi*), and "sordid intent" (*juanxia zhi zhi*). See also P. Yu, *Reading of Imagery,* p. 106.

6. Zhou Zizhi, "Preface to Yuefu Poets New and Old" ("*Gujin zhujia yuefu* xu") in *Li He shiji,* p. 362.

7. The two poems are "Autumn in the Boudoir, in Imitation of Li He" ("Qiugui, ni Li Changji"), *PSLJ* 1: 488; and "Mawei Hillock [the site of Yang Guifei's grave], in Imitation of Li He" ("Mawei po, ni Li Changji"), *PSLJ* 1: 499. The first poem is a generic boudoir poem. The second poem closely imitates Li He's "The Grave of Little Su Xiaoxiao" ("Su Xiaoxiao mu") in both prosody (a preponderance of three-character lines) and subject matter (the burial site of a beautiful woman and her ghostly apparition). The resemblance is most discernible in these lovely lines:

> Fog becomes sinew, ice becomes bone.
> Yellow pine-flowers stain her gauze stockings;
> Tinkling pendants dissolve with the mist.

8. *Youming lu* is a zhiguai collection attributed to Liu Yiqing (403–44) of the Southern Dynasties, the same prince under whose aegis *Shishuo xinyu* was compiled. Pu Songling has altered the second character in the original title (*ming*, bright) to its homophone (*ming,* dark, underworld), probably to enhance the gloominess of this line.

9. "Yizhi xu," *Yijian zhi,* p. 185. On the many reprints of this collection during the late Ming, see Barr, "Pu Songling and *Liaozhai,*" pp. 197–98.

10. Certeau charts the basic premises of travel literature in his essay "Montaigne's 'Of Cannibals,' " in *Heterologies,* p. 69. See also Campany's ("Chinese Accounts of the Strange," p. 85) discussion of zhiguai and collectors: "Spatially, the collector embarks on a pilgrimage of curiosity and wonder. . . . from the fixed, stable center into a wild, undomesticated terrain and back again."

11. It is worth recalling here the etymology given in the *Shuowen,* a first-century A.D. dictionary, for the character *shi* (history, historian): "The person who records events. His hand holds onto the center; the center means what is correct." Hence the term for unofficial history, *waishi,* which comes to connote fiction. On historical writing as "the discourse of authority" in China, see W. Y. Li, "Rhetoric of Fantasy," pp. 22–25. On the importance of the idea of the center in records of the strange, see Campany, "Chinese Accounts of the Strange," pp. 77–94.

12. I am inspired here by Certeau's (*Heterologies,* p. 69) insights into travel literature: "First comes the outbound journey: the search for the strange, which is presumed to be different from the place assigned it in the beginning by the discourse of culture."

13. *The Geography of the Imagination* is Guy Davenport's title for his 1981 collection of essays.

14. Campany ("Chinese Accounts of the Strange," p. 94) characterizes this attitude to the strange as "anti-locative"—"The distancing of the ordinary and the familiar, its revelation of a foreignness even in what is near."

15. "Preface to *A Catalogue of Ancient Inscriptions*" ("*Jigu lu mu xu*"), 1063, in *Ouyang Wenzhonggong quanji* 41.7a–8a.

16. Wu Cheng'en, "*Yuding zhi* xu," in Huang Lin and Han Tongwen, *Zhongguo lidai xiaoshuo lun* 1: 122.

17. I explore at length the paradigm of obsessive collecting and its importance for *Liaozhai* in Chapter 3.

18. See "Liu Liangcai" (6.798–99); "The Hungry Ghost" ("E gui"; 6.819); and "Yu Qu'e" (9.1166–72). Feng Zhenluan ("Du *Liaozhai* zashuo," in *Liaozhai,* p. 10) relates the story of a man from Shandong said to be Pu Songling's incarnation—his birth was foretold when *his* father dreamed of an old scholar who was holding reeds (*pu*) and standing under a willow tree (*liu*) next to a spring (*quan*). Together these punned objects spell Pu Liuquan, one of Pu Songling's sobriquets.

In *The Confucian's Progress* (pp. 164, 174), Wu Pei-yi mentions two Ming autobiographies in which the subject's mother dreamed about a monk on the day her son was born. Du Wenhuan's mother supposedly dreamed that a monk in a white robe ascended into the hall while shaking his staff; Mao Qiling's mother is said to have dreamed that a foreign monk came into her chamber and hung a certificate on the wall. Both reveal the archetypal nature of the dream ascribed to Pu Songling's father. For further examples of omens dreamed before a relative's birth, see Fang-tu, "Ming Dreams," p. 53.

19. Yuan Shishuo cites and discusses this letter, which also praises *Liaozhai*'s stylistic excellence, in *Pu Songling xinkao*, pp. 110–11; see Chapter 1, n34. Yuan points out that Gao Heng's heightened interest in the didactic uses of *Liaozhai* reflects his own preoccupations in his old age.

20. I follow W. Y. Li's translation of this phrase ("Rhetoric of Fantasy," p. 42).

21. Burton Watson translates *gu fen* as "the sorrow of standing alone." See his discussion and translation of Sima Qian's theory of literature in *Ssuma Ch'ien*, pp. 155–57.

22. Li Zhi, "Preface to *The Water Margin*" ("*Zhongyi Shuihu zhuan* xu"), in *Fen shu*, p. 109.

23. Confucius may be echoing the lovely lines from the *Odes* (Mao 65; trans. Waley, *Book of Songs*, p. 306):

> I go on my way, bowed down
> By the cares that shake my heart.
> Those who know me
> Say, 'It is because his heart is so sad.'
> Those who do not know me
> Say, 'What is he looking for?'

24. Trans. D. C. Lau, *Mencius*, p. 114 (slightly modified). Confucius's remark concludes: "Those who condemn me will also do so through the *Spring and Autumn Annals*."

25. Du Fu, *Du shi xiangzhu*, 2: 556. I have consulted Hawkes's translation in *Little Primer of Du Fu*, p. 92. In the *Liaozhai* tale "White Autumn Silk" ("Bai Qiulian"; 4.1488), the poetry-loving carp-heroine informs her husband that reciting Du Fu's "Dreaming of Li Bo" over her corpse will resurrect her from the dead.

26. See esp. "Being Moved on One Occasion" ("Ou gan," *PSLJ* 1:503, dated 1673), which concludes:

> My greatest regret in life
> Is the absence of a true friend.
> For if I had one true friend,
> Why need I grieve over failure?

27. The commentator is Feng Zhenluan (*Liaozhai* 1.85): "I say that in this piece Liaozhai is writing his own brief autobiography; that is why it is

recounted with so much pain." Similarities between the comment and the preface include the phrases about being laughed at by ghosts and scratching one's head in self-pity, the overall emotional intensity and pathos, and the use of parallel prose.

28. Wang Shizhen, *Chibei outan,* p. 6. Pu Songling was acquainted with Wang Shizhen but, as far as we know, never visited him or participated in his convivial gatherings. For an account of their relationship, see Yuan Shishuo, *Pu Songling xinkao,* pp. 187–219. I discuss the relationship at greater length in Chapter 5.

29. Wang Shizhen, *Chibei outan,* p. 6.

30. Of course, Pu Songling was by no means the only seventeenth-century author to dwell on the act of writing in his preface to a work or to suggest that it was composed in isolation and anguish.

31. Hervouet, "L'autobiographie," p. 111.

32. Guo Dengfeng, *Lidai zishuzhuan wenchao.* The "independent self-introduction" (*dandu zixu*) is another of his categories. Not all prefaces to a work written by the author himself are autobiographical in intent; the term *zixu* is ambiguous because it designates both any preface by the author himself and an autobiographical preface.

33. Wu Pei-yi, *The Confucian's Progress,* p. 166.

34. For an excellent discussion of *Liaozhai*'s formal debt to *Records of the Historian,* see W. Y. Li, "Rhetoric of Fantasy," chap. 1.

35. Emperor Wu of the Han sentenced Sima Qian to castration for supporting a defeated general in court. For a translation and discussion of "The Postface of the Grand Historian," see Watson, *Ssu-ma Ch'ien,* pp. 42–69.

36. Owen, "The Self's Perfect Mirror," p. 74.

37. See "A Biographical Account of [My Wife)] Miss Liu" ("Shu Liushi xingshi"), *PSLJ* 1: 250–52; and "Preface to *Sayings for Self-examination*" ("*Xingshen yulu* xu"), *PSLJ* 1: 60–61. In general, Chinese writers seem to expose more details about their private life when writing about someone else (especially a dead relative) than when writing about themselves.

38. "To 'know oneself' is to know oneself as other, a disjunction between the knower and the known . . . the act of autobiography irrevocably divides and subdivides the assumed unity of the self" (Owen, "The Self's Perfect Mirror," p. 74).

39. Of course, in offering earlier examples to illustrate his theory that literature is the product of suffering and indignation, Sima Qian also created a literary genealogy for himself.

40. See Wu Pei-yi, "Self-examination." In the overabundance of motives and darkness of tone, Pu Songling's preface vaguely resembles the Ming

loyalist Zhang Dai's confessional preface to his *Tao'an mengyi*. See Owen's discussion of this piece in *Remembrances*, pp. 135–36.

41. Yanling is the name of a mountain in present-day Zhejiang province. Taken literally as "steep funeral mounds," it adds to the rather ominous flavor of the opening.

42. Although there is no pronoun in this line, the sudden shift and empassioned declaration suggest direct address. Here Yu Ji's diction even seems to mimic Pu Songling's preface (*Liaozhai*, p. 3): "I vainly compose a sequel to *Records of the Underworld* [*You*ming zhi lu]. How sad [*bei*] it is that I must express [*jituo*] myself like this!" Yu Ji's exclamations repeat and embellish Pu Songling's self-appraisal: "How miserable and alone you must have been to entrust your intent [*tuo* zhi] so far beyond this world [*you* xia]. . . . I grieved deeply [*bei*] for this man's intent" (p. 6).

43. Gao Fenghan, who later became famous as one of the Eight Yangzhou Eccentrics (*Yangzhou baguai*), met Pu Songling some time between 1697 and 1699, when his father, Gao Yuegong (*juren* 1675), was serving as official instructor (*jiao yu*) in Zichuan. Although only in his teens, the precocious Gao Fenghan came to know most of the notable men in Zichuan's intellectual and artistic circles, several of whom were also close friends of Pu Songling's. See Li Jinxin and Guo Yu'an, "Gao Fenghan nianpu," pp. 280–81, 290–92. Gao's dedicatory verses for *Liaozhai* are preceded by a colophon dated 1723, which is omitted from Zhang Youhe's edition of *Liaozhai*. See Li Jinxin and Guo Yu'an, "Gao Fenghan nianpu," p. 297, for a transcription of the colophon. Based on Gao's own reckoning in the verses that his meeting with Pu Songling had taken place about twenty years previously, the authors of Gao's *nianpu* date the meeting to 1699, the last year Gao's father held office in Zichuan. Unfortunately, they erroneously calculate Pu Songling's age as 69 rather than 59 at the time.

Chapter 3

EPIGRAPH: *Yuan Hongdao ji*, p. 826.

1. Wang Qishu, *Shuicao qingxia lu*, quoted in Wang Xiaochuan, *Yuan Ming Qing sandai jinhui xiaoshuo*, p. 314. A portion of this chapter, with a somewhat different emphasis, appeared in my article "The Petrified Heart: Obsession in Chinese Literature, Medicine, and Art" in *Late Imperial China*.

2. Zhang Zilie, *Zhengzi tong*, wuji 24a. This dictionary was based on Mei Yingzuo's (1570–1615) *Lexicon* (*Zihui*), printings of which were still extensive ca. 1691. *DMB* (pp. 1061–62) calls *Zhengzi tong* "the most successful of a large number of vulgate versions of the *Tzu-hui* [*Zihui*] which circulated widely in late Ming and early Qing times and which dominated both

popular and professional Chinese lexicography until the *K'ang-hsi tzu-tien* [Kangxi dictionary] became available." The *Kangxi Dictionary* cites *Zhengzi tong*'s definition of pi. I am indebted to Mi-chu Wiens for calling my attention to the importance of Mei Yingzuo's work.

3. Unschuld, *Medicine in China: Pharmaceutics*, p. 20.

4. Chao Yuanfang, *Zhubing yuanhou lun* 20.113. This section introduces eleven varieties of pi diseases, including *pijie* (pi nodules), *yinpi* (fluid-induced pi), *hanpi* (cold-induced pi), and *jiupi* (chronic pi). On Chao Yuanfang, see *Zhongyi dacidian*, p. 233.

5. Wang Tao, *Waitai biyao* 12.329. See the entry "Pi ying ru shi fu man." This book synthesizes many pre-Tang works, including *Zhubing yuanhou lun*, whose discussion of pi is quoted verbatim at 12.321. For further information on this book, see *Zhongyi dacidian*, p. 53.

6. *Pi* written with the "person" radical has a long history in its own right extending back to the *Odes* (*Mao shi*, no. 254) and the *Jiu zhang* in *Chu ci*.

7. "No. 10: Connoisseurship" ("Shi: haoshi"), *Pingshi*, p. 846. "Peach Blossom Spring" alludes to a hidden utopian community in Tao Yuanming's famous account. For a complete French translation and discussion of *Pingshi*, see Vandermeesch, "L'arrangement de fleurs en Chine." Vandermeesch defines pi (written with the "person" radical) as "designating at once that which is distant and vague and that which diverges from the normal path."

8. *Shishuo xinyu* 4.15, p. 199; trans. Mather, *New Tales of the World*, p. 185. *New Tales* has no specially designated category for obsession. The term "pi" occurs only once in Liu Xiaobiao's early sixth-century commentary to the work and even *shi* (a taste for) occurs only rarely. The characters most commonly used to describe fondness or attachment are *hao* (to be fond of) and, less often, *ai* (to like, to love); *bing jiu* (to be addicted to liquor) is employed once.

9. Zhang Yanyuan, *Records of Famous Paintings Through the Ages* (*Lidai minghua ji*), in Yu Jianhua, ed., *Zhongguo hualun leibian* 2: 1225–26. Trans. Bush and Shih, *Early Chinese Texts on Painting*, pp. 73–74 (modified).

10. "*Jigu lu mu* xu," in *Ouyang Wenzhonggong quanji* 41.7a–b.

11. *Ouyang Wenzhonggong quanji* 40.1. For a translation of this essay, see Egan, *Literary Works of Ou-yang Hsiu*, pp. 217–18.

12. Ye Mengde, "*Pingquan caomu ji* ba"; trans. Hay, *Kernels of Energy*, p. 34.

13. Su Shi, "On the Hall of Precious Paintings" ("Baohuitang ji") in Yu Jianhua, *Zhongguo hualun leibian* 1: 48. I have modified Bush and Shih's translation in *Early Chinese Texts on Painting*, p. 233. Su Shi probably borrowed his concept of "lodging" from Ouyang Xiu's autobiographical essay,

"The Old Drunkard's Pavilion" ("Zuiweng ting ji,") (*Ouyang Wenzhonggong quanji* 39.9–10; trans. Egan, *Literary Works of Ou-yang Hsiu*, p. 216): "The Old Drunkard's real interest is not the wine but the mountains and streams. Having captured the joys of the mountains and streams in his heart, he lodges them in wine."

14. The locus classicus of the phrase *youwu* is *Zuo zhuan* Zhao 29 in which it refers to beautiful women: "Where there are beautiful creatures [*youwu*], they are capable of perverting men. Unless virtue and righteousness prevail there will surely be disaster" (trans. Dudbridge, *Tale of Li Wa*, p. 69).

15. Both men were powerful Tang chief ministers who were disgraced and executed. According to the editor of *Li Qingzhao ji*, Wang Bo must be an error for Wang Ya (ca. 760–835), who was renowned as a connoisseur of books and paintings. His collection was destroyed after his fall from power. Yuan Zai, who accumulated great wealth during his tenure in office, was executed in 777. An official raid on his home unearthed a cache of 800 piculs of pepper.

16. In a famous anecdote in the sixth-century commentary to *Shishuo xinyu* 20: 4, the scholar and general Du Yu tells the emperor that He Qiao has "an obsession with money"; he himself has "an obsession with the *Zuo Commentary*" (p. 381). Mather (*New Tales of the World*, p. 359) translates pi as "a weakness for."

17. "Postface to *Records on Stone and Bronze*" ("*Jinshi lu* houxu"), in *Li Qingzhao ji*, pp. 176–77.

18. For a partial translation and close reading of the postface, see Owen, *Remembrances*, pp. 80–98.

19. Ouyang Xiu, "Biography of the Retired Scholar of Six Ones" ("Liu-yi jushi zhuan"), in *Ouyang Wenzhonggong quanji* 44.7a–b. For a translation, see Egan, *Literary Works of Ouyang Hsiu*, pp. 217–18.

20. Xie Zhaozhe, *Wu za zu* 7.299. In an adjacent passage (7.296), Xie observes that human tastes and preferences have always differed and then erects a hierarchy of preferences drawing on historical examples. In the highest group he includes such benign passions as a fondness for roaming in scenic spots and for books one has never heard of before. This kind of thing, says Xie, "comes from natural disposition and doesn't warrant being considered an illness." His second group includes more problematic activities: a fondness for ox fights, braying like a donkey, and a love of rocks. "These," in Xie's words, "already verge on obsession, but are not yet harmful." Moving down the ladder, Xie covers weirder passions in his third category, such as a fetish for cleanliness, for taboo characters, and for ghosts. Here Xie allows himself a practical quibble: "These present obstacles for getting

along in the world." But he draws the line at his final category, eating filth and a taste for foot-bindings: "This is too much!"

21. Tang Binyin (1568–ca. 1628; *jinshi* 1595), "A Short Preamble to *History of Obsession*" ("*Pishi* xiaoyin"), in Hua Shu, *Pidian xiaoshi*. On Hua's publications, see Wang Zhongmin, *Zhongguo shanbenshu tiyao*, pp. 421, 425–26. Tang Binyin must have been a friend of Hua Shu's because we find a preface to Hua Shu's collected works ("Hua Wenxiu *Qingshuige ji* xu") in Tang Binyin's *Shui'an gao, juan* 5. Hua Shu reused part of Yuan Hongdao's famous essay on connoisseurship from *Pingshi* as Yuan Hongdao's preface to *Pidian xiaoshi*. I see no reason to doubt the attribution to Tang Binyin, although the preface to *Pishi* is not found in his *Shui'an gao;* it is possible that for this preamble, too, Hua Shu recycled some already existing essay of Tang Binyin's.

22. *Yuan Hongdao ji,* p. 846.

23. Zhang Dai, "The Obsessions of Qi Zhixiang" ("Qi Zhixiang pi"), in *Tao'an mengyi,* p. 39. Zhang was so taken with this aphorism that he repeated it in another piece, "The Biographies of Five Extraordinary Men" ("Wu yiren"), in *Langhuan wenji, juan* 4.

24. Zhang Chao, *Invisible Dream Shadows* (*Youmeng ying*) 164.6. After this work had been completed, Yagi Akiyoshi's article "Fools in *Liaozhai zhiyi*" ("*Ryōsai shii* no 'chi' ni tsuite") was brought to my attention. Yagi draws upon a number of the same sources to explore the close relationship between folly and obsession in Ming-Qing thought and the influence of this relationship on Pu Songling and *Liaozhai;* see esp. pp. 91–96.

25. Each of these famous connoisseurs was proverbial for his obsession. Yuan Hongdao's comment appears after the entry on obsessions with rocks ("shi pi") in Hua Shu's *Pidian xiaoshi*. Feng Menglong included an abridged version of Yuan's comment in his *Gujin tan'gai* 9.426. To avoid redundancy in English, I have followed Feng's abridgment in the last line of my translation.

26. Barr, "Pu Songling and *Liaozhai,*" p. 217.

27. Hanan, *Chinese Vernacular Story,* p. 79.

28. The development of this new conception of qing is still inadequately understood, but is generally ascribed to the influence of Wang Yangming's (1472–1529) thought. The best discussion of the Ming philosophical influence underlying qing in literature is W. Y. Li, *Enchantment and Disenchantment*.

29. *Qingshi leilüe* 23.17a. The comment is probably by Feng Menglong, who is thought to have published *Qingshi leilüe* under the pseudonym Zhan-zhan waishi. For a discussion of the authorship and contents of this book,

see Hanan, *Chinese Vernacular Story,* pp. 95–97; and Mowry, *Chinese Love Stories.* Barr ("Pu Songling and *Liaozhai,*" pp. 216–17) points out that the pseudonym Historian of Love parallels Pu Songling's Historian of the Strange and demonstrates that Pu was familiar with *Qingshi.* The resemblance between Pu's commentary and Feng's commentary goes even further; they sometimes express similar opinions, sometimes in similar language.

30. Tang Binyin, "*Pishi* xiaoyin," in Hua Shu, *Pidian xiaoshi.*

31. Gu Wenjian, *Fuxuan zalu,* under the entry "personal taste" ("xingshi") in *Shuo fu* 2.1319–20. The close connection between *shi* (a taste for), one of the main graphs associated with obsession, and food is indicated by the presence of the "mouth" radical. The Tang-Song encyclopedia *Bai-Kong liutie* places its entry on obsession in the food section under the heading "predilections" ("shihao") and primarily lists bizarre eating habits. The Song encyclopedia *Taiping yulan* also uses the heading "shihao," but it subsumes non-food-related obsessions in this category as well.

32. For two such lists, see Xie Zhaozhe, *Wu za zu* 7.296; and Feng Menglong, *Gujin tan'gai* 9.8b–10a. The interest in eating habits of a bizarre nature is manifested in two short *Liaozhai* anecdotes, "A Passion for Snakes" ("She pi"; 1.130) and "Nibbling Rocks" ("He shi"; 2.137). The frequency of obsessions in Chinese writing with eating filth on the one hand and cleanliness on the other seems to indicate some affinity with the obsessive-compulsive syndromes familiar from psychoanalytic literature, and it would be interesting to ponder the connection with obsessive collecting.

33. Homosexuality presents a special case in that it involves human beings rather than things, but even here I believe the emphasis is on a category of people or a mode of behavior rather than on a particular person. Although obsession with sex in general or with one's own wife does occasionally crop up in the literature, an obsession with a particular person, regardless of gender, is generally not interpreted as obsession but as qing. See, e.g., *Hairpins Beneath a Man's Cap (Bian er chai),* a 1517 collection of sentimental stories of male love, and the "Qingwai" (gay love) section of *Qingshi leilüe.* At the same time, only exclusive homosexuality qualifies as an idiosyncrasy or obsession; casual or occasional homosexual liaisons do not. See Zhang Dai's account (*Tao'an mengyi,* p. 39) of a friend said to have an obsession with homosexuality because he abandoned his wife to run off with a male lover during the fall of the Ming.

34. Pu Songling's preface to this work appears in *PSLJ* 1:53.

35. Barr, "Pu Songling and *Liaozhai,*" pp. 278–79. Yuan Hongdao's essay "Raising Crickets" ("Xu cuzhi," in *Yuan Hongdao ji,* pp. 728–29) cites

Jia Qiuhuo's *Cricket Manual* (*Cuzhi jing*) as an authority on different species of crickets and methods for raising them. For a translation of Yuan's essay, see Chaves, *Pilgrims of the Clouds,* pp. 83–88.

36. For a few of the pigeon varieties, I have followed G. Yang and Yang Xianyi's translations in *Selected Tales of Liaozhai,* p. 96.

37. It is possible that Pu Songling had consulted some version of Zhang Wanzhong's *Pigeon Handbook* (*Ge jing*). Pu's story displays some similarities in wording and content with this manual. The story's list of pigeon varieties by region closely parallels a section of the handbook that classifies pigeons by region of origin. The order of places in the story follows that in the handbook, and under each region it names at least one of the varieties named in the handbook. Another obvious similarity concerns the treatment of sick pigeons. In the story, we are told, "If a pigeon took cold," the pigeon fancier would "treat it with the finest variety of sweet grass [*Glycyrrhiza glabra*]"; "if a pigeon became overheated, he would offer it grains of salt" [*leng ze liao yi fencao, re ze tou yi yan ke*] (6.839). Under the heading "Cures" ("Liaozhi"), the handbook reads: "If a pigeon becomes overheated, treat it with salt; if it takes cold, treat it with sweet grass" [*re, liao yi yan; leng, liao yi gancao*] (50.5a). On the other hand, there are a number of places in which the story and the manual do not overlap, such as the etymologies given for the Nightwanderer ("yeyou") pigeon and the treatment of other diseases.

Pu Songling's familiarity with this manual also seems likely because the author of the manual, Zhang Wanzhong, styled Kouzhi, came from Zouping, one of the counties in Pu Songling's native Ji'nan prefecture. Zhang Wanzhong, son of the well-known official Zhang Yandeng, was a late Ming senior licentiate who distinguished himself for his heroism during the fall of the Ming. See the *Zouping xianzhi* (1696 ed.) 5.8b and (1837 ed.) 15.47b–49a.

The wealthy pigeon fancier of Pu's story, Zhang Youliang, is also surnamed Zhang and comes from Zouping. In fact, both the story's pigeon-fancier and the compiler of the pigeon handbook were members of the wealthiest and most prominent gentry family in Zouping, and both had renowned gardens. See Cheng Jinzheng's private gazetteer-memoir, *Zouping xian jingwu zhi,* section on "famous gardens" ("ming yuan"), 3.11a, 3.15a. It is possible that Pu Songling intended to call his pigeon-fancying protagonist after the author of the pigeon manual, but mistook or misremembered his name.

Curiously, Zhang Youliang, whose name appears on no gazetteer list of degree holders, was well known for his obsession not with pigeons but with *rocks*. Zhu Jiuding of Qiantang's preface to his rock catalogue, the *Ti'an shipu* (like the *Gejing,* printed in the *Tanji congshu* [*juan* 44]), recounts that his

friend and fellow rock-lover Zhang Youliang of Zouping had once had a
rock that he admired dragged from the mountains to his garden by a team of
300 oxen. The identical anecdote is recounted in both Wang Zhuo's *Jin
shishuo* (8.107) and Cheng Jinzheng's *Zouping xian jingwu zhi.*
Finally, Pu Songling's friend Gao Heng may have known Zhang Youliang because he composed a poem entitled "Zhang Youliang's Ancient
Sword" ("Zhang Youliang gujian pian"). See Lu Jianzeng, *Guochao Shanzuo
shichao* 6.12b–13a.
Pu Songling's story satirizes the pigeon collector for trying to curry favor
with a friend of his father, a high official. It is possible that in addition to a
general satire against obsessive collecting, spoiled rich sons of officials, and
brownnosing, Pu Songling is also directing some sort of topical satire
against the wealthy and powerful Zhangs of Zouping.

38. For the rock catalogue and the flower handbook, see *Liaozhai yiwen
jizhu,* pp. 151–58 and 107–23, respectively.

39. Ye Mengde, "*Pingquan caomu ji* ba." We know that Pu Songling was
familiar with the *Pingquan caomu ji,* because in 1707 he wrote a poem called
"Reading the *Record of the Pingquan Estate*" ("Du *Pingquan ji*"), *PSLJ* 1.613.

40. Kong Chuan, "*Yunlin shipu* xu." The allusion is to *Analects* 6.23:
"The wise find joy in water; the benevolent find joy in mountains. The wise
are active; the benevolent are still. The wise are joyful; the benevolent are
long-lived" (trans. D. C. Lau, p. 84).

41. *Yutai xinyong (Gyokudai shin'ei),* p. 705.

42. A simplified formulation of an important point in Chinese poetics.
See Siu-kit Wong, "Ch'ing and Ching in the Critical Writings of Wang Fu-
chih."

43. "Lament" ("Yuan shi"), attributed to Ban Jieyu, *Yutai xinyong,* p. 78.
For a translation, see Watson, *Chinese Lyricism,* pp. 94–95.

44. "No. 8: On Watering" ("Ba: ximu"), *Pingshi,* p. 824.

45. Zhang Chao, *Youmeng ying,* 4b–5a. Zhang's full list is quite long and
encompasses many of the best-known paragons of obsession.

46. For the original text, see *Liaozhai* 11.1575–79. For my translation,
see the Appendix. Giles's translation (*Strange Stories,* pp. 181–91) calls the
hero a "mineralogist" and his rocks "specimens," but these terms are misguided; the hero's love for rocks is emotional and aesthetic and not in the
spirit of Victorian science and its impartial interest in collecting "specimens." It is extremely interesting, however, that Giles, writing for a turn-
of-the-century English audience, tried to make sense of the Chinese obsession with rocks in terms of a *scientific* passion.

47. Originally said of Yu Rang, an assassin-retainer who commits suicide (Sima Qian, *Shiji* 86.2519).

48. Li Zhi, *Fen shu,* pp. 130–31.

49. Lu Xun (*Zhongguo xiaoshuo shilüe,* pp. 52–53) notes the revival of interest in *New Tales of the World* during the late Ming and early Qing. During this period, which was also the heyday of obsession, the predilections of the *New Tales* eccentrics were reinterpreted in light of the late Ming notion of obsession. Although as I have already mentioned, no category in *New Tales* was specifically devoted to obsession, the chapter heading "Blind Infatuations" ("Huo ni"), which recounted men's infatuations with women, was converted into a rubric for obsession in a number of the sixteenth- and seventeenth-century updates. For example, the "Blind Infatuations" chapter in He Liangjun's *Shishuo xinyu bu,* which was published with great success in 1556, constructs a history of famous obsessions up to the Ming. The entries under the heading "Blind Infatuations" in Wang Zhuo's *Jin shishuo* (preface dated 1683) have nothing to do with romantic love; all are examples of obsessions. A disproportionate number of the entries in Hua Shu's *Pidian xiaoshi* retell or simply reprint anecdotes from *New Tales.* The chapter on obsession in Feng Menglong's *Gujin tan'gai* also includes many anecdotes from *New Tales.*

According to his friend and biographer Yuan Zhongdao, Li Zhi himself had "an obsession with cleanliness" ("Li Wenling zhuan" in *Fen shu,* p. 3). Li Zhi was profoundly interested in drawing connections between the *New Tales* eccentrics and nonconformists of his own time (see Billeter, *Li Zhi,* pp. 232–33). In 1588 Li Zhi published his *Chutan ji,* which was based on his readings of *New Tales* and *Jiaoshi leilin,* a sequel to *New Tales* that his friend, the bibliophile and scholar Jiao Hong (1541–1620), had published the year before. In recognition of Li Zhi's association with the *New Tales* eccentrics in the eyes of the reading public, a late Wanli edition of He Liangjun's *Shishuo xinyu bu* was brought out with a commentary by Li Zhi. According to Wang Zhongmin (*Zhongguo shanbenshu tiyao,* p. 391), this commentary was based on Li Zhi's annotations to his personal copy of *New Tales,* the rough draft for his *Chutan ji.*

50. *Shishuo xinyu* 23: 46; trans. Mather, *New Tales of the World,* p. 388.

51. See Billeter, *Li Zhi,* on the acutely felt lack of a true friend as a major theme in Li Zhi's work.

52. *Bu shen*—a pun, for the meaning of *shen* as a noun and as an adjective differ. As a noun, *shen* means "spirit"; as an adjective, it is closer to "extraordinary," "amazing," "divine."

53. A reworking of the title and a line in the *Book of Documents (Shang shu)* concerning the flute songs of Shao.

54. Here, in the cleverest and most playful writing in the piece, Li Zhi creates a virtual pastiche of phrases and puns (such as *jie,* which means both

"integrity" and "a segment of bamboo") from the considerable corpus of inscriptions written on paintings of bamboo. The most famous is probably Su Shi's colophon on Wen Tong's painting "Bent Bamboos," which included the following poem:

> The ink gentlemen [bamboos] on the wall cannot speak,
> But just seeing them can dissipate one's myriad griefs;
> And further, as for my friend's resembling these gentlemen,
> The severity of his simple virtue defies the frosty autumn.
> (Trans. Bush and Shih, *Early Chinese Texts on Painting*, p. 35)

The piece that Li Zhi's description resembles most closely is Ke Qian's (1251–1319) preface to Li Kan's *Manual of Bamboos* (*Zhu pu;* 1319):

> How fortunate is it that in recent times the family of bamboo met up with Master Li K'an [Li Kan]. . . . Because Li absorbs the purest air in the world, his mind is clear and open, and his spirit is brilliant, both of which are congenial to the manner and disposition of the "Gentlemen." . . . What neither description nor painting can encompass are the virtues for which bamboo stands. Bamboo stems are hollow. . . . The nature of bamboo is to be straight. . . . Bamboo's joints are clear-cut.   (Trans. Bush and Shih, *Early Chinese Texts on Painting*, pp. 274–75)

55. In a short rock catalogue entitled *Encomia for Rock Friends* (*Shiyou zan,* in *Zhaodai congshu, ce* 77), Wang Zhuo compares himself unfavorably to the rocks whose histories he records. The allegorical associations of this phrase are apparent in Zhu Xi's (1130–1200) colophon on a scroll of rocks and bamboos painted by Su Shi: "As for Old Tung-p'o [Su Shi], he possessed lofty and enduring qualities and a firm and immovable nature. One might say that he resembled these 'bamboo gentlemen' and 'rock friends' (trans. Bush, *Chinese Literati on Painting*, p. 103).

56. "When he is alive, I uphold him in times of crisis; when he is no longer alive, I support his children and grandchildren: this is how to conduct 'a friendship of stone'" ("The Principles of Human Behavior" ["Weiren yaoze"], *PSLJ* 1: 291). It is significant that Pu Songling uses this phrase here in the context of personal friendship rather than in the context of Ming loyalism.

Barr ("Pu Songling and *Liaozhai,*" pp. 121–23) has sensibly placed Pu Songling, who was only four years old at the time of the Qing conquest, in a broad "middle" category of early Qing intellectuals who recognized the legitimacy of the new dynasty but did not flinch from expressing sympathy toward Ming loyalists and toward the suffering of the people during the takeover.

Hay (*Kernels of Energy*, pp. 92–96) discusses an album of rocks painted by Ni Yuanlu (1594–1644) entitled "A Friendship of Stone" ("Shijiao tu"), which he translates as "Rock Bound." The painter was a Ming statesman and loyalist martyr who hung himself in 1644. Given this background, it is not difficult to interpret these paintings as allegorical allusions to the painter's loyalty to the fallen Ming dynasty; rocks in the mid-seventeenth century could certainly connote Ming loyalism. Thus an early Qing collection of vernacular short stories with a strong loyalist theme is entitled *The Sobering Stone (Zuixing shi)*. It is likely that the presence of the rock in the title was intended to call attention to the collection's loyalist bent (see Hanan, "The Fiction of Moral Duty," p. 204).

Despite the strong association of rocks with Ming loyalist sentiments in some works of the mid-seventeenth century, however, we have no evidence to interpret "The Ethereal Rock" as topical allegory or as an expression of Ming sympathies. No hints or clues favoring such an interpretation can be found within the tale or in the Historian of the Strange's commentary. The same is true of other *Liaozhai* tales about flowers or dreams, which are devoid of the loyalist symbolism assigned them in the writings of Ming loyalists such as Gui Zhuang or Dong Yue. What becomes most apparent is the multivalence and flexibility of cultural symbols during this period.

57. *Qingshi leilüe*, comment following the chapter entitled "Qinghua" ("Metamorphosis through love"), *juan* 11.

58. Karl Kao (*IC*, p. 129) points out that *Liaozhai* contains what he calls "narrativized instances of figures." W. Y. Li ("Rhetoric of Fantasy," pp. 50–52) discusses "the literalization of metaphor" in *Liaozhai* as a way of naturalizing other worlds. For a more detailed discussion of the literalization of figurative language, see Chapter 5 and the Conclusion to this book.

59. See Wu Hung, "Tradition and Innovation," which discusses the literati vogue during the Ming for uncarved jade to capture the spiritual and visual "naturalness" of rock and to distinguish its owner from vulgar folk who could appreciate only "artificial" beauty.

60. Although there were other famous rock connoisseurs in Chinese history such as Niu Sengru of the Tang and the ubiquitous Su Shi, Mi Fu seems to have eclipsed them all. In the writings on obsession, it is Mi Fu's name that is invariably coupled with rocks, and in that role he is heavily featured in Feng Menglong's *Gujin tan'gai* and in the Ming sequels to *New Tales of the World*. For a discussion of different Ming editions of Mi Fu anecdotes, see van Gulik, *Mi Fu on Inkstones*, pp. 3–4.

61. *Song shi* 444.13124. In his preface to a collection of stories entitled *Rocks That Nod Their Heads (Shi dian tou*, p. 329), Feng Menglong provides a cosmological rationale for Mi Fu's appellation of his rock: "Now when Heaven gives birth to the myriad things, though their endowments of material may differ, they are alike in receiving qì [energy]. When qì congeals, it becomes a rock; when it melts it becomes a spring; when qì is

limpid, it becomes a human being; when it is turbid, it becomes an animal. It is simply that men and rocks are brothers." Feng then argues that rocks, too, have intelligence and reaches this rhetorical climax: "As for calling a rock 'my elder'—why shouldn't a rock be the equal of a human being?" Pu Songling's Historian of the Strange takes this position one step further: the rock shows himself not merely the equal but the superior of most men.

62. I am grateful to Professor Ma Ruifang of Shandong University for taking me to see this rock in June 1987.

63. There is a lacuna in the text in this line and the fifth character is missing. Pu Songling is making a play on words between clothes and the names of plants here.

64. A variation on a line from "The Mountain Spirit" in *Songs of the South*. This line must have been one of Pu Songling's favorites; he also included it in the opening of his powerful preface to *Liaozhai*.

65. According to ancient legend, Gong Gong knocked down the sky by bumping into the pillar of Heaven; the Goddess Nü Wa eventually repaired the damage with rocks.

66. *PSLJ* 1: 620.

67. For illustrations of Mi Fu bowing to his rock, see Hay, *Kernels of Energy*.

68. Contrast with Yuan Hongdao's poem "Shizong," no. 1: "The rock is one Mi Fu pulled from his sleeve" (*Yuan Hongdao ji*, p. 1460).

69. Niu Sengru, a Tang statesman and author of a book of strange tales, was one of the earliest famed rock collectors.

70. The two poems are "Inscribed on a Stone" ("Tishi"), *PSLJ* 1: 620; and "Stone Recluse Garden" ("Shiyin yuan"), *PSLJ* 1: 619.

71. According to Stein (*World in Miniature*, p. 37), the *Yunlin shipu* describes a stone shaped like a miniature mountain that could be made to emit smoke that looked like clouds: "There are high peaks and holes that communicate through twists and turns. At the bottom is a communication hole in which one may set up a two-story incense burner. [If one lights it,] it is as though clouds were buffeting each other among the summits." Stein traces the Chinese interest in stones as miniature mountains back to the mountain-shaped incense burners of the Han.

72. Trans. Hay, *Kernels of Energy*, p. 83. For a woodblock print of this ink stone with the inscriptions—it resembles the map of a mountain in a local gazetteer—see Tao Zongyi's (1316–1403) *Chuogeng lu* and Hay, *Kernels of Energy*, p. 81.

73. From an inscription on an album leaf by Li Liufang (1575–1629); the last leaf is signed by the artist and is dated 1625. Reproduced in Sotheby's *Catalogue of Fine Chinese Paintings* (New York, Dec. 6, 1989), p. 43. Accord-

ing to Schaefer (*Tu Wan's Stone Catalogue*, p. 8), the last Northern Song emperor, Huizong, "that notorious petromaniac," went so far as to "formally enfeoff a prodigious stone as 'marklord of P'an-ku,'" Pangu (P'an-ku) being "a primordial cosmogonic deity, fashioner of the earth and its rocky bones."

74. Taking the surname Xing as a pun for the verb *xing* "to move."

75. On Pu Songling's flower obsession stories, see W. Y. Li, *Enchantment and Disenchantment*.

76. This often-repeated definition of rocks appeared as early as a Jin dynasty work *A Discussion of the Pattern of Things* (*Wuli lun*). See Hay, *Kernels of Energy*, p. 128 n72.

77. Hay, *Kernels of Energy*, p. 97.

78. This handscroll is reproduced in Sotheby's *Catalogue of Fine Chinese Paintings* (New York, Dec. 6, 1989), pp. 38–39. I am indebted to Nancy Berliner for lending me additional photographs of the paintings and inscriptions.

79. *Zhongguo meishujia renming cidian*, p. 242.

80. Based on Mi Wanzhong's final inscription, dated 1510 (photograph of the handscroll).

81. An inscription on the painting by the influential painter and art theorist Dong Qichang (1555–1636) emphasizes this point.

82. A particularly interesting catalogue is Lin Youlin's 1603 *Suyuan shipu*, which features woodblock prints of famous rocks created from the artist's imagination. Unillustrated rock catalogues are well represented in collectanea such as *Shuofu*, *Tanji congshu*, *Zhaodai congshu*, *Meishu congshu*, and *Yushi guqi pulu*.

83. Mi Wanzhong's final inscription (photograph of the handscroll).

84. The Ming and Qing ideology of collecting, taken to such extremes in Pu Songling's tale and Wu Bin's handscroll, forestalls or diffuses the postmodernist critiques leveled against collecting by contemporary Western critics such as Susan Stewart in *On Longing*. In the Chinese idealization of obsession, the relationship between collectors and the objects of their collection is not arbitrary, because objects have become imbued with cultural significance, especially moral virtues. Nor is the relationship one-sided, because objects are said to need collectors as much as collectors need objects. Thus the conceit that the object itself deliberately "finds" the proper collector. Finally it is not luck or even connoisseurship that enables the collector to locate a rare object, but a moral causality. The sufficiently devoted collector comes to possess an object because he merits it.

85. In contrast to earlier medical books that treated pi as a category of digestive illness, pi is no longer a serious disease category in any stan-

dard nosological list that reflects contemporary sixteenth- or seventeenth-century practice, including Li Shizhen's encyclopedic *Classified Materia Medica* (see *juan* 3–4). When the term "pi" does crop up in sixteenth- and seventeenth-century medical literature, it is simply as a verb for tobacco or alcohol addiction. I am indebted to Charlotte Furth for alerting me to the eclipse of pi as a disease category. Of course, Ming dictionaries like *Zhengzi tong* still list the earlier medical meanings of pi in their definitions.

86. Li Shizhen, *Bencao gangmu* 52.96.

87. Ibid.

88. For a fuller discussion of this point and a more detailed reading of Li Shizhen's entry, see my article "The Petrified Heart."

89. Li Shizhen, *Bencao gangmu* 52.96–97.

90. Hay, *Kernels of Energy*, p. 84.

91. Li Shizhen, *Bencao gangmu* 52.96.

92. Xie Zhaozhe, *Wu za zu* 7.300.

93. Trans. Barr, "Pu Songling and *Liaozhai*," p. 223.

94. *Song shi* 444.13124.

95. A widely used allusion that refers to an anecdote in "The Biography of Dong Xian" ("Dong Xian zhuan") in Ban Gu, *Han shu* 13.3733. The emperor, wishing to get out of bed, chose to tear off the sleeve of his robe rather than awaken his favorite male lover.

96. Qian Xuan's (ca. 1235–after 1301) beautiful handscroll in the Metropolitan Museum depicts Wang Xizhi in a waterside pavilion watching geese (see Cahill, *Hills Beyond a River*, p. 353, color pl. 35).

97. *Shishuo xinyu* 30: 11; trans. Mather, *New Tales of the World*, p. 464. Pu Songling mentions this anecdote in an essay written in 1670 on behalf of Sun Hui, "Inscription on a Stela at the Pond for Releasing Life" ("Fangsheng chi bei ji"), *PSLJ* 1: 39.

98. *Peiwen yunfu* 3: 3456, under the entry "potted chrysanthemums" ("penju"); cited in Vandermeersch, "L'arrangement de fleurs," p. 83.

99. *PSLJ* 1:641.

100. Ibid.

101. Like most lower-degree holders, Pu Songling prided himself on his sensitivity to "vulgarity." This is particularly evident in his list of "unbearable things" ("bu ke nai shi") appended to a tale about a vulgar scholar who selects money over calligraphy when put to the test by two beautiful fox-maidens. See "A Licentiate of Yishui" ("Yishui xiucai"; 7.906).

102. In this, Pu Songling may be following the conventions of the drama. As Swatek has asserted in "Feng Menglong's *Romantic Dream*": "One of the paradigms of chuanqi drama is that the pursuit of love and the pursuit of fame are connected" (p. 232); and "in *Mudan ting*, the fulfillment

of sexual desire is the precondition for all other resolutions" (p. 214). *Liaozhai*'s interest in the mechanics of the hero's financial success, however, resembles as well the concerns of many vernacular stories that unfold in a mercantile milieu.

103. Tao Qian, *Tao Yuanming ji*, p. 89.

104. Trans. H. C. Chang, *Tales of the Supernatural*, p. 142.

105. Ibid., p. 147.

106. Barr ("Pu Songling and *Liaozhai*," pp. 217–26) discusses the influence of Li Zhi's "Tongxin shuo" on *Liaozhai*'s naive heroes and draws an explicit parallel to "The Bookworm."

107. "Exhortation to Study" (the locus classicus is a chapter title in *Xunzi*) was a favorite theme, especially during the Song. Wai-kam Ho ("Late Ming Literati," p. 26) notes the reasons for the popularity of cheap didactic primers in sixteenth- and seventeenth-century publishing: "The main purpose of course for children was to extol the glory of scholarship, to impress young minds with the power of wealth, even the 'face of jadelike beauty' that one could expect to find in books, or to rhapsodize about the joy of studying in poems such as 'Sishi dushu le' [The pleasures of studying in the four seasons]."

108. Liu Mengmei, the romantic hero of *The Peony Pavilion*, complains in his self-introduction about the false promises of "Exhortation to Study": "In books lie fame and fortune, they say, / Then tell me, where are the jade-smooth cheeks / the rooms of yellow gold?" (trans. Birch, *Peony Pavilion*, p. 3)

Chapter 4

EPIGRAPH: Xu Wei, *Ci Mulan*, in his quartet *Sisheng yuan* 12a.

1. I thank Charlotte Furth and the 1988–89 members of Yale University's Whitney Society for the Humanities for their suggestions regarding the first part of this chapter. I presented a shorter and earlier version of this essay at the 1987 Harvard Fukiyose Conference. For the original text of the tale, see *Liaozhai* 12.1711–13. A complete translation of the tale is presented in this chapter.

2. Following the reading *mou ao* of the 24-*juan* MS, rather than the *gua ao* (an old widow) of the Zhao Qigao edition. "The Human Prodigy" is not included in the extant half of the author's MS or in the Zhuxue zhai MS (preface dated 1751). See Yuan Shishuo's (*Pu Songling xinkao*, pp. 400–408) argument on the importance and reliability of the 24-*juan* MS.

3. Johnson, *Critical Difference*, p. 5.

4. Dan Minglun (*Liaozhai* 12.1711) uses a classical allusion from *A*

Garden of Anecdotes (*Shuo yuan*) to make this point: "An autumn cicada was being attacked by a praying mantis. The mantis was about to capture the cicada, not realizing that behind him was a sparrow."

5. See Sima Qian, "Huaiyin hou liezhuan, no. 32," *Shiji,* p. 2616; glossed by Lü Zhan'en, *Liaozhai* 12.1711. During the civil wars that followed the fall of the Qin dynasty, Han Xin, general of the Han forces, snatched victory from defeat by secretly sending a force to switch the flags at the Zhao camp to red Han flags. Assuming that their camp had already been captured by Han, the Zhao army panicked and lost the battle. See Watson, *Records of the Historian,* p. 184.

6. The *Liaozhai* tale "Qiao niang" (2.256) employs the term *tian an* in the sense of "natural eunuch" to describe a boy born with deformed genitals, who at age seventeen still had a "penis only the size of a silkworm."

The "natural" (*tian zhe*) figures as the first on Li Shizhen's list of the five sorts of men who cannot beget children in the "Human Anomaly" section of *Bencao gangmu* (52: 113): "The natural has an impotent penis that is useless. This is what the ancients called a 'natural eunuch' " (Li Shizhen uses the term *tian huan* rather than *tian an*). The second category in his list, "the gelding" (*jian zhe*) describes "a man whose genitals have been castrated" (the verb he employs for castrate is *an*). See Furth, "Androgynous Males and Deficient Females," p. 5, for a discussion of the category of natural eunuch, which she traces back to the *Neijing,* an ancient medical classic.

7. Barthes, *S/Z,* p. 164.

8. Other *Liaozhai* anecdotes that mention castration: "Shan Fuzai" (9.1197), a punning joke about sons who castrate their father; and "Li Sijian" (3.426), an item copied from the *Beijing Gazette* about a man who beat his wife to death. In remorse, he rushed into the temple to the city god and hacked off his ear and his fingers before finally castrating himself. See also *Shi dian tou,* no. 4, in which a man's response to his fraudulent wife's suicide is to castrate himself, and Ling Mengchu's *Pai'an jingqi erke,* no. 34, in which an official castrates his secretary on learning that the secretary has been enjoying the official's harem in his absence.

9. Two seventeenth-century exceptions that prove the rule: *The Biography of a Foolish Old Woman* (*Chi pozi zhuan*) and *Idle Talks Under the Bean Arbor* (*Doupeng xianhua*). See Hanan, *Chinese Vernacular Story,* pp. 192–93.

10. "A Discussion of Heaven" ("Tianlun pian"), *Xunzi,* 17.209. The graph *yao* is written throughout this chapter with the variant "sacred" radical rather than with the customary "woman" radical.

11. From at least the Northern Song on, the general meaning of human anomaly and the specialized meaning of sexual impersonator coexist and become subject to individual preference and usage. *TPGJ* (367.2912–25)

includes seventeen items in a supplement entitled "Human Prodigies" appended to the section on monsters and demons (*yaoguai*). Of these only four pertain to male impersonators; the rest concern human freaks such as women who give birth through unusual channels of the body or a child born with four hands and four feet. Feng Menglong, on the other hand, includes solely items about freaks in his entries on human prodigies in *Qingshi leilüe* and *Gujin tan'gai*.

Human prodigies may also be distinguished from the related and more general term *yaoren* or "prodigious humans." *Yaoren* usually refers to rebels and sorcerers rather than to sexual impersonators and freaks, but not always: Yuan Mei calls a female impersonator a *yaoren* in *Zi bu yu* 23.573–74.

12. Li Yanshou, "Liezhuan," no. 35, *Nan shi* 45.1143.

13. Henderson, *Development and Decline of Chinese Cosmology*.

14. Cao Cao, founder of the Wei dynasty during the Three Kingdoms period, became notorious in Late Imperial times for his villainy, especially through his portrayal in the theater and the novel.

15. This tendency to parody the serious forms of the classical tradition is characteristic of the late Ming and Qing. See, e.g., *Jokes on the Four Books* (*Sishu xiao*) with the unlikely attribution to Li Zhi. *Liaozhai* and Tang Xianzu's *Peony Pavilion* delight in twisting lines from the *Odes* into obscene puns. Li Yu's running commentary to his pornographic novel *Rou putuan* is one of the best examples of commentary turning into parody. See Hanan's translation, *The Carnal Prayer-Mat*. Hom ("The Continuation of Tradition," p. 134) notes that Pu "manipulat[ed] the commentary structure to express satire and humor," but incorrectly argues that Pu's comic commentaries are of his own invention.

16. See *DMB*, pp. 128–32, for a biography of this interesting figure.

17. Cited in Wang Liqi, *Lidai xiaohua ji*, p. 280.

18. The repetition of an image used in both tale and comment also occurs in stories such as "Gong the Immortal" ("Gong xian"; 7.895–901) and "Gongsun Jiuniang" (4.777–83), where it likewise helps bridge the disjunction between narrative and discourse.

19. Furth, "Androgynous Males and Deficient Females," p. 17.

20. Ibid., p. 18. Not all accounts conform to this distinction. One of Wang Shizhen's accounts of a widow who turns into a man and starts carrying on with "her" daughter-in-law is much closer to the hyper-eroticized view of male sexual transformations than to the moralistic interpretation of female-to-male transformation. Wang Shizhen's anecdote is more piquant because it is the erotically charged figure of the adulterous widow, not an unmarried adolescent, who undergoes transformation. See *Chibei outan*, no. 1193, 25.597. Both the erotic and moral possibilities of female-to-male

changes in sex coexist in Niu Xiu's "Shi gu," an anecdote included in Zhang Chao's *Yu Chu xinzhi* (17.264). The studious daughter of a village school-master has a dream in which a man informs her that he will transform her into a boy to reward her heirless father. What is particularly noteworthy is that the transformation is described: the man in the dream strokes the girl's lower body and feeds her a red pill. "She felt hot energy [qì] like flame pass down from her chest until it reached between her thighs." After a trance lasting seven days, she awakens to discover she has become a boy. The narrative continues the process of eroticization by describing her as wearing a male cap but with traces of makeup still visible.

21. Gan Bao, *Soushen ji*, no. 115, pp. 71–72.

22. Furth, "Androgynous Males and Deficient Females," p. 18 *n*43, likewise points out this interesting contrast between the European and Chinese interpretations.

23. Trans. Laqueur, "Orgasm, Generation, and the Politics of Repro-ductive Biology," p. 14. For the original text, see Paré, *Des Monstres et Prodiges*, p. 30.

24. As Zhang Chao (*Yu Chu xinzhi* 17.264) commented on Niu Xiu's story of the daughter of the heirless village schoolmaster who was trans-formed into a boy (see note 20 above): "Historians have designated those who magically underwent changes of sex as 'human prodigies.' Reading this now, I find that [such changes] were really a means to reward good-ness."

25. This massive work in 34 *juan* was compiled by Chen Shiyuan (*jinshi* 1544; preface dated 1564) and augmented by He Dongru (preface dated 1636). According to Chen's biography in *DMB*, p. 179, the *Siku quanshu* credits the compilation of *Menglin xuanjie* to Chen, with additional infor-mation provided by He Dongru. See Wang Zhongmin, *Zhongguo shan-benshu tiyao*, p. 292, on the tangled authorship of this book. See also Michael Lackner's study, *Der chinesische Traumwald*. I discuss *Menglin xuanjie* at greater length in the next chapter.

26. He Dongru, *Menglin xuanjie* 6.34a.

27. Sun Jianqiu, *Qingchao qi'an daguan* 1.40–41. (There is some confusion about the editor's name: the cover and the preface give it as Jianqiu, but the credits at back reverse it to Qiujian.) The case discussed here was written by a Mr. Mei. Written in simple Classical Chinese, this collection attests to the popularity of traditional zhiguai and crime case collections as late as 1919. Apparently, new zhiguai-type collections were still being compiled at the time for popular publishing ventures.

28. Li Qingchen, *Zuicha zhiguai* 2.3.

29. Thompson, *Motif-Index of Folk Literature*, D Magic, pp. 9, 54. This

motif has recently resurfaced in the espionage case of a French diplomat and his Chinese lover, a Peking Opera star and the supposed mother of their child. A French court investigation revealed that the "Chinese mother" was not a woman but a man. The Frenchman insisted that he had been ignorant of his lover's true sex. The Chinese-American playwright David Hwang has transformed the case into the prizewinning play *M. Butterfly*. See Garber, *Vested Interests*, for a sensitive analysis of the issues raised by the play.

30. *Lüchuang xinhua*, p. 59. The anecdote is entitled "Companion of Joy Deflowers Miss Zhang Chan" ("Banxi chu fan Zhang Channiang").

31. The Yuan version appears in Luo Ye's [*A New Printing of*] *Conversations with an Old Drunk* ([*Xinbian*] *Zuiweng tanlu*) included in *Lüchuang xinhua*, pp. 59–60.

32. Li Shizhen, *Bencao gangmu* 52.113.

33. O'Flaherty, *Women, Androgynes, and Other Mythical Beasts*, p. 284.

34. Ling Mengchu, *Pai'an jingqi chuke*, no. 34, vol. 2. Note the interesting parallel with the idea of male sexual heat caused by friction in the Galenic tradition.

35. Feng Menglong, *Xingshi hengyan*, no. 10, vol. 1. Hanan (*Chinese Short Story*, p. 242) attributes the story to Langxian, whom he originally identified as "x."

36. Lu Can is the only author who claims to have seen official documents pertaining to the case and to have copied them into his text. Since the notation books that I have seen do not usually cite legal documents verbatim, I am inclined to accept Lu Can's claim. Whether such a case actually took place, however, is less important than the fact that later readers like Pu Songling would have assumed that it had.

37. Lu Can, *Gengsi bian* (ca. 1520), 2910: 9.204–8. Tan Zhengbi also reprints the *Gengsi bian* account in *Sanyan liangpai ziliao* 2: 431–32.

38. The names of the seven gang members are also listed in Xie Zhaozhe, *Wu za zu*; and Chu Renhuo, *Jianhu ji* (*yuji* 4.14a–b).

39. See Furth, "Androgynous Males and Deficient Females," pp. 9–12, for translations of accounts of the case by Li Shizhen and Li Xu.

40. Li Yu, "Nan Mengmu jiaohe sanqian." For a discussion of this story and its possible connection to the Li Liangyu case, see Furth, "Androgynous Males and Deficient Females," pp. 12–13. For a translation, see Hanan, *Silent Operas*.

41. These are: Huang Wei, *Pengchuang leiji*, 1a/b; Xie Zhaozhe, *Wu za zu* 8.3739; and Zhao Shanzheng, *Bintui lu* 2.16. (Zhao Shanzheng's book should be distinguished from a Song work by Zhao Yushi with the identical title.)

42. It seems likely that Pu Songling had read at least two versions of the

case. The only Ming notation book account to include both the names of Sang Chong's gang *and* the premeditated seduction plot is Xie Zhaozhe's *Wu za zu*. But Xie employs a variant graph with a "feather" radical for Sang Chong's given name whereas Pu Songling employs a graph with an "ice" radical. Only *Gengsi bian* and Chu Renhuo's *Jianhu ji* employ Pu Songling's graph for Sang Chong's name, and the *Jianhu ji* account is clearly an abridgment of *Gengsi bian*. However, neither of these include the seduction subplot. It seems probable therefore that Pu Songling was familiar with the account in *Gengsi bian* (the *Jianhu ji* account also seems less likely because it appeared in the collection's last installment [preface dated 1703] and would have circulated late) *and* with one of the other accounts that included the seduction subplot. Access to the two accounts would not have been difficult. A Wanli publication, *Yanxia xiaoshuo,* for instance, conveniently reprints both *Gengsi bian* and Huang Wei's *Pengchuang leiji* in the same collection.

43. Barthes, *S/Z,* p. 36.

44. Eliade, *The Two and the One,* p. 100.

45. Yuan Mei, "The False Female" ("Jia nü"), in *Zi bu yu* 23: 573–74.

46. The female impersonator in "Two Brothers of Different Sex" is not called Sang Chong but Sang Mao, the name of Sang Chong's adoptive father in the *Gengsi bian* account. This may have simply been a careless error on the vernacular storywriter's part.

47. Feng Menglong, *Xingshi hengyan,* no. 10, p. 199.

48. Wang Shizhen also includes a version of this anecdote in *Chibei outan,* no. 1129, 24.571, but without the supplementary story in the *Liaozhai* comment.

49. Based on accounts in *Biographies from the Qing History (Qingshi liezhuan)* and Dong Hanzeng's *San'gang shilüe*. Barr (Bai Yaren, "*Liaozhai zhiyi* zhong," p. 158) demonstrates that Pu Songling made a number of errors in this story. Yang Fu's name should be written with a different character (also pronounced "fu" but meaning "wealth"), and the governor of Fujian's name was Dong Weiguo, not Cai. From Barr's research, it seems that Pu Songling's main innovation was to link both of the stories circulating about Yang Fu and to suggest an uncanny causality between them. Significantly, the figure of Yang Fu's manly wife attempting to avenge her husband's death seems to appear only in the *Liaozhai* account.

50. Xie Zhaozhe, *Wu za zu* 8.302.

51. Gan Bao, *Soushen ji,* no. 193, 7.79. *Juan* 6 and 7 contain many interesting items involving abnormality in dress and gender.

52. Li Yanshou, "Liezhuan," no. 35, *Nan shi,* 45.1143. The account of Bai Xiangya, a female bandit chief during the early Khitan attacks who

disguised herself as a man when she went to meet the barbarian king, makes the correlation between "human prodigies" and rebels against the state even more explicit: "The northern Rong barbarians wreaking havoc in the heartland, a woman calling herself a man: both are manifestations of excessive yin" (*TPGJ* 367.2925).

53. See Barr, "Pu Songling and *Liaozhai*," p. 198, on the popularity of *TPGJ* reprints beginning in the late Ming.

54. For *yiren*, see Xie Zhaozhe's list in *Wu za zu* 8; for *nüzhong zhangfu*, see Chu Renhuo's list in *Jianhu ji* 4.13. The principal source for such lists was *TPGJ*. See also *Jiyuan ji suoji, juan* 6, under "Extraordinary Persons of the Boudoir" ("Guizhong yiren"), which includes subsections on "women scholars" (*nü xueshi*), "women first-place graduates" (*nü zhuangyuan*), "women officials" (*nüzi wei nanguan*), "women disguised as men" (*nüzi zha wei nanzi*), and "women generals" (*nü jiangjun*). The same stories from *TPGJ* crop up in a number of late Ming compendia about women, such as *Lüchuang nüshi* and *Qi nüzi zhuan* 2.29a–31b. Although the latter classifies Lou Cheng as an "amazing woman," the postface dutifully repeats the historian's judgment that she was a human prodigy. But the label clearly has lost its sting.

55. The earliest reference to a "hero among women" occurs in *The Annals of Wu and Yue* (*Wuyue chunqiu* 3.16a): "Pure and enlightened, an upholder of virtue—surely this is a 'hero among women.'" Chu Renhuo's definition of the term (*Jianhu ji* 4.13) is the most restrictive: "women who masquerade as men and receive official posts [civil or military]." Clearly, Pu Songling does not subscribe to such a narrow definition of the term in *Liaozhai*. After an anecdote about a peasant woman who possesses the physical prowess and temperament of a knight-errant, he comments playfully: "When the world calls a woman 'a hero among women,' she still realizes that she is not a man, but this woman has completely forgotten that she's a woman!" (9.1243) Xie Zhaozhe (*Wu za zu* 8.301), on the other hand, classifies women who masquerade as men and serve as officials under the title "extraordinary persons," but elsewhere remarks that a love of fame and wealth is a masculine trait and that any woman who exhibits it deserves to be called "a hero among women." I suspect he is being facetious.

56. Mulan's story was retold in many different genres during the late Ming. The vernacular prologue to Feng Menglong, *Gujin xiaoshuo*, no. 28 (p. 417), which Hanan (*Chinese Short Story*, p. 238) dates as "late," recounts the story of Mulan and those of two other cross-dressers in the context of "extraordinary women" (*qinü*): "For now, I'll just tell you about that really weird, really bizarre sort of false male who lacks the proper tool, a real woman who binds her hair in a man's turban." The main story recounts a

well-known incident about an orphaned merchant's daughter named Huang Shancong who dressed as a boy for many years. Retaining her chastity throughout, she managed to raise the money to convey her father's body back to his native place for burial. The official *Ming History* recorded her biography in the "Exemplary Women" section, *juan* 301. Notation book accounts described her as a "second Mulan" or a "Mulan of our times." See Tan Zhengbi, *Sanyan liangpai ziliao*, pp. 154–57. Mulan's adventures were also a popular subject for the theater during the late Ming. See Xu Wei's *zaju* play *Maid Mulan Joins the Army in Her Father's Stead* (*Ci Mulan ti fu congjun*) in his *Sisheng yuan* quartet. For a translation of the play, see Faurot, "Four Cries of a Gibbon."

57. Trans. C. C. Wang, *Traditional Chinese Tales*, pp. 91–92 (slightly modified).

58. Ouyang Xiu and Song Qi, *Xin Tang shu, juan* 205. For the various versions of Xie Xiao'e's story, see Wang Pijiang, *Tangren xiaoshuo*, pp. 93–97.

59. In his comments on "Shang Sanguan" (3.375), Wang Shizhen points out the similarity between the heroine of this tale and Xie Xiao'e.

60. In traditional Chinese nomenclature, women retained their father's surname after marriage. Technically "Yanshi" means "of the Yan clan." See G. Dudbridge, *Tale of Li Wa*, pp. 39–40, on the canonical implications of omitting the hero's name as a sign of moral censure. Significantly, the only *Liaozhai* tale to begin with a formal biography of a woman is "Feng Sanniang" (5.610–17), the unique story of a lesbian love affair. The opening alerts us that the girl will assume the role customarily reserved for a young male scholar in *Liaozhai*.

61. *Hairpins Beneath a Man's Cap* (*Bian er chai*), the title of the sixteenth-century collection of sentimental homosexual stories, utilizes the same clash of symbols to represent a contradiction in gender identity. According to He Dongru, *Menglin xuanjie* 10.20, for an unmarried woman (*guinü*) to dream that she is capped like a man means that she is a "hero among women."

62. The prologue to the vernacular story "Two Brothers of Different Sex" imagines the training process through which a boy embarked on the path of female impersonation. In that version the young Sang meets a middle-aged woman when both take refuge in a temple during a rainstorm. The boy realizes that the woman is flirting with him and tries to take advantage of her, but the "woman" is of course really a man and easily overpowers the boy. Impressed, Sang becomes the disciple of this female impersonator and embarks on his fatal course.

63. Segregated dramatic troupes were a long-standing practice in China, and all-female troupes where women played men's parts existed during the Ming and Qing. See MacKerras, *Rise of Peking Opera*, pp. 45–47.

In Xu Wei's play, *The Female First-Place Graduate Declines a She-Phoenix and Gets a He-Phoenix* (*Nü zhuangyuan ci huang de feng*), the stage directions instruct the heroine and her maid to "mime a change of costume." In the very next line, the two of them set off on a journey, ready to pass as men. See *Sisheng yuan*, no. 4, scene 1, 3b. Women dressing as men to pass the examinations and gain official posts was also a theme of seventeenth-century chantefables written by and for women and in *caizi jiaren* fiction.

64. *Liaozhai*'s conservative nineteenth-century commentators are far less restrained about the couple's inversion than Pu Songling and cannot resist interpreting Miss Yan's term in office as an evil portent for the fall of the Ming. Picking up on the suggestion planted in the text about Miss Yan's retirement just before the change in dynasties, He Shouqi (*Liaozhai* 6.769) writes: "A woman acted as a man and openly served as an official—if it hadn't been for the fall of the Ming, there would have been no distinction between male and female. Wouldn't she then have been close to a human prodigy?" Dan Minglun (6.768) plays both sides of the fence; although he applauds Miss Yan's talents, he notes: "When she was promoted to censor, however, a hen was crowing in the state; yin was flourishing, and yang was declining: this was an inauspicious omen for the Ming dynasty."

65. An allusion from Li Yanshou, "Basic Annals of the Song Emperor" ("Song benji"), *Nan shi*. The lascivious princess of Shangyin complained to the emperor about the inequity in the number of their consorts. He gave her permission to bring in thirty handsome men.

66. Ma Ruifang (*Pu Songling pingzhuan*) points out that "The Ballad of a Swordswoman" ("Xianü xing") more closely resembles "Shang Sanguan" than the famous *Liaozhai* tale entitled "The Swordswoman" ("Xianü"; 2.210–16).

67. Literally, the allusion reads "a female Yu Rang," one of the assassin-retainers recorded in Sima Qian's *Shiji* (86.2519–21). The allusion is particularly apt because Yu Rang disguised himself as a eunuch, just as Shang Sanguan disguised herself as a boy. Yu Rang's scheme to avenge the death of his patron failed, but like Shang Sanguan, he committed suicide in the end.

68. *PSLJ* 2: 1035.

69. In the tale "Jiang Cheng" (6.860), the pretty shrew Jiang Cheng disguises herself as a man in order to keep her straying husband under surveillance during his visit to a brothel. Pu Songling manipulates point of view and suspense in a manner strikingly close to "Shang Sanguan." The narrative of "Jiang Cheng" also delays the revelation of the androgynous youth's true sex and depicts the admiration he arouses in the male customers present. In "Shang Sanguan" the disguise proves to be deadly both for Shang Sanguan and her enemy; the consequence of Jiang Cheng's cross-

dressing is to intensify her preternatural reign of terror over her cowed husband.

70. The same shift in narrative focus from the bully to his servants occurs in Pu Songling's vernacular play, but because the scenes in the play are so much longer and detailed, the effect is less striking.

71. In Xu Wei's dramatization of the Mulan story, the stage directions call for her to first "mime the gesture of painfully unbinding her feet" and then to "mime the gesture of changing her clothes and putting on a man's cap." She reveals that she has a secret family recipe to shrink her feet again when she resumes female identity and returns to get married (*Sisheng yuan*, no. 2, scene 1, 2b–3a).

In another late Ming comedy about cross-dressing, *The Male Empress* (*Nan wanghou*), the hero, who plays the female *dan* role, laments he has not been born a woman, boasting that he is more beautiful than any woman— all he lacks is "a pair of 3-inch curved shoes" (scene 1, 2a).

72. Most other accounts of the Sang Chong case describe in much greater detail the feminine attributes of the impersonator and specify that his feet were bound. Pu Songling is oddly reticent on this subject, but this omission may be explained as typical of his effort to streamline the merely descriptive elements in a story and to rely instead on the oblique perceptions of other characters in the story.

73. On the intensification of the chaste widow cult during the Qing period, see T'ien Ju-k'ang, *Male Anxiety and Female Chastity*, esp. pp. 126–48; and Mann, "Widows."

74. Wu Hung, *Wu Liang Shrine*, p. 269; for an illustration of Zhongli Chun, see p. 270. Once again Pu Songling streamlines the description in his version so as not to impede the narrative flow.

75. *Liezi* 8.95.

76. Y. Wu, "Marriage Destinies," chap. 2. See also her article based on this chapter, "Inversion of Marital Hierarchy."

77. Hu Shi, "*Xingshi yinyuan zhuan* kaozheng."

78. Y. Wu, "Marriage Destinies," chap. 1.

79. *PSLJ* 1: 308–10.

80. Y. Wu, "Marriage Destinies," chap. 2.

81. Interestingly, Li Yu's essay "Against the Absurd" ("Jie huangtang," in *Xianqing outan*, pp. 18–19), which argues that daily life offers the richest and most inexhaustible source of material for writers, selects the shrew as an example of a theme that can be endlessly varied.

82. Xie Zhaozhe, *Wu za zu* 8.309–10.

83. Charlotte Furth ("Androgynous Men and Deficient Women," p. 25) argues that in terms of sexual politics, "the Ming to Ch'ing transition

in gender norms encouraged the intensification of the chaste widow cult" and was not "connected to perceptions of new social assertiveness among women." In providing a way to integrate the two, however, Pu Songling's story of Qiu Daniang, like that of the hideously ugly widow Qiao who requites her true friend, suggests that the socially assertive woman and the chaste widow were not necessarily mutually exclusive categories but could operate in tandem and even reinforce one another.

Chapter 5

EPIGRAPHS: Dong Yue, "Mengshe yue," in *Fengcao'an qianji* 2.15b; comment following the chapter "Illusory Love" ("Qinghuan"), *Qingshi leilüe* 9.57b–58a.

1. Sometimes this "I" merely describes the author's relationship with an informant, as in "my friend Bi Yi'an" or "my brother-in-law's grandfather." Other more important cases narrate reminiscences of boyhood magic tricks in "Stealing Peaches" ("Tou tao"; 1.32), his observations during an earthquake ("Di zhen"; 2.170), and his skeptical attendance at a seance held by a fox-shamaness ("Shang xian"; 5.691). To employ Genette's (*Narrative Discourse*, p. 245) useful distinction, "The Goddess of Flowers" is really the only homodiegetic narrative in *Liaozhai*.

2. Bi Jiyou's garden, The Stone Recluse Garden (Shiyin yuan), must have enjoyed considerable local fame. It appears in the "Gardens and Parks" section of the Zichuan gazetteer along with Bi's own lengthy description of his garden's history and special features (*Zichuan xianzhi* 3.22a–24a). Pu Songling describes the pleasure he took in this garden in a number of poems; see, e.g., *PSLJ* 1: 491–93, 515–16, 543, 612.

3. See *PSLJ* 1: 296–98 for the text of this "call to arms" (with an additional opening line) under the title "A Call to Arms Challenging Auntie Wind, Written on Behalf of the Goddess of Flowers" ("Wei huashen tao Fengyi xi"). Alongside it appears another parodic piece that invokes the Goddess of Flowers, "The Flowers' Prosecution of Frankincense" ("Qunhui jie ruxiang zhazi," *PSLJ* 1: 298–99). Pu Songling's "Call to Arms" has Tang antecedents such as the widely read story "Cui Xuanwei," which was reprinted in a number of late Ming anthologies. The piece also has contemporary parallels in You Tong's "The Goddess of Flowers Presses Charges Against Auntie Wind" ("Huashen tan Fengyi wen"), *Xitang zazu* 3.11a–12b in *Xitang quanji*, and the vernacular prologue to *Xingshi hengyan*, no. 4 (cf. Tan Zhengbi, *Sanyan liangpai ziliao*, pp. 411–12).

4. Tale: "huanpei qiangqiang" (6.739); poem: "huanpei xiang qiangqiang" (*PSLJ* 1: 467).

5. *PSLJ* 1: 468. Wang Shizhen (*PSLJ* 1: 468) commented favorably on this poem, calling it "densely woven with seductive beauty."

6. Trans. Spence, *Death of Woman Wang,* p. 32; Spence admirably conveys the erotic flavor of this scene.

7. He Dongru's encyclopedic *Menglin xuanjie* devotes one subcategory to dreams about gardens, which are mainly amorous in orientation. Most interesting are the dreams "Wandering in a garden and encountering a beautiful woman" ("Youyuan yu meinü"; 3.41a) and "Mandarin ducks flying about a garden pond" ("Yuanchi zhong yuanyang fei"; 3.43). On the compilation of this book, see Chapter 4, *n25.*

8. See, e.g., Wang Zhuo's "A Strange Experience Viewing Flowers" ("Kanhua shuyi ji") in Zhang Chao, *Yu Chu xinzhi* 12.183–87. Zhang Chao's comment (12.187) on this story makes clear how common this fantasy was in literature of the period: "In the past when I read books like *A Compendium of Rare Beauties* [*Yanyi bian*] and saw how flower-spirits and moon-maidens always had a romantic affinity with men of letters, I was secretly envious. I've always regretted that in my own life I've never encountered any. Now reading this account makes my desire even keener!" Other Ming compendia of classical tales with stories about flower-spirits are *Love at First Sight* (*Yijian shangxin*) and *Embroidered Phrases About Beautiful Maidens* (*Huazhen qiyan*). This theme receives its most hilarious treatment in the main story of Feng Menglong's *Xingshi hengyan,* no. 4, "The Old Gardener's Nocturnal Encounter with Immortal Flower-Maidens" ("Guanyuan sou wan feng xiannü").

9. Being asked by a divinity to write extemporaneously on an assigned topic is a standard dream and appears in the "Poetry" ("Shici") category of He Dongru, *Menglin xuanjie,* and in the "Pen and Ink" ("Bimo pian") section of Chen Shiyuan, *Mengzhan yizhi.*

10. Although Pu Songling sometimes affixes long rhetorical pieces to his stories, these pieces either recapitulate the plot as in "Rouge" ("Yanzhi"; 10.1374–77) or develop more fully some issue in the story, such as bestiality in "The Dog Who Committed Adultery" ("Quan jian"; 1.49–50) or salt smuggling in "Wang Shi" (11.1560–62).

11. The contemporary interest in dreams as the source of literary composition is evidenced by a number of fragments of poems composed in dreams, identified as such by a title or preface. The late Ming dream encyclopedias devote a separate category to the relationship between dream and writing; see, e.g., "Bimo pian" in Chen Shiyuan, *Mengzhan yishi;* and "Shici" in He Dongru, *Menglin xuanjie.*

12. *PSLJ* 1: 616. The preamble does not make clear how much of the quatrain was dreamed or how it was altered, only that Pu Songling "completed" the poem upon waking. For other dream poems, see *PSLJ* 1:467, 550, 616, 623, 624, 632.

13. Influenced by Jin Shengtan's aesthetics, commentator Dan Minglun

tries to read "The Goddess of Flowers" as a conclusion (*Liaozhai* 6.740).

14. Cheng Yizhong "*Yu Chu zhi* de bianzhe," pp. 36–38) dates the earliest edition to the first decades of the sixteenth century and attributes its compilation to Lu Cai (d. 1537). An enlarged version attributed to Tang Xianzu was also in circulation.

15. See, e.g., Huang Wei, "Records of Dreams" ("Ji meng"), *Pengchuang leiji, juan* 4; Shen Defu, *Wanli yehuo bian* 28.718–20; and Cheng Shiyong, "Corroborated Dreams" ("Meng zheng") section, *Fengshi leibian*.

16. "A Sequel to the Yellow Millet [Dream]" ("Xu huangliang"; 4.518–27), based on "The Tale of the Pillow" ("Zhenzhong ji"); "Princess of the Lilies" ("Lianhua gongzhu"; 5.673–77), based on "The Governor of the Southern Branch" ("Nanke taishou zhuan"); and "A Gentleman from Fengyang" ("Fengyang shiren"; 2.187–90), based on "Dugu Xiashu." All are well known.

17. Parts of *Mengzhan leikao* are also incorporated into *Menglin xuanjie,* which reprints Zhang Fengyi's original 1585 preface. Zhang's preface asserts that the art of dream interpretation fell into decline during the Song and Yuan and was revived during the Ming.

18. As Dong Yue's essay "An Oneiric Pharmacopoeia" ("Meng bencao"; *Fengcao'an ji,* 3.12b) puts it: "If an obsession with dreams has already become chronic, it is not considered a disease but a medicinal drug." This volume features a number of Dong's writings on dream, including "A Gazetteer of Dreamland" ("Mengxiang zhi") and "Preface to *Zhaoyang's History of Dreams*" ("*Zhaoyang mengshi* xu"). For studies of Dong Yue, see Brandauer, *Tung Yüeh,* esp. pp. 109–29; and T. A. Hsia, "The *Hsi-yu pu* as a Study of Dreams in Fiction," in his "New Perspectives."

19. For example, Song Maocheng (*juren* 1612) includes a series of dreams relating to immortality in his *Jiuyue ji.* Several accounts of dream in both prose and verse appear in Yuan Hongdao's collected work; for translations of a few, see "Dreams" in Chaves, *Pilgrim of the Clouds,* pp. 77–79. Li Yingsheng's (Wanli *jinshi*) essay "Recording a Dream" ("Jimeng") models his account of a dream journey on the travel account (*youji*) (reprinted in Zhu Jianxin, *Wan Ming xiaopin xuanzhu,* pp. 212–13). Zhang Dai's *Tao'an mengyi* includes "Praying for a Dream at Nanzhen Temple" ("Nanzhen qimeng"; 3.20) and "The Mythical Stone Grotto Library" ("Langhuan fudi"; 8.79); Zhang's preface to this work is also a rumination on dreams and the past (see Owen, *Remembrances,* pp. 134–41). You Tong (1618–1704) discourses on the dream in the preface to his *Records of Autumn Dreams* (*Qiumeng lu*) in *Xitang quanji.* See also Fang-tu, "Ming Dreams"; and Wu Pei-yi, *Confucian's Progress.*

20. I am indebted to Ellen Widmer, who is engaged in a study of Huang Zhouxing's work, for permitting me to see her photocopies of Huang's rare dream diary, *A Selection of Dreams* (*Mengxuan lüeke*) and a long narrative of several interconnected dreams entitled "Mandarin Duck Dreams" ("Yuan-yang meng").

21. See Wang Shouren, *Wang Wenchenggong quanshu* 2: 19.49–50; 20.119–20, 133–34; Xu Wei, *Xu Wenchang quanji*, pp. 12, 41, 104, 128; Yuan Hongdao, *Yuan Hongdao ji*, pp. 1308, 1446–47; Tang Xianzu's dream records in verse, *Tang Xianzu shiwen ji*, pp. 244, 383, 534, 757, 882; Gao Heng, *Qiyunge ji*, esp. "Analyzing a Dream" ("Fen meng"), *juan* 2, "A Past Dream" ("Jiu meng"), *juan* 7, "Upon My Pillow" ("Zhenshang"), *juan* 11; and Zhu Xiang, *Ji'nan Zhushi shiwen huibian*. I suspect the collections of most Ming and Qing writers include poems on dream.

22. For reproductions of seventeenth-century paintings of dreams, see Cahill, *Chinese Painting,* pp. 138–39, and idem, *The Compelling Image,* p. 89. For Li Rihua, see Chu-tsing Li and J. Watt, *A Scholar's Studio* (pl. 3); Xiang Shengmo's "Five Pines" (pl. 17 in *A Scholar's Studio*) bears an interesting 1629 inscription by the artist relating that the painting was based upon a dream. See also *Asian Art* 3.4 (Fall 1990), special issue on the dream journey and Chinese art, esp. W. Y. Li, "Dream Visions of Transcendence in Chinese Literature and Painting," pp. 53–77.

23. The dream interpretation for the entry "Wandering in a Garden and Encountering a Beautiful Woman" (He Dongru, *Menglin xuanjie* 3.41a) appends a story about an unmarried youth who dreams of strolling through a beautiful garden. There he meets a beautiful woman and makes love to her beside the peonies. After awakening, he falls ill with longing for her, but his parents force him to go through the marriage they have already arranged for him. On his wedding night he discovers that his bride is none other than the girl in his dream. A final comment reads: "This story bears a remarkable resemblance to Liu Mengmei [the hero of *The Peony Pavilion*]."

24. *DMB*, p. 178. The preface recounts a dream dated to 1562. These works on dreams are also clearly related to the general late Ming trend toward scholarly compilation, stimulated both by the growth of the publishing industry and the beginning of the *kaozheng* movement.

25. Chen Shiyuan, *Mengzhan yizhi* 1.1.

26. Ibid., 1.4. Wang Chong (A.D. 27–97) provides the earliest skeptical refutation of prognostic dreams in his *Lun heng*.

27. Chen Shiyuan, *Mengzhan yizhi* 8.72.

28. Callois, "Logical and Philosophical Problems," p. 23. A shorter version of this essay also serves as an introduction to Caillois's anthology, *Dream Adventure*.

29. See the discussion of Chinese dream interpretation manuals and their standard symbolism in Drège, "Notes d'onirologie Chinoise."

30. Bai Xingjian (d. 827) emphasizes this point in the opening to his "Accounts of Three Dreams" ("San meng ji"): "There do exist dreams that differ from ordinary ones" and in his final comment that dreams like the one he has just narrated have never been described before (Wang Pijiang, *Tangren xiaoshuo*, pp. 108–9).

31. Chen Shou, "Weizhi," *Sanguo zhi*, pp. 510–11. See Ong, *Interpretation of Dreams in Ancient China*, pp. 128–30, for a somewhat different interpretation of this passage. Fang-tu ("Ming Dreams," pp. 65–66) also discusses a Ming anecdote in which a feigned dream comes true as interpreted. Cf. the *Mishna* (*Berakhot* 55b): "There were twenty-four interpreters of dreams in Jerusalem. Once I had a dream and went to everyone of them and what any one interpreted, none of the others interpreted in the same way and yet all of them were fulfilled. This is in pursuance of the saying: *The dream follows the mouth* (of the one who interprets it)" (quoted in Caillois, *Dream Adventure*, p. xii).

32. At the end of this passage, Zhou Xuan explains the rationale behind his interpretations. Since straw dogs were used in sacrifices, he simply followed the sequence of the ritual, substituting the person or household of the dreamer for the straw dog. Thus, the dreamer will first obtain food and drink because making an offering is the first step in the sacrifice. The straw dog is then run over by a cart, and so the second prognostication is that the dreamer will fall from a carriage and break his foot. The final step in the ritual is to burn the straw dog, and so the last dream foretold a fire.

33. Chen's three techniques, curiously placed in the category of "Dream Causes" ("Meng duan"; 2.13–15), are adapted from an oneirocritical typology drawn up by Wang Fu in his 2nd c. A.D. work, *Qianfu lun*, pp. 315–16. The convergence between Wang Fu and Artemidorus's classifications of oneirocritical methods is discussed at length in Ong's *Interpretation of Dreams in Ancient China*, pp. 134–41. On Artemidorus's categories, see the *Oneirocritica*.

34. This is not the only criterion, of course. There are many caveats in *Menglin xuanjie* about the need to take into account the identity, status, and sex of the dreamer.

35. An authorial note (3.428) credits Bi Zaiji (Jiyou) with recording this item. The same anecdote appears without significant variation in Wang Shizhen, *Chibei outan* 27.624.

36. "Lord of the Five Black Sheepskins" was the epithet of Bai Lixi. In later usage, it alluded to a ruler's respectful treatment of worthy ministers.

37. Dreams that predict the outcome of the civil service examinations are frequent in the literature, and Chen Shiyuan devotes a full section to this

type of dream ("Kejia pian," *Mengzhan yizhi* 6.43–46). See also Fang-tu, "Ming Dreams," pp. 60–62.

38. Had he consulted Chen Shiyuan under the category of "antithetical dreams," he would indeed have discovered that one dreams of a doctor when one is going to fall ill. Had he consulted He Dongru, *Menglin xuanjie*, p. 41b, however, he would have found his assumption confirmed: dreams of "heavenly doctors" (*tian yi*) are diagnosed as auspicious and foretell the healing of disease.

39. Another *Liaozhai* tale, "The Great Sage Equal to Heaven" ("Qitian dasheng"; 11.1459–63), also makes fun of mediocre doctors for killing rather than curing their patients.

40. Bergson defines "the metaphorical made literal" as "the comic effect obtained whenever we pretend to take literally an expression which was used figuratively or once our attention is fixed on the material aspect of the metaphor" (quoted in Stewart, *Nonsense*, p. 76, who offers a helpful analysis of this device in the operations of nonsense). See also Todorov, *The Fantastic*, pp. 76–90, on the importance of the metaphorical made literal in nineteenth-century fantastic narratives.

41. Lu Xun, "Diary of a Madman" ("Kuangren riji"), in *Lu Xun quanji* 1: 9–19. What makes Lu Xun's 1918 story "modern" is that the discourse itself has been destabilized. Because the narrator is a madman, the reader can no longer distinguish figurative and literal language with any degree of certainty.

42. Ong, *Interpretation of Dreams in Ancient China*, p. 19. For the range of possible Chinese terms, see Bauer, "Chinese Glyphomancy," p. 73. These include the terms "chaizi" (to dissect characters) and "pozi" (to break up characters).

43. A passage in Freud's *Interpretation of Dreams* (p. 330) comes remarkably close to describing unwittingly the Chinese process of ideographic analysis:

> The dream content seems like a transcript of the dream-thoughts into another mode of expression, whose characters and syntactic laws it is our business to discover. . . . The dream-content . . . is expressed as it were in a pictographic script, the characters of which have to be transposed individually into the language of the dream-thoughts. . . . Suppose I have a picture-puzzle, a rebus, in front of me. It depicts a house with a boat on its roof, a single letter of the alphabet, the figure of a running man whose head has been conjured away, and so on. . . . We can only form a proper judgment of the rebus . . . if . . . we try to replace each separate element by a syllable or word that can be represented by that element in some way or other. The words which are put together in this way are no longer nonsensical but may form a poetical phrase of the greatest beauty and significance. A dream is a picture-puzzle of this sort.

See also Ong, "Image and Meaning."

44. In *Researches into Chinese Superstition* (p. 356), Doré includes a chapter

on "divination by dissecting written characters," a method he says "consists in dissecting or writing out separately the distinct parts of which a character is composed, and with these elements making one or several new words which have a different meaning from the original." He cites both dream interpretation and etymology as precedents for this practice.

Both Mark ("Orthography Riddles, Divination, and Word Magic") and Bauer ("Chinese Glyphomancy," p. 59) point out that glyphomancy applies the structural device of riddles in reverse. The fact that all the Chinese terms for ideographic analysis relate to the idea of separation rather than to the idea of recombination, however, leads me to believe that the use of the technique in dream interpretation must have come later.

45. The first part of the dream riddle is not explicitly interpreted, for it is not susceptible to ideographic analysis; rather, it describes the innocent man's predicament of having "met with the inauspicious outside." Its main purpose is to present the dream riddle in the appropriate parallel couplet form and to obscure the interpretation.

46. The famous scholar-official Zhou Lianggong, who is called by his style name Yuanliang in the story, served as magistrate of Weixian, Shandong, in 1642–43 (ECCP, p. 173).

47. Bauer ("Chinese Glyphomancy," pp. 75–76) calls Zi chu the most famous of the Qing books on this subject and mentions that Zhou Lianggong "was celebrated as an excellent glyphomancer by later authors." According to the Harvard-Yenching Library catalogue, Zi chu consists of "anecdotes, facetiae, satire, etc. divination." The book reproduces stories from zhiguai collections such as Wang Tonggui's Ertan along with anecdotes from the dynastic histories; it has been reprinted in a number of collectanea.

48. "Snow trails" signifies "old" because it describes white hair; "clouds form" signifies "dragon" because dragons are rain divinities in China; "wood on the water" is obviously a "boat," because boats are fashioned from wood and float; "a door on a wall" describes a "portal" (hu), a character that is also used as a suffix to indicate an occupation, as in "chuanhu" (boatman) or "dianhu" (shopkeeper).

49. On Pu Songling's relationship with Zhu Xiang and Zhu's keen interest in Liaozhai, see Chapter 1, n43; and Yuan Shishuo, Pu Songling xinkao, pp. 220–43. Yuan (p. 241) argues that Zhu Xiang must have informed Pu Songling about the case.

50. Both documents are appended to "The Ferrymen of Laolong" in Zhang Youhe's variorum edition of Liaozhai (12.1613–14).

51. This is rather unusual; Chinese crime case literature usually reveals the identity of the murderer at the outset—the reader's pleasure derives from watching the detective-official solve the crime rather than from guess-

ing "whodunit." Another story in *Liaozhai* that thwarts this convention is "Poetry Solves a Crime."

52. Trans. C. C. Wang, *Traditional Chinese Tales*, p. 87. For original text, see Wang Pijiang, *Tangren xiaoshuo*, p. 93.

53. Trans. C. C. Wang, *Traditional Chinese Tales*, pp. 88–89. Wang Pijiang, *Tangren xiaoshuo*, p. 94.

54. Hutter, "Dreams, Transformations and Literature," p. 231.

55. One example is the Yuan play *Magistrate Qian Cleverly Investigates the "No Clothes" Dream (Qian Dayin zhikan feiyimeng zaju)*. The magistrate in the play prays for a dream to solve a murderer's identity and is given a cryptic statement that contains the characters for the murderer's name. See Zhuang Yifu, *Gudian xiqu cunmu huikao*, p. 163.

56. Shi Runzhang, who is called by his sobriquet Yushan in this story, was renowned not only as an educator but also as a poet, historian, and member of the Hanlin Academy. He became commissioner of education for Shandong in 1656 and granted Pu Songling his degree in 1658 (see *ECCP*, p. 651).

57. The characters seem to have exorcised the evil spirit. This sort of word magic is probably linked to the practice of writing "elaborately stylized and distorted" characters on protective amulets (Mark, "Orthography Riddles, Divination, and Word Magic," p. 63). Interestingly, Mark reprints an amulet used for the protection of boats and vehicles from a 1973 Hong Kong almanac that bears a vague similarity to the dreamed characters in "Tiny Coffins."

58. Graham, *Lieh-tzu*, p. 59. I follow Graham's dating of this book.

59. Trans. Watson, *Complete Works of Chuang Tzu*, p. 45. For original text, see *Zhuangzi* 2.7.

60. Trans. Graham, *Lieh-tzu*, p. 70. For original text, see *Liezi* 3.36–37.

61. According to Caillois ("Logical and Philosophical Problems," pp. 46–47), Marco Polo described an Islamic subterfuge in which fake dream experiences were staged to recruit assassins. The story provided the basis for a seventeenth-century Spanish play, *Life Is a Dream*.

62. Pu Songling's commentators remark upon this uncharacteristically "open" or indefinite instance of closure here. Wang Shizhen (*Liaozhai* 1.337) approves: "It comes to an end, but it doesn't end." Feng Zhenluan (ibid.) is bothered by the unfinished feeling of the ending, and he offers an explanation that Jin Shengtan would have understood only too well: "It seems as if there should still be a few lines after this. I imagine that Wang Shizhen has simply excised them."

63. In the mid-seventeenth century, Ming loyalists like Zhang Dai and Dong Yue drew upon the dream's traditional associations with the past and

with a renunciation of the world. Although the dream is not accorded any specific loyalist symbolism in *Liaozhai,* dreams do occasionally have an elegaic and melancholy flavor that recalls the loyalist mood, as in this story.

64. See, e.g., Hales, "Dreams and the Demonic," p. 71.

65. Unschuld, *Medicine in China: Ideas,* p. 216.

66. Chen Shiyuan, *Mengzhan yizhi* 2.13. On the Greek relationship between healing and dreams, see Hippocrates, *Regimen IV,* pp. 441–47.

67. *Shishuo xinyu* 4.14; trans. Mather, *New Tales of the World,* p. 98.

68. The first three categories are from Wang Fu, *Qianfu lun,* pp. 315–16. Chen's classification appears in *Mengzhan yizhi* 2.13. Judging from his examples, Chen seems to mean qing in the sense of desire or emotion (e.g., "If one is excessively afraid, one dreams of hiding").

69. *TPGJ* 281.2244–45. Wang Pijiang, *Tangren xiaoshuo,* pp. 108–12, conveniently gathers the Tang variants. "Dugu Xiashu" was also rewritten as a vernacular story in Feng Menglong, *Xingshi hengyan,* no. 25.

70. Barr, "Pu Songling and *Liaozhai,*" p. 273.

71. See "Li Bangzhi's Dream" ("Li Bangzhi meng") in Hong Mai, *Yijian zhi, jiazhi* 11.94: "Sticking a flower in her hair is the symbol of an engagement. The slipper means union. I will die before long, and you will marry Miss Sun." Tang Xianzu's play *The Purple Hairpin* (*Zichai ji,* in *Tang Xianzu xiqu ji* 1: 94) also incorporates a romantic dream interpretation that hinges on the pun between shoe and union. According to Nozaki Seikin (*Zhongguo jixiang tu'an,* pp. 262–63), a pair of shoes was supposed to be included in a woman's dowry as a punned symbol of "lifelong union" (tongxie daolao). Although Pu Songling employs the word lü rather than xie to denote shoes in this story, I believe the pun with union is obvious enough to be inferred.

72. The phrase "lüxi jiaocuo" occurs verbatim in "Dugu Xiashu" to describe the ribaldry of the banquet (see Wang Pijiang, *Tangren xiaoshuo,* p. 111). The borrowing of this phrase helps explain why Pu Songling chose to use the word lü rather than xie for slipper.

73. As Dan Minglun (2.188–89) observes: "Every line and every word were thought up by the wife when she was in a state of extreme longing, but now they are being sung by the beautiful lady; even if one said the lady's song was a flattering imitation [*xiao pin*], it ends up supplying the words to seduce the wife's husband—this is really hard to bear!"

74. For a discussion of the dreamer's perception that one's "personality is usurped by a double," see Caillois, "Logical and Philosophical Problems," p. 33.

75. Zhang Fengyi, "*Mengzhan leikao xu*" in *Menglin xuanjie* 2a–b.

76. Chen Shiyuan, *Mengzhan yizhi* 2.15.

77. Shen Defu, *Wanli yehuo bian* 28.720.

78. In "A Comparative Study of Early and Late Tales," Barr argues that horror is a theme only in the earliest *Liaozhai* stories.

79. The original anecdote appears in "Biographies of Singular Conduct" ("Duxing zhuan"), *Hou Han shu*, and was also included in Gan Bao, *Soushen ji*, no. 299, 11.144. The same anecdote was turned into a vernacular story in Feng Menglong, *Gujin xiaoshuo*, no. 6. See Tan Zhengbi, *Sanyan liangpai ziliao* 1: 90–91.

80. See Yuan Shishuo, *Pu Songling xinkao*, pp. 89–90; Yuan argues this point based on another of Pu Songling's poems, *PSLJ* 1: 531.

81. *PSLJ* 1: 580.

82. See Yuan Shishuo, *Pu Songling xinkao*, pp. 187–220. Yuan believes that one of Pu Songling's letters requested Wang Shizhen to write a preface for *Liaozhai*.

83. *PSLJ* 1: 632–33.

84. Alternatively, the title could be translated as "Cheng the Immortal." Note this story's similarities to "Scholar Chu," which I discussed in the Introduction.

85. Tang Yin's handscroll *Dreaming of Immortality in a Thatched Cottage* (see W. Y. Li, "Dream Visions," pp. 54–55) depicts a man asleep in a cottage at one end and the same man floating in a distant empty landscape on the other end. In Cahill's words (*Chinese Painting*, p. 139), "we are transported magically from a substantial world, made convincing by the strong modeling of rocks and superb rendering of detail, to a realm of space, an abyss ringed by dim peaks." The same sort of contrast between a substantial world and a marvelous world also operates in "Becoming an Immortal."

86. O'Flaherty, *Dreams, Illusions, and Other Realities*, p. 89.

87. A similar reversal occurs in the *Liaozhai* tale "Wu Qiuyue" (5.671). The hero has just rescued his ghost lover from hell in a daring and bloody jailbreak, when he awakens to find himself back at the inn. Just as he is marveling at the violence of his illusory dream, he sees his ghost lover standing by his side. After he relates his dream, she tells him: "It was real, it was no dream."

88. Owen (*Traditional Chinese Poetry*, pp. 14–15) has written of the pervasive bias against reading something as fiction in the Chinese poetic tradition, and Plaks ("Toward a Critical Theory," pp. 310–28) argues for the predominance of the historical model for Chinese fiction.

89. It seems to me no accident that the least ambiguous terms for "fictionality" in Classical Chinese are "Sir Fantasy" (Zi xu) and "Mr. No-Such"

(Wuyou xiansheng), allusions to the names of allegorical *characters*. Other terms, such as *xiaoshuo, yeshi,* and the like, are also used to indicate fiction as opposed to fact, but these, like *yuyan,* are far more ambiguous.

90. Trans. based on Widmer, *"Hsi-yu cheng-tao shu,"* pp. 44–45, which discusses Wang Qi's involvement in fiction publishing. Wang Siren (1575–1646), famous official, poet, and humorist (*DMB,* pp. 1420–25), is associated with an annotated edition of *The Peony Pavilion.* See his "Pidian Yumingtang *Mudan ting* cixu" (1623), reprinted in Mao Xiaotong, *Tang Xianzu yanjiu ziliao huibian* 2: 856–88.

91. One of the chief appeals of fiction at this time was its power to produce an emotional response in the reader. Thus, the preface to *Yu Chu zhi* attributed to Tang Xianzu praises the book on the grounds that "to read it opens the heart and releases the soul, stirring the senses to astonishment" (trans. Barr, "Pu Songling and *Liaozhai,*" p. 200). Zhang Chao's preface (p. 1) to his "sequel," *Yu Chu xinzhi,* iterates a similar claim: "Reading this book will make people feel joy and astonishment; it will make them want to sing and want to cry, all for no reason."

92. Stewart, *Nonsense,* p. 81.

93. Under the rubric "Personnages" ("Renwu," *Menglin xuanjie, juan* 5), He Dongru provides a series of interpretations of dreams about famous historical and fictional characters, ranging from Yang Guifei to Xie Xiao'e to Cui Yingying. Once characters enter the dreams of others, they have certainly escaped from their author's control!

94. Of course, the narrator in *Liaozhai* tales can and often does reverse himself, as in "The Scholar from Zhedong" ("Zhedong sheng"; 12.1701). In this slapstick tale, a braggart who prides himself on his courage keeps dying of fright and then coming back to life, like the children's toy that keeps springing back up again after being knocked down. In this story, everything—even death—is reversible; instead of everything coming true, nothing comes true. This is an alternative way of calling attention to the fictional nature of the tale, by exaggerating its reversibility.

95. For a discussion of the seventeenth-century references to the existence of this Fujian cult and its relationship to the novel *Journey to the West,* see Dudbridge, *The Hsi-yu Chi,* pp. 159–60. Dudbridge agrees that it was not "a priori impossible for cults to grow up around fictional heroes." Chu Renhuo records the existence of this religious cult in Fujian in his Kangxi period zhiguai collection, *Jianhu ji* (*yuji,* 2.7a) and quips: "Putting aside the question whether *Journey to the West* is of the "Sir Fantasy" or "Mr. No-Such" type—could it be that the Water Curtain Cave of the monkey kingdom is located in Fujian?"

96. "Qiu weng" (old Qiu) refers to the Daoist master Qiu Chuji (1148–1227), to whom was attributed the authorship of the novel *Journey to the West*. According to Plaks (*Four Masterworks*, p. 194), "This attribution was quite widespread during much of the Qing period," and it is mentioned in Yu Ji's preface to Wang Qi's *Xiyou zhengdao shu*. The current attribution of the novel to Wu Cheng'en is also apparently rather shaky.

97. Such conversion stories are related to the tradition of "the ghostly apologue" in which ghosts appear "in the flesh" to disabuse skeptics of their disbelief. See A. Yu, " 'Rest, Rest Perturbed Spirit!' "

98. Magical feats that Sun Wukong regularly performs in the novel. The embroidery needle is really a cudgel that he stores inside his ear for convenience.

99. This edition, which is still extant, was rather successful with the reading public, judging from the number of reprints published throughout the eighteenth and nineteenth centuries (see Fu Xihua, *Chuanqi quanmu*, pp. 63–66). I thank Sun Jiaxiu, Bu Jian, Shiba Yoshinobu, Valerie Hansen, and T. J. Ellermeier for helping me procure photocopies of the Kangxi edition of the commentary. In the original edition, Qian Yi's narrative is subtitled "The Return of the Soul: An Account of Events" ("Huanhunji jishi"). Zhang Chao anthologized Qian Yi's narrative in his *Yu Chu xinzhi* under the new title "The Story of a Shared Dream" ("Ji tongmeng") and also included it, along with the remaining materials framing the commentary, in his massive collectanea of contemporary writings, the *Zhaodai congshu*. Most of the framing materials, including Qian Yi's narrative, are conveniently reprinted in Mao Xiaotong, *Tang Xianzu yanjiu ziliao huibian* 2:889–906.

100. For the former, see "The Goddess of the Xiang" ("Xiang jun"), trans. Hawkes, *Songs of the South*, pp. 104–7; for the latter, see "Gaotang fu," attributed to Song Yu in *Wenxuan*.

101. Mao Xiaotong, *Tang Xianzu yanjiu ziliao huibian* 2: 902–3; Zhang Chao, *Yu Chu xinzhi* 15.223.

102. "The Great Clod [*da kuai*] belches out breath and its name is wind" (trans. Watson, *Complete Works of Chuang Tzu*, p. 36; for original text, see *Zhuangzi* 2.3).

103. "Hun you," in *Tang Xianzu xiqu ji* 1: 349–52. For a translation, see Birch, "Spirit Roaming," *The Peony Pavilion*, pp. 147–55. I diverge from Birch in translating "mei" not as "apricot" but as the more customary "flowering plum."

104. See Gan Bao, *Soushen ji*, no. 378, 16.189.

105. Li Yu, *Xianqing outan*, pp. 20–21.

106. Xie Zhaozhe (*Wu za zu* 15.308) argues that when someone tries to

point out the historical inaccuracies of a play, "it is really like relating a dream to a fool."

107. Ibid.

108. Giles, *Strange Stories*, p. 327.

109. In the Chinese shadow-puppet theater, brightly colored shadows cast by painted cut-out puppets were projected against a screen lit by lanterns. For examples, see Berliner's handsomely illustrated *Chinese Folk Art*, pp. 125–34.

110. The title of this opera, "Huafeng zhu," alludes to an anecdote in chap. 12 of *Zhuangzi*. Scholars have pointed out that titles of operas performed in novels such as *Jin Ping Mei* and *Honglou meng* frequently have a symbolic significance. Pu Songling probably invented both opera titles in "Mr. Gu" to suit the story. Neither I nor any of the commentators has been able to locate them in any drama catalogues.

111. As commentator He Shouqi (*Liaozhai* 8.1155) points out, "In a twinkling of an eye, the young became old."

112. No Chinese source I have seen differentiates dream and hallucination. Thus, Dong Yue's "Account of Wandering When Ill" ("Bingyou ji"; *Fengcao'an ji* 3.14.b–15) employs the category of dream to describe his experience of delirium.

113. This corresponds to Chen Shiyuan's (*Mengzhan yizhi* 2.13) category of "physical stimulus" (*tizhi*). Wang Fu provides no corresponding category in *Qianfu lun*, but *Liezi* gives several examples of this theory: "When you go to sleep lying on your belt, you dream of snakes; when a flying bird pecks your hair, of flying" (trans. Graham, *Lieh-tzu*, p. 66). See also Ong, *Interpretation of Dreams in Ancient China*, pp. 47–54.

114. Ong (*Interpretation of Dreams in Ancient China*, p. 54) relates a story from *Youyang zazu* about a man who dreamed that someone was beating a drum; when he awoke, it turned out that his brother was banging on the door.

115. Wang Fu (*Qianfu lun*, pp. 315–16) includes "the pathological" (*bing*) among his categories of dreams. Chen Shiyuan (*Mengzhan yizhi* 2.13–15) provides a more complex breakdown of this category in his list of dream causes: "repletion of qì" (*qisheng*); "deficiency of qì" (*qixu*) and "negative influences in an organ" (*xieyu*). See also Fang-tu, "Ming Dreams." In the *Liaozhai* story "Yang Dahong" (9.1256–57), a sick man dreams a line of poetry that predicts his cure.

116. This joke appears verbatim in both the late Ming *Forest of Jokes* (*Xiao-lin*) by Fubai zhuren (The Tippler) and in the late Kangxi *Knockdown Jokes* (*Xiaodao*) by Duoduo fu (Mister Ha-ha), later expanded by Chichi zi (Master Tee-hee); reprinted in Wang Liqi, in *Lidai xiaohua ji*, p. 221 and 444,

respectively. On the dating and authorship of these books, see pp. 204 and 442.

117. Virtually an identically worded anecdote is included in Wang Shizhen's *Chibei outan* under the title "The Miniature Man in His Heart" ("Xintou xiaoren"). (The 24-*juan* MS of the *Liaozhai* includes a comment by Wang Shizhen on this story that does not appear in the variorum edition: "Could this be Qi Yuan? Very strange" [p. 1139].) Although Barr ("Pu Songling and *Liaozhai*," p. 260) argues that the overlapping stories in *Liaozhai* and *Chibei outan* "do not appear to be the result of mutual borrowing for narrative variants suggest that the authors were drawing on independent sources," the wording of these two versions is close enough to suggest that in this case some sort of borrowing did take place. If we accept Wang's comment in the 24-*juan* MS as genuine, we would assume that Wang borrowed the story from Pu. At any rate the overlap suggests the shared appeal of such a story.

118. O'Flaherty, *Dreams, Illusions, and Other Realities*, p. 89.

119. He Dongru warns that even auspicious dreams about actors will come to naught, presumably because of the unreal nature of the theater (see the entry "Paiyou xinong zhi lei, sui ji cheng xu," *Menglin xuanjie, juan* 1, "Zhan you," 3a).

120. For instance, the hero in "Zhicheng" (11.1512) protests his unfair treatment at the hands of the Dragon King because the hero of the Tang tale "Liu Yi zhuan," whose surname he shares, was allowed to become an immortal whereas he himself has just been sentenced to death.

121. Campany, "Chinese Accounts of the Strange," p. 453.

122. Yuan Shishuo, *Pu Songling xinkao*, p. 173.

123. See, e.g., Ma Ruifang, *Pu Songling pingzhuan*, p. 153.

124. Barr, "Pu Songling and *Liaozhai*," p. 253.

125. Gao Heng, "The Biography of Liu Xianzhi" ("Liu Xianzhi zhuan"), in *Qiyunge ji, juan* 12. This biography of modern-day heroism (in which a tutor loyally retrieves the body of his patron, his "true friend") and several other of Gao's biographies of virtuous men and women share the themes and values of a number of *Liaozhai* tales. See also *n*8 to this chapter on Zhang Chao's keen desire to meet the flower-maidens described in *Yanyi bian* and *n*93 to this chapter on dreams about historical and fictional figures in *Menglin xuanjie*.

126. He Dongru, "*Menglin xuanjie* xu," *Menglin xuanjie* 3a.

127. Stewart, *Nonsense*, p. 73.

128. The entire banquet scene in which Bi plays drinking games with various pieces of intimate feminine apparel reads like a parody of brothel entertainment.

129. See Stewart's (*Nonsense,* pp. 72–76) discussion of games and discourse that denies itself.

130. Trans. Graham, *Chuang-tzu: The Inner Chapters,* pp. 59–60.

131. Interestingly, this is the same year and the same location provided for Pu Songling's dream in "The Goddess of Flowers."

132. The fox-maiden is not given a name, perhaps in tacit recognition of her fictional status, which makes it rather hard for her to be properly "commemorated." If anyone is the subject of the tale-biography, it is the elusive Bi Yi'an, who is caricatured as a plump and bewhiskered "wild scholar" (*kuang sheng*) type.

133. Li Zhi, "Zhuowu lunlüe," in *Fen shu,* pp. 86–87. See Wu Pei-yi's translation and discussion in *Confucian's Progress,* pp. 19–24, esp. pp. 20–21. Wu translates the surname Kong as "aperture" and convincingly demonstrates that Kong Ruogu must be taken as a fictional figure.

Conclusion

EPIGRAPH: Comment attributed to the first wife, Chen Tong, in *Wu Wushan sanfu heping Mudan ting* 1: 83a–b.

1. For example, Caillois includes Giles's bowdlerized translation of "The Painted Wall" in *Dream Adventure,* his anthology of world dream literature (pp. 37–39). The original text of this tale appears in *Liaozhai* 1.14–17. For a full translation, see the Appendix.

2. In Scene 26 of *The Peony Pavilion,* Liu Mengmei senses that Du Liniang is gazing back at him as he stares longingly at her self-portrait. A marginal comment in *The Three Wives* edition (1: 846) explains: "When one stares fixedly at an inanimate object, it will appear to move. And so indeed she seems to be gazing back at him, she seems to be holding him in her arms, she seems about to descend from the painting." In Scene 28, Liu Mengmei voices his desire to join his beloved in the painting: "Could I but urge / the transformation of this solitary image until our twin souls stood together / as on a painted screen" (trans. Birch, *Peony Pavilion,* p. 157).

3. "Zhu Ao" (*TPGJ* 334.2655) is reprinted as a "source" for "The Painted Wall" in *ZL,* pp. 9–10, along with an excerpt from the same tale that Chu Renhuo copied into his *Jianhu ji (yuji, juan* 4). *Qingshi leilüe (juan* 9) devotes a small subsection "Painting Illusions" ("Hua huan"), which concentrates on stories about paintings—mainly portraits of women—that come to life in response to their beholder's desire. "Zhu Ao" is not among these. Sawada (*Kishu dangi,* pp. 325–26) includes four stories from *TPGJ* and *Yijian zhi* about divine women painted on temple walls who come to life.

4. "Tanyue"—donor or almsgiver, a polite form used by a monk to address a layman.

5. This two-dimensional image of Zhu is reminiscent of several *Liaozhai* tales of magic mirrors that can trap images. In "The Tortoise King" ("Bada wang"; 6.868–75), a young man traps the image of a princess in a magic mirror and then marries her. In "Immortal Feng" ("Feng xian"; 9.1177–84), a beautiful fox-spirit inhabits a mirror so that her animated image can supervise her lover's studies in her absence.

6. Pu Songling may have drawn the inspiration for such a twist from a widely known Tang tale. In the tale, a man falls in love with a beautiful lady on a painted screen, who comes to life in response to his summons. He makes her his wife, and she bears him a son. When a friend advises the man to exorcise this "demon," the lady tearfully returns to the painted screen. Looking up once again at the screen, the man discovers that a portrait of a little boy has now been added to it. See "The Painter" ("Hua gong") in *TPGJ* 286.2283. Two important allusions to it occur in *The Peony Pavilion* (Scenes 14 and 26) in conjunction with Du Liniang's self-portrait. The story is also included in the "Painting Illusions" ("Hua huan") subsection in *Qingshi leilüe, juan* 9.

7. Giles (*Strange Stories*, p. 6 n1) likens Zhu's entry into the mural to Alice's adventures through the looking glass.

8. Hong Mai, *Rongzhai suibi* 1.218. See Zhang Shaokang, *Zhongguo gudai wenxue chuangzuo lun*, p. 176.

9. Zhang Shaokang, *Zhongguo gudai wenxue chuangzuo lun*, pp. 175–78.

10. *Records of Broad Learning* (*Bowu zhi*), an encyclopedic collection of notes compiled by Zhang Hua (232–308), survives only in fragments. Liu Bao was a Han dynasty painter. According to Huang Lin and Han Tongwen (*Zhongguo lidai xiaoshuo lun*), this particular anecdote is not preserved in the extant text of *Bowu zhi* but survives in Zhang Yanyuan's ninth-century *Lidai minghua ji, juan* 4.

11. Dragons are the traditional Chinese deities associated with water and storms. Zhang Sengyou was a great mural painter of the Six Dynasties; this story is also preserved in Zhang Yanyuan's *Lidai minghua ji*. Wu Daozi was one of the most famous painters of the Tang dynasty; Zhang Yanyuan wrote of him: "He painted as well five dragons in the Inner Hall, whose scaly armor moved in flight. Whenever it was about to rain, a mist would rise from them (trans. Bush and Shih, *Early Chinese Texts on Paintings*, p. 56).

12. Reprinted and annotated in Huang Lin and Han Tongwen, *Zhongguo lidai xiaoshuo lun*, pp. 259–60. The preface is attributed to the pseudonymous Layman of the Land of Nod (Shuixiang jushi), whom scholars have been unable to identify.

13. For legends about this monk, see *TPGJ* 90.594–97, under the alternative name "Shi Baogong."

14. Pu Songling was attracted to this phrase throughout his life. He not only utilized it in his 1679 preface to *Liaozhai* in reference to his previous incarnation as a monk, but also wrote a series of regulated poems in 1697 entitled "My minuscule hut completed, I follow my sons' suggestion and inscribe this name on a plaque: The Dwelling of Facing the Wall" ("Dou shi luo cheng, cong erbei yan zhi Mianbi ju," in *PSLJ* 1: 567). The poems describe a hut "as tiny as a fist" that he had built for himself at the age of 57. Hom ("Continuation of Tradition," p. 96, n12) suggests that "the name of the house alludes to Pu's personal belief that he was the rebirth of a suffering Buddha who sat facing the wall," as indicated in his preface to *Liaozhai*. But the first half of the poem sequence is comic and playfully laments that his "prayer mat will be empty day after day." We might rather take the allusion literally as an ironic joke: the house was so small and cramped that its occupant would perforce "face the wall." According to Barr's dating ("A Comparative Study of Early and Late Tales"), "The Painted Wall" is an early composition and would have been written far closer to the date of the preface (1679) than to the construction of the house (1697).

15. I am grateful for Barr's suggestion that the troublesome phrase "laopo xinqie" ("a bit too keen to see results"), which lacks an explicit subject, refers to the monk. In fact, the Zhao edition added the word for monk ("lao*seng* po xinqie"), presumably to specify the subject and make the meaning clearer. The expression "laopo xinqie" derives from an anecdote in *Jingde chuandeng lu*, a book of Chan Buddhist sayings by the Song monk Daoyuan. As Lü Zhan'en (*Liaozhai* 1.17) glosses the anecdote:

Chan Master Yiyuan once asked Huang Nie for what purpose the Venerable Teacher [Bodhidarma] had come from the West. He asked three times, and Huang Nie beat him each time. Then he asked for permission to leave. Huang Nie sent him to ask Great Stupidity [Da Yu]. Stupidity said: "How can Huang Nie be so *laopo xinqie?*" The Chan Master had a great realization and went back to Huang Nie. Huang Nie said: "You've returned too soon." Said the Chan Master: "It's just because I'm too *laopo xinqie.*" Huang Nie burst into uproarious laughter.

16. Dudbridge, *Tale of Li Wa*, p. 63.

17. McMahon, *Causality and Containment*, p. 20 n40, p. 26. McMahon is particularly fond of the example in Feng Menglong, *Xingshi hengyan*, no. 34, in which a man takes advantage of a crumbling wall to spy on girls playing on a swing next door. He duly climbs across the wall into their garden, and his erotic adventures begin.

18. Chinese houses were traditionally built as compounds surrounded by walls.

19. In "Qing E" (7.929–37), the hero uses a magic chisel, which can bore holes through solid stone "as though it were beancurd," to cross through the wall and enter his beloved's bedchamber.

20. There is a hilarious takeoff on this fantasy in "The Daoist of Laoshan" ("Laoshan daoshi"; 1.40–41), in which a stupid Daoist adept is duped into thinking he has acquired the power to go through walls. Naturally, when he returns home and attempts to demonstrate his newly learned skill to his wife, the wall remains solid, and he delivers himself a colossal blow on the head. In another tale, "Lotuses Under a Cold Moon" ("Hanyue furong"; 4.580), a Daoist magician draws a double-leafed door on a wall. When he raps sharply on it, it opens and the assembled company is able to glimpse the hustle and bustle of another world within. At the Daoist's bequest, the denizens of this other world quickly produce a sumptuous banquet for his guests on the opposite side of the wall.

21. I have been stimulated here by the operations that Susan Stewart (Nonsense, pp. 116–28) subsumes under the category "play with infinity," especially "nesting."

22. The definition of "jian" in this tale closely resembles the one offered by Han Daozhao of the Jin dynasty in his Wuyin jiyun: "When people die, they become ghosts, and when people see ghosts, they fear them. When ghosts die, they become jian, and when ghosts see jian, they are frightened. If one inscribes this character in seal script and fixes it above the doorway, then all baleful ghosts will keep their distance for a thousand li." Duan Chengshi (Youyang zazu) also notes the popular practice of inscribing the character jian above doorways, but glosses jian as the name of an official in the spectral bureaucracy, saying that the purpose of the inscription is to keep serious illness at bay. See Zhongwen dacidian, p. 11659.

23. Rebirth or reincarnation for a ghost in love with a living person is often represented as a kind of death in Liaozhai because it signals a permanent farewell just as death parts mortal lovers for eternity.

24. Stewart, Nonsense, p. 86.

25. See Swatek, "Feng Menglong's Romantic Dream," chap. 4, for the link between the strange and the erotic in The Peony Pavilion's language and imagery. Plaks ("Toward a Critical Theory," p. 329) notes "the impression of sensuality—the mild tinge of eroticism—that arises in connection with the best classical tales in Liao-chai Chih-i and similar collections."

26. A carnivalesque version of this conceit appears in chap. 7 of Journey to the West in which the monkey king makes a wager with the Buddha that he can somersault off his hand. When he arrives at what seems the end of the world, he sees five gigantic pink columns. To leave a "momento" of himself, he scrawls "The Great Sage was here" on one of the columns and then

piddles on another one. After his return, tiny characters can still be made out on the Buddha's middle finger, and the stench of monkey urine can still be whiffed between Buddha's thumb and forefinger, proving that he had never left the infinite expanse of Buddha's hand (for a translation, see A. Yu, *Journey to the West* 1: 173–74).

27. Pu Songling is master of the unexpected but perfect simile. It is one of the stylistic techniques that makes the language of his stories so effective. For instance, in the brief anecdote "A Passion for Snakes" ("She pi"; 1.130), a servant is said to devour raw snakes whole "as though swallowing a leek." Like the equation of writing and lice in "Gong the Immortal," this earthy simile instantly makes the aberrant familiar and convincing.

28. Campany, "Chinese Accounts of the Strange," p. 454.

29. The tendency toward fixed narrative conventions, especially in the case of zhiguai, is of course tied to these genres' claim to report hearsay or eyewitness events rather than to boast of literary inventiveness.

30. Compare Jauss's (*Toward an Aesthetic of Reception,* p. 23) emphasis on "the horizons of expectations": "The new text evokes for the reader (listener) the horizon of expectations and rules familiar from earlier texts, which are then varied, corrected, altered, or even just reproduced. Variation and correction determine the scope, whereas alteration and reproduction determine the borders of a genre-structure." Jauss has in mind the reader's experience rather than the writer's, but of course all writers are readers first.

31. This remark is itself a repetition or review because the lovers inside the sleeve had earlier incorporated the expression into one of the couplets they had inscribed on the wall.

32. Tao Qian, "Taohua yuanji," in *Tao Yuanming ji,* pp. 165–68. On the Chinese tradition of miniature representations of the universe and separate hidden worlds, see Stein, *World in Miniature,* esp. pp. 52–58.

33. Discussing the phenomenon of "micrographia" (miniature texts), Stewart (*On Longing,* p. 52) links the fantasy of *multum in parvo* (much in little) with "the miniaturization of language itself," for "it displays the ability of language to sum up the diversity of the sensual or physical world of lived expression."

Appendix

1. They are being hounded by Xing's avenging ghost.

2. In the 24-*juan* MS version of *Liaozhai,* the magistrate releases the grave robbers rather than sentencing them to death. This is clearly a less satisfying ending.

3. *Jinya huan* (lit., a "gold raven" bracelet). *Liaozhai*'s nineteenth-century annotators clearly have no idea what kind of bracelet this refers to. *Jinya* is a poetic kenning for the sun, but it also means a "golden raven"; it is possible that the bracelet was decorated with images of ravens or of the sun.

Selected Bibliography

For the abbreviations used here, see p. xiii.

Chinese and Japanese Sources

Bai-Kong liutie 白孔六帖 [Bai and Kong's encyclopedia]. Comp. Bai Juyi 白居易 (772–846) and Kong Chuan 孔傳 (12th c.). Facsimile reprint of Ming ed. 2 vols. Taipei, 1986.

Bai Yaren 白亞仁 (Allan Barr). "*Liaozhai zhiyi* zhong lishi renwu bukao (3)" 聊齋誌異中歷史人物補考 [New facts on historical figures in *Liaozhai zhiyi*]. *Zhonghua wenshi luncong* 中華文史論叢, no. 2–3 (1987): 158.

Ban Gu 班固 (32–92). *Han shu* 漢書 [History of the Former Han]. 20 vols. Beijing, 1962.

Beijing Fahai si Mingdai bihua 北京法海寺明代壁畫 [Ming dynasty wall paintings from the Fahai temple in Beijing]. Ed. Zhongguo gudian yishu chubanshe 中國古典藝術出版社. Beijing, 1958.

Bian er chai 弁而釵 [Hairpins beneath a man's cap]. By Zui Xihu xinyue zhuren 醉西湖心月主人, pseud. Early Qing ed. MQSB, Yanqing xiaoshuo zhuanji 艷情小說專輯 [Special series on erotic fiction].

Chao Yuanfang 巢元方 (fl. 605–16). *Zhubing yuanhou lun* 諸病源侯論 [The etiology and symptomatology of all diseases]. Comp. 610. Facsimile reprint of 1891 ed. Beijing, 1955.

Chen Shiyuan 陳士元 (16th c.). *Mengzhan yizhi* 夢占逸旨 [A treatise on dream interpretation]. Congshu jicheng 叢書集成, vol. 727. Changsha, 1939.

Chen Shou 陳壽 (233–97). *Sanguo zhi* 三國志 [Records of the Three Kingdoms]. 5 vols. Beijing, 1962.

Cheng Hao 程顥 (1032–85) and Cheng Yi 程頤 (1033–1107). *Er Cheng ji* 二程集 [Collected works of the Cheng brothers]. Ed. Wang Xiaoyu 王孝魚. Beijing, 1981.

Cheng Jinzheng 成晉徵 (*jinshi* 1649). *Zouping xian jingwu zhi* 鄒平縣景物志 [A record of the sights of Zouping county]. Preface dated 1692.

Cheng Shiyong 程時用. *Fengshi leibian* 風世類編 [A classified compendium of admonitions to the world]. 1601 ed. Academy of Sciences Library, Beijing.

Cheng Yizhong 程毅中. "*Yu Chu zhi* de bianzhe he banben" 虞初志的編者和版本 [*The Magician's Records*: its compiler and earliest edition]. *Wen xian* 文獻 36(1988.2): 36–38.

Chu ci jizhu 楚辭集註 [Annotated *Songs of the South*]. Annotated by Zhu Xi 朱熹 (1130–1200). Ed. Li Qingjia 李慶甲. Shanghai, 1979.

Chu Renhuo 褚人獲 (1630–1705). *Jianhu ji* 堅瓠集 [The useless gourd collection]. Prefaces dated 1690–1703. Facsimile reprint of 1926 ed. 4 vols. Hangzhou, 1986.

Dong Yue 董說 (1620–86). *Fengcao'an ji* 豐草庵集 [The Fengcao Hermitage collection]. In *Dong Ruoyu shiwenji* 董若雨詩文集 [Collected poetry and prose of Dong Yue]. Ed. Liushi of Wuxing 吳興劉氏. 1914 reprint.

Du Fu 杜甫 (712–70). *Du shi xiangzhu* 杜詩詳註 [Du Fu's poems with detailed annotation]. Ed. Qiu Zhao'ao 仇兆鰲. 5 vols. Beijing, 1985.

Du Wan 杜綰. *Yunlin shipu* 雲林石譜 [Rock catalogue of Cloudy Forest]. Zhibuzu zhai congshu 知不足齋叢書, vol. 217.

Duan Chengshi 段成栻 (ca. 800–863). *Youyang zazu* 酉陽雜俎 [The librarian's miscellany]. Beijing, 1981.

Feng Menglong 馮夢龍 (1574–1646). *Gujin tan'gai* 古今譚概 [Survey of talk old and new]. Facsimile reprint of Ming ed. 2 vols. Beijing, 1955.

———. *Gujin xiaoshuo* 古今小說 [Stories old and new]. Ed. Xu Zhengyang 許正揚. 2 vols. Beijing, 1981.

———. *Xingshi hengyan* 醒世恒言 [Constant words to awaken the world]. Ed. Gu Xuejie 顧學頡. Hong Kong, 1978.

Fu Xihua 傅惜華. *Chuanqi quanmu* 傳奇全目 [A complete catalogue of *chuanqi* drama]. Beijing, 1959.

Fujita Yūken 藤田佑賢 and Yagi Akiyoshi 八木章好. *Ryōsai kenkyū bunken yōran* 聊齋研究文獻要覽 [A bibliographic handbook for *Liaozhai* research]. Tokyo, 1985.

Gan Bao 干寶 (fl. 320). *Soushen ji* 搜神記 [Seeking the spirits]. Ed. Wang Shaoying 汪紹楹. Beijing, 1979.

Gao Heng 高珩 (1612–97). *Qiyunge ji* 捷雲閣記 [Records from the Lofty Perch Pavilion]. Qing ed. Shandong Provincial Library, Ji'nan.

Gu Wenjian 顧文薦 (Song). *Fuxuan zalu* 負暄雜錄 [Miscellaneous records under the sun]. In *Shuofu* 說郛 [Environs of fiction], vol. 2. Facsimile reprint. Hanfenlou 涵芬樓 ed. Taipei, 1972.

Guo Dengfeng 郭登峰. *Lidai zishuzhuan wenchao* 歷代自叙傳文鈔. [An

anthology of autobiographical writings through the ages]. Shanghai, 1937.

He Dongru 何棟如 (1527–1637), ed. *Menglin xuanjie* 夢林玄解 [Arcane explanations to the forest of dreams]. Preface dated 1636. Harvard-Yenching Library, Cambridge, Mass.

He Liangjun 何良俊 (1506–73), ed. *Shishuo xinyu bu* 世說新語補 [Supplement to *New Tales of the World*]. Ming Wanli ed. Academy of Sciences Library, Beijing. The Harvard-Yenching Library, Cambridge, Mass., holds a 1676 ed.

Hong Mai 洪邁 (1123–1202). *Rongzhai suibi* 容齋隨筆 [Informal notes from Rongzhai]. 2 vols. Shanghai, 1978.

———. *Yijian zhi* 夷堅志 [Records of the listener]. 4 vols. Beijing, 1981.

Hu Shi 胡適. "*Xingshi yinyuan zhuan* kaozheng" 醒世姻緣傳考證 [An investigation of *Marriage Destinies to Awaken the World*]. In Xi Zhou sheng 西周生, pseud., *Xingshi yinyuan zhuan*, 3: 1448–95. Shanghai, 1981.

Hu Yinglin 胡應麟 (1551–1602). *Shaoshi shanfang bicong* 少室山房筆叢 [Collected jottings from the Shaoshi Mountain Retreat]. Shanghai, 1958.

Hua Shu 華淑 (fl. late Ming). *Pidian xiaoshi* 癖顛小史 [A brief history of obsession and lunacy]. In both his *Xianqing xiaopin* 閑情小品 [Tidbits for idle moods], Wanli ed., and his *Qingshuige kuaishu shizhong* 清睡閣快書十種 [Ten amusement books from the Chamber of Untroubled Sleep], 1618. Library of Congress, Washington, D.C.

Huang Lin 黃霖 and Han Tongwen 韓同文, eds. *Zhongguo lidai xiaoshuo lunzhu xuan* 中國歷代小說論著選 [An annotated anthology of Chinese fiction criticism], vol. 1. Nanchang, 1982.

Huang Wei 黃暐 (b. 1438; *jinshi* 1490), *Pengchuang leiji* 蓬窗類記 [Classified records from an overgrown window]. Preface dated 1526. In *Hanfenlou miji* 涵芬樓密笈, ed. Wang Yunwu, 汪雲五. vol. 6. Facsimile reprint. Taipei, 1962.

Huazhen qiyan 花陣綺言 [Embroidered phrases about beautiful maidens]. Comp. Xiansou shigong 仙叟石公, pseud. MQSB, 2nd series.

Ji Yun 紀昀 (1724–1805). *Yuewei caotang biji* 閱微草堂筆記 [Notes from the Thatched Cottage of Careful Reading]. 2 vols. Tianjin, 1980.

Jiyuan ji suo ji 寄園寄所寄 [Expressions from the Garden of Self-expression]. Comp. Zhao Jishi 趙吉士 (*juren* 1651). Preface dated 1695. Qing ed. Harvard-Yenching Library, Cambridge, Mass.

[Jiaozheng] *Kangxi zidian* 校正康熙字典 [Kangxi dictionary]. 1716. 2 vols. Taipei, 1973.

Kong Chuan 孔傳 (12th c.). "*Yunlin shipu* xu" 雲林石譜序 [Preface to *Rock Catalogue of Cloudy Forest*]. Zhibuzu zhai congshu 知不足齋叢書, vol. 217, pp. 1–2.

Li Deyu 李德裕 (787–849). *Pingquan caomu ji* 平泉草木記 [Record of the plants of the Pingquan estate]. Tangdai congshu 唐代叢書, vol. 9.

Li He 李賀 (791–817). *Li He shiji* 李賀詩集 [Collected poems of Li He]. Ed. Ye Congqi 葉蔥奇. Beijing, 1984.

Li Jianguo 李劍國. *Tangqian zhiguai xiaoshuo shi* 唐前志怪小說史 [A history of pre-Tang zhiguai fiction]. Tianjin, 1984.

Li Jinxin 李金新 and Guo Yu'an 郭玉安. "Gao Fenghan nianpu" 高鳳翰年譜 [An annalistic biography of Gao Fenghan]. In *Yangzhou baguai yanjiu ziliao congshu* 揚州八怪研究資料叢書 [Research materials on the Eight Yangzhou Eccentrics], vol. 1, pp. 273–352. Jiangsu, 1990.

Li Qingchen 李慶辰. *Zuicha zhiguai* 醉茶誌怪 [Drunk on Tea's strange accounts]. Jinmen, 1892.

Li Qingzhao 李清照 (1084–ca. 1154). *Li Qingzhao ji jiaozhu* 李清照集校註 [A collated and annotated edition of Li Qingzhao's works]. Ed. Wang Xuechu 王學初. Beijing, 1979.

Li Shizhen 李時珍 (1518–93). *Bencao gangmu* 本草綱目 [Classified materia medica]. 6 vols. Shanghai, 1954.

Li Xin 李昕. "Jieshao Kong Jihan de 'Pu Songling *Liaozhai zhiyi xu*'" 介紹孔繼涵的蒲松齡聊齋誌異序 [Introducing Kong Jihan's "Preface to Pu Songling's *Liaozhai zhiyi*"]. *PSLK* 4 (1984): 349–51.

Li Yanshou 李延壽 (Tang). *Nan shi* 南史 [History of the Southern Dynasties]. Beijing, 1983.

Li Yu 李漁 (1611–80). "Nan Mengmu jiaohe sanqian" 男孟母教合三遷 [Male Mother Mencius]. In *Wusheng xi* 無聲戲 [Silent operas], vol. 2, no. 6. Facsimile reprint. MQSB, 1st series.

———. *Rou putuan* 肉蒲團 [The carnal prayer mat]. Kangxi ed. Harvard-Yenching Library, Cambridge, Mass.

———. *Xianqing outan* 閒情偶談 [Casual chats for idle moods]. In Zhongguo gudian xiqu lunzhu jicheng 中國古典戲曲論著集成 [Collected discourses on traditional Chinese drama], vol. 7. Beijing, 1959.

Li Zhi 李贄 (1527–1602). *Fen shu* 焚書 [A book for the burning]. 1590. Beijing, 1975.

Liezi 列子. Zhuzi jicheng 諸子集成, vol. 3. Beijing, 1986.

Lin Youlin 林有鄰. *Suyuan shipu* 素園石譜. [The Garden of Simplicity's rock catalogue]. Dated 1603. In Tuben congkan 圖本叢刊, ed. Ōmura Seigai 大村西崖. Tokyo, 1935.

Ling Mengchu 凌蒙初 (1580–1644). *Pai'an jingqi chuke* 拍案驚奇初刻 [Slapping the table in amazement, first collection]. Facsimile reprint of 1628 Shangyou tang 尚友堂 ed. 2 vols. Shanghai, 1985.

———. *Pai'an jingqi erke* 拍案驚奇二刻 [Slapping the table in amazement, second collection]. Facsimile reprint of 1628 Shangyou tang 尚友堂 ed. 2 vols. Shanghai, 1985.

Liu Xie 劉勰 (465–520). *Wenxin diaolong xuanzhu* 文心雕龍選註 [The literary mind and the carving of dragons]. Ed. Zhou Zhenfu 周振甫. Beijing, 1980.

Lu Can 陸燦 (1494–1551). *Gengsi bian* 庚巳編 [The Gengsi compendium]. Congshu jicheng 叢書集成, vol. 2910. Shanghai, 1937.

Lu Jianzeng 盧見曾 (1690–1768). *Guochao Shanzuo shichao* 國朝山左詩鈔 [A selection of Shandong poetry from our dynasty]. Preface dated 1758. Qing ed. Harvard-Yenching Library, Cambridge, Mass.

Lu Xun 魯迅. *Lu Xun quanji* 魯迅全集 [Collected works of Lu Xun]. Beijing, 1956.

———. *Zhongguo xiaoshuo shilüe* 中國小說史略 [A brief history of Chinese fiction]. Preface dated 1930. Beijing, 1973.

Lüchuang nüshi 綠牕女史 [The green window history of women]. Comp. Qinhuai yuke 秦淮寓客, pseud. Facsimile reprint of late Ming ed. MQSB, 2nd series.

Lüchuang xinhua 綠窗新話 [New tales from a green window]. By Huangdu fengyue zhuren 皇都風月主人, pseud. Ed. Zhou Yi 周夷. Shanghai, 1957.

Lunyu 論語 [Analects]. Harvard-Yenching Sinological Index, supplement no. 16. Reprinted—Taipei, 1965.

Ma Ruifang 馬瑞芳. *Pu Songling pingzhuan* 蒲松齡平傳 [The life of Pu Songling]. Beijing, 1986.

Maeno Naoaki 前野直彬. *Chūgoku shōsetsu shikō* 中國小說史考 [Studies in the history of Chinese fiction]. Tokyo, 1975.

Mao Xiaotong 毛校同, ed. *Tang Xianzu yanjiu ziliao huibian* 湯顯祖研究資料彙編 [Research materials on Tang Xianzu]. 2 vols. Shanghai, 1986.

Mei Dingzuo 梅鼎祚 (1549–1618). *Caigui ji* 才鬼記 [Records of talented ghosts]. Preface dated 1605. Microfilm. Harvard-Yenching Library, Cambridge, Mass.

Ming zhuangyuan tu kao 明狀元圖考 [An illustrated study of Ming dynasty first-place graduates]. Ed. Gu Zuxun 顧祖訓 (fl. 1571), expanded by Wu Cheng'en 吳承恩 (fl. 1607), and illustrated by Huang Yingcheng 黃應澄 (fl. 1607). 1607 ed. Expanded 1634. Harvard-Yenching Library, Cambridge, Mass.

Nan wanghou 男王后 [The male empress]. By Qinlou waishi 秦樓外史, pseud. (Wang Jide 王驥德). In *Shengming zaju sanshi zhong* 盛明雜劇 三十種 [Thirty *zaju* dramas of the High Ming]. Songfenshi congkan 誦芬室叢刊, 1916–22, vol. 84.

Nozaki Seikin 野崎誠近. *Zhongguo jixiang tu'an* 中國吉祥圖案 [Chinese auspicious designs]. Taipei, 1979.

Ouyang Xiu 歐陽修 (1007–72). *Ouyang Wenzhonggong quanji* 歐陽文忠公全集 [The complete works of Ouyang Xiu]. Sibu congkan 四部叢刊 ed. Shanghai, 1929.

Ouyang Xiu 歐陽修 and Song Qi 宋祁 (998–1061), eds. *Xin Tang shu* 新唐書 [New Tang history]. 20 vols. Beijing, 1975.

Pu Lide 蒲立德 (1683–1751). *Donggu wenji* 東谷文集 [Collected prose of Pu Lide]. Unpaginated Qing ms. Shandong Provincial Museum, Ji'nan.

Pu Songling 蒲松齡 (1640–1715). *Liaozhai yiwen jizhu* 聊齋佚文輯註 [Rediscovered writings of Liaozhai]. Ed. Sheng Wei 盛偉. Ji'nan, 1986.

————. *Liaozhai zhiyi* 聊齋誌異. Facsimile reprint of the author's ms. Beijing, 1955.

————. [*Zhuxue zhai chaoben*] *Liaozhai zhiyi* 鑄雪齋抄本聊齋誌異. Facsimile reprint of ms. copied by Zhang Xijie 張希傑. Preface dated 1751. Shanghai, 1974.

————. [*Ershisi juan chaoben*] *Liaozhai zhiyi* 二十四卷抄本聊齋誌異. Facsimile reprint of a 24-*juan* ms. Ji'nan, 1981.

————. *Liaozhai zhiyi huijiao huizhu huiping ben* 聊齋誌異會校會註會評本 [The complete collated and annotated *Liaozhai's Records of the Strange*]. Ed. Zhang Youhe 張友鶴. Rev. ed., 1978. Reprinted—Shanghai, 1983.

————. *Pu Songling ji* 蒲松齡集 [Collected works of Pu Songling]. Ed. Lu Dahuang 路大荒. 2 vols. 1962. Reprinted—Shanghai, 1986.

————. *Yishi* 異史 [A history of the strange]. Facsimile reprint of a Yongzheng (1723–35) ms. Beijing, 1991.

Qian Zhongshu 錢鍾書. *Guanzhui bian* 管錐編 [The brush and awl compendium]. 4 vols. Beijing, 1979.

Qingshi leilüe 情史類略 [A classified history of love]. By Zhanzhan waishi 詹詹外史, pseud. With the collaboration of Feng Menglong 馮夢龍. Facsimile reprint of early Qing ed. MQSB, 2nd series.

Qi nüzi zhuan 奇女子傳 [Biographies of amazing women]. Comp. Wu Zhenyuan 吳震元 (Ming). Facsimile reprint of Ming ed. MQSB, 2nd series.

Qu You 瞿佑 (1347–1433). *Jiandeng xinhua* 剪燈新話 [New tales under the lamplight]. In *Jiandeng xinhua wai erzhong* 剪燈新話外二種 [Three *Under the Lamplight* collections]. Ed. Zhou Yi 周夷. Shanghai, 1957.

Sasakura Kazuhiro 笹倉一広. "Bunken mokuroku: Ho Shōrei kankei bunken mokuroku 1985–1989 (kō)" 文獻目錄: 蒲松齡関係文獻目錄1985-1989 (稿) [Bibliographic materials concerning Pu Songling from 1985 to 1989 (draft)], in *Chūgoku koten shōsetsu kenkyū dōtai* 中國古典小說研究動態, no. 3 (Dec. 15, 1989): 90–96.

Sawada Mizuho 澤田瑞穗. *Kishu dangi* 鬼趣談義 [A discourse on ghosts]. Tokyo, 1976.

Shanhai jing jiaozhu 山海經校註 [The classic of mountains and seas]. Ed. Yuan Ke 袁珂. Shanghai, 1979.

Shen Defu 沈德符 (1578–1642). *Wanli yehuo bian* 萬歷野獲編 [Unofficial gleanings from the Wanli period]. 3 vols. Beijing, 1980.

Shi dian tou 石點頭 [Rocks that nod their heads]. By Tianran chisou 天然痴叟, pseud. (Langxian 浪仙). First published late Ming. Shanghai, 1985.

Shishuo xinyu jiaojian 世說新語校箋 [An annotated and collated edition of *New Tales of the World*]. Comp. under the aegis of Liu Yiqing 劉義慶 (403–44). Ed. Xu Zhen'e 徐震堮. Beijing, 1984.

Shuihu zhuan huiping ben 水滸傳會評本 [The complete annotated *Water Margin*]. Ed. Chen Xizhong 陳曦鐘 et al. 2 vols. Beijing, 1981.

[*Shanghai bowuguan cang*] *Si gaoseng huaji* 上海博物館藏四高僧畫集 [Paintings of the Four Monks in the Shanghai Museum collection]. Ed. Xie Zhiliu 謝稚柳. Shanghai and Hong Kong, 1980.

Siku quanshu zongmu 四庫全書總目 [General catalogue of the Qianlong imperial book collection]. 2 vols. Beijing, 1987.

Sima Qian 司馬遷 (ca. 145–ca. 85 B.C.). *Shiji* 史記 [Records of the Historian]. 10 vols. 1959. Reprinted—Beijing, 1985.

Song Maocheng 宋懋澄 (*juren* 1612). *Jiuyue ji* 九籥集. [The Daoist scroll-cover collection]. Ed. Wang Liqi 王利器. Beijing, 1984.

Sun Jianqiu 孫劍秋. *Qingchao qi'an daguan* 清朝奇案大觀 [An impressive array of amazing cases from the Qing dynasty]. Shanghai, 1919.

Sun Yizhen 孫一珍. "Ping Dan Minglun dui *Liaozhai zhiyi* pingdian" 評但明倫對聊齋誌異評點 [Evaluating Dan Minglun's commentary on *Liaozhai zhiyi*]. *PSLK* 2 (1981): 282–310.

Taiping guangji 太平廣記 [Accounts widely gathered in the Taiping era]. Comp. Li Fang 李昉 (925–96) et al. Reprint of 1961 ed. 10 vols. Beijing, 1981.

Taiping yulan 太平御覽 [Imperially reviewed encyclopedia of the Taiping era]. Comp. Li Fang 李昉 (925–96) et al. Facsimile reprint of the Hanfenlou 涵芬樓 ed. 4 vols. Beijing, 1985.

Tan Zhengbi 譚正璧. *Sanyan liangpai ziliao* 三言兩拍資料 [Research materials on the short story collections of Feng Menglong and Ling Mengchu]. 2 vols. Shanghai, 1980.

Tang Menglai 唐夢賚 (1627–98). *Zhihetang ji* 志壑堂集 [Collected works of Tang Menglai]. Kangxi ed. Harvard-Yenching Library, Cambridge, Mass.

Tang Xianzu 湯顯祖 (1550–1616). *Tang Xianzu shiwen ji* 湯顯祖詩文集 [Collected poetry and prose of Tang Xianzu]. Ed. Xu Shuofang 徐朔方. 2 vols. Shanghai, 1982.

———. *Tang Xianzu xiqu ji* 湯顯祖戲曲集 [Collected plays of Tang Xianzu]. Ed. Qian Nanyang 錢南揚. 2 vols. Shanghai, 1982.

Tao Qian 陶潛 (365–427). *Tao Yuanming ji* 陶淵明集. Ed. Lu Qinli 逯欽立. Beijing, 1979.

Tao Zongyi 陶宗儀 (1316–1403). *Chuogeng lu* 輟耕錄 [Records after ceasing to plow]. Ming ed. Harvard-Yenching Library, Cambridge, Mass.

Togura Hidemi 戸倉英美. "*Ryōsai shii*: yi o kokorozasu nagare no naka de" 聊齋誌異—異を志す流れの中で [On the concept of *yi* in *Liaozhai zhiyi*]. *Tōyō bunka* 東洋文化 61 (1981): 99–127.

Wang Fu 王符 (2nd c.). *Qianfu lun jianjiaozheng* 潛夫論箋校正. [Essays by Mr. Anonymous]. Ed. Peng Duo 彭鐸 et al. Beijing, 1985.

Wang Liqi 王利器, ed. *Lidai xiaohua ji* 歷代笑話集 [Anthology of jokebooks through the ages]. Hong Kong, 1959.

Wang Pijiang 汪辟疆, ed. *Tangren xiaoshuo* 唐人小說 [Tang fiction]. Shanghai, 1978.

Wang Shizhen 王士禎 (1634–1711). *Chibei outan* 池北偶談 [Occasional chats north of the pond]. 2 vols. Beijing, 1982.

Wang Shouren 王守仁 (1472–1529). *Wang Wenchenggong quanshu* 王文成公全書 [Collected works of Wang Yangming]. 2 vols. Shanghai, 1934.

Wang Tao 土燾. *Waitai biyao* 外臺秘要 [Secret prescriptions of the outer tower]. Comp. 752, redacted 1069 and 1640. Facsimile reprint. Beijing, 1955.

Wang Tonggui 王同軌 (ca. 1530–1608+) *Ertan* 耳談 [Tales of hearsay]. Preface by Jiang Yingke 江盈科 (1514–70). Taipei, 1977.

———. *Ertan leizeng* 耳談類增 [Tales of hearsay, enlarged and classified]. Ming ed. Academy of Sciences Library, Beijing.

Wang Xiaochuan 王曉傳. *Yuan Ming Qing sandai jinhui xiaoshuo xiqu shiliao* 元明清三代禁毀小說戲曲史料 [Historical materials prohibiting fiction and drama during the Yuan, Ming, and Qing dynasties]. Beijing, 1958.

Wang Zhongmin 王重民. *Zhongguo shanbenshu tiyao* 中國善本書提要 [Catalogue of Chinese rare books]. Shanghai, 1983.

Wang Zhuo 王晫 (b. 1636). *Jin shishuo* 今世說 [A modern *Tales of the World*]. Author's preface dated 1683. Shanghai, 1957.

Wu Wushan sanfu heping Mudan ting 吳吳山三婦合評牡丹亭 [Wu Wushan's three wives' combined commentary to *The Peony Pavilion*]. Kangxi ed. First printed 1694. Tōyō bunka kenkyūjo 東洋文化研究所, Tokyo.

Wuyue chunqiu 吳越春秋 [Annals of Wu and Yue]. Sibu congkan 四部叢刊 ed. Shanghai, 1930.

Xie Zhaozhe 謝肇淛 (1567–1624). *Wu za zu* 五雜組 [The fivefold miscellany]. 2 vols. Shanghai, 1935.

Xu Wei 徐渭 (1521–93). *Sisheng yuan* 四聲猿 [Four cries of the gibbon]. In *Sheng Ming zaju sanshi zhong* 盛明雜劇三十種 [Thirty *zaju* dramas of the High Ming]. Songfenshi congkan 誦芬室叢刊, 1916–22, vol. 77.

———. *Xu Wenchang quanji* 徐文長全集 [Collected works of Xu Wei]. Hong Kong, 1950's.

Xunzi jijie 荀子集解 [Collected commentaries on *Xunzi*]. Zhuzi jicheng 諸子集成, vol. 2. 1954 ed. Reprinted—Beijing, 1986.

Yagi Akiyoshi 八木章好. "*Ryōsai shii* no 'chi' ni tsuite" 聊齋誌異の痴について ['Fools' in *Liaozhai zhiyi*]. *Geibun kenkyū* 藝文研究 48 (1986): 81–98.

Yang Jialuo 楊家駱, ed. *Yushi guqi pulu* 玉石古器譜錄 [Catalogues and records of jades, rocks, and ancient vessels]. Taipei, 1968.

Yanxia xiaoshuo shisan zhong 烟霞小說十三種 [The fiction collection of mist and rainbows: thirteen varieties]. Wanli ed. Beijing Library.

Yanyi bian 艷異編 [A compendium of rare beauties]. Comp. attributed to Wang Shizhen 王世貞 (1526–90). 12 *juan*. Facsimile reprint of Ming ed. MQSB, 2nd series.

Yanyi bian 艷異編 [A compendium of rare beauties] and *Xu Yanyi bian* 續艷異編 [A continuation of *A Compendium of Rare Beauties*]. 40 *juan*. Comp. attributed to Wang Shizhen 王世貞 (1526–90). Facsimile reprint of Ming ed. MQSB, 2nd series.

Ye Mengde 葉夢德 (1077–1148). "*Pingquan caomu ji ba*" 平泉草木記跋 [Colophon on *The Record of the Plants of the Pingquan Estate*]. Tangdai congshu 唐代叢書, vol. 9.

[*Quanxiang xinjuan*] *Yijian shangxin* 全像新鐫一見賞心 [Love at first sight]. MQSB, 2nd series.

You Tong 尤侗 (1618–1704). *Xitang quanji* 西堂全集 [Collected works of You Tong]. Kangxi ed. Harvard-Yenching Library, Cambridge, Mass.

Yu Chu zhi 虞初志 [The magician's records]. Comp. attributed to Tang Xianzu 湯顯祖. Facsimile reprint of Ming ed. published by Ling Xingde 凌性德 of Wuxing 吳興. Taipei, 1956.

Yu Jianhua 俞劍華, ed. *Zhongguo hualun leibian* 中國畫論類編 [A classified anthology of Chinese discussions on painting]. 2 vols. Beijing, 1957.

Yu Wenlong 俞文龍. *Shiyi bian* 史異編 [A compendium of strange accounts from the dynastic histories]. Ming Wanli ed. Bibliothèque Nationale, Paris.

Yuan Hongdao 袁宏道 (1568–1610). *Pingshi* 瓶史 [A history of flower arranging]. In idem, *Yuan Hongdao ji jianjiao* (q.v.), 2: 817–28.

———. *Yuan Hongdao ji jianjiao* 袁宏道集箋校 [Collated and annotated works of Yuan Hongdao]. Ed. Qian Bocheng 錢伯城. 3 vols. Shanghai, 1981.

Yuan Mei 袁枚 (1716–98). *Xiaocang shanfang shiwen ji* 小倉山房詩文集 [Collected prose and poetry of Yuan Mei]. Shanghai, 1988.

———. *Zi bu yu* 子不語 [What the master didn't speak of]; (Alternative title: *Xin Qixie* 新齊諧 [The new Qixie]). Ed. Shen Meng 申孟 and Gan Lin 甘林. 2 vols. Shanghai, 1986.

Yuan Shishuo 袁世碩. *Pu Songling shiji zhushu xinkao* 蒲松齡事迹著述新考 [A new investigation into Pu Songling's life and work]. Ji'nan, 1988.

Yuan Xingpei 袁行霈 and Hou Zhongyi 侯忠義, eds. *Zhongguo wenyan xiaoshuo shumu* 中國文言小説書目 [A catalogue of fiction in Classical Chinese]. Beijing, 1982.

Yutai xinyong 玉臺新詠 [New songs from the jade terrace]. Comp. Xu Ling 徐陵 (507–83). Annotated and translated by Uchida Sennosuke 內田泉之助 as *Gyokudai shin'ei* 玉臺新詠. 2 vols. Tokyo, 1974.

Zeng Zuyin 曾祖蔭 et al., eds. *Zhongguo lidai xiaoshuo xuba xuanzhu* 中國歷代小說序跋選註 [An annotated anthology of prefaces and postfaces on Chinese fiction through the ages]. Xianning, Hubei, 1982.

Zhang Chao 張潮 (fl. 1676–1700). *Youmeng ying* 幽夢影 [Invisible dream shadows]. In idem, *Zhaodai congshu* (q.v.), vol. 164.

———, ed. *Yu Chu xinzhi* 虞初新志 [The new magician's records]. Zhang Chao's postface dated 1700. Beijing, 1954.

———. *Zhaodai congshu* 昭代叢書. [Collectanea of contemporary writings]. Re-edited by Yang Fuji 楊復吉 (1747–1820). 1919 reprint of 1876 ed.

Zhang Chao 張潮 and Wang Zhuo 王晫, eds. *Tanji congshu* 檀几叢書 [The sandalwood desk collectanea]. Preface dated 1695. Harvard-Yenching Library, Cambridge, Mass.

Zhang Dai 張岱 (1597–1684). *Langhuan wenji* 瑯嬛文集 [Zhang Dai's literary treasure trove]. Zhongguo wenxue zhenben congshu 中國文學珍本叢書. Shanghai, 1935.

———. *Tao'an mengyi / Xihu mengxun* 陶庵夢憶 / 西湖夢尋 [Tao'an's dream memories / Searching for West Lake in dream]. 2 vols. in 1. Shanghai, 1982.

Zhang Fengyi 張鳳翼 (1527–1613). *Mengzhan leikao* 夢占類考 [A classified investigation into dream interpretation]. Preface dated 1585. Wanli ed. Library of Congress, Washington, D.C.

Zhang Shaokang 張少康. *Zhongguo gudai wenxue chuangzuo lun* 中國古代文學創作論 [Theories of literary creation in China through the ages]. Beijing, 1983.

Zhang Wanzhong 張萬鍾. *Ge jing* 鴿經 [The pigeon handbook]. In Zhang Chao and Wang Zhuo, *Tanji congshu* (q.v.), *erji* 二集, *juan* 50.

Zhang Zilie 張自烈 (fl. 1627). *Zhengzi tong* 正字通 [A complete mastery of correct characters]. Preface dated 1670; 1685 ed. Library of Congress, Washington, D.C.

Zhao Shanzheng 趙善政 (Ming). *Bintui lu* 賓退錄 [Recorded after the departure of my guests]. Congshu jicheng 叢書集成, vol. 2831. Shanghai, 1939.

Zhongguo banhua shi tulu 中國版畫史圖錄 [An illustrated history of Chinese woodblock illustrations]. Ed. Zhou Wu 周蕪. Shanghai, 1988.

Zhongguo gudai banhua congkan 中國古代版畫叢刊 [Traditional Chinese woodblock illustrations]. Ed. Zheng Zhenduo 鄭振鐸. Vol. 4 on Yuan and Ming drama. Shanghai, 1988.

Zhongguo meishujia renming cidian 中國美術家人名辭典 [A dictionary of Chinese artists]. Ed. Yu Jianhua 俞劍華. Shanghai, 1981.

Zhongwen dacidian 中文大辭典 [Encyclopedic dictionary of the Chinese language]. Ed. Zhang Qiyun 張其昀 et al. 3d rev. ed. 10 vols. Taipei, 1976.

Zhongyi dacidian 中醫大辭典 [Encyclopedic dictionary of Chinese medicine]. "Wenxian" 文獻 [Documents volume]. Beijing, 1981.

Zhou Lianggong 周亮工 (1612–72). *Zi chu* 字觸 [A sense of words]. Preface dated 1667. Harvard-Yenching Library, Cambridge, Mass.

Zhu Jianxin 朱劍心, ed. *Wan Ming xiaopin xuanzhu* 晚明小品選註 [Annotated anthology of informal essays from the late Ming]. Taipei, 1964.

Zhu Xiang 朱緗 (1670–1707). *Ji'nan Zhushi shiwen huibian* 濟南朱氏詩文彙編 [Collected poetry and prose of Mr. Zhu from Ji'nan]. Qing ed. Shandong Provincial Library, Ji'nan.

Zhu Yixuan 朱一玄, ed. *Liaozhai zhiyi ziliao huibian* 聊齋誌異資料滙編. [A *Liaozhai* sourcebook]. Henan, 1986.

Zhuang Yifu 莊一拂. *Gudian xiqu cunmu huikao* 古典戲曲存目彙考 [A comprehensive catalogue of existing traditional drama titles]. 3 vols. Shanghai, 1982.

Zhuangzi 莊子. Harvard-Yenching Sinological Index Series, no. 20. Cambridge, Mass.: Harvard-Yenching Institute, 1947.

Zichuan xianzhi 淄川縣志 [Zichuan gazetteer]. 1743.

Zouping xianzhi 鄒平縣志 [Zouping gazetteer]. Preface dated 1696.

Zouping xianzhi 鄒平縣志 [Zouping gazetteer]. 1837.

Western-Language Sources

Allan, Sarah, and Alvin P. Cohen, eds. *Legend, Lore, and Religion in China: Essays in Honor of Wolfram Eberhard.* San Francisco: Chinese Materials Center, 1979.

Artemidorus (2nd c. A.D.). *Oneirocritica: The Interpretation of Dreams.* Trans. Robert J. White. Park Ridge, N.J.: Noyes Press, 1975.

Asian Art 3.4 (Fall 1990). "The Dream Journey in Chinese Art."

Barr, Allan. "A Comparative Study of Early and Late Tales in *Liaozhai zhiyi.*" *HJAS* 45.1 (1985): 157–202.

————. "Pu Songling and *Liaozhai zhiyi*: A Study of Textual Transmission, Biographical Background, and Literary Antecedents." Ph.D. dissertation, Oxford University, 1983.

————. "The Textual Transmission of *Liaozhai zhiyi.*" *HJAS* 44.2 (1984): 515–62.

Barthes, Roland. *S/Z.* Trans. Richard Miller. New York: Hill & Wang, 1974.

Bauer, Wolfgang. "Chinese Glyphomancy." In *Legend, Lore, and Religion in China*, ed. Sarah Allan and Alvin P. Cohen. San Francisco: Chinese Materials Center, 1979, pp. 71–96.

Berliner, Nancy Zeng. *Chinese Folk Art.* New York: New York Graphic Society, 1986.

Billeter, J.-F. *Li Zhi, philosophe maudit.* Geneva: Librairie Droze, 1979.

Birch, Cyril, ed. *Anthology of Chinese Literature*, vol. 1. New York: Grove Press, 1965.

————, trans. *The Peony Pavilion.* Bloomington: Indiana University Press, 1980.

Brandauer, Frederick. *Tung Yüeh.* New York: Twayne, 1978.

Brooke-Rose, Christine. *A Rhetoric of the Unreal: Studies in Narrative and Structure, Especially of the Fantastic.* Cambridge, Eng.: Cambridge University Press, 1981.

Bush, Susan. *The Chinese Literati on Painting: Su Shih (1037–1101) to Tung Ch'i-ch'ang (1555–1636).* Cambridge, Mass.: Harvard-Yenching Institute, 1971.

Bush, Susan, and Hsio-yen Shih, comps. and eds. *Early Chinese Texts on Painting*. Cambridge, Mass.: Harvard-Yenching Institute, 1985.

Cahill, James. *Chinese Painting*. New York: Rizzoli, 1977.

———. *The Compelling Image: Nature and Style in Seventeenth-Century Painting*. Cambridge, Mass.: Harvard University Press, 1982.

———. *Hills Beyond a River: Chinese Painting of the Yüan Dynasty, 1279– 1368*. New York: John Weatherhill, 1976.

Caillois, Roger. "Logical and Philosophical Problems of the Dream." In *The Dream and Human Societies*, ed. G. E. von Grunebaum and Roger Caillois. Berkeley: University of California Press, 1966.

———, ed. *The Dream Adventure*. New York: Orion Press, 1963.

Campany, Robert F. "Chinese Accounts of the Strange: A Study in the History of Religions." Ph.D. dissertation, University of Chicago, 1989.

Campbell, Robert J. *A Psychiatric Dictionary*. 6th ed. New York: Oxford University Press, 1989.

Certeau, Michel de. "Montaigne's 'Of Cannibals.'" In idem, *Heterologies*, trans. Brian Massumi. Minneapolis: University of Minnesota Press, 1986.

Chang, H. C. *Chinese Literature 3: Tales of the Supernatural*. Edinburgh: Edinburgh University Press, 1973.

Chaves, Jonathan, trans. *Pilgrim of the Clouds: Poems and Essays by Yüan Hung-tao and His Brothers*. New York: Weatherhill, 1978.

Ch'en, Tokoyo Yushida. "Women in Confucian Society—A Study of Three T'an-tz'u Narratives." Ph.D. dissertation, Columbia University, 1974.

Chen Hsiao-chie et al., trans. *Shan hai ching*. Taipei, 1985.

Congreve, William. *Incognita*. In *Shorter Novels: Jacobean and Restoration*, ed. Phillip Henderson. London: J. M. Dent, 1949, pp. 237–303.

Davenport, Guy. *The Geography of the Imagination*. San Francisco: North Point Press, 1981.

DeWoskin, Kenneth J. "The Six Dynasties *chih-kuai* and the Birth of Fiction." In *Chinese Narrative*, ed. Andrew Plaks. Princeton: Princeton University Press, 1977, pp. 21–52.

Doré, Henri. *Researches into Chinese Superstitions*. Shanghai, 1914. Reprinted—Taipei, 1966.

Drège, Jean-Pierre. "Notes d'onirologie chinoise" [Notes on Chinese dream interpretation]. *Bulletin de l'Ecole Française d'Extrême Orient*, no. 70 (1981): 271–89.

Dudbridge, Glen. *The Hsi-yu Chi*. Cambridge, Eng.: Cambridge University Press, 1970.

———. *The Tale of Li Wa*. London: Ithaca Press, 1983.

Egan, Ronald. *The Literary Works of Ou-yang Hsiu*. Cambridge, Eng.: Cambridge University Press, 1984.

Eight Dynasties of Chinese Painting: The Collections of the Nelson-Gallery-

Atkins Museum, Kansas City, and the Cleveland Museum of Art. Cleveland and Bloomington, Ind., 1980.

Eliade, Mircea. *The Two and the One.* Trans. J. M. Cohen of *Mephistophèle et l'androgyne.* London: Harvill, 1965.

Elman, Benjamin. *From Philosophy to Philology: Intellectual and Social Aspects of Change in Late Imperial China.* Cambridge, Mass.: Harvard University Council on East Asian Studies, 1984.

Fang-tu, Lien-che. "Ming Dreams." *Tsing-hua Journal of Chinese Studies,* n.s., June 1973: 55–72.

Faurot, Jeannette. *"Four Cries of a Gibbon:* A Tsa-chü Cycle by the Ming Dramatist Hsü Wei (1521–1593)." Ph.D. dissertation, University of California, Berkeley, 1972.

Freud, Sigmund. *The Interpretation of Dreams.* Trans. James Strachey. New York: Avon, 1965.

———. "The Uncanny." In *The Standard Edition of the Complete Psychological Works of Sigmund Freud,* trans. and ed. James Strachey. London: Hogarth Press, 1955, 17: 219–52.

Furth, Charlotte. "Androgynous Men and Deficient Females: Biology and Gender Boundaries in Sixteenth- and Seventeenth-Century China." *Late Imperial China* 9.2 (Dec. 1988): 1–31.

Garber, Marjorie. *Shakespeare's Ghostwriters.* New York: Methuen, 1987.

———. *Vested Interests: Cross-dressing and Cultural Anxiety.* New York: Routledge, 1992.

Genette, Gérard. *Narrative Discourse: An Essay in Method.* Trans. Jane E. Lewin. Ithaca: Cornell University Press, 1979.

Giles, Herbert A., trans. *Strange Stories from a Chinese Studio.* Shanghai, 1916. Reprinted—New York: Dover, 1969.

Goodrich, L. Carrington, and Chaoying Fang, eds. *Dictionary of Ming Biography, 1368–1644.* New York: Columbia University Press, 1976.

Graham, A. C., trans. *Chuang-tzu: The Inner Chapters.* London: George Allen & Unwin, 1981.

———. *Lieh-tzu.* London: John Murray, 1960.

Gulik, Robert H. van. *Mi Fu on Inkstones.* Peking: Henry Vetch, 1938.

Hales, Dell. "Dreams and the Daemonic in Traditional Chinese Short Stories." In *Critical Essays on Chinese Literature,* ed. William Nienhauser, Jr. Hong Kong: Chinese University of Hong Kong, 1976, pp. 71–88.

Hanan, Patrick D. *The Chinese Short Story.* Cambridge, Mass.: Harvard-Yenching Institute, 1973.

———. *The Chinese Vernacular Story.* Cambridge, Mass.: Harvard University Press, 1981.

———. "The Fiction of Moral Duty." In *Expressions of Self in Chinese Literature,* ed. Robert E. Hegel and Richard C. Hessney. New York: Columbia University Press, 1985, pp. 189–213.

————. "The Making of 'The Pearl-sewn Shirt' and 'The Courtesan's Jewel Box.'" *HJAS* 33 (1975): 124–53.

————, ed. *Silent Operas*. Hong Kong: Chinese University Press, 1990.

————, trans. *The Carnal Prayer-Mat*. New York: Ballantine, 1990.

Hansen, Valerie. *The Changing Gods of Medieval China*. Princeton, N.J.: Princeton University Press, 1990.

Hawkes, David. *A Little Primer of Tu Fu*. Hong Kong: Chinese University of Hong Kong, 1987.

————, trans. *Songs of the South*. Harmondsworth, Eng.: Penguin, 1985.

————. *The Story of the Stone*, vol. 1. Harmondsworth, Eng.: Penguin, 1973.

Hay, John. *Kernels of Energy, Bones of Earth*. New York: China Institute of America, 1985.

Henderson, John B. *The Development and Decline of Chinese Cosmology*. New York: Columbia University Press, 1984.

Hervouet, Yves. "L'autobiographie dans la Chine traditionelle." In *Etudes d'histoire et de littérature chinoise: Offertes au professeur Jaroslav Průšek*. Paris: Bibliothèque de l'Institut des Hautes Etudes Chinoises, 1976, pp. 107–42.

Hippocrates. *Regimen IV*. Trans. W. H. S. Jones. Loeb ed. Cambridge, Mass.: Harvard University Press, 1957.

Ho, Wai-kam. "Late Ming Literati: Their Social and Cultural Ambience." In *The Chinese Scholar's Studio: Artistic Life in the Late Ming Period*, ed. Chu-tsing Li and James C. Y. Watt. New York: Asia Society, 1987, pp. 23–36.

Hom, Marlon. "The Continuation of Tradition: A Study of *Liaozhai zhiyi* by Pu Songling (1640–1715)." Ph.D. dissertation, University of Washington, 1979.

Hsia, T. A. "New Perspectives on Two Ming Novels: *Hsi-yu chi* and *Hsi-yu pu*." In *Wen-lin: Studies in the Chinese Humanities*, ed. Chow Tse-tsung. Madison: University of Wisconsin Press, 1968, pp. 239–45.

Hummel, Arthur, ed. *Eminent Chinese of the Ch'ing Period (1644–1912)*. 2 vols. Washington, D.C.: Government Printing Office, 1943, 1944. Reprinted—Taipei: Ch'eng Wen, 1976.

Hutter, Albert. "Dreams, Transformations, and Literature: The Implications of Detective Fiction." In *The Poetics of Murder*, ed. Glenn W. Most and W. Stowe. San Diego: Harcourt Brace, 1983, pp. 230–51.

Irwin, Richard. *The Evolution of a Chinese Novel*. Cambridge, Mass.: Harvard-Yenching Institute, 1953.

Jauss, Robert Hans. *Toward an Aesthetic of Reception*. Trans. Timothy Bahti. Minneapolis: University of Minnesota Press, 1982.

Johnson, Barbara. *The Critical Difference*. Baltimore: Johns Hopkins University Press, 1981.

Kao, Karl S. Y., ed. *Classical Chinese Tales of the Supernatural and the Fantastic*. Bloomington: Indiana University Press, 1985.

Ko, Dorothy Yin-yee. "Toward a Social History of Women in Seventeenth-Century China." Ph.D. dissertation, Stanford University, 1989.

Lackner, Michael. *Der chinesische Traumwald: Traditionelle Theorien des Traumes und seiner Deutung im Spiegel der Ming-Zeitlischen Anthologie "Meng-lin hsuan-chie"* [The Chinese world of dreams: traditional theories of dreams and their meanings as reflected in the Ming anthology *The Forest of Dreams*]. Frankfort: Peter Lange, 1985.

Laqueur, Thomas. "Orgasm, Generation, and the Politics of Reproductive Biology." In *The Making of the Modern Body*, ed. T. Laqueur and Catherine Gallagher. Berkeley: University of California Press, 1987, pp. 1–41.

Lau, D. C., trans. *The Analects*. Harmondsworth, Eng.: Penguin, 1979.

————. *Mencius*. Harmondsworth, Eng.: Penguin, 1979.

Li, Chu-tsing, and James C. Y. Watt. *The Chinese Scholar's Studio: Artistic Life in the Late Ming Period*. New York: Asia Society, 1987.

Li, Wai-Yee. "Dream Visions of Transcendence in Chinese Literature and Painting." *Asian Art* 3.4 (Fall 1990): 53–77.

————. *Enchantment and Disenchantment: Love and Illusion in Chinese Literature*. Princeton: Princeton University Press, forthcoming.

————. "The Rhetoric of Fantasy and of Irony: Studies in *Liao-chai chih-i* and *Hung-lou meng*." Ph.D. dissertation, Princeton University, 1987.

Lu, Xun. *A Brief History of Chinese Fiction*. Trans. Yang Hsien-yi and Gladys Yang. Beijing: Foreign Languages Press, 1976.

Ma, Y. W., and Joseph Lau, eds. *Traditional Chinese Stories: Themes and Variations*. New York: Columbia University Press, 1978.

MacKerras, Colin. *The Rise of Peking Opera, 1770–1870*. London: Oxford University Press, 1972.

Mann, Susan. "Widows in the Kinship, Class, and Community Structures of Qing Dynasty China." *Journal of Asian Studies* 46 (1987): 37–56.

Mark, Lindy Li. "Orthography Riddles, Divination, and Word Magic." In *Legend, Lore, and Religion in China*, ed. Sarah Allan and Alvin P. Cohen. San Francisco: Chinese Materials Center, 1979, pp. 43–69.

Mather, Richard B., trans. *Shih-shuo hsin-yü: A New Account of Tales of the World*. Minneapolis: University of Minnesota Press, 1976.

McKeon, Michael. *The Origins of the English Novel, 1600–1740*. Baltimore: Johns Hopkins University Press, 1987.

McMahon, Keith. *Causality and Containment in Seventeenth-Century Chinese Fiction*. Leiden: Brill, 1988.

Montaigne, Michel de. *The Complete Essays of Montaigne.* Trans. Donald M. Frame. Stanford: Stanford University Press, 1978.

Most, Glenn W., and William H. Stowe, eds. *The Poetics of Murder: Detective Fiction and Literary Theory.* San Diego: Harcourt Brace, 1983.

Mowry, Hua-yuan Li, trans. *Chinese Love Stories from "Ch'ing-shih."* Hamden, Conn.: Archon Books, 1983.

Nienhauser, William H., Jr., ed. *Critical Essays on Chinese Literature.* Hong Kong: Chinese University of Hong Kong, 1976.

————. *The Indiana Companion to Traditional Chinese Literature.* Bloomington: Indiana University Press, 1986.

O'Flaherty, Wendy Doniger. *Dreams, Illusions, and Other Realities.* Chicago: University of Chicago Press, 1986.

————. *Women, Androgynes, and Other Mythical Beasts.* Chicago: University of Chicago Press, 1980.

Ong, Roberto K. "Image and Meaning: The Hermeneutics of Traditional Dream Interpretation." In *Psycho-Sinology: The Universe of Dreams in Chinese Culture,* ed. Carolyn T. Brown. Clanham, Md.: University Press of America, 1988, pp. 47–54.

————. *The Interpretation of Dreams in Ancient China.* Bochum, Germany: Studienverlag Brockmeyer, 1985.

Owen, Stephen. *Remembrances: The Experience of the Past in Classical Chinese Literature.* Cambridge, Mass.: Harvard University Press, 1985.

————. "The Self's Perfect Mirror: Poetry as Autobiography." In *The Vitality of the Lyric Voice,* ed. Shuen-fu Lin and S. Owen. Princeton: Princeton University Press, 1986, pp. 71–102.

————. *Traditional Chinese Poetry and Poetics: Omen of the World.* Madison: University of Wisconsin Press, 1985.

Paré, Amboise. *Des Monstres et Prodiges.* 1573. Critical ed. by Jean Céard. Geneva: Librairie Droze, 1971.

Plaks, Andrew. "Allegory in *Hsi-yu chi* and *Hung lou-meng.*" In *Chinese Narrative,* ed. A. Plaks, pp. 163–202.

————. *The Four Masterworks of the Ming Novel.* Princeton: Princeton University Press, 1988.

————. "Toward a Critical Theory of Chinese Narrative." In *Chinese Narrative,* ed. A. Plaks, pp. 309–52.

————, ed. *Chinese Narrative.* Princeton: Princeton University Press, 1977.

Průšek, Jaruslav. *Chinese History and Literature: Collection of Studies.* Dordecht: Reidel, 1970.

Rickett, Adele, ed. *Approaches to Chinese Literature.* Princeton: Princeton University Press, 1978.

Rolston, David, ed. *How to Read the Chinese Novel.* Princeton: Princeton University Press, 1990.

Schaefer, Edward. *Tu Wan's Stone Catalogue of Cloudy Forest: A Commentary and Synopsis*. Berkeley: University of California Press, 1961.

Sotheby's Catalogue of Fine Chinese Paintings. New York, Dec. 6, 1989.

Spence, Jonathan D. *The Death of Woman Wang*. Harmondsworth, Eng.: Penguin, 1978.

Stein, Rolf A. *The World in Miniature: Container Gardens and Dwellings in Far Eastern Religious Thought*. Trans. Phyllis Brooks. Stanford: Stanford University Press, 1990.

Stewart, Susan. *Nonsense: Aspects of Intertextuality in Folklore and Literature*. Baltimore: Johns Hopkins University Press, 1978.

————. *On Longing: Narratives of the Miniature, the Gigantic, the Souvenir, the Collection*. Baltimore: Johns Hopkins University Press, 1984.

Swatek, Catherine C. "Feng Menglong's *Romantic Dream*: Strategies of Containment in His Revision of *The Peony Pavilion*." Ph.D. dissertation, Columbia University, 1990.

Thompson, Stith. *Motif-Index of Folk Literature*. Rev. ed. Bloomington: Indiana University Press, 1955.

T'ien, Ju-k'ang. *Male Anxiety and Female Chastity*. Leiden: Brill, 1987.

Todorov, Tzvetan. *The Fantastic: A Structural Approach to a Literary Genre*. Trans. Richard Howard. Ithaca: Cornell University Press, 1975.

Unschuld, Paul. *Medicine in China: A History of Ideas*. Berkeley: University of California Press, 1985.

————. *Medicine in China: A History of Pharmaceutics*. Berkeley: University of California Press, 1986.

Vandermeesch, L. "L'arrangement de fleurs en Chine" [Flower arranging in China]. *Arts Asiatiques* 11.2 (1965): 79–123.

Waley, Arthur, trans. *The Book of Songs*. New York: Grove Press, 1987.

Wang, Chi-chen, trans. *Traditional Chinese Tales*. New York: Columbia University Press, 1977.

Wang, John Ching-yu. *Chin Sheng-t'an*. New York: Twayne, 1972.

Watson, Burton. *Chinese Lyricism*. New York: Columbia University Press, 1971.

————. *Ssu-ma Ch'ien: Grand Historian of China*. New York: Columbia University Press, 1958.

————, trans. *The Complete Works of Chuang Tzu*. New York: Columbia University Press, 1968.

————. *Records of the Historian*. New York: Columbia University Press, 1969.

Widmer, Ellen. *The Margins of Utopia: "Shui-hu hou-chuan" and the Literature of Ming Loyalism*. Cambridge, Mass.: Harvard University, Council on East Asian Studies, 1987.

————. "*Hsi-yu cheng-tao shu* in the Context of Wang Ch'i's Publishing Enterprise." *Chinese Studies* 6.19 (1988): 37–64.

Wong, Siu-kit. "Ch'ing and Ching in the Critical Writings of Wang Fu-chih." In *Approaches to Chinese Literature*, ed. Adele Rickett. Princeton: Princeton University Press, 1978, pp. 121–50.

Wu, Hung. "Tradition and Innovation: Ancient Chinese Jades in the Godfrey Collection." *Orientations*, Nov. 1986: 36–45.

———. *The Wu Liang Shrine: The Ideology of Early Chinese Pictorial Art.* Stanford: Stanford University Press, 1989.

Wu, Pei-yi. *The Confucian's Progress: Autobiographical Writings in Traditional China.* Princeton: Princeton University Press, 1990.

———. "Self-Examination and the Confession of Sins in Traditional China." *HJAS* 39.1 (1974): 5–38.

Wu, Yenna. "The Inversion of Marital Hierarchy: Shrewish Wives and Henpecked Husbands in Seventeenth-Century Chinese Literature." *HJAS* 48.2 (Dec. 1988): 363–82.

———. "Marriage Destinies to Awaken the World: A Literary Study of *Xingshi yinyuan zhuan*." Ph.D. dissertation, Harvard University, 1986.

Yang, Xianyi, and Gladys Yang, trans. *Selected Tales of Liaozhai*. Beijing: Panda, 1981.

Yu, Anthony. "'Rest, Rest Perturbed Spirit!' Ghosts in Traditional Chinese Fiction." *HJAS* 47.2 (Dec. 1987): 397–434.

———, trans. *Journey to the West*, 4 vols. Chicago: University of Chicago Press, 1977–84.

Yu, Pauline. *The Reading of Imagery in the Chinese Tradition.* Princeton: Princeton University Press, 1987.

Zeitlin, Judith T. "The Petrified Heart: Obsession in Chinese Literature, Medicine, and Art." *Late Imperial China* 12.1 (June 1991): 1–25.

———. "Pu Songling's *Liaozhai zhiyi* and the Chinese Discourse on the Strange." Ph.D. dissertation, Harvard University, 1988.

Character List

Entries are alphabetized letter by letter, ignoring word and syllable breaks.
Not listed here are authors who appear in the Selected Bibliography.

"A Bao" 阿寶
ai 愛
an 闇
Bada shanren 八大山人
"Bada wang" 八大王
Bai Lixi 百里奚
"Bai Qiulian" 白秋練
Bai Xiangya 白項鴉
Bai Xingjian 白行簡
ban (companion) 伴
ban (half) 半
Ban Jieyu 班婕妤
"Banxi chu fan Zhang
    Channiang" 伴喜初犯章禪娘
"Baohuitang ji" 寶繪堂記
"Bao shen" 電神
Bao Yu 寶玉
"Ba: ximu" 八洗沐
bei 悲
Bencao gangmu 本草綱目
Bencao jing 本草經

"Bian sao" 嬪騷
biji 筆記
Bi Jiyou 畢際有
"Bimo pian" 筆墨篇
bing 病
bing jiu 病酒
"Bingyou ji" 病遊記
bishuyuan jiantao 秘書院檢討
bixiang 比象
Bi Yi'an 畢怡庵
Bi Zaiji 畢載積
bizhen ruhua 逼真如畫
Bowu zhi 博物志
"bu ke nai shi" 不可耐事
bu shen 不神
caizi jiaren 才子佳人
Cao Cao 曹操
cezi 測字
chaizi 拆字
chang 常
Chang tan 常談

"Cheng xian" 成仙
Chen Hongshou 陳洪綬
Chen Tong 陳同
Chen Zhensun 陳振孫
chi 癡
"Chichi zi" 嗤嗤子
Chidu xinyu 尺牘新語
Chi pozi zhuan 癡婆子傳
chuanhu 船戶
chuanqi 傳奇
Chu Ni 鉏麑
chun meng 春夢
Chuogeng lu 輟耕錄
Chuoran tang 綽然堂
"Chu sheng" 褚生
Chutan ji 初潭集
ci jun 此君
Ci Mulan 雌木蘭
Ci Mulan ti fu congjun 雌木蘭替父
從軍
"Cui Xuanwei" 崔玄微
"Cuzhi" 促織
Cuzhi jing 促織經
daji 大吉
da kuai 大塊
dan 旦
dandu zixu 單獨自序
Dan Minglun 但明倫
Daoyuan 道原
Dayi 大異
dian 顛
dianhu 店戶
Dijing jingwu lüe 帝京景物略
dinghai 丁亥
"*Diwu caizi shu* dufa" 第五才子書
讀法
"Di zhen" 地震
Dong Hanzeng 董含曾
Dongpo zhilin 東坡志林
Dong Qichang 董其昌
Dong Weiguo 董衛國

"Dong Xian zhuan" 董賢傳
Doupeng xianhua 豆棚閑話
"Dou shi luo cheng, cong erbei
yan zhi Mianbi ju" 斗室落成從兒
輩顏之面壁居
"Du fu" 賭符
"Dugu Xiashu" 獨孤遐叔
Dule yuan 獨樂園
"Du *Liaozhai* zashuo" 讀聊齋雜說
Du Mu 杜牧
Duoduo fu 咄咄夫
"Du *Pingquan ji*" 讀平泉記
Du Wenhuan 杜文煥
duxing zhuan 獨行傳
Du Yu 杜預
"E gui" 餓鬼
Erlu 耳錄
Ertan 耳談
Erxi 二喜
Fahai si 法海寺
Fang Junyi 方濬頤
"Fangsheng chi bei ji" 放生池碑記
fangshi 方士
"Fangzhu tujuan wen" 方竹圖卷文
fanji 反極
Fan Juqing 范巨卿
"fanli" 凡例
Fan Ye 范曄
Fan Zhuan 范磚
"Feng Sanniang" 封三娘
"Feng xian" 鳳仙
"Fengyang shiren" 鳳陽士人
Feng Zhenluan 馮鎮巒
"Fen meng" 分夢
Fubai zhuren 浮白主人
fusheng beise 服聲被色
fu yu zhuzuo de zixu 附於著作的
自序
"Gan fen" 感憤
Ganzeyao 甘澤謠
Gao Fenghan 高鳳翰

qingyi 情溢
"Qinse le" 琴瑟樂
qinü 奇女
qisheng 氣盛
"Qitian dasheng" 齊天大聖
Qiu Chuji 丘處機
"Qiu Daniang" 仇大娘
"Qiugui, ni Li Changji" 秋閨擬李
　　長吉
Qiumeng lu 秋夢錄
"Qiu shui" 秋水
Qiu weng 丘翁
Qiu Ying 仇英
qi wen 奇文
Qixie 齊諧
qixu 氣虛
qiyi 奇異
Qi Yuan 杞園
"Qi Zhixiang pi" 祁止祥癖
quan 泉
Quan Changru 權長孺
"Quan jian" 犬姦
"Quanxue pian" 勸學篇
"Qunhui jie ruxiang zhazi"
　　群卉揭乳香劄子
Qu Yuan 屈原
re, liao yi yan; leng, liao yi gancao
　　熱療以鹽冷療以甘草
renwu 人物
"Ren Xiu" 任秀
"Renyao" 人妖
"Renyao gongan" 人妖公案
Rongzhai suibi 容齋隨筆
Rou putan 肉蒲團
Ruan Zhan 阮瞻
ru hua 如畫
San'gang shilüe 三岡識略
Sang Chong (feather radical)
　　桑蚪
Sang Chong (ice radical) 桑冲

Sang Mao 桑茂
Sanguo zhi 三國志
"San meng ji" 三夢記
"Shan Fuzai" 單父宰
"Shang Sanguan" 商三官
Shang shu 尚書
"Shan gui" 山鬼
"Shang xian" 上仙
Shanhai jing 山海經
"Shan Hu" 珊瑚
Shao 韶
"Shao nü" 邵女
shen 神
sheng 盛
Sheng Shiyan 盛時彥
"Shen xushi" 審虛實
"She pi" 蛇癖
shi (history) 史
shi (poetry) 詩
shi (rock) 石
shi (solid) 實
shi (taste for) 嗜
"Shi Baogong" 釋寶公
"Shici" 詩詞
Shi dian tou 石點頭
"Shi gu" 事觚
shihao 嗜好
"Shi: haoshi" 十好事
Shi ji 史記
shijiao 石交
"Shijiao tu" 石交圖
shi pi 石癖
"Shi Qingxu" 石清虛
Shi Runzhang 施閏章
Shishuo xinyu 世說新語
Shitou ji 石頭記
shi xiong 石兄
"Shi yan" 詩言
shi yan zhi 詩言志
"Shiyin yuan" 石隱園

shi you 石友

Shiyou zan 石友贊

"Shiyue Sun Shengzuo zhaizhong shang ju" 十月孫聖佐齋中賞菊

shi zhang 石丈

"Shizong" 石淙

"Shu chi" 書癡

Shui'an gao 睡庵稿

Shuicao qingxia lu 水曹清暇錄

Shuihu zhuan 水滸傳

Shuixiang jushi 睡鄉居士

"Shu *Liaozhai zhiyi* Zhu ke juanhou" 書聊齋誌異朱刻卷後

"Shu Liushi xingshi" 逃劉氏行實

Shuofu 說郛

Shuowen 說文

Shuo yuan 說苑

Siku 四庫

Sima Guang 司馬光

simeng 思夢

"Sishi dushu le" 四時讀書樂

Sishu xiao 四書笑

"Song benji" 宋本記

Song Yu 宋玉

Soushen ji 搜神記

Sun Hui 孫蕙

Sun Wukong 孫悟空

Su Shi 蘇軾

Su Xiaoxiao mu 蘇小小墓

Taiping guangji 太平廣記

"Taixu sikong zhuan" 太虛司空傳

Tang Binyin 湯賓尹

Tang Yin 唐寅

Tanji congshu 檀几叢書

tanyue 檀越

"Taohua yuan ji" 桃花源記

Tao Yuanming 陶淵明

Tao Zongyi 陶宗儀

tian zhe 天者

tian an 天閹

"Tian gong" 天宮

tian huan 天宦

"Tianlun pian" 天論篇

Ti'an shipu 愓庵石譜

tianyao 天妖

tian yi 天醫

"Tishi" 題石

tizhi 體滯

tong (generalize) 通

tong (same) 同

tongsu xiaoshuo 通俗小說

Tongwei zhuren 通微主人

tongxie daolao 同諧到老

"Tongxin shuo" 童心說

tongzi xin 童子心

"Tou tao" 偷桃

tuo zhi 托志

waishi 外史

Waishi shi 外史氏

Waitai biyao 外臺秘要

Wang Bo 王播

Wang Chong 王充

Wang Daxi 王大喜

Wang Fu 王符

"Wang Gui'an" 王桂菴

Wang Huizhi 王徽之

Wang Jinfan 王金范

Wang Qi 王淇

Wang Qishu 汪啓淑

Wang Rushui 王如水

"Wang Shi" 王十

Wang Suidong (Siren) 王遂東 (思任)

Wang Xizhi 王羲之

Wang Ya 王涯

Wang Yan 王衍

Wang Yangming 王陽明

"Wei huashen tao Fengyi xi" 為花神討封姨檄

"Weiren yaoze" 為人要則

"Wei youren xiemeng bashi yun" 為友人寫夢八十韻

weizhi 微志
"Weizhi" 魏志
Wen Tong 文同
Wen xuan 文選
wenyan xiaoshuo 文言小說
Wu Bin 吳彬
Wu Cheng'en 吳承恩
Wu Daozi 吳道子
"Wugu dafu" 五殺大夫
Wuli lun 物理論
"Wuliu xiansheng zhuan" 五柳先
　生傳
wu qing 無情
"Wu Qiuyue" 伍秋月
Wu Sangui 吳三桂
Wu Wushan 吳吳山
*Wu Wushan sanfu heping
　Mudan ting* 吳吳山三婦合評牡
　丹亭
Wuyin jiyun 五音集韻
"Wu yiren" 五異人
Wuyou xiansheng 無有先生
Wuyue chunqiu 吳越春秋
"Wuyue huiri, ye meng Yuyang
　xiansheng wangguo, bu zhi
　ershi yi sun binke shuri yi"
　五月晦日夜夢漁陽先生枉過, 不知爾時
　已損賓客數日矣
Wu za zu 五雜組
xiang 舡
"Xiang jun" 湘君
Xiang Shengmo 項聖謨
"Xianü" 俠女
"Xianü xing" 俠女行
Xiaodao 笑倒
"Xiao guan" 小棺
"Xiao liegou" 小獵狗
Xiaolin 笑林
xiao pin 效顰
xiaoshuo 小說
Xiao zan 笑贊

xie (shoe) 鞋
xie (union) 諧
"Xie Xiao'e" 謝小娥
xieyu 邪寓
Xi Kang 嵇康
xing 行
"Xingshen yulu xu" 省身語錄序
"xingshi" 性嗜
Xingshi yinyuan zhuan 醒世姻緣傳
Xing Yunfei 邢雲飛
Xin Tang shu 新唐書
"Xintou xiaoren" 心頭小人
xiong 凶
Xitang zazu 西堂雜俎
Xixiang ji 西廂記
"Xi yi" 戲縊
Xiyou bu 西遊補
Xiyou ji 西遊記
Xiyou zhengdao shu 西遊證道書
xizi jiemeng 析字解夢
xu 虛
xuan 喧
Xuanying 玄應
xu ci 虛辭
"Xu cuzhi" 畜促織
"Xu huangliang" 續黃粱
Xu Ling 徐陵
Xu Ruhan 徐如翰
Xu Yao 徐瑤
yan 贗
"Yang Dahong" 楊大洪
Yang Fu 楊輔
Yangzhou baguai 揚州八怪
Yanling 嚴陵
Yan Ruyu 顏如玉
"Yanshi" 顏氏
Yanxia xiaoshuo 煙霞小說
Yanyi bian 艷異編
"Yanzhi" 臙脂
yao (sacred radical) 祅
yao (women radical) 妖

yaoguai 妖怪
yaoren 妖人
Yaosui shu 藥祟書
"*Yaosui shu xu*" 藥祟書序
"*Yaoyi*" 妖異
yege 噎膈
yehe 夜合
Ye Mengde 葉夢德
"Ye sheng" 葉生
yeshi 野史
"Ye yin zaifu" 夜飲再賦
yeyou 夜遊
yi (different) 異
yi (righteousness) 義
Yijian shangxin 一見賞心
Yijian zhi 夷堅志
yijing 意精
Yinglie zhuan 英烈傳
"Yingning" 嬰寧
Yingying 鶯鶯
"Yin jiu" 飲酒
yinpi 飲癖
Yiqie jing yinyi 一切經音義
yiren 異人
Yi shi 異史
yishi 逸史
Yishi shi 異史氏
"Yishui xiucai" 沂水秀才
yi wen sheng shi 以文生事
yi wen yun shi 以文運事
"Yizhi xu" 乙志序
youji 遊記
Youmeng ying 幽夢影
Youming lu 幽明錄
Youming zhi lu 幽冥之錄
you qing 有情
you shi 友石
youxia 幽遐
youwu 尤物
Youyang zazu 酉陽雜俎
"Youyuan yu meinü" 遊園遇美女

yu 寓
"Yuanchi zhong yuanyang fei" 園池中鴛鴦飛
Yuan Jiao 袁郊
"Yuan shi" 怨詩
"Yuanyang meng" 鴛鴦夢
Yuan Zai 袁載
Yuan Zhongdao 袁中道
Yu Chu xinzhi 虞初新志
Yu Chu zhi 虞初志
"Yuding zhi xu" 禹鼎志序
yuefu 樂府
"Yue Shen" 岳神
Yu Ji 余集
yuji 餘集
"Yunhe qizong xu" 雲合奇踪序
Yunlin shipu 雲林石譜
"Yunlin shipu xu" 雲林石譜序
"Yunluo gongzhu" 雲蘿公主
"Yu Qu'e" 于去惡
Yu Rang 豫讓
Yushi guqi pulu 玉石古器譜錄
Yutai xinyong 玉臺新詠
yuyan 寓言
zaji 雜記
zaju 雜劇
"Zhang Aduan" 章阿端
"Zhang gongshi" 張貢士
Zhang Hua 張華
Zhang Sengyou 張僧繇
Zhang Shenzhi xiansheng zheng Bei xixiang miben 張深之先生正北西廂秘本
Zhang Wanzhong 張萬鍾
Zhang Yandeng 張延登
Zhang Yanyuan 張彥遠
Zhang Youliang 張幼量
"Zhang Youliang gujian pian" 張幼量古劍篇
Zhang Yuan 張元
Zhang Yuanbo 張元伯

zhao 兆

Zhaodai congshu 昭代叢書

Zhao Mengfu 趙孟頫

Zhao Mingcheng 趙明誠

Zhao Nanxing 趙南星

Zhao Qigao 趙起杲

"*Zhaoyang mengshi* xu" 昭陽夢史序

Zhao Yushi 趙與峕

"Zhedong sheng" 浙東生

zhen 真

zheng 正

Zhengzi tong 正字通

"Zhenshang" 枕上

"Zhenzhong ji" 枕中記

Zhenzong 真宗

"Zhicheng" 織成

Zhi gong 誌公

zhiguai 志怪

zhiji 知己

"Zhi meng" 誌夢

zhi wo zhe, qi tian hu? 知我者其天乎

zhi wo zhe, qi zai *Chunqiu* hu? 知我者其在春秋乎

zhi wo zhe, qi zai qinglin heisai jian hu? 知我者其在青林黑塞間乎

zhixie 直叶

zhiyin 知音

Zhizhai shulu jieti 直齋書錄解題

Zhongli Chun 鍾離春

"*Zhongyi Shuihu zhuan* xu" 忠義水滸傳序

Zhongzhu zhai 種竹齋

Zhou Lianggong 周亮工

Zhou Xuan 周宣

Zhou Zizhi 周紫芝

zhuan 傳

Zhuang-Lie xuanlüe 莊列選略

zhuangyuan 狀元

zhuanji 傳記

"Zhu Ao" 朱敖

Zhubing yuanhou lun 諸病源候論

Zhu Da 朱耷

Zhu Hongzuo 朱宏祚

Zhu Jiuding 諸九鼎

"Zhu *Liaozhai zhiyi* xu" 注聊齋誌異序

"*Zhuowu lunlüe*" 卓吾論略

Zhu pu 竹譜

Zhu Xi 朱熹

Zhuxue zhai 鑄雪齋

Zichai ji 紫釵記

Zi chu 字觸

Zichuan 淄川

Zihui 字彙

Zi xu 子虛

zixu 自序

Ziyuan 梓園

Zongkong sheng 宗空生

Zuicha zhiguai 醉茶志怪

[*Xinbian*] *Zuiweng tanlu* [新編]醉翁談錄

"Zuiweng ting ji" 醉翁亭記

Zuixing shi 醉醒石

zuowen 作文

Zuo zhuan 左傳

Index

In this index an "f" after a number indicates a separate reference on the next page, and an "ff" indicates separate references on the next two pages. A continuous discussion over two or more pages is indicated by a span of page numbers, e.g., "57–59." *Passim* is used for a cluster of references in close but not consecutive sequence. Chinese personal names are alphabetized under the surname; other Chinese-language entries are alphabetized letter by letter, ignoring word breaks.

"Gaotang fu" 高唐賦
"Ge" 蛤
"Ge Jin" 葛巾
"Ge yi" 鴿異
Gong Gong 共工
gongsheng 貢生
"Gongsun Jiuniang" 公孫九娘
"Gong xian" 鞏仙
gua ao 寡媼
guai 怪
"Guaidan" 怪誕
guaiyi 怪異
"Guanyuan sou wan feng xiannü"
    灌園叟晚逢仙女
"Gua yi" 瓜異
gu fen 孤憤
guicai 鬼才
guinü 閨女
"Guiyan qinsheng" 閨艷琴聲
guiyi zhi ci 詭異之辭
"Guizhong yiren" 閨中異人
Gui Zhuang 歸莊
"Gujin zhujia yuefu xu" 古今諸家
    樂府序
"Guo An" 郭安
Guo Pu 郭璞
"Gu sheng" 顧生
Guwang ting 姑妄聽
Han Daozhao 韓道昭
Han Fei 韓非
hanpi 寒癖
Hansen qu 寒森曲
Han shu 漢書
Han Xin 韓信
Han Yu 韓愈
"Hanyue furong" 寒月芙蓉
hao 好
He Qiao 和嶠
"He shi" 盉石
He Shouqi 何守奇
He Tongwen 何肜文

He Yin 何垠
Hou Han shu 後漢書
"Hou Jingshan" 侯靜山
hu (fox) 狐
hu (nonsense) 胡
hu (portal, suffix) 戶
"Hua bi" 畫壁
"Huafeng zhu" 華封祝
"Hua gong" 畫工
"Hua huan" 畫幻
"Huai mudan" 懷牡丹
"Huaiyin hou liezhuan" 淮陰侯
    列傳
"Hua ma" 畫馬
huan 幻
"Huang Jiulang" 黃九郎
Huang Shancong 黃善聰
"Huangtang" 荒唐
"Huang Ying" 黃英
huangyin zhi yi 荒淫之意
Huang Zhouxing 黃周星
"Huanhunji jishi" 還魂記紀事
"Huan Niang" 宦娘
huanpei qiangqiang 環珮鏘鏘
huanpei xiang qiangqiang 環珮響
    鏘鏘
Huanshi shi 幻史氏
"Hua pi" 畫皮
"Huashen tan Fengyi wen" 花神彈
    封姨文
huashi gang 花石綱
"Hua Wenxiu Qingshuige ji xu"
    華聞修清睡閣集序
hua yao 畫妖
Huazhen qiyan 花陳綺言
Hugui shi 狐鬼史
Huizong 徽宗
"Hu meng" 狐夢
"Hun you" 魂遊
"Huo ni" 惑溺
"Hu Sijie" 胡四姐

Li Kan 李衎
Li Liangyu 李艮雨
Li Liufang 李流芳
Lin Bu 林布
Linchuan simeng 臨川四夢
ling 靈
"Lingji" 靈跡
"Lingxi shi ji" 菱谿石記
lingzhi 靈芝
liqu 俚曲
Li Rihua 李日華
"Li sao" 離騷
Li Shangyin 李商隱
"Li Sijian" 李司鑑
liu (detaining) 留
liu (willow) 柳
Liu Bao 劉褒
Liu Bolong 劉伯龍
"Liu Liangcai" 劉亮采
Liu Mengmei 柳夢梅
"Liuquan Pu xiansheng mubiao" 柳泉蒲先生墓表
"Liu Xianzhi zhuan" 劉顯之傳
Liu Xiaobiao 劉孝標
"Liu Xiaoguan cixiong xiongdi" 劉小官雌雄兄弟
"Liu-yi jushi zhuan" 六一居士傳
Liu Yiqing 劉義慶
"Liu Yi zhuan" 柳毅傳
Liu Yong 劉雍
Liu Yushu (Qingyuan) 劉玉書 (青園)
"Li Wenling zhuan" 李溫陵傳
Li Xu 李詡
Li Yingsheng 李應昇
long 龍
Lou Cheng 婁逞
lü 履
Lu Cai 陸采
Lüchuang nüshi 綠窗女史
Lüchuang xinhua 綠窗新話

Lun heng 論衡
"Luosha haishi" 羅利海市
Luo Ye 羅曄
lüxi jiaocuo 履舄交錯
Lü Zhan'en 呂湛恩
"Ma Jiefu" 馬介甫
Mao Qiling 毛奇齡
"Mao Ying zhuan" 毛穎傳
"Mawei po, ni Li Changji" 馬嵬坡擬李長吉
mei 梅
Meishu congshu 美術叢書
Mei Yingzuo 梅膺祚
"Meng bencao" 夢本草
"Meng bie" 夢別
"Meng duan" 夢端
"Meng lang" 夢狼
"Meng Li Bo" 夢李白
"Meng Rushui" 夢如水
"Mengshe yue" 夢社約
Meng xian 夢仙
"Mengxiang zhi" 夢鄉志
Mengxuan lüeke 夢選略刻
Mengyuan congshuo 夢園叢說
Mengzhan leikao 夢占類考
Mengzhan yizhi 夢占逸旨
"Meng zheng" 夢徵
mian bi 面壁
"Miaoyin jing xuyan" 妙音經續言
Mi Dian 米顛
Mi Fu 米芾
ming (bright) 明
ming (dark, underworld) 冥
ming bi 命筆
"ming yuan" 名苑
Mi Wangzhong 米萬鍾
mojie 魔劫
mou ao 某媼
mozhi 墨誌
Mudan ting 牡丹亭
Mulan 木蘭

Nancun 南邨

nangri waibian xiong, muxia libian ji 曩日外邊凶，目下裡邊吉

"Nanke taishou zhuan" 南柯太守傳

Nanling wushuang pu 南陵無雙譜

"Nan qie" 男妾

"Nan sheng zi" 男生子

Nan shi 南史

Nan wanghou 男王后

"Nanzhen qimeng" 南鎮祈夢

Neijing 內經

"Nian yang" 念秧

"Ni gui" 泥鬼

"Niu fei" 牛飛

Niu Sengru 牛僧孺

Niu Xiu 鈕琇

Ni Yuanlu 倪元潞

"Nü bian nan an" 女變男案

nü jiangjun 女將軍

Nuogao 諾皋

Nü Wa 女媧

nü xueshi 女學士

nüzhong zhangfu 女中丈夫

nü zhuangyuan 女狀元

Nü zhuangyuan cihuang de feng 女狀元辭凰得鳳

nüzi wei nanguan 女子爲男官

nüzi zha wei nanzi 女子詐爲男子

"Ou gan" 偶感

Pai'an jingqi 拍案驚奇

"Paiyou xinong zhi lei, sui ji cheng xu" 俳優戲弄之類雖吉成虛

Pangu 盤古

"Papo jingshu" 怕婆經疏

Peiwen yunfu 佩文韻府

Peng Zu 彭祖

penju 盆菊

pi 癖

pianpi 偏僻

Pidian xiaoshi 癖顛小史

"Pidian Yumingtang Mudan ting cixu" 批點玉茗堂牡丹亭詞叙

pihao 癖好

pijie 癖結

"*Pingquan caomu ji* ba" 平泉草木記跋

Pingshi 瓶史

pi shi (indigestion) 癖食

pishi (obsession) 癖嗜

pishi (*pi* stone) 癖石

pi, shihao zhi bing 癖嗜好之病

"*Pishi* xiaoyin" 癖史小引

pixing 癖性

pi ying ru shi fu man 癖硬如石腹滿

pozi 破字

pu 蒲

qì (energy) 氣

qi (marvelous) 奇

Qian Dayin zhikan feiyimeng zaju 錢大尹智勘緋衣夢雜劇

"qianji" 前集

Qian Xuan 錢選

Qian Yi 錢宜

"Qiao niang" 巧娘

"Qiao nü" 喬女

"Qie ji zei" 妾擊賊

qiguai 奇怪

"Qi gui" 棊鬼

qing 情

"Qing E" 青娥

"Qingfeng" 青鳳

"Qinghua" 情化

"Qinghuan" 情幻

Qinghuige pidian Mudan ting 清暉閣批點牡丹亭

Qingshi leilüe 情史類略

Qingshi liezhuan 清史列傳

Qingshi shi 情史氏

"Qingwai" 情外

Qingxu, tianshi 清虛天石